Tyndale Commentaries

Volume 17

Proverbs

Dedicated to Clarissa,
Her godly wisdom is an encouragement to me and many others.
'An excellent wife who can find?
She is far more precious than jewels.'
(Prov. 31:10)

Tyndale Old Testament Commentaries

Volume 17

Series Editor: David G. Firth
Consulting Editor: Tremper Longman III

Proverbs

An Introduction and Commentary

Lindsay Wilson

Inter-Varsity Press

IVP Academic
An imprint of InterVarsity Press
Downers Grove, Illinois

InterVarsity Press, USA
P.O. Box 1400
Downers Grove, IL 60515-1426, USA
Website: www.ivpress.com
Email: email@ivpress.com

Inter-Varsity Press, England
36 Causton Street
London SW1P 4ST, England
Website: www.ivpbooks.com
Email: ivp@ivpbooks.com

InterVarsity Press®, USA, is the book-publishing division of InterVarsity Christian Fellowship/USA® and a member movement of the International Fellowship of Evangelical Students. Website: www.intervarsity.org.

Inter-Varsity Press, England, is closely linked with the Universities and Colleges Christian Fellowship, a student movement connecting Christian Unions throughout Great Britain, and a member movement of the International Fellowship of Evangelical Students. Website: www.uccf.org.uk.

Unless otherwise indicated, Scripture quotations are from the Holy Bible, English Standard Version®, copyright ©2001 by Crossway Bibles, a publishing ministry of Good News Publishers. Used by permission. All rights reserved.

Scripture quotations marked NIV *are taken from the HOLY BIBLE, NEW INTERNATIONAL VERSION® NIV®. Copyright © 1973, 1978, 1984, 2011 by Biblica®. Used by permission of Biblica®. All rights reserved worldwide.*

Scripture quotations marked NRSV *are from the New Revised Standard Version Bible, copyright © 1989 the Division of Christian Education of the National Council of the Churches of Christ in the United States of America. Used by permission. All rights reserved.*

First published 2018

Image: © Erich Lessing/Art Resource, NY

USA ISBN 978-0-8308-4267-4 (print)
USA ISBN 978-0-8308-8755-2 (digital)

UK ISBN 978-1-78359-556-3 (print)
UK ISBN 978-1-78359-557-0 (digital)

Printed in the United States of America ∞

InterVarsity Press is committed to ecological stewardship and to the conservation of natural resources in all our operations. This book was printed using sustainably sourced paper.

Library of Congress Cataloging-in-Publication Data

A catalog record for this book is available from the Library of Congress.

P	18	17	16	15	14	13	12	11	10	9	8	7	6	5	4	3	2	1
Y	33	32	31	30	29	28	27	26	25	24	23	22	21	20	19	18		

CONTENTS

GENERAL PREFACE

The decision completely to revise the Tyndale Old Testament
Commentaries is an indication of the important role that the series
has played since its opening volumes were released in the mid-1960s.
They represented at that time, and have continued to represent,
commentary writing that was committed both to the importance of
the text of the Bible as Scripture and a desire to engage with as full
a range of interpretative issues as possible without being lost in the
minutiae of scholarly debate. The commentaries aimed to explain
the biblical text to a generation of readers confronting models of
critical scholarship and new discoveries from the Ancient Near East,
while remembering that the Old Testament is not simply another
text from the ancient world. Although no uniform process of
exegesis was required, all the original contributors were united in
their conviction that the Old Testament remains the word of God
for us today. That the original volumes fulfilled this role is evident
from the way in which they continue to be used in so many parts of
the world.

A crucial element of the original series was that it should offer
an up-to-date reading of the text, and it is precisely for this reason
that new volumes are required. The questions confronting readers
in the first half of the twenty-first century are not necessarily those
from the second half of the twentieth. Discoveries from the Ancient
Near East continue to shed new light on the Old Testament, whilst
emphases in exegesis have changed markedly. Whilst remaining true
to the goals of the initial volumes, the need for contemporary study

of the text requires that the series as a whole be updated. This updating is not simply a matter of commissioning new volumes to replace the old. We have also taken the opportunity to update the format of the series to reflect a key emphasis from linguistics, which is that texts communicate in larger blocks rather than in shorter segments such as individual verses. Because of this, the treatment of each section of the text includes three segments. First, a short note on *Context* is offered, placing the passage under consideration in its literary setting within the book, as well as noting any historical issues crucial to interpretation. The *Comment* segment then follows the traditional structure of the commentary, offering exegesis of the various components of a passage. Finally, a brief comment is made on *Meaning*, by which is meant the message that the passage seeks to communicate within the book, highlighting its key theological themes. This section brings together the detail of the *Comment* to show how the passage under consideration seeks to communicate as a whole.

Our prayer is that these new volumes will continue the rich heritage of the Tyndale Old Testament Commentaries and that they will continue to witness to the God who is made known in the text.

David G. Firth, Series Editor
Tremper Longman III, Consulting Editor

AUTHOR'S PREFACE

It was with some hesitation that I accepted David Firth's kind invitation to write the replacement volume on Proverbs for the Tyndale Old Testament Commentaries series. I have personally found Derek Kidner's volume very helpful, especially for his 'subject studies', and Derek himself was a wonderful wordsmith. They seemed very big shoes to fill, but it is now over fifty years since his Proverbs commentary appeared, based on the King James Version. Recent studies in Hebrew poetry, biblical theology and canonical readings of texts meant, however, that it was fitting for a new volume to be prepared. David has waited patiently for the completion of this project through some unplanned delays. His comments, observations and questions have always been gracious and helpful.

For me personally, it has been a worthwhile yet humbling experience, grappling in particular with the issues of structure in the sentence sayings, and working out how to make them more accessible to Christian believers in the contemporary world. At one level, proverbs sound like they are irredeemably old-fashioned, but in fact our world is full of their modern equivalents – slogans, advertising jingles and bumper sticker mottos. So I thought to myself, 'Just do it!' I believe that Proverbs is an important but neglected book, like the wider wisdom literature of which it is a foundational part. At a time when the church is increasingly marginalized, here is a book that speaks openly about those everyday realities of life (work, speech, money, the good life, friends, etc.) that are so significant for ordinary people in our society and in our churches. What rich resources there are here to equip believers with an important part of what they will need in order to live successfully in the twenty-first century in both the Western and the Majority World. The teaching of this book will cross cultural and national boundaries, and is still so clearly relevant. I have constantly been reminded of God's goodness in his concern that every part of our lives needs to be shaped by his active kingly rule, even if his activity is behind the scenes. Proverbs helps us to explore what it means for God to care about every aspect of our daily lives.

Of course, such a project can never be undertaken as a solo adventure. Many have contributed – some unaware and even unthanked – to this book, although they are not to blame for its shortcomings. Students over many years, and in three continents, have not only listened to my thoughts on Old Testament wisdom, but also asked many challenging questions. I am grateful to my Old Testament teachers, especially Barry Webb and John Woodhouse, for encouraging my interest in this vital part of God's word, and for my Old Testament colleagues at Ridley College in Melbourne over the last twenty-six years (Robin Payne, Paul Barker, Andrew Sloane, Andrew Reid, Andrew Abernethy and Jill Firth), as well as those lecturing in other areas. I particularly want to thank the four Principals at Ridley that I have worked under (Maurice Betteridge, Graham Cole, Peter Adam and Brian Rosner), for their personal and professional encouragement in many ways. I am grateful to the Board of Ridley College for granting several periods of study leave, during which time much of this book has been written. I continue to enjoy working within the fellowship of Australian College of Theology network, and I also would like to thank those who have interacted with my ideas at conferences in Australia, the United Kingdom, Asia and the United States. Iron sharpens iron (Prov. 27:17)! Those who have written on Proverbs before me have provided a rich source of possibilities and, at times, a correction to my overly speculative ideas. Librarians are God's gifts to scholars, and I would like to thank Ruth Millard and Alison Foster for their friendly and professional assistance, which has helped greatly.

At a personal level, it is a great delight to dedicate this book to one who exemplifies its principles of wise, godly living in such an attractive way – my wife Clarissa. My previous commentary was on the book of Job, and I did not want to dedicate that book to her as Job's wife gets such bad press. The book of Proverbs, however, ends with a wonderful poem of a woman who demonstrates wisdom, the excellent wife of 31:10–31, and so this seems like the ideal book to dedicate to Clarissa. You are 'an excellent wife . . . far more precious than jewels' (31:10), and I am grateful to God for you. I also want to thank my now-adult children, Samara, David (and Tina), Melanie (and Tristan), for the richness they have added to my life over the years, together with our recent granddaughter, Aivie Wren.

Finally, I would like to express my gratitude to our great God, the Father of our Lord Jesus Christ. His persevering grace and constant love give me strength to keep on living for him day after day.

Lindsay Wilson
Ridley College
May 2017

ABBREVIATIONS

AB	Anchor Bible
AbOTC	Abingdon Old Testament Commentary
ACC	Ancient Christian Commentary on Scripture
ANE	Ancient Near East(ern)
BBRSup	Bulletin for Biblical Research Supplement Series
BCOTWP	Baker Commentary on the Old Testament Wisdom and Psalms
BDB	Brown, F., S. R. Driver and C. A. Briggs, *A Hebrew and English Lexicon of the Old Testament* (Oxford: Clarendon, 1906)
BibSac	*Bibliotheca Sacra*
BIS	Biblical Interpretation Series
BST	The Bible Speaks Today
BTCB	Brazos Theological Commentary on the Bible
CBOTS	Coniectanea Biblica Old Testament Series
CBQ	*Catholic Biblical Quarterly*
DCH	*Dictionary of Classical Hebrew*, ed. D. J. A. Clines, 8 vols. (Sheffield: Sheffield Phoenix, 1993–2011)
DTIB	*Dictionary for Theological Interpretation of the Bible*, ed. K. J. Vanhoozer (Grand Rapids: Baker; London: SPCK, 2005)
EVV	English versions
GKC	*Gesenius' Hebrew Grammar*, eds. E. Kautzsch and A. E. Cowley, 2nd edn (Oxford: Clarendon, 1910)

HALOT	*The Hebrew and Aramaic Lexicon of the Old Testament*, eds. L. Koehler et al., trans. and ed. M. E. J. Richardson, 2 vois. (Leiden: Brill, 2001)
HBT	*Horizons in Biblical Theology*
ICC	International Critical Commentary
Int	*Interpretation*
ITC	International Theological Commentary
JBL	*Journal of Biblical Literature*
JETS	*Journal of the Evangelical Theological Society*
JNSL	*Journal of Northwest Semitic Languages*
JSOT	*Journal for the Study of the Old Testament*
JSOTSup	Journal for the Study of the Old Testament Supplementary series
JTISup	Journal of Theological Interpretation Supplementary series
KPG	Knox Preaching Guides
NAC	New American Commentary
NCBC	New Century Bible Commentary
NICOT	New International Commentary on the Old Testament
NIVAC	New International Version Application Commentary
NSBT	New Studies in Biblical Theology
NT	New Testament
OT	Old Testament
OTG	Old Testament Guides
OTL	Old Testament Library
OTM	Old Testament Message
PTW	Preaching the Word
SBLDS	Society of Biblical Literature Dissertation Series
SOTSMS	Society for Old Testament Study Monograph Series
THOTC	Two Horizons Old Testament Commentary
TOTC	Tyndale Old Testament Commentaries
TrinJ	*Trinity Journal*
TynB	*Tyndale Bulletin*
UBSHS	United Bible Society Handbook Series
VTSup	Vetus Testamentum Supplements
WBC	Word Biblical Commentary

Bible versions

ESV	English Standard Version, © 2001 by Crossway, a division of Good News Publishers
HCSB	Holman Christian Standard Bible®, copyright © 1999, 2000, 2002, 2003, 2009 by Holman Bible Publishers
KJV	King James Version (Authorized Version), the rights in which are vested in the Crown; extracts are reproduced by permission of the Crown's Patentee, Cambridge University Press.
LXX	Septuagint (pre-Christian Greek version of the Old Testament)
NIV	New International Version, copyright © 1973, 1978, 1984, 2011 by Biblica Inc.
NKJV	New King James Version, copyright © 1982 by Thomas Nelson, Inc.
NRSV	New Revised Standard Version, Anglicized edition, copyright © 1989, 1995 by the Division of Christian Education of the National Council of the Churches of Christ in the USA
REB	Revised English Bible, copyright © Oxford University Press and Cambridge University Press 1989
RSV	Revised Standard Version, copyright © 1946, 1952 and 1971 the Division of Christian Education of the National Council of the Churches of Christ in the United States of America

BIBLIOGRAPHY

Commentaries

Aitken, K. T. (1986), *Proverbs* (Louisville: Westminster John Knox).

Alden, R. L. (1983), *Proverbs* (Grand Rapids: Baker).

Atkinson, D. (1996), *The Message of Proverbs*, BST (Leicester: Inter-Varsity Press).

Bland, D. L. (2002), *Proverbs, Ecclesiastes & Song of Songs*, College Press NIV Commentary (Joplin: College Press).

Clifford, R. J. (1999), *Proverbs*, OTL (Louisville: Westminster John Knox).

Cox, D. (1982), *Proverbs with an Introduction to Sapiential Books*, OTM (Wilmington: Michael Glazier).

Farmer, K. A. (1991), *Proverbs and Ecclesiastes*, ITC (Grand Rapids: Eerdmans).

Fox, M. V. (2000), *Proverbs 1–9*, AB 18A (New York: Doubleday).

—— (2009), *Proverbs 10–31*, AB 18B (New Haven: Yale University Press).

Garrett, D. A. (1993), *Proverbs, Ecclesiastes, Song of Songs*, NAC 14 (Nashville: Broadman).

Goldsworthy, G. (1993), *The Tree of Life: Reading Proverbs Today* (Sydney: AIO).

Hubbard, D. A. (1989), *Proverbs*, Communicator's Commentary (Dallas: Word).

Kidner, D. (1964), *Proverbs*, TOTC (London: Tyndale Press).

Koptak, P. E. (2003), *Proverbs*, NIVAC (Grand Rapids: Zondervan).

Lane, E. (2000), *Proverbs*, Focus on the Bible (Fearn: Christian Focus).

Longman, T. (2006), *Proverbs*, BCOTWP (Grand Rapids: Baker Academic).

Lucas, E. C. (2015), *Proverbs*, THOTC (Grand Rapids: Eerdmans, 2015).

McKane, W. (1970), *Proverbs*, OTL (London: SCM).

Murphy, R. E. (1998), *Proverbs*, WBC 22 (Nashville: Thomas Nelson).

Ortlund, R. C. (2012), *Proverbs: Wisdom that Works*, PTW (Wheaton: Crossway).

Perdue, L. G. (2000), *Proverbs*, Interpretation (Louisville: John Knox).

Reyburn, W. D. and E. McG. Fry (2000), *A Handbook on Proverbs*, UBSHS (New York: UBS).

Scott, R. B. Y. (1965), *Proverbs, Ecclesiastes*, AB (Garden City: Doubleday).

Steinmann, A. E. (2009), *Proverbs*, Concordia Commentary (Saint Louis: Concordia).

Toy, C. H. (1899), *The Book of Proverbs*, ICC (Edinburgh: T. & T. Clark).

Treier, D. J. (2011), *Proverbs and Ecclesiastes*, BTCB (Grand Rapids: Brazos).

Van Leeuwen, R. C. (1997), 'The Book of Proverbs', in L. E. Keck and R. J. Clifford (eds.), *The New Interpreter's Bible*, vol. 5 (Nashville: Abingdon), 17–264.

Waltke, B. K. (2004), *The Book of Proverbs: Chapters 1–15*, NICOT (Grand Rapids: Eerdmans).

—— (2005), *The Book of Proverbs Chapters 15–31*, NICOT (Grand Rapids: Eerdmans).

Whybray, R. N. (1994), *Proverbs*, NCBC (Grand Rapids: Eerdmans).

Wright, J. R. (2005), *Proverbs, Ecclesiastes, Song of Solomon*, ACC IX (Downers Grove: IVP Academic).

Yoder, C. R. (2009), *Proverbs*, AbOTC (Nashville: Abingdon).

Other books and articles

Alster, B. (2005), *Wisdom of Ancient Sumer* (Bethesda: CDL).

Bartholomew, C. G. (2001), *Reading Proverbs with Integrity*, Grove B22 (Cambridge: Grove).

Bartholomew, C. G. and R. P. O'Dowd (2011), *Old Testament Wisdom Literature* (Downers Grove: IVP Academic; Nottingham: Apollos).

Boström, L. (1990), *The God of the Sages*, CBOTS 29 (Stockholm: Almqvist & Wiksell).

—— (2016), 'Retribution and Wisdom Literature', in D. G. Firth and L. Wilson (eds.), *Exploring Old Testament Wisdom. Literature and Themes* (Nottingham: Apollos), 134–154.

Brown, W. P. (1996), *Character in Crisis* (Grand Rapids: Eerdmans).

Brueggemann, W. A. (2003), *An Introduction to the Old Testament: The Canon and Christian Imagination* (Louisville: Westminster John Knox).

Bryce, G. E. (1972), 'Another Wisdom "Book" in Proverbs', *JBL* 91: 145–157.

Byargeon, R. W. (1997), 'The Structure and Significance of Proverbs 9:7–12', *JETS* 40: 367–375.

Collins, J. J. (1980), *Proverbs, Ecclesiastes*, KPG (Louisville: John Knox).

Dahood, M. J. (1963), *Proverbs and Northwest Semitic Philology* (Rome: Pontifical Biblical Institute).

Dell, K. (2000), *'Get Wisdom, Get Insight'* (London: Darton, Longman & Todd).

—— (2002), *Seeking a Life that Matters* (London: Darton, Longman & Todd).

—— (2006), *The Book of Proverbs in Social and Theological Context* (Cambridge: Cambridge University Press).

Estes, D. J. (1997), *Hear, My Son: Teaching and Learning in Proverbs 1–9*, NSBT (Leicester: Apollos; Downers Grove: InterVarsity Press).

—— (2005), *Handbook on the Wisdom Books and Psalms* (Grand Rapids: Baker).

Finkbeiner, D. (1995), 'An Analysis of the Structure of Proverbs 28 and 29', *Calvary Baptist Theological Journal* 11: 1–14.

Foster, B. R. (1993), *Before the Muses: An Anthology of Akkadian Literature*, 2 vols. (Bethesda: CDL).

Goldingay, J. (1994), 'The Arrangement of Sayings in Proverbs 10–15', *JSOT* 61: 75–83.

—— (2014), *Proverbs, Ecclesiastes and Song of Songs for Everyone* (Louisville: Westminster John Knox).

Goldsworthy, G. L. (1987), *Gospel and Wisdom* (Sydney: Lancer).

—— (2000), *Preaching the Whole Bible as Christian Scripture* (Grand Rapids: Eerdmans).

Gowan, D. E. (1980), *Reclaiming the Old Testament for the Christian Pulpit* (Atlanta: John Knox).

Hallo, W. W. and K. L. Younger (eds.) (1996–2003), *The Context of Scripture*, 3 vols. (Leiden: Brill).

Hatton, P. T. H. (2008), *Contradiction in the Book of Proverbs*, SOTSMS (Aldershot: Ashgate).

Hawkins, T. R. (1996), 'The Wife of Noble Character in Proverbs 31:10–31', *BibSac* 153: 12–23.

Heim, K. M. (2001), *Like Grapes of Gold Set in Silver: An Interpretation of Proverbial Clusters in Proverbs 10:1 – 22:16* (Berlin: de Gruyter).

—— (2013), *Poetic Imagination in Proverbs*, BBRSup 4 (Winona Lake: Eisenbrauns).

Hildebrandt, T. (1988), 'Proverbial Pairs: Compositional Units in Proverbs 10–29', *JBL* 107: 207–224.

Holmgren, F. (1979), 'Barking Dogs Never Bite, Except Now and Then: Proverbs and Job', *Anglican Theological Review* 61/3: 341–353.

Hybels, B. (1988), *Making Life Work* (Leicester: Inter-Varsity Press).

Jenks, A. W. (1985), 'Theological Presuppositions of Israel's Wisdom Literature', *HBT* 7: 43–75.

Kidner, D. (1985), *The Wisdom of Proverbs, Job and Ecclesiastes* (Downers Grove: InterVarsity Press).

Kim, S. (2007), *The Coherence of the Collections in the Book of Proverbs* (Eugene: Pickwick).

Kitchen, K. A. (1977), 'Proverbs and Wisdom Books of the Ancient Near East: The Factual History of a Literary Form', *TynB* 28: 69–114.

—— (2008), 'Proverbs 2: Ancient Near Eastern Background', in T. Longman III and P. Enns (eds.), *Dictionary of the Old Testament: Wisdom, Poetry & Writings* (Downers Grove: IVP Academic; Nottingham: Inter-Varsity Press), 552–566.

Kruger, P. (1987), 'Promiscuity or Marriage Fidelity? A Note on Prov 5:15–18', *JNSL* 13: 61–68.

Lambert, W. G. (1996), *Babylonian Wisdom Literature* (Winona Lake: Eisenbrauns).

Landes, G. M. (1974), 'Creation Tradition in Proverbs 8:22–31 and Genesis 1', in H. N. Bream, R. D. Heim and C. A. Moore (eds.), *A Light unto My Path* (Philadelphia: Temple University Press), 279–293.

Lichtheim, M. (1973–1976), *Ancient Egyptian Literature*, 3 vols. (Berkeley: University of California).

Long, T. G. (1989), *Preaching and the Literary Forms of the Bible* (Philadelphia: Fortress).

Longman, T. (2002), *How to Read Proverbs* (Downers Grove: InterVarsity Press).

Longman, T. and P. Enns (eds.) (2008), *Dictionary of the Old Testament: Wisdom, Poetry & Writings* (Downers Grove: IVP Academic; Nottingham: Inter-Varsity Press).

Lucas, E. C. (2003), *Exploring the Old Testament 3: The Psalms* and *Wisdom Literature* (London: SPCK).

—— (2016), 'The Book of Proverbs: Some Current Issues', in D. G. Firth and L. Wilson (eds.), *Exploring Old Testament Wisdom: Literature and Themes* (Nottingham: Apollos), 37–59.

McKenzie, A. M. (1996), *Preaching Proverbs* (Louisville: Westminster John Knox).

—— (2002), *Preaching Biblical Wisdom in a Self-Help Society* (Nashville: Abingdon).

McKinlay, J. E. (1996), *Gendering Wisdom the Host: Biblical Invitations to Eat and Drink* (Sheffield: Sheffield Academic).

Malchow, B. V. (1985), 'A Manual for Future Monarchs', *CBQ* 47: 238–245.

Martin, J. D. (1995), *Proverbs*, OTG (Sheffield: Sheffield Academic Press).

Messenger, W. (ed.) (2015), *Theology of Work Bible Commentary*, vol. 2, Theology of Work Project (Peabody: Hendrickson).

Moberly, R. W. L. (2000), *The Bible, Theology, and Faith: A Study of Abraham and Jesus*, Cambridge Studies in Christian Doctrine (Cambridge: Cambridge University Press).

Murphy, R. E. (1966), 'The Kerygma of the Book of Proverbs', *Int* 20/1: 3–14.

—— (1986), 'Proverbs and Theological Exegesis', in D. G. Miller (ed.), *The Hermeneutical Quest* (Allison Park: Pickwick), 87–95.

—— (2002), *The Tree of Life*, 3rd edn (Grand Rapids: Eerdmans).

O'Connor, K. M. (1988), *The Wisdom Literature*, Message of Biblical Spirituality 5 (Wilmington: Glazier).

O'Donnell, D. S. (2011), *The Beginning and End of Wisdom* (Wheaton: Crossway).

Peels, H. G. L. (1994), 'Passion or Justice? The Interpretation of *beyom naqam* in Proverbs vi 34', *VT* 44: 270–274.

Perdue, L. G. (1994), *Wisdom and Creation* (Nashville: Abingdon).

Pilch, J. J. (2016), *The Cultural Life Setting of the Proverbs* (Minneapolis: Fortress).

Sandoval, T. J. (2006), *The Discourse of Wealth and Poverty in the Book of Proverbs*, BIS 77 (Leiden: Brill).

Schwáb, Z. S. (2013), *Toward an Interpretation of the Book of Proverbs*, JTISup 7 (Winona Lake: Eisenbrauns).

Sheriffs, D. (1996), *The Friendship of the Lord: An Old Testament Spirituality* (Milton Keynes: Paternoster).

Skehan, P. W. (1967), 'Wisdom's House', *CBQ* 29: 162–180 [468–486].

Smith, G. V. (1992), 'Is There a Place for Job's Wisdom in Old Testament Theology?', *TrinJ* 13NS: 3–20.

Tan, N. N. H. (2008), *The 'Foreignness' of the Foreign Woman in Proverbs 1–9* (Berlin: de Gruyter).

Taylor, A. (1994), 'The Wisdom of Many and the Wit of One', in W. Mieder and A. Dundes (eds.), *The Wisdom of Many: Essays on the Proverb*, 2nd edn (Madison: University of Wisconsin Press), 3–9.

Van Leeuwen, R. C. (1988), *Context and Meaning in Proverbs 25–27*, SBLDS 96 (Atlanta: Scholars).

—— (2005), 'Proverbs, Book of', in K. J. Vanhoozer (ed.), *Dictionary for Theological Interpretation of the Bible* (London: SPCK; Grand Rapids: Baker), 638–641.

Voorwinde, S. (1996), *Wisdom for Today's Issues* (Phillipsburg: P&R).

Waltke, B. (2002), 'Friends and Friendship in the Book of Proverbs: An Exposition of Proverbs 27:1–22', *Crux* 38: 27–42.

Walton, J. H. (2008), 'Retribution', in T. Longman and P. Enns (eds.), *Dictionary of the Old Testament: Wisdom, Poetry & Writings* (Downers Grove: IVP Academic; Nottingham: Inter-Varsity Press), 467–655.

Weeks, S. (2010), *An Introduction to the Study of Wisdom Literature* (London: T. & T. Clark).

Whybray, R. N. (1990), 'Yahweh-sayings and Their Contents in Proverbs, 10, 1–22, 16', in M. Gilbert (ed.), *La Sagesse de l'Ancien Testament*, 2nd edn (Leuven: Leuven University Press) 153–165.

—— (1990b), *Wealth and Poverty in the Book of Proverbs*, JSOTSup 99 (Sheffield: Sheffield Academic).

—— (1994b), *The Composition of the Book of Proverbs*, JSOTSup 168 (Sheffield: JSOT).

—— (1995), *The Book of Proverbs: A Survey of Modern Study* (Leiden: Brill).

—— (2002), *The Good Life in the Old Testament* (London: T. & T. Clark).

Williams, J. G. (1981), *Those Who Ponder Proverbs* (Sheffield: Almond).

Wilson, L. (1995), 'The Book of Job and the Fear of God', *TynB* 46: 59–79.

—— (2011), 'Spirit of Wisdom or Spirit of God in Proverbs 1:23', in D. G. Firth and P. D. Wegner (eds.), *Presence, Power and Promise: The Role of the Spirit of God in the Old Testament* (Nottingham: Apollos), 147–158.

—— (2015), *Job*, THOTC (Grand Rapids: Eerdmans).

Witherington III, B. (1994), *Jesus the Sage: The Pilgrimage of Wisdom* (Minneapolis: Fortress).

Wolters, A. (2001), *The Song of the Valiant Woman* (Carlisle: Paternoster).

Wright, C. J. H. (2015), *Sweeter than Honey: Preaching the Old Testament* (Carlisle: Langham).

INTRODUCTION

1. Historical issues

a. Authorship

The heading in 1:1 (*The proverbs of Solomon, son of David, king of Israel*) does not necessarily mean that the entire book is written by Solomon. The precise way in which they are proverbs *of Solomon* is not made clear, so it could imply either that he wrote them or collected them. It may be only a dedication, saying that this collection is in memory of Solomon, since it could also be translated 'proverbs *for* Solomon'. However, the association of Solomon with proverbial sayings supports the option of Solomonic authorship. We know from 1 Kings 4:29–34 that he 'spoke 3,000 proverbs' (more than in this book), which implies that he was more than capable of writing the proverbs found in this book.

However, this heading may refer only to chapters 1 – 9, since other headings are also found in 10:1 (also *The proverbs of Solomon*), 22:17 (*the words of the wise*) and 24:23 (*the sayings of the wise*). The last two non-Solomonic headings suggest that these parts were either incorporated by Solomon or added to his collection at a later date. In 25:1 there is explicit mention of the men of Hezekiah (late eighth–early seventh centuries BC) who copied or edited some further proverbs of Solomon. Finally, chapters 30 – 31 have separate authorship titles (*The words of Agur, The words of King Lemuel*), which preclude him from being the author of the entire book. So as a book it claims to be substantially, but not entirely, Solomonic.

Some evangelical authors dispute the Solomonic authorship of chapters 1 – 9 (e.g. Lucas 2015: 6, 'probably another anonymous, non-Solomonic, collection'), and it certainly cannot be finally established. But what has drawn scholars into disputing a Solomonic connection with chapters 1 – 9 has been the longer wisdom instructions found there, unlike the sentence sayings of chapter 10 onwards. However, Waltke (2004: 31–36) builds an argument for Solomonic authorship based on considerable evidence cited by Kitchen and Kayatz from parallel ANE (mainly Egyptian) wisdom sources. These attest to similar long instructional material well before the time of Solomon, so there would be nothing anachronistic about him writing these longer instructions as well as the shorter proverbs. Steinmann (2009: 1–19) has also argued robustly for the consistency of thought and vocabulary between chapters 1 – 9 and 10 – 24, supporting Solomon's authorship of both parts.

In the end, authorship is not a major focus in scholarship on the book; it is acknowledged by all that proverbs usually have a long oral prehistory before they are written down. What we have in proverbial literature is 'the wisdom of many, and the wit of one'.[1] It takes a whole community to formulate and validate a proverb, even if only one person finally captures that wisdom in a pithy and memorable set of words. God has seen fit to include in Scripture these literary genres that express God-given insights developed over many years. Indeed, Agur and Lemuel (the authors of 30:1 – 31:9) were probably not Israelites, and some of chapters 22 – 23 appear to be based on (but adapted from) an Egyptian wisdom text, the *Instructions of Amenemope*. Certainly, Solomon has put his significant stamp on the shape and structure of at least chapters 1 – 22,

---

1. On this expression, see Taylor (1994: 3–9).

but it is highly unlikely that these chapters were written from scratch by Solomon.[2]

b. Date of writing

All this makes the question of the date of Proverbs a little problematic. Much of it would have circulated in oral form before Solomon collected, edited and crystallized the contents. Solomon's theological structuring of the first twenty-two or twenty-four chapters would have taken place in the tenth century BC, while chapters 25 – 29 were compiled by the men of Hezekiah's time (late eighth–early seventh centuries BC). It appears that materials from Agur (ch. 30) and Lemuel (31:1–9), as well as the closing poem (31:10–31), were added after this time, but our lack of information about the identities of these authors make it very difficult to date. Even Waltke (2004: 36–37) and Steinmann (2009: 17–19) suggest that this final editing could have taken place as late as the post-exilic Persian period (fifth–fourth centuries BC). Proverbs is thus a book that had its core established in the time of Solomon, but its final form took shape some centuries later.

c. Proverbs and wisdom in the Ancient Near East

The wisdom literature of Israel, which includes Proverbs, shares much in common with a broader interest in wisdom, scribes and instruction in the ANE. The strongest links with Proverbs occur in Egypt, where there are clear parallels between the longer instructions or lectures of Proverbs 1 – 9 and a wide variety of Egyptian texts. The Egyptian instructions are first found well before Solomon (e.g. Hardjedef, Kagemni, Ptahhotep, Merikare) and continue for many centuries thereafter. While it is beyond the aims of this commentary series to explore these in any depth, this has been done elsewhere in an accessible way.[3] The individual sentence sayings are less common

---

2. However, we need to hear Longman's caution (2002: 159) that 'if we are quite honest, the authorship and date of the book have little or no impact on our interpretation of it'.

3. See e.g. Murphy (2002: 151–179); Longman (2006: 42–56); Kitchen (1977: 69–114; 2008: 552–566). Most of the texts for Egyptian wisdom can be found in Lichtheim (1973–1976). The Mesopotamian texts can be

in Egyptian wisdom, but were present in Mesopotamian wisdom at a very early stage in the Sumerian proverbs (see Alster 2005). However, even in the Egyptian texts the basic pattern of a teacher (called 'father') handing down instruction to his 'son' is reflected throughout Proverbs. There is ongoing dispute over whether the court setting of wisdom in Egypt was reflected in Israel, but at least some of Proverbs seems to reflect a similar setting (see Dell 2006: 67–79). There is fairly general agreement that at least part of 22:17 – 24:22 is a filtered adaptation of the earlier Egyptian *Instructions of Amenemope* (but see the cautions of Kitchen 2008: 562–563 and the discussion of Lucas 2015: 32–38). Other parallels between Proverbs and Egyptian wisdom include thematic links like those between retribution and the Egyptian concept of *Ma'at* ('truth/order'), a prominent focus on speech, and similar lists of virtues and vices.

2. Literary issues

a. What kind of literature is a proverb?

The nature of a proverb needs to be understood in light of the various literary forms actually used in the book. There is such a variety, including sentence sayings (what we normally understand as a proverb, especially in chapters 10 – 22), longer didactic discourses (common in chapters 1 – 9), numerical sayings (e.g. 6:16–19; 30:21–31), 'better than' sayings (e.g. 12:9; 15:16–17) and even an acrostic poem (31:10–31). Both the word *māšāl*, 'proverb', and the book itself can refer to this wide range of wisdom forms (see the next section).

A proverb makes an observation that must be confirmed by those who hear or read it. As a comment about how things are, it usually lacks an imperative. It is a generalization based on experience, or a distillation of knowledge gained by experience – it is not a revealed truth (although God may be behind the discernment process), or a law or a promise.

Chapter 26 warns us that a proverb is not automatically effective, as it can be misused. Thus a proverb in the mouth of a fool can be as

---

(note 3 *cont.*) accessed in Lambert (1996), Foster (1993) and Alster (2005). See also Hallo and Younger (1996–2003).

useless as a lame man's legs (26:7) or as dangerous as a thorny branch in the hand of a drunk (26:9). The key here is the phrase *in the mouth of fools*. Within chapters 1 – 9, fools are those who reject the starting point of the fear of the Lord (1:7), who keep on choosing the path of folly not the way of wisdom (9:1–6, 13–18), and who refuse to allow their character to be shaped by wisdom (2:1–11). In other words, a proverb is not fully useful unless its hearer or reader has made the fundamental and ongoing choices called for in chapters 1 – 9.

One way to misuse a proverb is to assume that it applies all the time. While the Mosaic law or a prophetic word must always be obeyed, wisdom is needed to know when to use which proverb. In Proverbs this is seen most clearly in the so-called 'contradictory proverbs' in 26:4, 5:

> *Answer not a fool according to his folly,*
> *lest you be like him yourself.*
> *Answer a fool according to his folly,*
> *lest he be wise in his own eyes.*

We cannot 'obey' verse 4 and verse 5 at the same time; we need to work out which truth is best for the situation we face.[4] This 'sometimes applicable and sometimes not applicable' aspect can be seen in contemporary English proverbs as well:[5]

> 'Many hands make light work' vs 'Too many cooks spoil the broth'
> 'He who hesitates is lost' vs 'Look before you leap'
> 'Out of sight, out of mind' vs 'Absence makes the heart grow fonder'

Proverbs are presented in an absolute, unqualified form, and we need to discern when to apply one and not another. Some promises

---

4. Holmgren (1979: 343) notes, 'Both of these sayings are true, but it is the wise person who recognizes the situation when it is better to listen to the one proverb rather than the other.'

5. It is also the case in the NT. At one point Jesus says, 'Let your light shine before others' (Matt. 5:16), but he also cautions, 'Do not let your left hand know what your right hand is doing' (Matt. 6:3–4). We need to work out when to do one, and when to do the other.

(e.g. God will forgive the sins of those who trust in Jesus) are always true and apply to all circumstances. A proverb, on the other hand, is not intended to cover every situation and often needs to be fleshed out by other perspectives.[6] A proverb is, however, still true, even if it does not always apply. This will mean that it is useful to balance the varying perspectives of different proverbs on the same theme (e.g. money, speech, work). Thus, we need to read the observations of the poor having few friends (14:20) together with an encouragement to be generous to the poor (14:21). In the wider canon the books of Job and Ecclesiastes give us a nuancing of the teaching of Proverbs, especially on the idea of retribution (i.e. that God rewards the righteous and punishes the wicked). This nuancing is present even within the book of Proverbs itself, for in 24:16 the writer insists that the righteous will rise and the wicked will be brought down, but that the righteous person may fall down seven times. Similarly, someone's wealth can be taken by wrongdoers without any hint that the person deserved it (13:23).

Indeed, sometimes Proverbs observes an aspect of society without either commending or criticizing (e.g. 25:20; 20:14), although at other times the lesson is clearly implied even though not stated (e.g. 11:22). Yet Proverbs is content at times simply to describe how life is, such as the difficulty of making friends when you are poor (14:20; 19:4, 7), or the effectiveness of a bribe (18:16; 21:14). They are making sense of the world by observing what works in life and what does not.

It is also vital to understand that proverbs do not operate as guarantees. Many parents rightly value 22:6:

> *Train up a child in the way he should go;*
> *even when he is old he will not depart from it.*

Yet, this is not a promise to 'claim', but an observation that this sequence typically happens. It should not be pressed so hard as to deny that the child has any responsibility for his or her actions. It

---

6. Holmgren (1979: 341–342) observes that 'generally speaking, proverbs are not infallible statements that are valid for every person or situation. Rather they tell us what generally, usually, or often is the case.'

needs to be qualified by seeing that the child also has a role to play. The proverb helps us to see that parental training has a strong impact, not that it bears sole responsibility. So the proverbs impart godly wisdom to us when they are rightly understood as proverbs, not promises.

Proverbs also observes that living wisely often lengthens the years of your life (3:1–2; 9:10–11). Yet this is not meant as a 'guarantee' of long life for the godly (remember that Jesus died young), but is based on observations that godly persons use good sense and do not indulge in riotous living. Their lifestyle will promote health in body and mind. Thus, generally speaking, they live longer. Similarly, 3:9 urges us,

> *Honour the LORD with your wealth*
> *and with the first fruits of all your produce;*
> *then your barns will be filled with plenty,*
> *and your vats will be bursting with wine.*

While we know there are exceptions, it is true that careless living will often lead to poverty (21:17). Yet Proverbs recognizes that some will be poor because they were cheated by the wicked (13:23), so that you cannot diagnose a person's spiritual condition from their wealth. This was the mistake of Job's friends.

b. Poetry and parallelism

The book of Proverbs is written according to the conventions of Hebrew poetry. Even the didactic narrative in 7:6–27 is a narrative poem. The basic individual proverb is bilinear, that is, a two-line saying usually found in one verse. Hebrew poetry does not rhyme, but there is a kind of 'thought-rhyme' (and sometimes other features like alliteration or assonance) in which the second line echoes the first, but in a variety of ways. This is technically called parallelism.

Many proverbs have been regarded as using one of three main types of parallelism, and this remains a helpful place to start.[7] In

---

7. Since the 1980s scholars like O'Connor and Kugel have argued that all parallelism is of one sort: 'A, and what's more, B', suggesting that the

synonymous parallelism, the second line is conveying a similar idea to
the first, with only a slight variation. Proverbs 18:15 is a good example:

> *An intelligent heart acquires knowledge,*
>   *and the ear of the wise seeks knowledge.*

Antithetical parallelism occurs where the second line contrasts with
the first. Proverbs 13:3 observes,

> *Whoever guards his mouth preserves his life;*
>   *he who opens wide his lips comes to ruin.*

Most of chapters 10 – 15 are of this sort, and it is often expressed
in the English versions by the conjunction 'but', as in 13:6:

> *Righteousness guards him whose way is blameless,*
>   *but sin overthrows the wicked.*

Step (or synthetic) parallelism is found when the second line is
neither expressing the same idea, nor a contrasting truth, but rather
developing the idea of the first line into a fuller one by taking it one
step further. So in 19:14:

> *House and wealth are inherited from fathers,*
>   *but a prudent wife is from the LORD.*

The 'better than' sayings have a distinctive form, and are used to make
a striking comparison (a form of antithetical parallelism), as in 17:1:

> *Better is a dry morsel with quiet*
>   *than a house full of feasting with strife.*

Some proverbs are simple comparisons (possibly a type of synonymous parallelism), often using the word 'like', as in 26:23:

(note 7 *cont.*) 'what's more' has a greater number than just three variations.
For a survey of this debate as it affects Proverbs, see Heim (2013: 19–32).

Like the glaze covering an earthen vessel
   are fervent lips with an evil heart.

The numerical sayings are an elaborate form of comparison, often
commenced by successive numbers (x; x + 1), as in 6:16 or 30:18:[8]

There are six things that the LORD hates,
   seven that are an abomination to him.
(6:16)

Three things are too wonderful for me;
   four I do not understand.
(30:18)

The alphabetic acrostic form is also found in the final poem of
31:10–31. Here each of the twenty-two verses begins with a different
letter of the Hebrew alphabet and occurs in alphabetical order.

While the discussion of parallelism can become very technical
and esoteric, most readers will find that identifying the kind of
parallelism used in a proverb will help them to read it with more
understanding.

c. What is the flavour of the book of Proverbs?

Proverbs paints a picture of the good life – or better, the good
community – in its daily patterns and activities. The focus on the
present can be seen in its teaching about God. In terms of God's
actions in the past, they only concern the creation of the world
(e.g. 3:19–20; 8:22–31) and nothing since. Most of the explicit statements about God in Proverbs speak to the present and the future –
what the Lord is doing and can be expected to do: for example, he
weighs the spirit (16:2), tries hearts (17:3) and searches the innermost
parts (20:27). God is expected to dole out material rewards and
punishments to people during their lifetime (e.g. 3:9–10; 22:4). There
is no emphasis on end-time judgment, and the great majority of

---

8. Often, but not always, the focus is on the final example cited. Sometimes
there is no ascending set of numbers, as in 30:15 and 30:24–28.

statements concerning consequences of behaviour does not mention God by name. In 13:21a, for example, it is not that God will punish wrongdoers, but simply that *disaster pursues sinners*. This is not to shut God out of causing the consequences, but rather to concentrate on the here-and-now effects of what we do in our everyday lives.

Goldsworthy points out that Proverbs is fundamentally an optimistic book, teaching that wisdom and life are within our grasp. They are so because they are God's gift, and the human task. He suggests that 'Proverbs defines goodness in terms that are wider than morality and ethics. It is the order that underlies the creation' (1987: 85). Proverbs does not speak of the fall of humanity into sin, although it may be presupposed from earlier OT books. What Proverbs affirms is that any chaos brought by sin has not conquered, and that the order in creation can still be perceived. Wisdom is about living life to the full, and Proverbs calls us to a decision to stand with either the wise person or the fool.

Proverbs assumes that people are free to choose their course of action in life and are being urged to choose the way of wisdom. While a moral code undergirds the book of Proverbs, its real intent is to train a person, to actively form character, to show what life is really like and how best to cope with and manage it. Yet its flavour is so different from the stern prohibitions of the law and the strong rebukes of the prophets. Murphy (2002: 15) says, 'It does not command so much as it seeks to persuade, to tease the reader into a way of life.' The urging of Proverbs is not based on appeals to God's saving acts, nor Israel's history, nor even the distinctives of Israel as God's chosen people. While it is addressed to Israelites, it has in view the followers of God as human beings seeking to make sense of life before the one who has created and sustains them.

While there are clear warnings about the way of folly, the book as a whole focuses more on the patterns that will lead to living well in God's creation. This emphasis on the regularities and normal activities of daily life is a significant part of the book's appeal to contemporary readers. While some of the OT seems foreign in its concerns, the issues explored in Proverbs are familiar and topical. McKenzie (1996: xi–xiv) has described us as living in 'a proverb-filled world'. She imagines what our life would look like if it were shaped by the book of Proverbs, proposing what might be written on our tombstone (McKenzie 2002: 108):

> I lived with a listening heart, attentive to God's wisdom all around and within me. With my attention on Divine Wisdom, I was able largely to close my ears to the influence of foolish people and my own unruly appetites. I was faithful to my spouse and controlled my appetites for food and drink. I was industrious, controlled my temper and curbed my unruly tongue. While I came to realize that life contains a measure of mystery and that God is ultimately in charge of things, I focused on those areas of life where, by making wise choices, I could usually ensure auspicious outcomes. I ordered my life so that I knew a measure of peace of mind and worked for harmony in my community. While I respected the poor as those whom God created and loves, I worked to ensure that I would not share their lot. As a result, I secured a reputation for integrity and prudence among my peers.

That is the flavour of the book of Proverbs.

3. Structural issues

a. Structure in chapters 1 – 9

Some aspects of the structure of the book are very clear, but others are quite controversial and disputed. There is general agreement that chapters 1 – 9 are distinct from the following chapters as they contain longer, more cohesive instructions or lectures rather than the shorter sentence sayings of chapters 10 – 29. The final two chapters (30 and 31) round off the book with two further collections and a poem on wisdom exemplified as a woman.

Proverbs 1 – 9 contains long, cohesive units of thought, unlike the sentence sayings of the rest of the book. A number of scholars have identified ten major units of thought in Proverbs 1 – 9. Whybray (1994: 25) labelled them as 'instructions' (on analogy with Egyptian texts), but McKane (1970: 9) argues that, unlike the Egyptian texts, they are not instructions for court officials, but for young men in the broader community, with the aim of promoting a particular way of life.

Fox (2000: 45) calls them lectures (i.e. a father lecturing his son or sons on moral behaviour), comprising three parts:

a. exordium (i.e. introduction) containing an address (my son), an exhortation (e.g. 1:8) and a motivation (e.g. 1:9);
b. lesson, i.e. the body of the teaching (e.g. 1:10–16);
c. conclusion, i.e. a summarizing statement generalizing the teaching of the lesson (e.g. 1:17–18), sometimes ending with a capstone (e.g. 1:19).

Fox (2000: 44–45) suggests that these ten lectures (I–X) are interlaced with five interludes (*A–E*), which are largely reflections on wisdom. He sets out the components as follows:

Prologue (1:1–7)

I		1:8–19	Avoid gangs
	A	*1:20–33*	*Wisdom's warning*
II		2:1–22	The path to wisdom
III		3:1–12	The wisdom of piety
	B	*3:13–20*	*In praise of wisdom*
IV		3:21–35	The wisdom of honesty
V		4:1–9	Loving wisdom, hating evil
VI		4:10–19	The right path
VII		4:20–27	The straight path
VIII		5:1–23	Another man's wife and one's own
	C	*6:1–19*	*Four epigrams on folly and evil*
IX		6:20–35	Adultery kills
X		7:1–27	Beware the seductress
	D	*8:1–36*	*Wisdom's self-praise*
	E	*9:1–18*	*Two banquets*

While there may need to be further discussion about the titles given to each section, the essential outline of these chapters seems well described by his proposal.

b. Structure in 10:1 – 22:16
The remainder of the book (chapters 10 – 31) can be broadly structured by the headings found there. The first major section

(10:1 – 22:16) is introduced by the title *The proverbs of Solomon.* This section is comprised of one- or two-line sentence sayings, which are not neatly arranged in terms of content. Every now and then there are small clusters of proverbs around a single theme, such as the use of words in 10:18–21 or the mention of kings in 16:12–15, but these are clear exceptions to the dominant, seemingly random pattern.[9]

There is, however, a growing desire among some scholars to read the book of Proverbs as a meaningful book, not just a waste-paper bin of gathered wisdom. Bartholomew (2001: 6–7) notes that just as in Psalms or Isaiah, attention is being paid to the shape of the book as we have it in its canonical form, with evidence of editing, gathered collections and interconnections. While clearly not every proverb is linked to the one it follows or precedes, many more are linked than was once thought, as Van Leeuwen (1988) has demonstrated in relation to chapters 25 – 27. Hildebrandt (1988: 209–218) has also drawn attention to a number of proverbial pairs (10:15–16; 13:21–22; 15:1–2, 8–9; 26:4–5), giving hints of a more cohesive structure in chapters 10 – 29. Bartholomew's suggestion is that we should read the book of Proverbs like other books, starting at the beginning and allowing the meaning to accrue as we move along. While this is easily done in relation to chapters 1 – 9, we should ask if it is more possible in chapters 10 – 31.

A key proponent of this new trend is Knut Heim's *Like Grapes of Gold Set in Silver* (2001).[10] He noted that seven out of nine commentaries he surveyed acknowledged that there is some structure in this section that should affect how it is interpreted (even if there is no agreement about the details). The kind of features he points to include the following (Heim 2001: 63): 'chapter divisions,

---

9. In the later sentence proverbs there is also a higher incidence of this topical clustering, especially in chapters 25 – 27. Here we can find distinct sections dealing with the king (25:2–7), the lazy person (26:13–16) and mischief-making (26:20–28).

10. The title is taken from Prov. 25:11: a word fitly spoken is like grapes or apples of gold set in silver. He uses this analogy to explain the structure of this section. The subtitle of his book is *An Interpretation of Proverbial Clusters in Proverbs 10:1 – 22:16.*

"educational" sayings, paronomasia (the use of a word in different senses or the use of words similar in sound to achieve a specific effect, as humour or a dual meaning; commonly a pun of some form) and catchwords, theological reinterpretations, proverbial pairs, and variant repetitions'. While Heim concludes that none of these is sufficient on their own, the combination of phonological, semantic, syntactic and thematic repetition factors mounts a powerful case for a deliberate attempt to structure this section into clusters of between two and thirteen verses. In developing the analogy found in 25:11, he says, 'The cluster forms an organic whole linked by means of small "twiglets", yet each grape can be consumed individually. Although the grapes contain juice from the same vine, each tastes slightly different. It doesn't matter in which sequence the grapes are consumed, but eating them together undoubtedly enhances the flavour and enriches the culinary experience.'[11]

Longman (2006: 38–42) has criticized Heim's approach, saying that the criteria are so broad and varied that different scholars will come up with different clusters. These clusters can therefore be just as much a projection of the commentators as a reality that emerges from the text. Longman concludes that the sentence sayings are, in the end, arranged in a more or less random fashion, especially when it comes to their content. Each proverb is on its own for meaning.

More recently, Fox has produced his commentary on chapters 10 – 31, and has pointed out that this programme of trying to find clusters goes back to medieval Jewish commentators (twelfth century), or perhaps even earlier. He observed that Heim relied on linking devices rather than clear boundary markers. His conclusion is that the process that best explains the grouping we can find in this part of the book is that of associative thinking, that is, a word or sound or root or phrase triggers off for the compiler another proverb

---

11. Heim (2001: 107). He adds, 'The primary criteria for the delimitation of proverbial clusters are consequently not boundary markers, as commonly thought, but linking devices (the "twiglets" in the grape analogy) ... The most fundamental such device, of course, is repetition – repetition of sound and sense: consonants, word roots, words, synonyms, etc.'

which is then included. He gives an example of how this process works in 19:11–14. Here patience in verse 11 triggers the thought of wrath, the opposite of patience (v. 12); which is an irritation, leading to the thought of an irritable wife (v. 13); which provokes the thought of a virtuous one (v. 14).[12] Fox suggests that there is no reason to look for or assume the existence of any larger patterns, as there are other forms of literary artistry which also give unity. His image is not one of clusters of grapes, but of each proverb being like a jewel, with the book like a heap of different kinds of jewels. They do not need to be sorted into neat rows or separate piles in order to be attractive.

While Waltke (2004; 2005) has identified a number of units and subunits, this has been taken further by Lucas (2015: 15–22; see also 2016: 37–42). Lucas divides much of this Solomonic collection into 'proverbial clusters', but has tried to base this more on thematic connections. In this commentary I also have tried to develop some connections and groupings, largely on the basis of thematic or content links. In this matter, to quote a proverb, the proof of the pudding is in the eating. While the exact boundaries differ in these various scholarly attempts to identify groups of proverbs, the many connections identified do suggest that these proverbs have come together over a period of time rather than in a single and simple work of editing. Longman's conclusion is to go back to the idea of interpreting the proverbs as randomly structured; mine is to assume that first the proverb is to be read on its own, but there is always a need to see if it might connect to surrounding proverbs.

There are a number of other indicators of some structuring happening in this section. Many commentators have pointed out the preponderance of antithetical parallelism in chapters 10 – 15 (on one count, 163 out of 183 proverbs), while chapters 16 – 22 are more characterized by either synthetic or synonymous parallelism. Bartholomew (2001: 11–13) has suggested that character-consequence link is very strong in chapters 10 – 15, with a stress on the contrast between the lifestyles of the righteous and the wicked. He then observes that most of the exceptions to this pattern of retribution

---

12. Fox (2009: 480). He gives another worked example on 26:1–12.

(God rewarding the righteous and punishing the wicked) are found in chapters 16 – 22. Van Leeuwen (2005: 638) has concluded that 'Prov. 10–15 teaches the elementary pattern of acts and consequences, while chs. 16–29 develop the exceptions to the rules.'

There are other patterns as well. With the exception of two instances in the linking passage (14:28, 35), the king is not mentioned in chapters 10 – 15, but there are many references in chapters 16 – 22 (16:10, 12, 13, 14, 15; 17:7; 19:12; 20:2, 8, 26, 28; 21:1). Chapters 16 – 22 also contain more 'better ... than' sayings (12:9; 15:16–17; 16:8, 16, 19, 32; 17:1; 19:1, 22; 21:9, 19; 22:1; see also 25:7, 24; 27:5, 10; 28:6) than the rest of the book. This provides a form of prioritization as one thing is judged better than another.

These differences suggest that there is some structure in chapters 10 – 22 after all. Of particular significance here is Whybray's observation of a high concentration of 'Yahweh sayings' at the seam of the two sections (chapters 10 – 15 and 16 – 22) in 15:33 – 16:9. In 10:1 – 22:16 one third of all the sayings containing the Lord are found in chapters 15 and 16, with nine out of ten verses in 15:33 – 16:9 using the Lord, making it the largest group of sayings with thematic unity (Whybray 1990; see also Dell 2006: 106 for some minor recounting). This not only gives a theological flavour to the final form of the whole Solomonic section, but also provides structure and cohesion. On balance, then, there are enough indicators of a variety of structuring devices to suggest that the proverbs of 10:1 – 22:16 are not *simply* randomly arranged.

c. Structure in 22:17 – 31:31

Structure is less problematic in the rest of the book. Further titles are found in 22:17 (*the words of the wise*, covering 22:17 – 24:22) and in 24:23 (*These also are sayings of the wise*, covering 24:23–34). These titles introduce collections of sentence sayings. The *words of the wise* can be grouped into an introduction in 22:17–21 and three sections (22:22 – 23:11; 23:12–35; 24:1–22). The 'further sayings' are only a small section of twelve verses that are best seen as having three parts (24:23–25, 26–29 and 30–34).

They are followed by chapters 25 – 29, given the title in 25:1: *These also are proverbs of Solomon which the men of Hezekiah king of Judah copied.* Many have concluded that there are two collections here, as chapters 25 – 27 contain many striking metaphors and comparisons, and little antithetic parallelism, while these features are reversed in chapters 28 – 29. Van Leeuwen (1988) has done a careful analysis of chapters 25 – 27 and identified a coherent structure there, made up of six parts (25:2–27 [1–28]; 26:1–12, 13–16, 17–28; 27:1–22, 23–27). Chapters 28 – 29 can be divided into four sections (28:1–12, 13–28; 29:1–15, 16–27; so Finkbeiner 1995: 3–4).

The book finishes with the sayings of Agur (ch. 30) and Lemuel (31:1–9). Chapter 30 is a collection of wisdom proverbs, using mainly numerical sayings.[13] The oracle to Lemuel is a short section of nine verses, with three parts (31:1–3, 4–7, 8–9). Finally comes a description of the perfect wife in 31:10–31, which is quite a distinct section, but possesses no title. In the opening chapters wisdom is personified as a woman, and this acrostic poem shows an example of wisdom lived out in practice. The idea of the fear of the Lord makes an important structural contribution to the book, as it brackets chapters 1 – 9 (1:7; 9:10), is found in the 'theological kernel' (15:33; 16:6) and here finally at the close of the book. This is a coherent unit with an introduction (31:10–12), an outline of her activities (31:13–27) and a description of those who praise her (31:28–31).

4. Theological issues

a. Reading Proverbs theologically

Looking for theology in Proverbs may seem to be an ambitious task. Back in 1986 Roland Murphy (1986: 87–88) wrote, 'The Book of Proverbs would seem to be a very modest candidate for theological exegesis.' Yet, while he concedes that the theology of Proverbs is different from the focus of 'modern theology', he insists that its concern with understanding people in terms of their relationship with God is deeply theological.

A number of scholars have taken the view that the book of Proverbs – and especially the sentence sayings of chapters 10 – 29 – are simply examples of 'secular', non-theological wisdom. Yet Alan Jenks (1985: 87–88) has argued that instead of wisdom becoming

---

13. The LXX, however, places 30:1 – 31:9 at the end of chapter 24.

more 'theological', it was *originally* theological. Three basic theological presuppositions or principles undergird even what is usually understood to be the oldest section of Proverbs (chapters 10 – 29):

1. That this is an orderly world, ruled by Yahweh, its wise Creator;
2. That knowledge of this order is possible to the people who open themselves to wisdom;
3. That the wise who thus align themselves with God's order will experience good things, while the fools will suffer for their folly.

Norman Whybray (1990: 153–165) examined the 'Yahweh-sayings' in the book to explore what they taught about God. He finds a clear insistence that God is the Creator. Thus, 3:19–20 shows that he is the Creator of heaven and earth; also 8:22–31 Creator of earth, mountains, sky and sea; in 20:12 he gave people the ability to see and hear. The way the poor are treated matters to God (they are all his creatures, 16:4; 22:2; 29:13; those who mock the poor insult God, 14:31; 17:5; and those who are generous honour him, 14:31). Furthermore, he sees all (15:3) even into human hearts (5:21; 15:11) and he tests the human heart (16:2; 17:3; 21:2). He determines events (16:33; 20:24), often frustrating human plans (16:9; 19:21; 21:31).

Having a cluster of Yahweh sayings at the centre and seam of the largest collection in the book (15:33 – 16:9) implies that all the proverbs on either side of the seam need to be understood in the light of these theological truths, thus proposing a theological grounding for the sentence sayings. They are not just secular wisdom, good or bad; instead, they are observations that require the reader first to understand the bigger picture of where God fits in.

Lennart Boström notes that God is referred to by name throughout the book. Of the ninety-four references, twenty-one are in chapters 1 – 9; fifty-seven in 10:1 – 22:16; five in 22:17 – 24:34; seven in chapters 25 – 29 and four in chapters 30 – 31. Boström argues that God is pictured in Proverbs as both the supreme God (transcendent and sovereign) and as a personal God (seen in his attitude to the weak and to the righteous human). The idea of God as the sole Creator is not in dispute in the book, and hence creation theology is prominent. Proverbs views God as involved in the world and responsible for maintaining justice. He is simultaneously transcendent over, and engaged in, the world, intimately related to it and to individuals in it.[14] The theological perspectives established by the prologue may not always be referred to specifically, but they are assumed, applied and unpacked in the many observations about how to choose wisdom and avoid folly in daily life.

Daniel Treier has undertaken an explicitly theological commentary on the text.[15] His analysis of chapters 1 – 9 is guided by the theme of the 'two ways', which is a clear contrast drawn in the text. However, he also has a major focus on 8:22–36 because of its significance for later Christological debates (i.e. its significance for systematic theology, rather than because of its significance in the book).

Treier is at his most creative in suggesting a novel way of approaching chapters 10 – 29. Here he uses as his classification categories not topics but the classical virtues and vices. The four cardinal virtues (prudence, justice, temperance and fortitude) are derived from Greek thought, and the three theological virtues (faith, hope and charity) are derived from the Christian church during the Roman period. Thus, these are the virtues with a strong Greek aroma and a Latin aftertaste, having little real connection with Hebrew thinking. These seven virtues are matched by an equal number of capital vices (also called 'cardinal' or 'deadly sins'), namely lust, gluttony, greed, sloth, wrath, envy and pride. Again these vices have been derived from Greek origins, but are shaped by Latin thought.

In the end Treier's cardinal virtues and vices miss out on the fundamental relational dimension of Hebrew thought, as well as its social or community rather than individual focus. He majors on what kind of person should *I* be, rather than what kind of community should *we* be. In addition, from a cross-cultural point of view, his understanding echoes a modern Western right/wrong value system rather than an ANE honour/shame culture. In the end Treier's analysis loses too much of the ecology (and so, theology) of the text.

---

14. Boström (1990).

15. Treier (2011).

20 P R O V E R B S

Four specific areas of the book's theology deserve further discussion: the idea of retribution, the fear of the Lord, God's active involvement as Creator/Sustainer in everyday life, and the place of Proverbs in biblical theology.

b. Retribution

The doctrine of retribution is a theory of justice often used in legal circles to justify the punishment of wrongdoers. While this dimension is present in the OT, the focus in the book of Proverbs is on the connections between our character and the consequences that follow. The way in which God orders the world (in Proverbs, largely behind the scenes rather than overtly) is that the righteous are rewarded and the wicked punished. It is part of the explanation of God's sustaining the created, human world. In the books of the Law this retribution is seen more at a national level: God blesses his chosen people when they are obedient, and activates the covenant curses when they rebel (Deuteronomy 28).

Proverbs, however, is more concerned with the individual rather than the nation. In addition, their obligations to God and others are not specifically based on Israel's covenant law, but on God's broader ordering and sustaining of the creation.[16] Furthermore, the link in Proverbs is not just between specific actions and consequences, but between a person's character and the consequences that will flow.[17] Proverbs simply insists that there is a correlation between character/ actions and consequences without necessarily outlining the means used to reward or punish.

Proverbs clearly teaches both that the righteous will be rewarded and that the wicked will be punished. This can partly be seen in 3:9–10, where honouring God with your wealth and produce will lead to overflowing barns and bursting wine vats. In a cluster of Proverbs at the end of chapter 10 (10:27–32) there is a sustained contrast between a positive outcome for those of righteous character

---

16. Walton (2008: 650–651) also distinguishes between a corporate level retribution theology as a covenant theme, and a retribution principle at an individual level being a wisdom theme.

17. See Boström (1990: 138).

(life, joy, strength, security, wisdom, truth) with the opposite for the wicked. Righteousness and wickedness generally lead to different consequences (e.g. 10:3; 11:23).[18] The purpose of this doctrine of retribution is to provide an incentive for readers and listeners to embrace the way of wisdom in our daily lives.

However, this does not mean that righteousness will always be rewarded and its opposite punished. Those who see an *absolute* correlation between our righteousness and our rewards have forgotten that proverbs were never intended to be promises or guarantees. This explains why we can find so-called 'contradictory proverbs' (e.g. 26:4, 5) in the book, because each proverb is not applicable in every situation or at all times. More specifically, the book itself nuances the connection between righteousness and rewards, and between bad outcomes and wickedness. So wealth may come from either wickedness (10:2; 16:8, 19; 22:16) or diligence (10:4; 12:27), and our wealth at any given instant cannot be a reliable measure of our righteousness or wisdom. There is even the explicit mention of the righteous falling seven times (24:16). If we are part of a city or nation or community, the wickedness of others can bring disaster (11:11), even if we are a righteous person. Moreover, justice can be perverted by false witness (12:17), greed, dishonesty or bribes (15:27; 16:28; 17:8; 20:10, 14, 17, 23), while lies and slander (which characterize a fool, 10:18) can bring personal and social calamity. Innocent people can meet a violent end (1:11; 6:17) or be cheated of their rights (17:23, 26; 18:5) or livelihood (13:23) (so Kidner 1985: 118). A (righteous) person may be shamed by a foolish wife (12:4), son (19:13), prostitute (22:14; 23:27) or dishonourable servant (14:35), while strife can be stirred up by a person with a hot temper (15:18). The poor can be people of integrity (19:1, 22).[19] The book as a whole endorses the principle of retribution, but it does not describe all the ways in which God is at work in his world.

c. The fear of the Lord
The fear of the Lord is the starting point or first principle of wisdom. Messenger (2015: 159) notes that 'the central concern of the

---

18. This is amplified in Boström (2016: 137–146).
19. Much of this section is lightly adapted from Wilson (2015: 219–222).

book is the call to live life in awe of God. This call opens the book (Prov. 1:7), pervades it (Prov. 9:10), and brings it to a close (Prov. 31:30).' The frequency of the expression *the fear of the Lord* is quite remarkable, being found in the gateway chapters 1 – 9 (1:7, 29; 2:4–5; 8:13; 9:10; the verb *fear the Lord* is found in 3:7), the sentence sayings (10:27; 14:26–27; 15:16, 33; 16:6; 19:23; 22:4; 23:17; the verb is found in 24:21) and the epilogue (31:30).[20] Furthermore, its structural location is very significant. The concentration of occurrences in the foundational first nine chapters is itself important, but made more so by a similar proverb at the climax to the prologue (1:7) and between the invitations of wisdom and folly in chapter 9 (9:10). These two instances bracket the first nine chapters, which also form an inclusio with its occurrence at the end of the epilogue (31:30). The concept is also structurally important in the Solomonic sayings, being found towards the beginning and end (10:27; 22:4), and concentrated in the theological seam in the middle (15:16, 33; 16:6; strengthened by the number of other Yahweh sayings here). Even the subsequent words of the wise (22:17 – 24:22) begin with the similar idea of *trust . . . in the Lord* (22:19), close with *fear the Lord* (24:21) and have an exhortation to continue in the *fear of the Lord* (23:17) in the middle. The expression is not found in the brief further sayings of the wise (24:23–34), the later proverbs edited in Hezekiah's time (25 – 29) or the words of Agur and Lemuel (30:1 – 31:9), but the crucial importance of the idea has already been established. The important structural positioning of the motif testifies to the centrality of the idea in the book as a whole.

The concept of the fear of the Lord is potentially open to mis-understanding. It does not imply being terrified by, or living in dread of, God. Rather, it has a range of meanings that centre on respecting God as God and treating him as he deserves. It is this underlying attitude of treating God as God that is the only true foundation for knowledge and living wisely as outlined in the book, and is a necessary condition for living successfully in God's world. This inner attitude is closely connected to humility (15:33; 22:4), or rightly

---

20. On this theme in Proverbs and the wider wisdom books, see Wilson (1995: 59–79).

acknowledging that the Lord is God in his world. Those who wish to be shaped by wisdom are urged to embrace this right response to God (1:29; 3:7; 24:21). It is the beginning or first principle of wisdom (1:7; 9:10), but is also our ongoing response as well (23:17). The fear of the Lord is the foundation for a godly character (2:4–5 in the setting of 2:1–11) and is a moral category that will involve the rejection of arrogance and evil actions (8:13; 16:6). As instruction in wisdom (15:33) and a fountain of life (14:27; see the parallel with the teaching of the wise in 13:14), it is to be prized highly, since it is a more valuable possession than earthly riches (15:16). It results in a satisfying life (19:23), and is amply rewarded (22:4). As such, it is fitting that the virtue of fearing the Lord (31:30) climaxes the description of wisdom lived out in practice in the closing poem of 31:10–31.

d. God's active kingly rule in everyday life

Murphy (1986: 88–89) noticed two key theological ideas in Proverbs. First, the creation theology of the book, which establishes that 'Wisdom is more than well-turned nuggets of human observation.' Second, there is a key concept that God (who in Israelite wisdom must be Yahweh) reveals himself in human experiences. Similarly, Brueggemann (2003: 307–308) has argued that 'Wisdom theology in the book of Proverbs is thoroughly theological. That is, it refers every aspect of life to the rule of God.' He comments, 'The fact that the teaching is inductive and established case by case, however, makes the teaching no less formidable theologically, because wisdom asserts that the God who decrees and maintains a particular ordering of reality toward life is a sovereign beyond challenge whose will, purpose, and order cannot be defied or circumvented with impunity.'

    In seeking to identify the theological content of the book, Van Leeuwen (2005: 638) has argued that 'Proverbs raises the theological question of the relation of ordinary life in the cosmos to God the Creator.' As can be seen in the thematic studies in the next section, the focus of the book does not centre on the covenant, the law or even Israel and its institutions. Rather, it concerns those areas of everyday life such as wealth, speech, families, friends, work and our inner goals (the heart) which make up 'the good life'. Much of the rest of the OT deals with God's active rule as King over his chosen people, living in (and sometimes travelling towards or exiled from) the Promised Land, and being under the authority of God's law. Proverbs, like the other wisdom books, has a wider vista on all humanity, the whole earth (at times, the cosmos), and living in response to God's ordering of his creation (see Wilson 2015: 310–312). God the Creator is pictured as the one who sustains and orders his creation, and it is in this everyday life context that we have to live wisely.

This makes the book of Proverbs a rich source of teaching about how to live in a godly and wise way in our daily lives. God is clearly the one in charge (16:1–2, 9), and he is actively at work in his work (16:4, 7). While the law is dominated by commands and prohibitions ('you shall not . . .') and the prophets thunder at the people 'thus says the Lord', Kidner (1964: 13) notes that there is in wisdom books like Proverbs a concern with those everyday details which are too small to be trapped in the mesh of the law or attacked by the broadsides of the prophets. Proverbs deals with how to approach God and especially other people, but in quite a distinctive way. It is less confined to religious actions, and more orientated to the whole of life – what we spend most of our time doing. This is why generations of believers have found it such a profitable book. Moreover, it is concerned with our character (see especially on ch. 2) and not simply with our external actions. Who we are counts just as much for Proverbs as what we do. Proverbs takes our faith out of our church buildings and into the world, arguing that God is interested in us living under his active kingly rule in that context as well. There are rich resources here for a theology of everyday life.

e. Proverbs and biblical theology

The Bible, including the OT, is about God revealing and establishing his active kingly rule (= the kingship or kingdom of God), teaching and enabling God's people to live under this kingly rule. It outlines God's people, living in God's place, under God's rule. As such, it concerns God's active involvement in history, in creation, in everyday life, in the world, in God's people, in the future – and outlining the implications of God's kingly rule – for God's people and for others, in terms of how we are to respond to him as King, how we are to live, what we are to look forward to, and back to. The Bible is not just about God, but about his ordering, ruling, controlling his creation and his people, regulating life in his creation and calling for response from people. It outlines God's kingly rule past, present and future, exercised through special people and through his word, in the world and among his people, and climaxes in the life, death and victorious resurrection of Jesus.

What part does Proverbs play in such a biblical theology? It focuses on everyday life: what works, what brings success and so on. It speaks about God being in control, but not acting visibly in the world to accomplish his purposes. However, rather than God directly intervening as in the history books, there is a focus on the natural processes. In 10:3–4 God prospers the righteous, but it is achieved through their diligence. Similarly, the lazy will come to poverty through their slackness, although this is also the work of the Lord. Often Proverbs simply asserts that God does or will do something, without outlining the means he uses (e.g. 12:2–3; 15:25; 16:3, 5). There is no hint of God's overt intervention, but in all this he is actively at work, achieving his outcomes and controlling these natural processes as he brings about his purposes behind the scenes. It is describing the work of the same God as the rest of the OT, but focuses on the regular and orderly patterns of his sustaining work, rather than on his more specific, spectacular redemptive activity that is dominant in much of the rest of the OT. Of course, other parts of the OT explore God's work in creation, such as the creation accounts of Genesis 1 – 2, God's power over creation in Exodus 1 – 15, some psalms (e.g. 19, 104), and even the image of the new creation in Isaiah 65:17–25. Proverbs mentions in passing God's action in bringing creation into being (3:19–20; 8:22–31), but the main emphasis is on his sustaining activity. The one who brought creation into being now also keeps it going, and urges people to learn from how he sustains it.

Thus, Proverbs (as part of wisdom literature) adds a distinctive richness to a biblical understanding of God at work in his world. It must be read on its own terms first (so Longman 2006: 64), and in so doing it reveals that God's purposes are broader than simply saving sinners. While this will always be at the heart of the Bible, God has seen fit to include a book like Proverbs which describes him as actively at work in shaping individuals and the community in accordance with his values, and giving much instruction for daily living. Since all of life must come under Christ's lordship (since he is in Col. 1:15–20 Lord of both creation and redemption), then the teaching of Proverbs must be brought to the NT and reread in the light of Christ (Luke 24:27, 44). Jesus builds on the teaching of Proverbs (e.g. parts of the Sermon on the Mount) in arguing that our new life in Christ must result in a radically transformed way of daily living. Some later NT books develop that in terms of life in the church, as well as in our everyday lives in the world (e.g. James).[21]

5. Thematic issues

Many preachers and teachers use thematic studies on the sentence sayings of the book (see Ministry issues, pp. 48–51). I will explore the issue of wealth and poverty at greater length as a guide for how this can be done, with briefer analyses of some other key themes.[22]

a. Wealth and poverty
In Proverbs wealth is viewed positively, neutrally and negatively, and we must not simply 'cherry-pick' those sayings that suit us. Moreover, the explicit teaching of the book is that there are other matters that are of greater value than wealth.

---

21. Two examples of tracing through the concerns of Proverbs (e.g. on speech) in the light of the NT are given by Lucas (2015: 363–382) and Longman (2002: 145–155). See also the thematic studies in the next section, which need to be developed by reflections on how the coming of Christ and the explicit teaching of the NT enrich and apply the teaching of Proverbs.
22. Several other books will provide topical studies of these and other issues. See Kidner (1964: 31–56); Aitken (1986: 144–231); Farmer (1991: 73–102); Dell (2002: 34–115); Estes (2005: 221–261); Longman (2006: 549–578); Lucas (2015: 232–314). Voorwinde (1996) has helpfully grouped the proverbs without comment into a variety of topics. Another way of grouping the proverbs has been to study the various characters or stereotypes mentioned in the book. On this see Aitken (1986: 93–144); Lucas (2015: 219–232).

The link between godliness and wealth is already clear in 3:9–10, where honouring the Lord with your wealth and produce leads to full storage barns and overflowing vats of wine. Wisdom is seen to be the possessor (and giver) of riches and enduring wealth (3:16; 8:18), although in these proverbs wisdom holds this wealth together with honour, righteousness and long life. This gift of wealth is viewed as an inheritance arranged by wisdom (8:21). Other sayings view riches as a blessing or reward from God (10:22; 13:21). The normal expectation according to 15:6 is that the righteous will receive treasure. However, Sandoval (2006: 156–157) notes that the proverbs which promise well-being, such as 11:18 and 15:6, require a figurative reading rather than one in dollar or shekel terms. They are true as generalizing proverbs, but should not be read as promises. Yet the normal pattern remains that embracing knowledge and wisdom will lead to riches (24:4).

So the book of Proverbs does make a connection between righteousness and wealth, and between wickedness and poverty, but it does much more than this. Waltke (2004: 463) notes that half the occurrences of wealth, *hôn*, in the Solomonic collection concern prizing wealth (10:15; 12:27; 13:7; 19:14; 29:3), and the other half make the balancing point of not trusting in it. Its teaching on riches is much more nuanced than is suggested by some proponents of prosperity theology.

At times, the book of Proverbs simply provides a descriptive, neutral or non-evaluative observation about money or wealth. Proverbs 10:15 observes that wealth can provide a certain measure of safety and security. This proverb is not arguing that people should trust in their wealth for security. It is simply observing that wealth provides insulation from setbacks in life, without any judgment about this being right or wrong. The proverb of verse 15a is used in 18:11–12 to warn against pride, but here it serves to ground the observation in verse 16 that the character of a person will determine whether wealth will be beneficial or harmful. Proverbs 14:20 observes that the rich have more friends than the poor (Murphy 1998: 105, 'riches create differences in social life'), without any implication that this ought to be the case. There is no command to follow, or goal to strive for. The proverb just describes the reality that those who are rich can lavish good things on their friends, but a poor person has little to give. It is also clear that economic power is real. Proverbs 22:7 outlines a society stratified by power linked to money, but the proverb neither condemns nor commends it. It simply observes that economic power is part of reality, whether that be the greater opportunities the rich have compared with the poor, or the dependency that results when a person takes out a loan from another.

There are various observations that negate or significantly qualify a connection between righteousness and wealth. These fall into a number of groups. First, there are the many references to wicked people being wealthy. Second, there are examples of people who gain wealth wrongfully, such as through bribes, injustice, assault, adultery or even just too hastily. Corresponding to these are depictions of those who are poor, whose poverty is not due to unrighteousness. Lastly, there are some warnings about the dangers of wealth itself.

Yet the fact that Proverbs mentions those who are both wicked and rich makes it clear that there is no automatic connection between righteousness and wealth. If righteousness is always rewarded with riches, and wickedness punished by poverty, then there should be no wicked rich, but there are (11:7; 22:16; 28:6, 8, 22).

There are also a number of general descriptions of people wrongfully gaining wealth (10:2; 11:4; 21:6). Wealth cannot be pursued without weighing up the means used to attain it. Thus, we see the problem of wealth gained by bribes (17:8, 23; 29:4), dishonesty (20:10), injustice (18:5; 22:22, 28; 28:21), physical attacks on others (1:8–19; 16:19), adultery or prostitution (5:8–12; 6:29–32) and even acquired too hastily (13:11; 20:21; 28:20). The flip side of this is that there are those who are poor, not because of wickedness, but due to the wrong actions of others (13:23). It is clear, then, that Proverbs does not exclusively teach that God will always financially reward the wise/righteous and financially punish the foolish/wicked. Life does not work that way, and neither does the book of Proverbs.

So people are warned not to trust in riches (11:28) since God is the one who is to be trusted (16:20; 28:25; 29:25). Riches are seen to be fleeting (23:4–5). One of the seductions of wealth is that it offers the lure of becoming self-sufficient (18:10–11), presumably by insulating the possessor from having to worry about daily needs. Yet

sometimes having wealth leads to greater danger, such as being the
target of kidnappers (13:8).

The book of Proverbs also insists that there are other things more
valuable than 'mere money'. Some obvious examples will suffice:
wisdom is of greater worth than wealth (8:10–11, 19), as are
wholesome relationships (17:1), godly character (22:1; 28:6), righteousness (11:4) and honour (11:16). Furthermore, wealth is only of
value if it is combined with the more crucial category of a godly
character, grounded in the fear of the Lord, and issuing in a life of
justice and righteousness. Thus, if wisdom is allowed to shape our
character, then the way we use wealth must be consistent with a
godly character. When it comes to money, that will involve not being
greedy, or coveting what others have, not having as our goal in life
to make as much money as possible (i.e. worshipping it). It will
lead us to think in community terms (a godly character builds up
community), and be committed to justice and righteousness. Lucas
(2015: 293) notes that the prologue sets out the purpose of the book
and 'there is no indication that it offers the attainment of material
wealth.' Instead, 'the point the prologue makes is that what you *are*
is foundational to the good life. What you *have* is a secondary matter.'

A closer look at 3:1–12 is in order. Waltke (2004: 238–240)
helpfully shows that verses 1–10 are a celebration of what flows
from the changed character outlined in chapter 2. In the odd verses
(vv. 1, 3, 5, 7, 9), he discerns the outline of a godly character, while
the even verses (vv. 2, 4, 6, 8, 10) draw attention to the outcomes
that will follow. When read together, the even-numbered verses
announce that those who are shaped by wisdom will receive a
long and peace-filled life, favour and success in the sight of both
God and others, a straight path through life, physical health and
healing, and abundant material prosperity. But that cannot be independent of trusting in the Lord (v. 5), fearing the Lord (v. 7) and
honouring the Lord (v. 9). Indeed, the material prosperity in 3:9–10
is not linked with the size of a monetary gift, but with character
(honouring the Lord, v. 9; see also *trust in the LORD*, v. 5; *fear the LORD*,
v. 7). Lucas (2015: 295) comments that 'the enjoyment of wealth is
subordinated to, and dependent on, honouring the LORD.' Of course,
there is no *promise* of abundant wealth in 3:9–10, any more than there
was a promise of long life and peace in 3:2. In fact, verses 1–10 are

also followed immediately by verses 11–12, which address the situation when the prosperity, life and success of verses 1–10 do not seem to be happening.

While the faithful use of material possessions often leads to further material blessing (3:9–10), this must always be based on honouring the Lord (3:9). The depiction of character in Proverbs would involve not wanting to give wealth an inordinate place in one's desires, so that truly honouring God would entail keeping your life free from the love of money. One clear goal of 'the good life' is the virtue of contentment (15:16–17; 16:8; 30:8–9).

In the book as a whole, the appropriate response to gaining wealth is not the accumulation of further riches, but rather generosity to those in need (22:9). It is clear in 11:24–26 that any growth in wealth is simply an added bonus and not the goal of the enterprise (see also 14:22). Proverbs, like the rest of the OT, endorses care for, rather than exploitation of, the poor and needy in their own community (14:31; 19:17; 22:22–23; 31:20).

b. Family and marriage

Proverbs 6:16–19 lists a series of matters that are abominable to the Lord, and these climax (or reach their low point) in a person who stirs up division between brothers. Hybels (1988: 161–193) suggests that forging strong families is a key theme of the book. However, it seems to talk more about godly families – those which have been worked over or shaped by God. Godly families are certainly important for the good life. Many Western cultures define a good family as one where children are well provided for and given a lot of opportunities and experiences so that they can reach their full potential. Proverbs thinks more in terms of training children to respect others, handing down the truths of the faith and modelling the service of God. The goal is that children become people who fear the Lord and develop a godly character.

Parents have a responsibility to teach and train their children. This is part of our role and responsibility before God, and given to both fathers and mothers (1:8). One well-known saying is *Train up a child in the way he should go; even when he is old he will not depart from it* (22:6). While this is not a guarantee (remember it is a proverb, not a promise) that the children of godly parents will become believers themselves, it does give parents encouragement that diligent parenting is valuable and has enduring effects. Notwithstanding the exceptions that we all know, it is generally true that good teaching and discipline in a family will strike a positive response from a child. However, this proverb should not be pressed so far that we ignore either the sovereign election of God, or the real responsibility of children themselves. Proverbs 22:15 points out that *folly is bound up in the heart of a child*. A child can be too opinionated to learn (13:1; 17:21), idle (10:5) or self-indulgent (29:3). Children might mock or curse (30:11, 17) and waste their parents' money (28:24; 29:3). It is unkind to leave them like that, and so parents have a responsibility to teach and train their children (23:13–14).

References to the rod are not primarily an endorsement of corporal punishment, but rather a call to teach and correct those in our charge. In ancient Israel it involved the use of the rod, but each generation needs to apply the principle of correcting children in ways that work best in their society. The warning that if we do not use the rod, we hate the child (13:24; 29:15, 17) is really an out-working of the book's real concern to mould children to live wisely. A hard road to wisdom is better than a soft road to death (19:18; 23:14), and their character needs shaping (22:15). The encouragement of training a child (22:6) is based on the view that character is like a plant that grows better by pruning (5:11, 12; 15:32, 33).

Yet there is also the positive dimension of encouraging the next generation. We do not only prune plants, but also fertilize, feed and water them. With our children we train them by instruction (7:2, 3), having the aim of equipping them for life (3:23; 4:8–9, 12). Of course, parents must themselves model godly behaviour. As 20:7 expresses it,

The righteous who walks in his integrity –
blessed are his children after him!

The children of godly parents are blessed because they have an example to follow. Thus *the glory of children is their fathers* (17:6b).

Children – even youths or adult children – must respect their parents and their teaching. They are called to give due honour to their parents (23:22), which at least involves listening to them and not despising them (19:26; 20:20; 28:24; 30:11). The consequences of mocking or scorning obedience to parents are set out memorably in 30:17! So children must learn to live wisely day by day, and to adopt healthy patterns for the rest of their lives (23:19–21). The ideal is to live in such a way that their (godly) parents or grandparents delight in them (10:1; 15:20; 23:24–25; 17:6a). This focus on others rather than self is part of the counter-cultural summons of the book, then and especially now. Godly families are set in the wider context of a transformed community.

The book of Proverbs does not aim to give a comprehensive study of marriage, but it does shed light on some aspects of this particular relationship. A few matters are dealt with in passing, such as the covenantal nature of marriage (2:17), even if issues like divorce are not covered. Again, the marriages in view are between one man and one woman (5:15–20; 31:10–31), but there is no explicit polemic against polygamy, let alone the contemporary issue of same-sex marriage. There is much emphasis on the loose or foreign woman (including the prostitute and adulteress) in chapters 1 – 9 (e.g. 2:16–19; 5:1–23; 6:20–35; 7:1–27; 9:13–18). While these passages are primarily about folly personified in its clearest example, they do also disclose something about sexual relationships outside of marriage. This is not largely the focus of the later sentence sayings, but occasionally surfaces (e.g. 22:14; 23:27–28; 30:20). It is clear that young men are warned against both the prostitute and the adulteress, and that succumbing to either is a failure of both wisdom and discipline (e.g. 5:12–13, 23). However, more significant is the positive endorsement of sex (developed in the Song of Songs) within the context of marriage in 5:15–20. The explicit commendation of one's wife in 5:18–19 suggests that chapters 5 – 7 can be used to speak not only about folly personified but also sexual temptation and transgression.

A spouse is a good gift from God (18:22; 19:14; 30:18–19), and men are urged not to stray from their home (27:8). Young people are urged to choose their spouse carefully, as a good wife enriches a person's life (12:4), just as a poor choice makes life constantly difficult (e.g. 11:22; 19:13; 21:9, 19; 25:24; 27:15–16).[23] Of course,

---

23. In relation to 21:9, Dell (2002: 107) rightly notes that 'This
    maxim would of course be equally applicable to an autocratic

many of the truths about friendship will apply to marriage as well. The book concludes with a long poem about an excellent wife (31:10–31). While this concluding section is mainly intended to exemplify wisdom (a counterbalance to folly 'enfleshed' in chapters 5 – 7), it also draws attention to a number of positive attributes in a wife (see below on the 'good life'). Of special significance is the statement that she fears the Lord (31:30), which presumably is the foundation for her actions full of energy, care and initiative.

c. Friends

We need godly advice about friendship because this is a key area in which we often hurt others by our shortcomings. Indeed, most of us can tell of times when we chose the wrong friends and got hurt.[24] Given the increasing strength of peer pressure, this teaching is more vital than ever. The opening chapters of the book have a repeated emphasis on young men avoiding bad male company. The negative counter-example to embracing wisdom (1:20–33; 4:10–13) is joining a gang (1:8–19; 4:14–17), while the result of the shaped character (2:1–11) is being rescued from wicked men and their ways (2:12–15). The danger of simply drifting into a bad friendship is also enunciated later in the book (13:20; 28:7b).

What kind of friend is commended in the book? A key feature of a good friend is loyalty. A true friend has an ongoing commitment and is not put off by adversity (*loves at all times*, 17:17). Such a friend can establish a relationship that is even stronger than our family bonds (18:24). The relationship between David and Jonathan was this type of friendship (1 Sam. 20, especially vv. 17, 41–42). They do not cease to be friends when it no longer suits them, or they no longer receive material benefit from it (e.g. gifts, 19:6). Thus, the closeness of our relationships is more important than the number of friendships we have (18:24). So friends are to be greatly valued (27:10).

---

and quarrelsome male, whose wife might prefer to spend a night on the roof!'

24. The common Hebrew word for 'friend' (*rēaʿ*) can also mean 'neighbour'. I have focused on friendship, but it is always wise to keep this alternative meaning in mind.

Genuine or earnest advice is a valuable aspect of friendship (27:9). The best kind of friend is not one who will always agree with, flatter or affirm us, but rather one who has our best interests at heart. Thus, our friends will be those who will be honest and open with us. Kidner (1964: 44–45) reminds us that they need to say both 'yes' and 'no' – 'yes' to a proper request (3:27–28), but 'no' when it would lead to folly (6:1–5). We do not benefit from deceptive flattery (26:24–25), but we can certainly grow in character when those committed to us are brave enough to rebuke and challenge us (27:5–6; 28:23). Our wisdom 'sharpness' grows as we interact with our friends, like iron sharpening iron (27:17). Friends do not simply indulge us, but also hold us accountable. The words a friend uses may hurt (*wound*, 27:6), but they come from a faithful desire that we grow. As our friends help us to grow in wisdom, they will no doubt also help us to grow in our relationship with God.

Finally, some characteristics of others militate against establishing valuable friendships. Thus, a gossip is a person to be avoided (16:28; 17:9; 20:19; 26:20–21). Gossip is often a 'respectable sin' in Christian circles, sometimes disguised by 'sharing a matter for prayer', but it is destructive of community and of faith.

Someone who is inconsiderate or insensitive will make a poor friend. A person loudly 'blessing' another early in the morning (the community equivalent of waking a teenager), will not be appreciated (27:14). Humour is a great source of enjoyment in relationships, but one who does not know when to stop, or how to use humour, will also make a poor friend (26:18–19). Saying 'I was only joking' does not fix the hurt or betrayal. Other indications of a poor friend include overstaying a welcome (25:17) and being insensitive to someone's pain (25:20).

Friendship is one of God's good gifts and is too important a gift to treat lightly. Proverbs urges us to be wise in the friends we choose, for they will influence us greatly, for good or bad. We need to choose those friends who will help make our character and actions reflect the values of wisdom. Yet, in the end, the emphasis should fall not on how we should choose our friends, but on what kind of friend we should be to others (3:27). Lucas (2015: 239) comments, 'We are not all parents, but all are children. We are not all married but are all family members. So, we all can play our part in creating functional families.'

d. Speech and words

The discussion of family and friends leads naturally to the issue of speech, possibly the most prominent theme in the book. While a contemporary English proverb says that 'sticks and stones may break my bones, but words will never hurt me', the book of Proverbs sees that speech has great power for both good and harm. Words have the power to bring life and cause death (18:21; 12:6); they can cause healing or inflict damage like a sword (12:18; 14:25; 15:4); they can restore joy to an anxious person (12:25). They are seldom 'mere words'. Grace-filled words have a sweetness that revives and restores (16:24), but worthless speech is like a scorching fire, and brings strife and division (16:27–28). Wisdom and folly personified are able to be distinguished by their life-giving or life-taking words (9:5–6, 17–18). Wise words reflect what we are like inside – wise of heart (16:23; 18:4).

Proverbs both warns against the wrong use of words, and affirms the right use of words. In 6:16–19 three out of the seven things God hates have to do with false speech (*a lying tongue, a false witness who breathes out lies* and *one who sows discord among brothers*). A worthless or wicked person is characterized by crooked speech (6:12). Scoffers epitomize the wrong use of words, as their mocking speech leads to quarrels, strife and abuse (22:10; 29:8). They react angrily to correction (9:7–8a; 15:12), making them an abomination (24:9), spoilt by their pride and arrogance (21:24).[25] Close to the scoffer are those who slander or insult others (10:18b). Their words reveal other people's secrets (11:13), or wrongly curse those who deserve their loyalty (20:20).

There is a significant focus on lying in the book. The Lord hates lies and false witness (6:17, 19; 12:22), and the righteous should do

---

25. McKane (1970: 399) comments, 'No man earns more universal detestation or deserves it more than he who . . . supposes it is his mission in life to promote the corrosion of the values by which individuals and society lives.'

so too (13:5). There are explicit or implied exhortations not to speak
crookedly or lie (4:24; 12:17, 19). Agur asks for two things: neither
poverty nor riches, and falsehood and lying to be removed far from
him (30:7–8). Telling lies is harmful (25:18), and we should not lie
to get out of an obligation (3:28; 12:13).[26] It has been pointed out
that 'Throughout the book of Proverbs, the importance of telling
the truth is a steady drumbeat' (Messenger 2015: 164). It is better to
be poor than a liar (19:22), which includes not keeping a promise
(25:14). Lying is closely related to its more socially acceptable cousin
– flattery (26:28; 28:23). This too should not characterize those who
want to walk in the way of wisdom. Furthermore, we should not
listen to, or tolerate, the mischievous lies of others (17:4).

There are a number of other ways in which words can be abused.
We are not to use them to boast about ourselves (27:2), or to show
off before others (12:23). Nor are we to speak too hastily before we
have heard the full picture (18:13, 17; 29:20). A wise character is
needed to know when to speak and when to refrain from speaking
(26:4, 5). Words used in gossip are harmful and pointless (11:13; 18:8;
26:22), and speaking behind the backs of others is destructive (25:23).
We should beware of the seductive use of words by those enticing
us to do wrong. This is most clearly seen in the book in the figure
of the forbidden woman with her silky smooth words (2:16; 5:3;
6:24; 7:21–22; 22:14), but others can also cause damage by disguising
their harmfulness behind gracious words (e.g. 26:23–26).

However, there is also much written in the book about how words
are to be used in a positive way. Indeed, the assumption is that godly
speech will prevail (10:31). We need to listen to, and be shaped by,
the words of wisdom as she speaks (e.g. 1:20–21; 2:1–2; 8:1–11).
Wisdom's words are true and life-giving (8:7–8, 32–35), just as every
word from God is true (30:5–6). Our righteous words are designed
to give life (10:11), commend knowledge (15:2) and show a winsome
grace (22:11). We are to speak up for the helpless poor and needy
(31:8–9), and utter true words of confession before God and others
when we have done wrong (28:13). Self-control should be a feature

---

26. In relation to 12:13, Alden (1983: 101) cites the rabbinic saying: 'If you
always tell the truth, you don't have to remember what you said.'

of our speech, as we carefully weigh up when to speak and what to say (13:3; 17:27–28; 21:23). This may often lead to us speaking fewer words, as we ponder carefully how to answer a person (15:28). With fewer words we can pay more attention to their quality or truth or helpfulness (10:19). A timely comment or 'word in season' can be very beneficial (15:23; 25:11).

Certainly, our words should be honest (24:26), although this does not preclude us from giving correction when needed (27:5). Although our words may seek to be persuasive (16:21, 23), they must also be gentle (15:1, 4) and gracious (16:24; 31:26). A civil tongue should not simply be dismissed as a relic of a bygone era. There should be a calmness (or *cool spirit*, 17:27) in how we speak, as we attempt to do good and bring wholeness with our words.

e. Work and laziness

The focus on daily life in Proverbs makes it a rich source of teaching about the neglected topic of daily work.[27] A counterpoint to this information about work is the comic portrayal of the one who refuses to work – the lazy person or sluggard.[28] The two themes are sometimes discussed separately (e.g. hard work in 27:23–27; laziness in 26:13–16), but also woven together into one for a sharper analysis (e.g. 6:6–11).

On the topic of work, the book deals extensively with a wide range of workplaces: 'agriculture, animal husbandry, textile and clothing manufacture, trade, transportation, military affairs, governance, courts of law, homemaking, raising children, education, construction and others' (Messenger 2015: 159–160). The woman of 31:10–31 is active in many of these areas, making it clear that the issue of work is a vital one for both men and women. The book contains reflections both on work itself, and on how workers should work.

---

27. On this see Messenger (2015: 155–197). The main contributors to this section of *Theology of Work Bible Commentary* were Bruce Waltke and Alice Mathews. It helpfully contains the text of all verses in the book related to work (187–197).

28. On the sluggard, see Lucas (2015: 227–228); Waltke (2004: 114–115); Aitken (1986: 116–121).

Work is seen as the appropriate way to provide wealth and sustenance (10:4; 12:11; 28:19). It is, at the very least, a fitting way to avoid poverty (14:23), and a failure to work will result in a person not having enough to eat (20:4). A memorable example is given of the hard-working ant (6:6–8) who works without a supervisor forcing her to focus, and who plans ahead for future lean times. An interesting feature of the book of Proverbs is that there is almost no focus on job satisfaction, nor of the value of work or the danger of overworking. However, it affirms the rightness of working skilfully (i.e. performing a job well), and the observation is made that this will lead to professional advancement in future (22:29). It also indicates that work to meet our basic needs should take priority over work to make life more comfortable (24:27).

There is much greater emphasis on the attitudes we bring to our work. The Theology of Work Project helpfully draws out a number of descriptions of the wise worker (Messenger 2015: 161–186). Those shaped by wisdom will be trustworthy or honest in their work, both in their words (8:6–7; 10:18–19; 12:17–20; 14:25; 21:6) and actions (11:1; 16:11; 23:10–11). They will be diligent, working hard (10:4–5), planning for the future (6:6–8; 21:5; 24:27; 27:23–27) and contributing to the profitability of the workplace (18:9; 31:18a). Such a worker will also be shrewd (1:4–5) in the sense of showing good judgment (31:13–14), preparing for contingencies (31:21–22) and seeking good advice (15:22; 20:18). Wise workers will be both generous (11:24–26; 19:17; 28:27) and just (3:27–28; 16:8; 22:8–9, 16, 22–23). They will be careful in their speech (21:23), avoiding gossip (11:12–13; 16:27–28; 18:6–8; 20:19; 26:20–21), speaking kindly (15:1, 18; 16:32; 31:26) and using words to build up others (12:25; 15:4; 18:21). Finally, they will be modest rather than proud (11:2; 16:18–19; 21:4; 29:23) or even wealth-seeking (11:28; 22:1; 23:4; 28:22; 30:8–9).

On the issue of laziness, the book concentrates on the lazy person or sluggard rather than laziness itself.[29] Longman (2006: 561) notes that 'Proverbs is intolerant of lazy people; they are considered the

---

29. Dell (2002: 43) notes that warnings against being lazy outweigh those that promote hard work. She concludes, 'Warnings against laziness, then, are more important to the sages than praise of the work ethic itself.'

epitome of folly.' Sluggards are caricatured throughout the book. They make up fanciful stories (*There is a lion in the road/outside*, 22:13; 26:13) to justify their inactivity.[30] They reach out for food but cannot be bothered to bring the food back to their mouth (26:15). Their only exercise is to turn over in bed (26:14). The sluggard owns a vineyard, but neglects it so much (almost as if he did not notice) that it becomes overgrown with thorns and nettles, and its protective walls are broken down (24:30–31). No other stereotype is denigrated quite as much as the lazy person. Dell (2002: 37) expresses it well: 'Laziness is a barren land that leads nowhere.' In an honour/shame culture, the lazy bring shame on their family (10:5) and destroy their family's inheritance (19:13–15; 24:30–31).

Kidner (1964: 42, followed by Lucas 2015: 228) suggests that the sluggard's problem is threefold: 'he will not begin things . . . he will not finish things . . . he will not face things'. He prefers sleep to effort (6:9–10; 24:33); he is an irritant to those around him (10:26, *like vinegar to the teeth and smoke to the eyes*); he is unsatisfied (13:4; 21:25–26) and destructive (18:9); and is heading nowhere in life (12:24; 24:34). Waltke (2004: 115) notes that the sluggard is never equated with the poor whom we should help, and that the only thing he has plenty of is poverty (28:19). Being lazy causes us to miss out on the good life which hard work is intended to bring about.

f. The good life

The whole of the book of Proverbs could be covered under the heading of 'the good life' (see e.g. Whybray 2002: 161–185). While this would be both worthwhile and comprehensive, my aim in this section is to examine one cameo – that of the excellent wife in 31:10–31 – as a source of insights about the good life according to the book. This could be a very fruitful topic for a final sermon or Bible study on the book. This approach is based on the assumption (argued for in the commentary) that the wife of 31:10–31 is not simply a (possibly composite and certainly overwhelming) model

---

30. Aitken (1986: 118) comments, 'Clearly the sages enjoyed poking fun and pouring ridicule on this lazy fellow. They saved some of their best humour and liveliest imagery for him.'

of what a wife should be like, but is rather a worked example of
what it means to live wisely in the world. As such, it is a useful
source of instruction for both men and women who seek to live
the 'good life'.

She embodies many of the themes picked up in this section of
the commentary. The Proverbs 31 woman models the achievement
of a secure life for herself and her dependants, principally security
from a life of poverty. She gains prosperity because of her entrepreneurial skills, hard, persistent work, good management and her
business acumen (vv. 13–19, 24, 27). She trades and transports
her goods (vv. 13–14, 24), buys land and starts a business (v. 16). She
rises early (v. 15a), works until late (v. 18b) and provides food for
her family and servants (v. 15b) as well as clothing (vv. 17, 19). Verse
27 summarizes her diligence in work:

> *She looks well to the ways of her household*
> *and does not eat the bread of idleness.*

Her family can live securely without anxiety about the future as *she
laughs at the time to come* (v. 25b). While there is no explicit mention of
her exercising civic power, her work builds up her husband's situation
(vv. 11b–12), and he has a leading role in the community (v. 23 – the
gate is the place of civic and legal decision-making). Thus, the family
is wealthy as a result of her effort. There is no lack of gain (v. 11b);
she trades profitably (v. 18a); her family is warmly clothed and her
house furnished (vv. 21–22). Of course, this is not at the expense
of the rest of the community, as she provides food for her servants
(v. 15b) and gives generously to the poor and needy (v. 20). In
financial terms she cares for those around her. There is no specific
mention of good health and long life, but she must have had
many years of energy-filled living in order to do all the things she
accomplished.

She also excels in relational terms. Her speech is characterized by
kindness and wisdom (v. 26). The passage as a whole paints a full
picture of a contented and prosperous family, with their needs
provided for by her initiatives. Her spouse and children value her
highly (v. 28), and she enables the family to flourish (vv. 11–12). In
the end, her key relationship is with God, and the climactic

description of her is that she is *a woman who fears the LORD* (v. 30). Her experience of the good life is predicated on that foundation or building block. She is testimony to the fact that there is more to people than charm and beauty (v. 30a – although she apparently likes nice clothes, vv. 21b, 22b), as instead she grounds her life on giving God the respect and trust due to him (the fear of the Lord).

The surrounding thematic studies highlight many of these characteristics in the rest of the book. Diligent work is commended as fitting for those shaped by wisdom (6:6–8; 18:9; 22:29). Wealth is a good gift (3:9–10), but is not the most important aspect of life (23:4–5), so that contentment is better than excessive riches (30:8–9). Thus, it is important to care for the poor (11:24–25; 21:13; 22:9; 29:7). Relationships – including an active trust in God – are more valuable than great wealth (15:16–17). Positive care for family, friends and neighbours is part of the fabric of the book. Friends and neighbours are to be valued highly (17:17; 18:24; 27:5–6, 10), and it is much better to be a supportive wife (12:4; 18:22) than one who constantly nags (19:13; 21:9, 19; 25:24; 27:15). A long, respected life (3:2; 16:31) and good health (3:7b–8) are greatly valued in the book, but they must be built on lives of wisdom, integrity and righteousness (8:35; 13:6; 16:6, 8, 11, 17; 21:21). A good name is preferable to great riches (22:1), and godly humility is crucial (16:18–19; 22:4). All this must be built on the foundation of a proper respect and trust in the Lord (1:7; 9:10; 15:33; 22:4). The good life in Proverbs is available to those whose entire lives are controlled by God.

So the book of Proverbs as a whole echoes the rich source of teaching about the good life given in 30:10–31. They are both memorable portrayals of what it means to be a person fully alive.

g. The heart
The theme of the heart is a neglected one in studies of Proverbs.[31] This is surprising since the two Hebrew words for heart (usually *lēb*,

---

31. Goldingay (2014: 165–167) lists, without comment, a series of proverbs under the heading, 'The Inner Person (Mind and Heart)'. Longman (2006) has a long appendix on topics in the book, but there is nothing on the heart. However, his subject index outlines where he deals with

occasionally *lēbāb*) are used over ninety times in the book. The 'heart' has a different sense in Hebrew than in English, where it often has romantic connotations ('matters of the heart'). In Proverbs it is occasionally used metaphorically (e.g. 'the heart of the sea', 30:19), and sometimes refers to 'common sense' (especially in the phrase *hăsar lēb, lacking sense* in 7:7; 9:4, 16; 10:13; 11:12; 12:11; 15:21; 24:30, etc.). However, overwhelmingly in the book (and the rest of the OT) it refers to the core of one's being and decision-making, the centre of our will and thinking, what drives us. Farmer (1991: 40) observes that 'the "heart/mind" represents the place within the human body where both rational and emotional decisions are made.'[32] This is the sense we need to explore. Estes (1997: 69) notes that 'because the heart controls all of life, it is the key to personal success or failure.'

Despite the book's concern for wise and foolish actions, it is also aware of the underlying attitudes of the heart. It is an integral part (2:10) of the shaped character (2:9–11) of the wise, and linked with both wisdom (2:10) and understanding (2:2). The outward commands and actions have to be internalized (3:1, 3; 4:4, 21), while trusting the Lord must be grounded in what we are like on the inside, being our core commitment (3:5). Chapters 2 – 4 are concerned with our fundamental choice to embrace wisdom and have our character shaped. The central role of the heart in this is set out clearly in 4:23:

> *Keep your heart with all vigilance,*
> *for from it flow the springs of life.*

In the warnings against the forbidden women in chapters 5 – 7, 'heart problems' can lead to harmful choices. The heart can despise

---

(note 31 *cont.*) the idea in the book (also Waltke 2005). Significantly, in Voorwinde (1996: 38–42), the heart is one of the longer entries of the book, larger than topics like parents, friends and neighbours or wealth.

32. Waltke (2004: 90–91) has noted that in the biblical doctrine of humanity, the heart is seen to control the body. It involves 'the complex interplay of intellect, sensibility, and will', but also includes the spiritual dimension of trusting God.

correction (5:12); it can be perverted (6:14); it can devise wicked
plans (6:18 – indeed, the prostitute can be wily of heart, 7:10); it can
cause us to desire the beauty of the 'forbidden woman' (6:25) or to
turn aside to her ways (7:25). Seduction, adultery and their underlying
folly all start in the heart.

In the sentence sayings the *wise of heart* is contrasted with the
babbling fool (10:8), or fools more generally (11:29; 14:33). The heart
of the righteous clashes with the mouth of the wicked (15:28).
Proverbs 16:21–23 links the wise of heart (16:21) and the heart of
the wise (16:23) with winsome speech, and the two sayings bracket
verse 22 where the prudence of a wise person is a life-giving fountain.
A wise heart has the effect of gladdening the hearts of others (23:15).

The heart is to be applied to instruction or shaping (*mûsār*) in
23:12, while in 23:19 it is linked with listening and being wise so that
the young person will be directed in the right way. The words of the
wise open with a call to apply ourselves to knowledge at the core of
our being (22:17), and a right heart is connected to the fear of the
Lord (23:17). Our hearts reflect who we really are (27:19), like a
reflection in a pool of water. A good heart is characterized as
contented or tranquil (14:30), glad (15:13; 27:9, 11), cheerful (15:15),
joyful (15:30; 17:22), discerning and leading to winsome speech
(16:21, 23), intelligent (18:15) and pure (22:11). A wicked heart
is depicted instead as worthless (10:20), crooked (11:20; 17:20),
deceitful (12:20; 26:24), foolish (12:23; 15:7; 22:15), anxious (12:25),
backsliding (14:14), sorrowful (15:13), arrogant (16:5), proud (18:12;
21:4), raging against the Lord (19:3), impure and sinful (20:9), stingy
(23:7), envious (23:17), perverse (23:33), devising violence (24:2),
evil (26:23), full of abominations (26:25) and hardened (28:14). The
two ways of chapters 1 – 9 parallel the two hearts of chapters 10 –
29. God is described as the one who tests or weighs our hearts (15:11;
17:3; 21:1–2; 24:12), that is, what we are really like, not what we
pretend to be. Whybray (1990) has persuasively argued that the
theological thrust of the sentence sayings of chapters 10 – 22 is
established by the concentrations of 'Yahweh sayings' at the seam
in 15:33 – 16:9. Significantly, three of these ten verses (16:1, 5, 9;
indeed, heart is mentioned fifteen times in chapters 15 – 16) occur
in this theological kernel, reminding readers that God will determine
whether the deepest longings of our hearts will be actioned

successfully (16:1, 9), while those who are arrogant of heart will be punished (16:5).

The book of Proverbs is therefore concerned with our inner attitudes and core ambitions, and not simply with right outward actions. One of the key building blocks of chapters 1 – 9 is the importance of a shaped character, and this introduces the focus on who we are on the inside. Scaffolded to this is our ongoing commitment to our heart wisely embracing wisdom and her ways, and rejecting the path of folly. Proverbs has much to say about our outward words and actions, but this is all based on our hearts being informed, reformed and transformed.

6. Ministry issues

The important area of practical theology is often overlooked. How should we use this book in pastoral ministry and in preaching? Until we have earthed Proverbs in this way, we have not fully understood its theology. Using Proverbs as a ministry resource will be of great value because it deals with many aspects of everyday life and daily decisions not covered elsewhere. Its issues are those of contemporary men, women and children – friendship, neighbours, money, how we speak, what kind of people we want to be and so on. Proverbs not only gives us advice, but challenges our character. As Ortlund (2012: 16) has pointed out, 'What God is going after through this book is change deep inside our hearts.' There is nothing superficial about Proverbs' perspectives on daily life. In a 'Google age' we have an abundance of information, but Proverbs wants to move beyond this to transformation.

Gowan (1980: 104) sums up the attitude of many preachers:

> Of what use can the Old Testament proverbs be to the preacher? Their very nature suggests they ought not to be taken as texts to be expounded in a sermon . . . They are like the punch line of a joke; if they have to be explained, better not to bother with it in the first place.

Long has noted that '"A soft answer turns away wrath, but a harsh word stirs up anger" is a famous biblical saying, a noble thought, and in some cases a useful piece of advice. But can it serve as the basis for a sermon?' He suggests that, for many, 'the book of Proverbs appears to be a dry and barren spot among lush biblical gardens.'[33] Yet McKenzie (1996: xiii–xiv) has observed that, while our world is full of 'proverbs' (think of the many slogans like 'Just do it!'), the book of Proverbs is strangely missing from many contemporary preaching programmes.

> Proverbs! Constantly used by the people, consistently ignored by many preachers. Proverbs, which have been found almost everywhere in the world and in almost every period in human history . . . About the only place proverbs do not seem to be found today is in the pulpit . . . As Thomas G. Long points out, 'The question is not will people live by proverbs, but what kind of proverbs will they cherish?' . . .The answer, in large part, depends on the contemporary preacher.

a. Some principles for preaching Proverbs

The following guidelines will assist in using Proverbs in ministry more generally, but will have a specific focus on how to deal with those of chapters 10 – 29 in the context of a sermon or Bible study.

  i. Always approach the individual proverbs through the gateway of chapters 1 – 9. Proverbs 1 – 9 establishes the framework needed for understanding each particular proverb, based on three main messages: the fear of the Lord, choosing wisdom not folly, and the need to have our character transformed (see below for more detail). Once we have these three features in place, we are ready to interpret the individual proverbs.
  ii. Proverbs are not promises or guarantees.[34]
  iii. Proverbs do not apply all the time and in every context.
  iv. Proverbs often describe reality rather than urge action.
  v. Proverbs often have to nuance, and be nuanced by, each other.

---

33. Long (1989: 53). At fifty-five, he rightly concludes that 'People need the kind of portable and memorable wisdom of the nuts-and-bolts variety that a proverb is designed to provide.'
34. The principles outlined in ii–v are developed under Literary issues above.

vi. Each proverb must be read in the broader context of OT
wisdom literature, and as part of the OT as a whole. It can
be useful to do a series combining either Job or Ecclesiastes
with Proverbs, since this highlights the connections between
the books.

vii. Every proverb must ultimately be read in the light of Christ.
This does not mean that we need to read Christ into the
book of Proverbs (e.g. where is Christ in *Go to the ant,
O sluggard* in 6:6–11?), but it acknowledges that all Scripture
climaxes in Christ, even though the wisdom books do not
focus on God's saving rescue of his chosen people. Christ,
however, is the Lord of creation as well as the Lord of
redemption (Col. 1:15–20), so that the creation theology
of Proverbs (i.e. God sustaining his creation) finds its goal
in Christ. In addition, Christ is also the wisdom of God
(1 Cor. 1:21–24, 30), and the one 'in whom are hidden all the
treasures of wisdom and knowledge' (Col. 2:3). Witherington
(1994: 155–156) has also made the ambit claim that at least
70% of what we learn about Jesus in the Synoptic Gospels
has come from OT wisdom. While this is to overestimate the
connection, it is certainly true that his emphasis on character,
and building on the right foundation (rock not sand, Matt.
7:24–27), is strongly reminiscent of the book of Proverbs
(see Bartholomew 2001: 22–23). A number of important
parallels can be made between the key ideas of Proverbs
1 – 9 and the Christian life:

Build on the right foundation – the fear of the Lord.	The only foundation for Christians is Christ's death for our sin (Rom. 5:8; 6:23; Col. 1:21–22).[35]
Keep on choosing the way of wisdom, not the path of folly.	Live under the lordship of Jesus in our daily lives (Col. 2:6–7).
Allow wisdom to shape our character, not just change our actions.	Allow the Spirit to transform us more and more into the likeness of Christ (2 Cor. 3:18), growing in us the fruit of the Spirit (Gal. 5:22–23).

This table gives us a framework for applying the book of Proverbs to Christians, and for seeing how it can be a bridge to various cultures around the world today.[36]

b. Preaching on chapters 1 – 9

We have mentioned the three main messages of the opening nine chapters. First, we must start with the fear of the Lord, that is, respecting God for who he is. This is the initial and ongoing foundation for wise living. Second, we must keep on choosing the way of wisdom and rejecting the path of folly (personified by Lady Wisdom and Dame Folly respectively). Third, we must allow wisdom to shape our character. Any preaching on the book of Proverbs needs to cover these issues first. These emphases must be set out clearly in the initial (and perhaps final) sermons in a series on Proverbs.

The first nine chapters can clearly be worked through expositionally rather than topically. The prologue (1:2–7) can lead into a discussion of the purpose of the book, climaxing in the idea of the fear of the Lord.[37] The value of character and its consequences

---

35. Walter Moberly (personal comment) has suggested the NT equivalent of the fear of the Lord is faith in the Lord Jesus Christ. While this probably overstates the case (since the fear of the Lord is also used in the NT, e.g. Acts 9:31; 2 Cor. 5:11; 7:1; Col. 3:22; 1 Pet. 2:17; Rev. 14:7), it does point to a clear parallel between the foundations of trust in the book of Proverbs and the message of Jesus. See Moberly (2000).

36. Wright (2015: 250–251) notes that 'the Wisdom literature is very useful for building contact and relationships with other cultures. The Thai Bible Society, for example, has recently published the book of Proverbs (on its own) in the Thai language because it is such a useful tool for starting conversations with others in that society.' However, he also observes that we need to cross the bridge and talk of what Christ has done.

37. Goldsworthy (2000: 188) notes that 'No series of sermons on Proverbs should be attempted without at least making clear reference to the prologue of the book. This passage is important for indicating a purpose for the whole collection.'

is set out in chapters 2 – 4. The strong encouragement to find
wisdom of chapters 3 – 4 is developed in chapter 8 as well, while
the warnings of folly (and specifically sexual unfaithfulness as the
paradigm example of folly) are explored at length in chapters 5 – 7.
Proverbs 6:1–19 deals with several cameos about financial folly,
laziness and troublemakers. Both 1:8–33 and 9:1–18 draw a strong
contrast between the way of wisdom and the path of folly. There is
rich material here for preachers, and it will be foundational for the
subsequent sermons. We need not rush too quickly to the many
interesting topics covered in chapters 10 – 29. There is value too in
using Job and Ecclesiastes as conversation partners in these sermons.
While we need to be careful not to read Christ into every passage
(even 8:22–31),[38] the preacher needs to put each passage in the
context of the Bible as a whole, which climaxes in Christ, especially
as the one who actively sustains and orders his creation (Col. 1:15–17).

c. Preaching on chapters 10 – 31

One of the most common questions people ask about Proverbs is
how to preach on the sentence sayings in the last two-thirds of the
book. Preachers often recommend tracing a topic (e.g. friends,
speech, money) through the whole section, rather than focusing on
a specific passage. The previous thematic section will be useful for
this. This is generally quite fruitful, although it is helpful in each
sermon to remind listeners of the key guidelines of chapters 1 – 9
as the book's setting for these sayings. Our listeners will not understand the book's teaching on friendship, for example, without the
foundation of the fear of the Lord (1:7), the foolish choice to join
with the wrong kind of friends (1:8–19), and the need to have our
character strong enough to resist the lure of those who would lead
us astray (2:1–15). What is said from chapter 10 onwards is building
on these principles.

---

38. On 8:22–31, even Goldsworthy (2000: 189) writes, 'This passage has
    been traditionally interpreted as a reference to Christ, which of course
    in the Old Testament it isn't . . . While this passage . . . is not about
    Christ directly, it certainly foreshadows the role of Christ as the wisdom
    of God in creation (Col. 1:15–17).'

While it is possible to follow these topics through chapters 10 –
29 using the same template, it is always an act of kindness by
preachers to put variety in sermons. There are a number of different
ways to cover the many topics in the book. With some themes, there
are small clusters of proverbs such as use of words in 10:18–21;
kings in 16:12–15 and 25:2–7; the lazy person in 24:30–34; 26:13–16;
mischief-making in 26:20–28. These could be used as a preaching
unit, but not all the topics can be covered in this way.

A second way is to use a 'string of beads' approach – using a
number of proverbs on a particular theme, for example money, the
tongue and so on, and stringing them together into one sermon. It
is based on the assumption that not everything about a topic can be
said in one proverb, so that all proverbs are meant to be balanced
and nuanced by what other proverbs say about the topic. This seems
to be the most common approach used for the sentence sayings,
and is often the only approach used by preachers. It works especially
well with those topics which are not covered by a cluster of sayings,
but which are prominent in the proverbs, for example wealth,
friends, family. Longman (2006: 573–576; 2002: 117–130) gives an
example of this in relation to wealth and poverty:

a. God blesses the righteous with wealth (8:18–19).
b. Foolish behaviour leads to poverty (10:4–5).
c. The wealth of fools will not last (11:4, 18; 13:11).
d. Poverty is the result of injustice and oppression (13:23).
e. Those with money must be generous (28:27; 29:7, 14).
f. Wisdom is better than wealth (16:16; 28:6).
g. Wealth has limited value (11:4; 13:8).
h. There needs to be a balance (23:4–5; 30:7–9).

McKenzie (1996) has suggested a number of additional ways to
deal with topics that can be found in individual proverbs (or
sometimes a cluster on the one topic). A proverb may be used as a
'roving spotlight' shedding light on one narrow scenario (McKenzie
2002: 93 calls this a 'freeze-dried narrative') rather than a floodlight
which illuminates the whole area. In this approach we focus in on
(usually) one proverb and show how it resonates with life today. One
preacher compares it to looking at a jewel, seeing all its facets from

different angles, turning it in every direction and probing each facet to determine gradually the richness of the meaning of the proverb. This makes it very easy to have a clear focus in the sermon. Examples could be 15:4, 9 or, as a cluster passage, 10:18–21.

Variations on this 'roving spotlight' would include the 'sometimes but not always' and the 'too good to be true' approaches. The 'sometimes but not always' approach works well for those proverbs that are clearly partial generalizations, designed for some situations but not all. We might explain where this proverb sheds light, but also a number of experiences where using this proverb would not be helpful. This model shows both the helpfulness of a saying but also its boundaries or limitations. With this approach you are not balancing this proverb with another proverb, or with all other proverbs on the topic. You simply focus on the single proverb. This could be used with, for example, 15:1 or 15:24.

The 'too good to be true' approach can be used where we might experience a double take when we first hear a proverb, since it seems to be contradicted too often by our observations and experiences. Proverbs that talk about the righteous always prospering, or God always protecting the godly (e.g. 15:6, 19) come to mind. The crucial issue is not whether the preacher might find it hard to believe, but whether those in our congregation will. What happens here is that we must look at it again, work out what is really being said, digging deeper to discover the truth it contains, while acknowledging that it does not sound right at the surface level.

McKenzie (1996: 127–133) also deals with how to preach on more than one proverb on a topic. In terms of the 'proverbs that subvert order' (McKenzie's term for those proverbs that nuance or qualify traditional wisdom views), she proposes a model of 'dueling proverbs'. 'Dueling' proverbs involve placing two contrasting proverbs or groups of proverbs side by side. This is clearly done in the book itself (e.g. 26:4, 5), but there is a broader sense in which we can use a variety of views on a topic as conversation partners. This can be a useful way of engaging people, as the preacher chooses two or more proverbs in tension with each other, and works through them. Thus, not everything that can be said about speech can be covered in a single proverb. The emphasis on placating words in 15:1 needs to be heard alongside the importance of giving a rebuke (25:12).

These are not simply unconnected 'beads on a string', but views in counterpoint. Listening to both helps us to explore when to use soft speech and when to take a stand. Similarly, in relation to money, we could explore the interplay between honouring God leading to wealth in 3:9–10, and wealth being taken away unjustly in 13:23. This can help us unravel the complex reasons why some people are rich and others are poor. Attitudes to the poor could be examined by reading 14:20 alongside 14:21, and attitudes to wealth by juxtaposing 10:15 and 16:8. None of these conversations will exhaust their respective topics, but will enable the preacher to engage the listener with at least some of the key perspectives.

A proverb can also be used to ask hard questions about our society, or speak out on behalf of the voiceless. McKenzie (1996: 134–149) also proposes the 'challenger' sermon, in which a 'subversive' proverb is allowed to ask hard questions of both our church and culture (e.g. 15:15–17; 19:21; 21:30). Similarly, she refers to the 'advocate' sermon, in which the preacher uses a proverb to champion an oppressed people or cause against a dominant culture in our setting (e.g. 14:31; 17:5; 31:8–9).

Longman (2002: 157) has made a number of other useful suggestions about the framing of sermons on Proverbs. He proposes that we could, on occasions, seek to pair a particular proverb with a biblical person (e.g. Joseph or Daniel) who might embody or illustrate its truth. We might also use the NT as a conversation partner (e.g. Jas 3 about the tongue, or the teaching of Jesus) to explain a proverb and make connections with the Bible as a whole.

Chapters 30 and 31 contain more cohesive groups of sayings, with the words of Agur in chapter 30, the words of Lemuel in 30:1–9, and an acrostic poem in 31:10–31. Each of these can again be viewed as preaching units. The final poem, most likely incorporated as an inclusio with chapters 1 – 9, is an excellent place to finish a series on the book, as this excellent wife exemplifies wisdom itself, recapitulating many of the descriptions of wisdom in the rest of the book. As such, it is a splendid summary and reminder.

These are not meant as exhaustive suggestions, but as some specific ways that might encourage you to explore more creatively (and faithfully) how we can use all of the book of Proverbs to bring wisdom to the contemporary world.

ANALYSIS

1. THE GATEWAY TO THE SAYINGS (1:1 – 9:18)
A. The prologue (1:1–7)
B. The choice between two calls (1:8–33)
    i. Avoid the company of wrongdoers (1:8–19)
    ii. Respond to the call of wisdom (1:20–33)
C. The value of character (2:1–22)
D. The rewards of wisdom (3:1–35)
E. A plea to embrace wisdom (4:1–27)
F. Adultery as folly (5:1–23)
G. Other examples of folly (6:1–19)
    i. Financial folly (6:1–5)
    ii. Laziness and hard work (6:6–11)
    iii. Troublemakers (6:12–15)
    iv. A numerical saying (6:16–19)
H. The danger of adultery (6:20–35)
I. The enticing words of the immoral woman (7:1–27)
J. A fuller picture of wisdom (8:1–36)
K. Two invitations (9:1–18)

2. THE SAYINGS OF SOLOMON (10:1 – 22:16)

A. The first half of Solomon's sayings (10:1 – 15:33)
(A mixture of clusters and individual proverbs [see the commentary])
B. The theological heart of the sayings (16:1–9)
C. The second half of Solomon's sayings (16:10 – 22:16)
(A mixture of clusters and individual proverbs [see the commentary])

3. THE SAYINGS OF THE WISE (22:17 – 24:34)

A. The thirty sayings of the wise (22:17 – 24:22)
   i. Introduction (22:17–21)
   ii. Key life choices (22:22 – 23:11)
   iii. The temptations of youth (23:12–35)
   iv. The destinies of the wise and the wicked (24:1–22)
B. More sayings of the wise (24:23–34)
   i. The role of the judges in administering justice (24:23–25)
   ii. Promoting community in speech and work (24:26–29)
   iii. The folly of laziness (24:30–34)

4. MORE PROVERBS OF SOLOMON COMPILED DURING THE TIME OF HEZEKIAH (25:1 – 29:27)

A. Living wisely in public (25:1 – 27:27)
   i. Living in the community and in the court (25:1–28)
   ii. How to deal with a fool (26:1–12)
   iii. The lazy person (26:13–16)
   iv. The damage done by false words (26:17–28)
   v. Relationships, good and bad (27:1–22)
   vi. Advice to leaders (27:23–27)
B. The righteous and the wicked (28:1 – 29:27)
   i. The wicked (28:1–12)
   ii. The character of the righteous and the wicked (28:13–28)
   iii. Wisdom in the midst of wickedness (29:1–15)
   iv. Improper speech and attitudes (29:16–27)

5. THE SAYINGS OF AGUR AND LEMUEL (30:1 – 31:9)
  A. The sayings of Agur (30:1–33)
     i. Testimony and prayer (30:1–9)
     ii. Proverbs and numerical sayings (30:10–33)
  B. The sayings of King Lemuel (31:1–9)
     i. The role of the king (31:1–3)
     ii. A potential distraction (31:4–7)
     iii. Do good for the poor (31:8–9)

6. EPILOGUE: THE WIFE OF NOBLE CHARACTER (31:10–31)
  A. Her great value (31:10–12)
  B. Her actions (31:13–27)
     i. Her work at home (31:13–19)
     ii. Her involvement in the community (31:20–27)
  C. The praise she receives (31:28–31)

COMMENTARY

1. THE GATEWAY TO THE SAYINGS (1:1 – 9:18)

A. The prologue (1:1–7)

Context

The title (v. 1) sets out the genre and composer of the book, but is also syntactically linked to the rest of the prologue. The purpose infinitives in verses 2–6 hang from the word *proverbs* (*mišlê*) in verse 1. These are proverbs 'for' (NIV) a specified purpose or *to* (ESV) a given end. The clearly stated aim of verses 2–6 is meant to shape our reading of the book. The first purpose of the book (v. 2a) is to form our character, and this aspect is amplified in verses 3–5. The second half of verse 2 draws attention to the intellectual or academic purpose of the book, which is explained in verse 6. After the purpose of the book has been outlined, we find the foundational principle or motto about the fear of the Lord as the beginning of wisdom (v. 7). This important structural location is highlighted by the presence of a similar saying as an inclusio in 9:10, by the occurrence of the fear of the Lord elsewhere in chapters 1 – 9 (1:29; 2:5; 8:13) and in the closing poem (31:30), and in the concentration of Yahweh

sayings in what has been called the 'theological kernel' of the book
(15:33; 16:6; Whybray, 1990). The shaping of character and intellect
outlined in verses 2–6 is built upon this indispensable foundation,
so that wisdom rightly understood and used can never be separated
from the fear of the Lord.

Comment

1. The book's contents are described as *proverbs*. The Hebrew
word used (the plural of *māšāl*) can include proverbs as we know
them in English (e.g. 'a stitch in time saves nine'), but does have a
wider meaning than simply a proverb. The title tells us that Solomon
is the author or perhaps editor of most of it (see the Introduction),
or perhaps of only chapters 1 – 9 at this stage. The precise way in
which they are proverbs *of Solomon* is not made clear, so it could imply
either that he wrote them or collected them. We know from 1 Kings
4:32 that he 'spoke 3,000 proverbs' (more than are in this book).

Interestingly, despite being wisdom literature, and thus in a sense
international, the sayings are here tied to a particular country, and
to a specific historical person. In fact, none of the details mentioned
here (the person of Solomon, Davidic ancestry, kingship or Israel)
forms any significant part of the book's contents, even though it is
assumed throughout that these proverbs are primarily addressed to
the people of the God of Israel.

2. A twofold goal is set out here. The purpose outlined in verse
2a is to experience skilful living and discipline, which is a matter of
shaping the reader's character. The verb *yd'*, 'to know', often has the
sense of 'experience' or 'come to know'. Its twin objects are 'wisdom'
(*ḥokmâ*), which is practical skill in living, and 'instruction' (*mûsār*),
which has the nuance of 'discipline' or 'shaping'. Although we
connect these English words with the intellect, the underlying
Hebrew words do not primarily refer to academic or 'head knowledge'
matters, for they describe the realities of daily living more than
thinking.

Wisdom is used to describe the ability or know-how to make
clothes and other objects (Exod. 28:3; 31:3, 6), to do engraving
(Exod. 35:35), to build the tabernacle (Exod. 36:1–2), to shape metal
(1 Kgs 7:14) or to trade shrewdly (Ezek. 28:4–5). *Instruction* (v. 2a) is
commonly used in the sense of discipline (Job 5:17), correction (Jer.

5:3), even punishment (Isa. 53:5). An interesting use is found in
Proverbs 5:23, where the young man who succumbs to the adulteress
is described as dying from lack of discipline. He had the head
knowledge or instruction that adultery was deadly, but had not
allowed it to shape his life. The need for discipline arises because
character does not come naturally to a person. All of us need to be
shaped, corrected and trained. The process is not simply to set us
free to become our natural selves, but rather to discipline us so that
we become better people. The two words together probably constitute a cluster expression meaning 'disciplined wisdom'.

In verse 2b the intention of the collection of proverbs is to aid
in understanding their insights and so to shape the reader's thinking.
Their purpose is to cause the reader to understand or comprehend
words of insight. This implies insightful or wise sayings (lit. 'to
understand sayings of understanding') which comprise the bulk of
Proverbs.

3-5. Verse 3 begins to outline the process of shaping our
character, continuing the purpose construction of verse 2 ('to/for').
The proverbs are for receiving or taking in their discipline (*instruction*)
or shaping. They are intended to shape the reader in *wise dealing*
(ESV) or 'prudent behaviour' (NIV). The underlying Hebrew root
(*śkl*) has the sense of being skilful, and the nature of the skill is
set out in verse 3b: skill in *righteousness, justice and equity* (ESV). The
proverbs are meant to work on the character so that the reader will
be able to act in a way that is 'right and just and fair' (NIV). Righteousness and justice are a common Hebrew word pair in the
prophets, but they are also found here in a wisdom book. Righteousness (*ṣedeq*) in Hebrew thinking is fundamentally fulfilling the
demands of your relational obligations, while justice (*mišpāṭ*) and
equity (*mêšārîm*) imply fairness and uprightness. The process
envisaged in Proverbs is that one's character is transformed so that
one can lead a successful life which is fundamentally about integrity.
Fox (2000: 60) helpfully notices that these virtues are not being
demanded but being promised.

The target audience of the book is the *simple* one or *youth* (v. 4).
The term 'simple' is often popularly misunderstood to refer to intellectual impairment. It does not refer in Proverbs to those of limited
intelligence, but rather to those who are not (yet) formed in their

thinking, their moral purpose, their life direction. It is a matter of age or maturity, not lack of intelligence. This can also be seen here in the parallel with the youth in the next phrase. They are gullible, inexperienced or able to be taken in by others, but are distinct from the fool or mocker in that they are able to be taught and shaped.

The purpose construction ('for') is continued in verse 4. The proverbs are designed to give *prudence* (*'ārmâ*) to these unformed young men. Today prudence sounds old-fashioned, but it commonly means 'shrewdness' or 'cunning', referring to the ability to work out clever ways of achieving a goal. Interestingly, the term is used of the serpent in Genesis 3, where we see the other side of shrewdness, one separated from the fear of the Lord. This ability can be a virtue or a vice, depending on how it is used. The parallel expression in verse 4b (*knowledge and discretion*) clarifies that it is meant positively here. Knowledge and discretion is a cluster expression (hendiadys) meaning knowledge with discretion, and so is not just an intellectual feature, but a matter of character which will guard and guide a person (e.g. 2:11).

Verse 5 is a break from the purpose construction (resumed in v. 6), and functions as an exhortation to respond to verses 3–4. The three verbs (listen, add to, obtain) probably have a jussive sense, urging the recipients to embrace the teaching of the book. The call is not simply to listen or hear, for the Hebrew word *šm'* often includes the sense of obey or pay attention. This response is pictured as adding to their learning and obtaining guidance. In other words, it describes a process of allowing the proverbs to shape the way they are and the way they act. It is worth noting that those who are wise and understanding need further transforming by the proverb-ial teaching (see also 16:23, *persuasiveness*, ESV; 'instruction', NIV = 'teaching'), so that the book is not only intended for the unformed simple person or youth (v. 4) but for all. The term for guidance (lit. 'steering') is used only a handful of times in the OT, mostly in Proverbs, and speaks of direction or strategic advice.

6. The resumption of the purpose construction here shows that it has not been abandoned, but rather that it takes a new turn at this point. Just as verses 3–5 unpacked verse 2a's emphasis on the shaping of character, now verse 6 picks up verse 2b's thrust on transforming thinking. The intellectual purpose of the book is that its readers will

understand the various types of 'proverbs' and the meaning they
convey. The category of proverb is a fairly generic one, which can
be used as in verse 1 to mean all the various genres in the book. The
saying (ESV; 'parable', NIV) is an uncommon word, found elsewhere
in the OT only in Habakkuk 2:6.[1] Its precise meaning is unclear, but
the context shows that it describes a subgroup of sayings in the
book. The *words of the wise* (or perhaps 'wise words') probably refer
to the collection of sayings, such as that given this heading in 22:17
(see also 24:23). The final category is the riddle, or puzzling,
enigmatic saying. However, the key point of the verse is not in dif-
ferentiating the various types of sayings, but rather in exhorting the
reader to learn from the whole range of literary types and groups
of proverbs found in the book.

The prologue as a whole thus urges the formed and unformed
learners to grow in their understanding, but also in their character, so that they will be able to manage daily life rightly and
successfully.

7. The concept of the fear of the Lord is the motto of the book,
but is potentially open to misunderstanding. As outlined in the Introduction, it does not imply being terrified by, or living in dread
of, God. Rather, it has a range of meanings that centre on respecting
God as God and treating him as he deserves. It is this underlying
attitude of treating God as God that is the only true foundation for
knowledge and living wisely as outlined in the book. This is a
necessary condition for successful living in God's world.

Respecting God as God is seen in verse 7 as the starting point or
foundation of knowledge. *Beginning* (*rē'šît*) could be translated as
either 'starting point' (first chronologically) or 'chief part' (first in
importance). The different word used in the parallel saying in 9:10
can only mean 'starting point', and so it is likely that this is its main
thrust here as well, since the two verses act together to bracket the
opening nine chapters.

The concept of the fear of the Lord is clarified by noticing the
second half of verse 7. Those who fear the Lord are contrasted with

---

1. Longman (2006: 98) translates it as 'difficult saying', Fox (2000: 63–64)
as 'epigram', and Waltke (2004: 173) as 'parable'.

fools. This is the first mention of the fool, and they will become a key stereotype within the book. Fools are not just the unformed simple youths of verse 4, but rather those who reject or ignore the path of wisdom. In verse 7b they are described as despising wisdom and instruction. This word pair was also found in verse 2, tying the prologue with the motto to make up the introduction of the book. We have seen in verse 2 that these words refer primarily to skill in living and the shaping of character, and this is precisely what the fools have not only rejected but despised.

Meaning

The prologue (vv. 2–6) establishes that the book has a specific purpose. It is designed to shape both our character and our thinking. This twin purpose is set out in verse 2, and amplified in verses 3–5 and verse 6. The book claims to be not simply filled with interesting observations, but is presented in such a way as to change its readers. Like the rest of Scripture, it is useful for 'teaching, reproof, correction and training in righteousness' (2 Tim. 3:16). Also at the outset of the book, the motto of verse 7 asserts that there is a fundamental choice in life between the way of wisdom built on respecting God as God and allowing him to shape our character, and the way of folly which treats such matters as of little value. Our foundational stance (fearing the Lord) and our fundamental choice to embrace the way of wisdom are presented as the only pathway to life in the book of Proverbs. The remainder of chapters 1 – 9 will expand on these underlying principles.

B. The choice between two calls (1:8–33)

Context

Immediately after the prologue in 1:2–7 comes the first of a number of calls to embrace wisdom and reject folly, which takes up the rest of chapter 1. Initially, it concerns embracing wisdom rather than joining with bad companions (vv. 8–19). The next section (vv. 20–33) speaks of embracing wisdom personified as a woman, an image found frequently in chapters 1 – 9. What is crucial is to see that this section is opening up the issue of choice, especially the foundational choice we make in life between wisdom and folly. Verses 8–19 certainly highlight the issue of where people take their basic stand in life, warning the individual child or student against falling into bad company.

Verses 8–9, an introductory call to listen, are essentially an appeal for a response, urging the young person to see the benefits of embracing wisdom and rejecting folly. They are followed by the core of the first lesson (vv. 10–18), and capped off by a conclusion (v. 19). The lesson is essentially in the form 'if … then … because': *if* sinners seek to lure you away (vv. 10–14), *then* do not follow them (v. 15), *because* their outcome is self-destruction (vv. 16–18).[2] The scenario of their enticing invitation is set out in verses 11–14. The kind of enticements such a group of *sinners* would offer are expressed in verses 11–14 as power, wealth, greed, camaraderie. This is portrayed as an alternative way of living, a different pathway through life.

The enticements of folly (vv. 8–19) are then balanced by the bold call of wisdom personified (vv. 20–33). The flow of thought is fairly clear. After the setting is established (vv. 20–21), the nature of wisdom's call is briefly outlined (vv. 22). The substance of the teaching is given in verses 23–31, which has two parts (vv. 23–27, the 'you' section in the second person and vv. 28–31, the 'they' section in the third person) with a similar pattern of reasons (vv. 24–25, 29–30) and consequences (vv. 26–27, 31). The core lesson is then drawn out in verses 32–33, which outlines the benefits of embracing wisdom and the disastrous outcome for those who reject her.

Comment
i. Avoid the company of wrongdoers (1:8–19)
8–9. This begins with a call to hear, which is the common first element in the longer speeches of chapters 1 – 9 (so Fox 2000: 79, who notes that a verb for listen or a synonym begins each lecture). *Hear* often means not only listen but also obey, and the mention of instruction and teaching, with the warning not to forsake it, implies

---

2. Fox (2000: 92) outlines a similar structure in more detail. Whybray (1994: 37) notes that there is a brief statement of the theme in v. 10. He sees the warning of v. 15 extending into v. 16.

that it has that sense here. The words *my son* are used in Egyptian instructions by a teacher to speak to a pupil, but the use of father and mother in this verse implies an actual son and a family setting for this instruction.[3] Interestingly, the mother is included here (and in a parallel introduction in 6:20), which implies that she has some authority and role in instruction at home. While the focus through chapters 1 – 9 is on the father as the shaper of his son (*my son*, 1:10, 15; *my words/commands*, 2:1; see also 3:1; 4:1; 5:1; 6:1; 7:1), the twin reference to the mother's teaching (1:8; 6:20) makes her contribution clear. The father's discipline or shaping (*instruction*, v. 8) is the same word used in the prologue and motto (1:2, 3, 7) and is parallel here to the mother's teaching (*tôrâ* in the sense of instruction).[4] The form of the prohibition in Hebrew (do not forsake, v. 8) implies an urging or pleading not to abandon this teaching, rather than a stern command. The substance of the instruction and teaching is set out in verses 10–19, and is an attempt to shape the unformed youth.

The motive clause of verse 9 (it begins with 'for/because', omitted in NIV) implies that this parental shaping will benefit and reflect well on the youth. The garland or wreath and the necklace are physical objects representing adornment, and the garland graces the youth (lit. 'a garland of grace'), suggesting that it gives its wearer favour in the eyes of others. The picture is of the youth growing in the esteem of others as a result of being shaped by his parents' instruction. Similar imagery about garlands and necklaces is found most clearly in 4:9, but also in 3:3, 22; 6:21, and commonly refers to learning and its rewards.[5]

---

3. Whybray (1994: 37) notes that mother is not mentioned in Egyptian or Mesopotamian texts, which implies a family setting here.

4. Fox (2000: 79) says that in Proverbs *tôrâ* like *miṣwâ* (command, as in 2:1) 'are basically secular words and carry with them no allusion to divine law'. Steinmann (2009: 66) also notes that *tôrâ* never has the article in Proverbs, implying that it refers to teaching in general rather than the teaching of the law.

5. The ESV translates necklace as *pendants*, while the NIV uses 'a chain'. Fox (2000: 83) notes that the Hebrew word means 'chain' and the plural form here implies an ornament of many chains or multiple strands.

10. The key instruction is outlined here. The father alone is now addressing his son and faces the reality that youth – even good young people – may be enticed, persuaded or lured to join the wrong company. Van Leeuwen (1997: 38) notes that good families are not immune to these possibilities, which is a hint for the pastoral use of this passage. The use of *sinners* elsewhere suggests habitual wrong-doers, and so perhaps criminals not just sinners (so Fox 2000: 85). This verse expresses in summary terms, do not consent or give in to this pressure.

11–14. Just as this 'gang' calls on the youth to 'come with us' (v. 11), so later the adulteress – the key image of folly in chapters 1 – 9 – will also urge the unshaped youth to come with her (7:18). Folly herself will call out to the undecided to come into her house (9:16), a call to be resisted because of Wisdom's call at the same time to come to her house (9:4). The purpose of going with the gang is to lie in wait for someone to ambush. The introductory words, *If they say*, begin a graphic, vivid call to benefit financially from plundering others. To *lie in wait for blood* implies a willingness to physically injure or even kill someone, with verse 16 making explicit that it is shedding blood that is in view. The NIV translates it as 'innocent blood', which is possible if the phrase *without reason* at the end of the verse applies to both *let us lie in wait* and *let us ambush*. The person to be ambushed is described as innocent, which makes it clear that this is not a justified or even revenge attack, but rather one just 'for fun' (as Longman 2006: 91 translates it). 'Lie in wait for' and 'ambush' are synonyms, making it likely that these are not two separate activities proposed, but two different ways of proposing the same thing.

The words of the enticers continue in verse 12. The parallel images of *Sheol* (the place of the dead; NIV = 'grave') and *those who go down to the pit* (= those who die) reveal the destructive nature of their plan. Before they are attacked, their victims are alive and whole; afterwards they are like the dead, literally or metaphorically. The word *whole* normally means 'blameless' (as in 2:21), but the parallelism in this verse implies its broader meaning of whole or complete. The lure of gaining much wealth is dangled before the youth, who is urged to chase after riches (v. 13). The attraction is of possessing costly or valuable treasures, and of taking them without apparent cost, like a conquering army takes plunder from its defeated enemies.

The concluding plea for a response is accompanied by a change from the first person (vv. 11–13) to the second person (v. 14), showing a greater sense of urgency. Verse 14 begins with a call to *throw in your lot among us*. This could mean either literally 'cast lots with us' (so NIV), or metaphorically to mean 'join us'. If the first is intended, then it might refer to the 'thrill' of gambling for the one purse mentioned in the second half of the verse, holding out the promise of even further riches. This is the end of the evildoers' words which began in verse 11, making the teacher's response begin in verse 15 with the resumptive *my son*.

15–18. The teacher/father explains the outcome of this downward spiral. Verse 15 exhorts the young man not to go down this path, before explaining where it will lead in verses 16–18. Again it is the wisdom language of urging and dissuasion rather than stern command (the form is the weaker form of prohibition in Hebrew, not the absolute prohibitions of the Ten Commandments). The intent is to train the youth to see the consequences for himself, rather than simply forbid a course of action. Yet the father is clear and strong in his warning not to choose this direction in daily living. Both *way* and *path* are metaphors for one's behaviour or course of life. It could also have a further meaning of not going down the literal road to the place of ambush (so Fox 2000: 87).

The use of *for* ('because') at the beginning of verse 16 indicates that reasons will now be given for this advice. The people in such a gang (feet being a metaphor of their actions) run to evil or perhaps run to do what is morally wrong (evil). They *run/make haste* (ESV; NIV, 'rush . . . are swift'). The nature of their intended harm is explained as shedding blood, implying that this is the real attraction even more than the promise of wealth. It is not yet explained whether the blood that will be shed is their victim's or their own.[6]

Verse 17 'is an exceptionally difficult verse, and the commentators are divided about its meaning' (Whybray 1994: 41). The imagery is based on catching birds, but often used metaphorically of evildoers trapped in their wrongdoing. If your aim is to trap birds, then it is

---

6. Fox (2000: 87) suggests that the failure to specify 'innocent' blood, as in the parallel Isa. 59:7, creates this ambiguity.

futile to set out a net that they can see. A net might be stretched out
on trees to catch or entangle the birds flying past or through. The
verb does not normally mean 'stretched or spread out', so Murphy
(1998: 8) proposes that it may refer to grain being scattered on a net
to attract and trap the birds. Fox (2000: 89) suggests that the image
has a double sense. First, the birds are compared to the naive youths
who are lured, but after verse 18 it also seems to apply to the robbers
as well, who are shown to be more witless than the birds.

Irony emerges as the gang who had planned an ambush (v. 11)
are themselves ambushed (v. 18). The verbs here are synonyms for
those used in verse 11, which draws attention to this being a fitting
but deadly end to their earlier misdoings. To go down that path is
seen as a dead-end, destructive way of life. It is to have missed the
shaping offered by the book of Proverbs. In seeking to hurt the lives
of others, they put their own lives at risk, and the youth is warned
about such a likely outcome.

19. The lesson is here drawn out in more abstract terms. Such
are the results or consequences for those who are greedy for the
wealth of others. The term *unjust* (or 'ill-gotten') *gain* always refers
to an illegally or wrongly obtained profit or gain. Such a gain is
attractive and enticing when it is offered, but it takes away rather
than gives life. It promises life but delivers death.

ii. Respond to the call of wisdom (1:20–33)

20–22. Wisdom is described by four verbs of speaking (*cries aloud,
raises her voice, cries out, speaks*) in order to build up anticipation of her
message. The use of a plural form for wisdom together with a
singular subject (as in 9:1) indicates that this is a personification of
wisdom who speaks in this passage. A variety of settings in the city
are given, but all are in busy, prominent locations where people can
hear her call. Wisdom speaks in the streets outside the houses, and
raises her voice in the city squares. While the ESV translates this word
as *markets*, the real thrust is that this is a broad, open space where
public decisions will be made (so NIV, 'public square'). Verse 21a
sees wisdom also at the busy crossroads (ESV, *the head of the noisy
streets*), although the LXX represents a slightly emended text and
translates as 'from the top of the walls' (followed by the NIV). On
either reading, it describes a place where many people can hear. The

final setting is at the entrance to the city at the gates. These were substantial, multi-roomed structures in ANE cities, and constituted the place of justice, community decisions and various public discussions. The cumulative effect of all this is that wisdom's cry is a very public, inescapable call. No-one can say they did not hear her words.

Verse 22 outlines the essence of wisdom's call in the settings of verses 20–21.[7] It begins with a straight question, even rebuke, to various people who have not yet embraced the path of wisdom. In asking *How long?* Wisdom is urging her hearers to delay no more. Three types of individuals, or perhaps three stages of rejection of wisdom, appear at first to be in view: the simple, the scoffers and the fools. The simple are those who have not developed their pathway through life, generally because of their youth. They are not yet shaped by wisdom and are open to folly, but have not yet embraced or rejected either one. The danger for them is not to move on from this stage (= loving being simple), and if they persist in this, they will move into being either a fool or a scoffer. Fools are those who have rejected the call of wisdom and embraced the path of folly. They are described as hating knowledge, which implies that they are adopting the lie that self-focused folly is preferable to wisdom built upon respecting God as God. One form of fool is the scoffer or one who mocks wisdom and those who seek to live by it. If the mocker is simply one representative of the path of folly, then this reduces those addressed to two groups.

These two ways may well be different, sequential stages instead of different groups. Thus, while young people begin as simple or unformed, if they keep on rejecting wisdom's attempts to shape them by her words, then they become fools and perhaps even scoffers.[8]

---

7. While Clifford (1999: 40–41) views it as merged with v. 23, it is better to view v. 22 as the foundational challenge question addressed to the simple one (second person) and the fool/scoffer (third person).

8. In favour of this view is the presence of *then* at the beginning of v. 28, which implies that the response of vv. 28–31 occurs after that of vv. 23–27. This would also account for the mention of only two figures (the simple and the fool) in the summary of v. 32. The use of the second

23–27. Verse 23 is difficult to interpret, and has been variously translated. What is clear is that wisdom is calling on the simple, unformed youth to turn (or perhaps repent) in response to her correction. The key debate is whether, if they respond to wisdom, there is held out a promise that *I will pour out my Spirit to you,* or whether it simply refers to my 'thoughts' (NIV) or *spirit* (ESV). The main clue is in the use of the words *pour out,* a different verb from the one in Joel 2:28. It is used eleven times in the OT, all but one in Psalms and Proverbs, and the overwhelming image is of pouring out words or what comes out of the mouth (Pss 19:2; 59:7; 78:2; 94:4; 119:171; 145:7; Prov. 15:2, 28; 18:4).[9] Thus, most modern scholars and translations (the ESV is a notable exception) see wisdom here indicating that she wants to pour out her thoughts to the simple ones, which makes a nice parallel with *I will make my words known to you* in the last part of the verse. Of course, even if it were to be translated 'spirit' here, it would be a reference not to the Holy Spirit of God, but to the spirit or essence of wisdom. This verse, then, is an encouragement and challenge to turn to wisdom, so that she can shape the simple person by her ideas through her words.

Verses 24–25 outline the current stance of the unformed person, which is not a depiction of innocence, but initially resisting wisdom's call. The simple ones have refused to listen or pay attention to wisdom's invitation (v. 24). In verse 25 they are described as letting go of, or brushing aside, wisdom's counsel/advice and not accepting the correction or rebuke, which in verse 23 was aimed at people turning to wisdom to be formed by her. These verses lay the foundation for the consequences which are set out in verses 26–27.

---

person (you) in addressing the simple in v. 22a is developed in the 'you' section of vv. 23–27. *If* the simple have not turned at wisdom's reproof, *then* their ongoing refusal to be shaped by wisdom will put them in another camp – the fools and scoffers of v. 22b–c (spoken about in the third person) whose outcome is explained in the 'they' section of vv. 28–31.

9. See Wilson (2011: 153). The only time the verb is used without words being in view is in Eccl. 10:1, where it describes ointment 'giving off' a bad odour.

The implied 'then' (v. 26) draws attention to what flows from their failure to be shaped by wisdom. The outcome for rejecting wisdom is not a lifetime of uncomplicated and innocent simplicity, but rather one of calamity and terror. This has already been illustrated in 1:18–19, and is developed further in verse 27. The sudden or unanticipated nature of the disasters is implied here, striking like a storm or whirlwind that is unable to be predicted. These metaphors hint at uncontrollable devastation, and the end result is an atmosphere of distress and anguish.

28–31. *Then* (v. 28) is either resumptive after verses 23–27, or sequential, outlining what happens next. The *they* of verses 28–31 describes the fools (who hated knowledge, vv. 22c, 29a) either as a second group of people or as the next stage for the simple who have rejected wisdom's correction. There is an interesting parallel with verse 24 where wisdom called them; now in verse 28 they call on her. They did not answer her; she will not answer them. Fools do not miss out on wisdom because of a lack of trying, but rather because they only begin to respond once the unpalatable outcomes of their way of life begin to take place. At that point they are stuck with the consequences of their choices. They now seek wisdom diligently (v. 28b, so ESV, which captures the nuance better than the NIV's 'look for'), but in vain.

Verse 29 begins with 'instead' (*because*, ESV; 'since', NIV), which draws attention to what supplanted the embrace of wisdom at an earlier stage. As in verse 22c, they (the fools) hated knowledge, which has the force of rejecting a relationship with wisdom or God. Their hate or rejection of wisdom clearly has implications for their relationship with God, for the parallel expression is that they did not choose the fear of the Lord. By the time the simple have become self-sufficient fools, it is clear that they have failed to build on the foundation of respecting God as God as set out in 1:7. Everyday wisdom must be based on a relationship with God. The recurrence of fear of the Lord language draws attention to the contrast in this opening chapter between the path of folly (1:8–19) and the way of wisdom (1:20–33).

It is clear from verse 30 that the persistent dismissal of wisdom's advice and correction (mentioned in the earlier stage or example of the simple in v. 25) also characterizes the fool. This unwillingness to be shaped by wisdom is the natural (or perhaps unnatural) outcome of ignoring or rejecting God. 'Instead' at the beginning of verse 29 hovers over verses 29–30, and the construction is then finished with verse 31 which explains the outcomes that flow from their prior choices and values. The irony in verse 31 is that the fools get what they wanted, and are stuck with it! Their attempt at a godless self-sufficiency is precisely all they have when they finally realize that they need more. But it is now apparently too late. The imagery of fruit suggests that the seeds they have sown yield the only product they can, but that is not what they need in the midst of a disaster. Their failure to respond appropriately to God (v. 29) has left them without God's help now that they come to understand their need.

32–33. The concluding lesson is then set out in the last two verses, and again the figures of the simple and fools emerge (v. 32). The summary of verse 32 is that both the simple and fools, or perhaps the simple who become fools, are destroyed by their complacency and turning away from wisdom. Their claim that they have no need of wisdom is shown to be short-sighted folly. However, there is not only a warning to the simple, but also encouragement to those who embrace wisdom (as in 8:34–36). The key is listening to wisdom (v. 33a), which implies not only hearing her words, but being shaped by them. Those who accept wisdom in this way will be secure, at ease and not dreading any future disaster. This highlights the importance of the foundation call of the fear of the Lord, as well as the ongoing challenge to have our character and actions transformed by wisdom.

Meaning

The juxtaposition of the way of folly (vv. 10–19) and the call of wisdom (vv. 20–33) sets up the fundamental choice of chapters 1 – 9. The reader is given a reading strategy for the book as a whole: start with the foundation of the fear of the Lord (v. 7), allow your character and thinking to be shaped (vv. 2–6), and now reject the path of folly (vv. 10–19) in order to embrace the way of wisdom (vv. 20–33). The tone of warning is the more dominant one, as even in the call to follow wisdom there is greater focus on the folly of not doing so, rather than on the benefits of walking her way.

C. The value of character (2:1–22)

Context

Understanding the flow of the chapter is quite crucial to its meaning. In verses 1–4 there are the conditions (the protasis, *if* . . .), followed by a twofold consequence (each is an apodosis, beginning with *then* . . .) in verses 5–8 and 9–11. This results in three major sections in the first half: an extended set of provisos (vv. 1–4; *if* . . . in vv. 1, 3, 4), conditions that must be fulfilled in order to gain wisdom (vv. 5–8) and be protected by an upright character (vv. 9–11). In the second half there are promises for protection from the two tempters, male and female (vv. 12–15 and 16–19), followed by a summarizing conclusion (vv. 20–22, beginning with 'thus'/'so'). Both verses 12 and 16 begin with the infinitive 'to save/deliver you' and in both cases with an implied subject ('wisdom' supplied in NIV). The use of the infinitive, a purpose construction ('in order to deliver you'), draws attention to the fact that what is outlined in the previous verses is the subject of the verb. While this may refer to an abstract idea of wisdom, the flow of thought in this chapter is that wisdom linked with the fear of the Lord will lead to a shaped character which will be the means God uses to protect people. Thus, it is this shaped character that will preserve a person from evil men (vv. 12–15) and the strange woman (vv. 16–19). These are both manifestations of folly. The evil men have already been seen to have this role (1:8–19), and in chapters 5 – 7 the loose/strange woman will have this task as well.

An acrostic pattern may also be present, but it does not seem to have any major implications. Clifford and Murphy both suggest that there is a different kind of acrostic pattern found in this chapter. Verses 1–11 constitute the first half, and the three stanzas all begin with the first Hebrew letter, aleph (if, then, then). In the second half (vv. 12–22) the three stanzas each begin with a lamed, the twelfth letter of the alphabet. However, despite the presence of twenty-two verses, no such acrostic has been found elsewhere, and it does not seem to be of any interpretive significance.[10] This chapter is detailing

---

10. So Longman (2006: 117); Tan (2008: 84) calls it a 'pseudo-acrostic'.

the importance of character as anticipated in the prologue (vv. 2a, 3–5). It has also been suggested that 'Prov 2 functions as a sort of agenda for Proverbs 1–9' (Tan 2008: 84).

Comment

1–4. This section also commences with the term *my son*, an indicator of either a family or a school context. The diligence required in the conditions draws attention to the seriousness of the quest for wisdom. Each verse contains a pair of parallel expressions outlining another key ingredient of the search. The first condition (v. 1) is accepting the teacher's words and properly valuing his instructions. The force of receiving or accepting these words is that their teaching must be taken on board or adopted, a deliberate choice not to reject or ignore them, but rather to embrace them (see the parallel in 7:1). The nuance offered in the second half of the verse is that they must be highly valued (ESV, *treasure*; the image is of accumulating something of value) and internalized ('with[in] you').[11] While the ESV translates the teacher's words as *commandments* (which implies the Ten Commandments and so OT laws), it is better to regard them in a wisdom context as the teacher's commands (so NIV). They are authoritative but not legal commands or instructions.

The conditions continue in verse 2 with an explanation or unpacking of the meaning of accepting and treasuring the teacher's words. It includes paying careful attention to the content of these words, that is, wisdom, and developing a right internal attitude (*inclining your heart*, which refers to the centre of one's being and thinking, not one's emotions).

Verses 3–4 draw attention to the fact that understanding must be actively pursued. There are two different words for understanding in verse 3 (translated by many versions as 'insight' and 'understanding'), both equally common but with no real difference between them. The thrust of the verse is not on describing different subtleties of wisdom, but rather on the verbs. There is a need to pursue understanding energetically, to call out and raise your voice for it. Verse 4

---

11. Steinmann (2009: 89) translates as 'inside you' and suggests that it speaks of the inner appropriation of the words by faith.

picks up the language of seeking and searching, and again the force
rests on the verbs. The quest must be diligently and thoroughly
undertaken, based on the belief that what is being sought is of great
value. It is to be pursued as if you were desperately searching for
lost money, or treasure that is hidden from sight. Indeed, the picture
that emerges from verses 1–4 is that the quest for wisdom is one that
requires great effort and hard work. The willingness to learn in verses
1–2 must be matched by a willingness to work (vv. 3–4). A character
shaped by wisdom does not fall into one's lap, but must be actively
sought.

5–8. The first consequence of searching wholeheartedly for
wisdom is revealed in verse 5, while verses 6–8 outline how God
works in his world. The result of striving hard for wisdom is understanding the fear of the Lord and finding the knowledge of God.
This was the foundation and starting point in 1:7, but is now also
the goal of the process. Knowing God and respecting him as God
is clearly not left behind as wisdom is pursued. The search for
wisdom will result in knowing and treating God as he is, for this is
the ongoing assumption of the godly wisdom promoted by this
book. Wisdom is never an end in itself. God's activity is set out in
more detail in verses 6–8. He is the giver of what people need to
strive for – wisdom, knowledge and understanding. People do not
earn wisdom by their own activity, for they are recipients of what
God graciously gives. Seeking wisdom involves hard work, but it is
not achieved by hard work alone. While OT wisdom literature tends
to focus on human actions, the underlying theological presupposition is always that God is working in the background, and usually
through human activity to accomplish his active kingly rule. Part of
this divine ordering of his world is set out in verses 7–8. He treasures
or stores up (*ṣāpan*, the same verb used in v. 1) for the upright the
successful use of wisdom skills (ESV, *sound wisdom*; NIV, 'success').[12]
The second image of verse 7 is that God is a protective shield for
those with integrity. There is no explanation at this stage about how
God protects or stores up success, but it is clear that this is what he

---

12. Fox (2000: 114) notes that this verb has the sense of setting something
aside for a favoured person, which implies exclusivity.

does for those whose character is shaped by uprightness and integrity. It is not a promise of success and protection for the self-indulgent, but for those who respect God as God and who follow the path of wisdom. Verse 8 amplifies the imagery of the shield, stating that God (the continuing subject of vv. 6–8) guards and watches over/protects those who are loyal and who act justly. This means that God is actively involved behind the scenes as people seek to live uprightly. These two verbs (guard, *nāṣar* and protect/watch over, *šāmar*) will recur with a different subject in verse 11.

9–11. The second set of consequences of diligently seeking wisdom (vv. 1–4) are set out in verses 9–11. Verses 9–10 outline the shaped character of those who seek wisdom linked with the fear of the Lord, and they do so in terms already used in the prologue. This is particularly seen in the triple expression *righteousness, justice and equity*, which is an exact quotation from 1:3. These words in 1:3, as well as wisdom and knowledge (v. 10; 1:2, 4), were seen to refer to a transformed character that results in godly action. The relational meaning of many of these words has already been set out. In verse 10 the focus appears to be on the changed, internal character (*into your heart*) that comes from the pursuit of wisdom, while verse 9 outlines the actions or pathway in life that issues from this shaped character.

The protective power of this character and life orientation is then outlined in verse 11. Discretion, already used in 1:4, operates here as a summary term for the character of those who seek wisdom. While the term can have a wider sense of a plan (e.g. Job 42:2), it most commonly refers to character in Proverbs (so 1:4; 3:21; 5:2; cf. 12:2; 14:17). The cluster of terms from the prologue used in this section establishes its character sense here. Waltke (2004: 228) makes the important observation that, while verse 8 claims that God guards and watches over those loyal to him, now verse 11 asserts that their shaped character does so. The same verbs are used in both verses 8 and 11. In other words, the character that comes from being formed by wisdom is the means by which God protects or guards people committed to him. What is true of God theologically (v. 8) is true of one's shaped character instrumentally (v. 11). God preserves people through transforming their character as they pursue wisdom linked with the fear of the Lord.

12–15. As noted above, the wisdom-shaped character is the subject of verse 12. The focus is now on those who seek to entice or trap the one being instructed by the teacher. The first part of the verse could refer abstractly to the *way of evil* (so ESV), or the 'way of the evildoer' (NIV, 'ways of wicked men'). However, even if it has this abstract sense, the second half of the verse makes it clear that individuals (a single human or person but used generically) are in view. A central feature of the loose woman in chapters 1 – 9 is that she attempts to seduce by her speech (2:16; 5:3; 6:24; 7:5, 14–18), and the first description of the evildoers here is that they have perverted speech. In the earlier warning against a gang of men there is a similar focus on words as the means of luring the youth away from the way of wisdom (1:10–14). Here, the speech, not the men, is 'of perversity'. This word for 'perversity' (*tahpukôt*) is found only in Proverbs (except for Deut. 32:20), and refers to words that are twisted. It is formed from a root meaning 'to turn upside down' and so refers to 'things turned upside down' or perverted. The evil men (now plural) are further described in verses 13–15. They are those who have abandoned paths of moral uprightness so that they can be free to act reprehensibly (*walk in the ways of darkness*). They rejoice and delight in doing what is wicked or twisted (the same root as in v. 12). Not only do they act badly, but they also delight and possibly even gloat over their wrongdoing, implying that their underlying attitudes (v. 14) make their actions (vv. 13, 15) even worse. Verse 15 rounds off this section by describing their paths and ways (i.e. the direction of their lives) as morally crooked and devious.

16–19. This formed character is also effective in delivering a person from the strange or foreign woman (v. 16). The ESV translates one of these words as adulteress, while the NIV translates the other, but neither should be confined to an adulteress. When the first term (*zārâ*) is used as a noun, it often means a stranger or foreigner, but when used adjectivally (as here), it refers to a foreign or forbidden object, usually an idol or a woman. The phrase is used again in 7:5, and the adjective is also used of this female figure in 5:3, 20.[13] The

---

13. Whybray (1994: 55) notes that in some places (e.g. Job 19:27; also Prov. 14:10; 27:2) it simply means 'another' person, not yourself.

second description (*nokriyyâ*) means 'foreigner' at its base level, but is often seen as a technical term for a prostitute, since they were often foreigners. It is best not to prejudge her identity and to translate here as 'the strange woman . . . the foreign woman'. As mentioned above, her main tool of seduction is her smooth or slippery words. Fox (2000: 119) comments, 'The woman's allure lies less in her looks (mentioned only in 6:25) than in her words.' Smooth speech is a metaphor for flattery. It is clear that she is not just any foreign woman but rather one who has left behind broken commitments (v. 17). She has abandoned the (intimate) friend of her youth, who is not immediately identified. The parallel phrase in the second half of the verse sheds light on his identity, for to abandon this friend is to ignore the covenant of her God. This is the only time that covenant is used in this wisdom book, and most likely refers to the idea of marriage as a covenant (as in Ezek. 16:8; Mal. 2:14).[14] Most commentators therefore identify the friend as her (former) spouse or partner, and thus see this as a description of marital unfaithfulness leading to a ruptured relationship.

This section is rounded off by pointing out the deadly end to following her lead in life (vv. 18–19). This is a crucial reason to avoid her, so as not to succumb to her enticements. The phrase *her house sinks down to death* is not initially transparent, and the image of a house sinking down to death is not present elsewhere.[15] However, a connection between her path and her house is found in Proverbs 5:8, as is a link between her house and the way down to death (7:27). The second part of verse 18 uses imagery of the spirits of the dead (as in Isa. 26:19), but without explanation. What is clear is that the

---

14. Fox (2000: 120–121) mentions the two other possibilities of
a covenant or marriage guaranteed by a pagan god, or a reference
to the Sinai covenant, in which case it may refer to religious
unfaithfulness.

15. This leads some to emend the text to read 'her path leads down or
inclines to death', a description found in 5:5; 7:27; 14:12; 16:25. There
is also a disagreement between the masculine noun for house and
a feminine verb. For a lengthy evaluation of the problems, see Waltke
(2004: 232).

teacher is warning that following such a woman will lead to premature death. The description, those *who go to her* (v. 19a), could simply refer to people visiting her house, but it may also be a euphemism for sexual intercourse ('those who have sex with', or 'go into' her; so Steinmann 2009: 98). The point being made is that such people do not, or will not, come back (alive), which is clarified by saying they do not regain the paths of life.

20–22. The word *so* or 'thus' is used resumptively in verse 20 to put all these principles back on the table as the teacher winds up the lesson. Having just been reminded of folly's deadly path, there is now a focus on being committed to the more positive way through life. It is variously described as the way of the good people (the plural prevents it from meaning 'the way of the [ideal of] good') and the paths of the righteous. The reason for embracing this path is set out in verse 21 (beginning with *for*), and the picture is one of settledness and security. In these verses the right path is described as that taken by the good, the righteous, the upright and the blameless/those with integrity. Some see the reference in verse 21 (living and remaining in the *land*) to refer to the land of Israel, which would mean that being cut off or torn from the land (v. 22) would be a reference to the historical threat or reality of exile (as in Deut. 28:63). However, the distinctives of Israel's covenant faith such as the Promised Land are bracketed out rather than discussed in the wisdom books, and the covenant focus (unlike here) is on national rather than individual use of the land. Thus, it is likely that another interpretation should be adopted. 'Land' (*'ereṣ*) is also commonly used in the OT to speak about the earth, not just the land of Canaan. If so, inhabiting the land refers to living on the earth (i.e. remaining alive).

In contrast, there is the way of the wicked in verse 22 (the first of seventy-eight uses of 'wicked' in Proverbs). Those on this deadly path are also described as the *treacherous* or 'unfaithful'. Clearly, there are varying outcomes for the two groups of people, but the precise meaning has been debated. If the consequence for the first group is that they will remain alive, the outcome for this second group is that they will be cut off from the earth (i.e. experience premature death). This seems to parallel the conclusion found in 8:34–36, and yields good sense as this passage ends.

Meaning

This chapter describes the process and benefits of forming a godly character. The conditions include giving wisdom its true value (vv. 1–2), and working hard to acquire it (vv. 3–4). The immediate consequence is that we will acquire God's gift of wisdom and be protected and preserved (vv. 5–8). Verses 9–11 make it clear that this protection comes about through the wisdom-shaped character that is built upon respecting God as God (vv. 9–11).

The wisdom-shaped character is then the means God uses to deliver us from two groups of people who will seek to entice us into the ways of folly. Neither perverse men who do evil (vv. 12–15) nor the strange or foreign woman (vv. 16–19) will be successful in their attempts to spoil our lives.

The chapter concludes with a summary reminder of the two ways to do life (vv. 20–22), as a way of commending the one path that flows from linking the fear of the Lord with the search for wisdom, and allowing wisdom to shape your character.

D. The rewards of wisdom (3:1–35)

Context

The presence of three *my son* addresses (vv. 1, 11, 21) suggests a threefold outline.[16] Waltke (2004: 238–240) helpfully shows that verses 1–10 are a celebration of what flows from the changed character outlined in chapter 2. In the odd verses (vv. 1, 3, 5, 7, 9) he discerns the outline of a godly character, while the even verses (vv. 2, 4, 6, 8, 10) draw attention to the outcomes that will follow. When read together, the even-numbered verses announce that those who are shaped by wisdom will receive a long and peace-filled life, favour and success in the sight of both God and others, a straight path through life, physical health and healing, and abundant material prosperity.

The second section (vv. 11–20) begins with a brief exhortation about the value of God's discipline (vv. 11–12), presumably in

---

16. However, some structure this chapter differently. Fox (2000: 152) and Garrett (1993: 80), for example, argue that the break should be after v. 12 rather than v. 10.

seeking wisdom. Verses 13–18 then show that wisdom is incomparable, and that the consequences of embracing the path of wisdom include long life, wealth and honour (v. 16), days of delight and contentment (v. 17) and life as it is meant to be lived (v. 18). This reinforces and at times amplifies what was said in the even verses of verses 1–10. Verses 19–20 outline the role of wisdom in creation, probably as an encouragement to embrace wisdom since we live in this wisely made world.

The third *my son* section (vv. 21–25) is comprised of three parts. Verses 21–24 urge the adoption of a character shaped by wisdom (v. 21), on account of the positive consequences outlined in verses 22–24: life, safety, absence of fear, contented sleep. Verses 25–31 define a series of actions they are to refrain from doing (not being afraid, withholding good, plotting harm, falsely accusing, etc.), while the chapter concludes (vv. 32–35) by summarizing the different outcomes for the wicked and the upright.

Comment

1–4. The teacher/father exhorts the young person not to forget his teaching or instruction (*tôrâ* – see comments on 1:8). This warning is an important one, for both remembering and forgetting have moral aspects in the OT. People are responsible for choosing to remember (to bring to mind the great truths about God and act accordingly), and held accountable for choosing to forget (to fail to do so). One key to not forgetting is to internalize the teacher's commands (not commandments, see 2:1), which requires diligence or vigilance (so Steinmann 2009: 107). This is a matter of the heart, that is, the drive or inner workings of a person.

The consequences of being moulded by this instruction (*they will add to you*) are long life and peace (v. 2). *Length of days* (repeated in v. 16) does not mean long days but rather many of them. The phrase *years of life* is found only in Proverbs (also in 4:10; 9:11) and refers to life in its fullest sense, a life that is enjoyable and worthwhile. The word *šālôm* (*peace*) is a rich and complex word in Hebrew thinking, and the NIV translates it as 'peace and prosperity'. It can refer to well-being, the absence of conflict, even material prosperity. Garrett (1993: 79) suggests 'wholesomeness' is better than prosperity here

– rich in health and relationship to others – and so the picture is of a life that is healthy in every way.

This robust image should not, however, lead to presumption, for immediately there is a command to embrace steadfast love and faithfulness. The word for *steadfast love* (*ḥesed*) speaks of loyal and merciful kindness, a strong commitment to the well-being of the other in relationship.[17] *Faithfulness* has a core sense of 'truth' and here has the sense of a firm, constant commitment to the truth of the commands (v. 1). These twin virtues are so crucial to a wisdom-shaped character that the pupil is urged not to let them abandon you. The image of binding them around your neck speaks of the public adopting of these characteristics, wearing them with boldness. This is balanced by the picture of them being not just outward, but internalized, engraved permanently on the tablets of your heart. They are to be made an enduring part of your character.[18]

The result of adopting these virtues into your character is a life of favour/grace and *good success* (ESV; 'good name', NIV, v. 4). In the light of the subsequent phrase *in the sight of God and others*, the term *success* appears to mean reputation or regard in their eyes. This was more highly valued in their culture than ours, probably to our loss.

5–6. Verse 5 urges the pupil to have wholehearted trust in God rather than being self-reliant. This dependence on God is the obvious corollary to having your foundation built on the fear of the Lord, and is again an issue of character leading to action. The pairing of trusting God and not leaning on your own understanding seems to be referring to the specific choice that needs to be made when your insight points in a different direction from God's

---

17. It is often, but not always, used in a covenant context. Fox (2000: 144) asserts that it can only be God's kindness towards the pupil, not the pupil's towards others. He thinks that this kindness could not abandon you, but it is not clear why this would be so. In the end it could refer to either or both, and probably has a primary reference to the pupil's character.

18. Garrett (1993: 80) says the overall image is one of making sound teaching and virtues part of the fabric of your life. Similar language is used in 6:21; 7:3, perhaps recalling Deut. 6:8.

instructions. In other situations one of the distinctives of wisdom
is that there is often an endorsement of relying on your God-given
understanding. In verses 5, 7, 9 (and also in vv. 11, 19, 26 and 33 in
the chapter) God is referred to as the LORD, Yahweh, the distinctively
Israelite name for God. This reminds us that while the proverbs are
designed for all human beings, they have been gathered here with a
particular focus for the people of God.

Verse 6 is a slight deviation from the pattern in verses 1–10, as
the first part of it still refers to a call to character (as begun in v. 5)
and not the outlining of consequences. This first part urges the pupil
to live out his relationship with God (*acknowledge him*, i.e. keep him
in mind) in his actions (*your ways*).[19] In light of verse 5's call to trust in
him rather than be self-reliant, this would mean to act consistently
with trusting God. The outcome of this mindful trust is that God
will make straight your paths. The intensive form of the verb 'to be
straight' has the force of 'to *make* (morally) straight'. It is not describing a smooth or easy path through, one free from obstacles or
hardship, but rather a life that is righteous, morally straight and
worthwhile.

7–8. Verse 7 begins with a call to humility or not being wise in
your own eyes. It draws attention to the truth that not all wisdom is
godly, such as when Solomon separates his wisdom from the fear
of the Lord in 1 Kings 11. It is appropriate, then, that the parallel
line includes the call to fear the Lord. In order to be humble, one
must respect God as God, rather than trying to supplant him and
become self-legislating. Longman points out that this verse clearly
shows the connection between the fear of the Lord and humility,
which is also made clear in 22:4.[20] If humility is at least a prerequisite
for the fear of the Lord, then rejecting evil is its necessary corollary.

---

19. Waltke (2004: 244) translates this as 'in all your ways, desire his presence',
    arguing that 'acknowledge' does not capture enough of the sense, which
    includes an intimate experience of another's reality.
20. Waltke (2005:193) notes there that, although our English versions often
    translate as 'the fear of the LORD and humility', there is no conjunction
    and the two words are in apposition. The NIV translates 22:4a as 'humility
    is the fear of the LORD'.

This is the flip side to fearing God – making a decisive break with the alternative sources of loyalty.

This transformed character will lead to physical health and perhaps nourishment (NIV) or refreshment (ESV) as well. While it is literally 'healing will be to your navel', it is clear that 'navel' should either be emended to 'flesh' or that the whole body is actually in view, despite the mention of only one part of it.[21] In addition, there will be refreshment or nourishment to your bones (again presumably meaning the physical body as a whole). The base meaning of *refreshment* is a drink, but it is used figuratively for refreshment in an ANE culture. Whybray (1994: 63) suggests that it may even mean 'medicine' here, a particular kind of drink that would restore health.

9–10. These verses outline how the faithful use of material possessions leads to further material blessing. Again this outcome is based on a character trait, on this occasion honouring the Lord (v. 9). It does not specify how you are to honour the Lord with your wealth, but it seems at least to involve handing over the firstfruits. Both your wealth (or accumulated capital) and a share of your crops and livestock (your income during the year) are targeted as areas for honouring God. The word for wealth or sufficiency is almost exclusively used in wisdom literature, and especially in Proverbs. The besetting danger of wealth in any generation is that it can lead to self-sufficiency. The giving of the firstfruits is a thankful acknowledgment to God for his provision, set out in the law (e.g. Deut. 26:1–11) but also predating it (e.g. Gen. 4:4).[22]

---

21. *BDB* gives the meaning as 'navel-string' (umbilical cord?). Fox (2000: 151) notes that 'navel' never stands for the entire body (although Steinmann 2009: 110 argues that it does), and the notion of health for the navel makes no sense. Fox supports emendation from 'your navel' to 'your flesh', which is a similar word. Driver, supported by McKane (1970: 293), suggests that 'healing' can mean 'health' on the basis of cognate languages. Garrett (1993: 81) proposes the translation 'strength', implying soundness of body and mind and not just physical health, but it is not clear that mental health is implied by 'flesh'.

22. Some note that this is the only place in Proverbs where the language of ceremonial worship is used. Waltke (2004: 247) notes that other

The ensuing picture (v. 10) is one of abundant prosperity in an agricultural context, but the mechanism of the process is not explained – just that it happens. The images are clear and evocative. The storehouses (but in the context of a harvest, barns or silos) will be 'filled to capacity' (Steinmann 2009: 111) or even 'overflowing' (NIV). The word *śābā'*, used to describe how it is filled, comes from the root 'to satisfy'. With reference to food it means plenty or abundance. The fresh or new wine was a symbol of fertility, and a valuable product. The wine vat is not our image of a wooden barrel, but an excavated section at the end of a stone winepress. What is pictured is that the wine trough is so full that the wine is bursting forth from it. They are images of abundance and plenty.

These verses in Proverbs are sometimes used by proponents of 'prosperity gospel' teaching, but this is to misuse them. First, there is no *promise* of abundant wealth, any more than there was a promise of long life and peace in verse 2. To claim a proverb as a promise is to misunderstand the type of literature it is. A proverb describes only part, not the whole, of life, and so is not always applicable in a given situation or at a given time. Thus, Jesus, despite honouring the Father with his whole life, had neither a long life (v. 2), nor barns filled with plenty (v. 10). Second, the material prosperity is not linked with the size of a monetary gift but with character (honouring the Lord). Such a character trait would involve not wanting to give wealth an inordinate place in one's desires, so that truly honouring God would entail keeping your life free from the love of money. The prosperity gospel misses the important emphasis in the book of Proverbs on the theme of contentment (e.g. Prov. 30:8–9).

11–12. These verses address the situation when the prosperity, life and success of verses 1–10 do not seem to be happening. Instead, the pupil may be undergoing hard times, which are described as times of discipline and rebuke. Murphy (1998: 21) suggests that only here in Proverbs is the problem of suffering touched upon, but it is

---

(note 22 *cont.*) verses in Proverbs do refer to sacrifice, but only this
one refers to cultic sacrifice. However, Garrett (1993: 81) comments
that it is not very explicitly cultic, with a bigger focus on demonstrating
gratitude.

not likely that this section is intending to explore that philosophical issue. These two words have been met before. Discipline (*mûsār*) was first encountered in 1:2, 3, where it had the sense of 'instruction'. Rebuke or reproof (*ykḥ*) occurred in 1:23, 25, 30 and has had the meaning of 'correction'. Thus, while they may both refer to setbacks and obstacles, the focus is on using these sufferings to redirect or shape a person's life. The pupil is therefore urged not to reject them or *be weary of* (ESV; better, 'resent', NIV) them, for this would prevent the individual from learning. In 9:7–12 it will be the fool who rejects correction. This is not a consideration of suffering in itself, or of punishment for wrongdoing, but of purposeful discipline with the goal of bringing about change. Thus, these two verses are appropriately quoted in Hebrews 12:5–6 in a setting not of suffering, but of the benefits of discipline in God's purposes for his people. That is exactly the context here, where the main point is that such discipline is purposeful and evidence of God's kindness. Verse 12 makes it clear that God's attitude towards the person who is disciplined is one of love and delight.

13–18. This is a self-contained section, beginning and ending with related words for blessed. However, it also follows on nicely from the preceding pair of verses. The reason why discipline is to be valued so highly (vv. 11–12) is that it is needed in order to achieve wisdom. Now it is asserted (vv. 13–18) that wisdom is worth whatever it takes, so no price is too high. The beatitude of verse 13 sets out the basic tenet about the value of wisdom and understanding. These twin words take their now-familiar sense of skilful living based on the shaping of character and grounded on respecting God as God.

What follows in verses 14–18 is a series of assertions about the value of wisdom, both in itself (vv. 14–15) and as a result of the benefits that flow from embracing wisdom (vv. 16–18). There are two claims in verses 14–15 (so Garrett 1993: 82). Wisdom yields better returns than money (v. 14), and it is more precious than the most exquisite wealth (v. 15). The 'better than' saying in verse 14 draws attention to the sustained comparison between wisdom and anything else of apparent value. The dividends she yields are better than those of precious metals (v. 14), the standard measure of trade in those days. Silver and gold (lit. 'yellow', but the root is often used in poetry to mean gold) simply do not compare. She is more valuable than precious stones or jewels.[23] Even your strongest desires or most ardent longing cannot surpass wisdom. This appears to be a wisdom theme, as Proverbs 8:11 seems to repeat verse 15 with only a slight rewording. Wisdom is incomparable.

The first set of consequences for embracing wisdom is a *long life* (*length of days*, as in v. 2), *riches and honour* (v. 16). Kayatz (cited in Lucas 2015: 64) notes that the picture of holding the ankh, a symbol of life, in one hand, and a sceptre, symbolizing power and wealth, in the other, is an image derived from the Egyptian goddess *ma'at*. In Proverbs, wisdom has replaced *ma'at*, resulting in a picture of wisdom as the giver of gifts to her followers. Verse 17 adds that wisdom's paths are ways of peace and pleasantness. As in verse 2, peace involves well-being or wholesomeness in a very broad sense. The term 'pleasant ways' (NIV) is also fairly general, but the overall thrust of the verse is a strong, positive commendation of the fullness of life that wisdom brings. The image of verse 18 may also be dependent on an Egyptian parallel, but could also be based on Genesis 3.[24] There are many wisdom terms or ideas in Genesis 3 (life, shrewd, wise, knowing good and evil), which implies that the image here is of ongoing life, life as it was meant to be. This tree of life needs to be held on to tightly, which builds on the diligent search of 2:1–4.[25]

---

23. Garrett (1993: 82) says that it is not clear if it means 'rubies' (in Lam. 4:7 they are said to be red; see NIV) or 'corals', but both are expensive, rare and beautiful. Longman (2006: 137) opts for pearls but does not explain why.

24. Garrett (1993: 82) suggests that, in the light of Genesis 3, and the plant of immortality in the Gilgamesh epic, it is surely not just a symbol of happiness, but rather the removal of the curse of death itself and so refers to life beyond the grave. While belief in life beyond death was also a feature of Egyptian religion, there is no indication that this concept came into OT wisdom. Murphy (1998: 22) is probably right in concluding that it is just a metaphor for the happiness associated with the good life.

25. Longman (2006: 137) proposes that 'those who hold her tight' is a sexual metaphor of embracing or holding a woman tight to you, which would be clearly understood by young men to whom it was addressed. The root *ḥzq* in this form means 'to make strong', but is commonly used in the sense of 'to take hold of, seize, grasp'.

It most likely refers to the effort needed in staying close to wisdom. This is brought out in the second half of verse 18, where it is paralleled with 'holding wisdom fast'. The choice to embrace wisdom is one to be envied and imitated.

19–20. The Lord's connection with creation is an additional motive to walk on the path of wisdom. Wisdom's active involvement in the creation means that she can provide clues about what is needed to live in accordance with the order set out in creation. The Lord used our familiar twins, wisdom and understanding, as he set the sky and land in place (v. 19). Wisdom also seems to be an aspect of God's nature, for it is by his knowledge (another key wisdom word) that the seas and clouds gave forth their water.[26] The core elements of creation are linked to wisdom and to God's wise purposes. This has echoes of Genesis 7:11 (so Garrett 1993: 83), when in the time of Noah the depths were divided. Thus, it pictures the destructive power of nature, with the following expression of the falling dew restoring the image of the beneficent creation. However, it is more likely in this positive context to be another image of wisdom being woven into the Genesis creation account.

21–24. The teacher starts in the verse 21 by urging the pupil not to turn aside his eyes from (*lose sight of*) these aspects of wisdom mentioned in the second half of the verse: sound wisdom and discretion.[27] The term for sound wisdom has previously appeared in 2:7 and has the sense of abiding success, perhaps even 'resourcefulness' (Longman 2006) or the 'inner power that helps one escape a fix' (Fox 2000). Discretion has already been used as a summary term for a wisdom-shaped character (2:8; see also 1:4) and retains that sense here. In verse 22 the result of focusing on these character traits is that they will bring life and grace (ESV *adornment*; NIV 'an

---

26. Waltke (2004: 262) notes that the verb *rʿp* in its two other occurrences (Job 36:28 and Ps. 65:12[13]) means 'pour down', not just trickle, and so refers to the regular watering of the earth.

27. So ESV, also Longman (2006) and Murphy (1998). There are a number of textual variants here, but it does not significantly change the meaning. The NIV inserts 'wisdom and understanding' in the first part, perhaps seeing a reference back to v. 19.

ornament to grace') to you both inwardly (your soul) and outwardly (your neck).[28]

Verses 23–24 set out the positive outcomes that flow as a result of preserving sound wisdom and discretion. Longman sees the same theme in both verses – that wise behaviour creates a safe environment which breeds confidence. Verse 23 speaks of living securely or safely, and of not stumbling over obstacles.[29] The safety of daily living in verse 23 is followed by confidence in sleep in verse 24. You will be able to lie down without fear of being attacked, and enjoy a sleep that is restful and refreshing.

25–31. A series of pleas to refrain from something begin all of these verses except verse 26, which then provides the key positive rationale that the Lord can be your confidence. The pupil is urged in verse 25 not to be afraid of an unexpected terror or disaster, or even less so, of the ruin of the wicked. Tragedies may come, but the reason for not being afraid is set out in verse 26: *the LORD will be your confidence* (ESV; 'at your side', NIV). The word translated 'confidence' has a range of meanings (including 'stupidity') and is used only here in Proverbs. It could mean either that God will be your source of confidence, or simply 'at your side', which would give you confidence.[30] The second half of verse 26 also implies that the parallel first half is an image of protection or safety. This reason also stands behind the remainder of the pleas in verses 27–31. The present help of God gives strength to live wisely in trust.

Garrett (1993: 83) sees verses 27–30 as concerning goodwill and helpfulness, noting that verses 27–28 urge not failing to do good, while verses 29–30 prohibit malicious activity. However, the section arguably continues to verse 31, which has the same construction, and is a

---

28. Garrett (1993: 83) also opts for 'grace for your neck', since the word 'grace' is not otherwise used as a noun for an ornament. This would make grace parallel to life.

29. Steinmann (2009: 126) says the equivalent English idiom for v. 23b would be 'you will not stub your toe'. The verb *ngp* means 'to strike', but is often used of striking your foot against a stone, or stumbling.

30. Waltke (2004: 265) opts for 'at your side', and notes a Ugaritic parallel to this.

warning against another malicious activity, namely the path of violence. The general theme appears to be about 'how to act in community'.

While verses 27–28 have the form of a prohibition, it is easy to discern the flip side that is being commended. Verse 27 describes the importance of fulfilling your obligations to others if you are able to do so (lit. 'when it is in the power of your hand[s] to do so'). Verse 28 describes the common scenario of having promised to lend, or having borrowed something, but it seems too much trouble to you to do it now. Your obligation to your neighbour is seen to override your own convenience.

Verse 29 speaks against betraying your neighbour's trust by apparently extending goodwill to him, but actually devising a treacherous plan. That would be a contravention of neighbourly trust. Even an argumentative spirit is ruled out in verse 30, where an unjustified (*for no reason*) personal or even legal dispute with another is prohibited. The reason given is that the person has not dealt with you wrongly. Finally, verse 31 warns against envy of a person who could presumably gain many possessions from acting violently, as in the gang of youths in 1:8–19. The pupil is warned not to be enticed by their apparent success, or to follow in their way of life. Thus, all the warnings of verses 27–31 speak about letting your wisdom-shaped character determine the way you act.

32–35. The entire chapter, and especially this speech, is summed up in this final section. The central lesson is to make sure that you pursue the way of the upright and reject the path of the wicked. This is an anticipation of chapter 9. Garrett (1993: 84) notes that in verses 32–34 the first line of each verse sets out God's opposition to evil, while the second talks of his favour to the righteous. This order is reversed in the concluding verse 35.

Verse 32 contrasts the (morally) devious or twisted person with the morally upright. God's different attitudes towards the two are clear – the first he regards in strong language as an abomination, while the second is *in his confidence*, his trusted ones. The image of being *in his confidence* is one of belonging to the inner circle of trusted friends.[31]

---

31. Sheriffs (1996) uses this phrase, which he translates in Ps. 25:14 as 'the friendship of the Lord' as the key motif of OT spirituality.

The language of curse and blessing is applied respectively to the wicked and righteous in verse 33. This is not an impersonal, automated process for, as in verse 32, there is a specific reference to the Lord. God is involved in this righting of wrongs. Verse 33 implies that there are only two categories of people, and that all must fit in one or the other, with each group experiencing fitting consequences. The same two groups are described differently in verse 34 – the scorners or mockers and the humble (NIV, 'humble and oppressed'). The person who scorns (God and humans?) receives what they give out to others. On the other hand, God extends grace to the humble poor, reversing their afflictions by showing his favour towards them. The core categories are mentioned in verse 35 – the wise and the fools – and their respective outcomes are honour and shame. The Hebrew word for 'honour' (*kābôd*) can also mean 'glory', and so some see here an indication of a magnificent or glorious outcome for the wise (e.g. Longman 2006: 143, 'the wise possess glory'). It is likely that those of us in the individualistic Western world undervalue the significance of honour and shame. Ours is a right/wrong culture, but many cultures, including those in the ANE, are based largely on the categories of honour and shame. To us this seems a little anti-climactic, but for those to whom it was originally written it goes to the core of their societal values.

Meaning
The value of wisdom, and of walking in her ways, is the central theme of this chapter. This is not, however, simply a neutral description of what wisdom is like, but an exhortation to embrace wisdom and find a fuller life. This 'good life' is pictured in relational, physical and material terms (vv. 2, 4, 6, 8, 10), showing why the pathway of wisdom makes such good sense. While it requires discipline (vv. 11–12), the goal of wisdom is always worth more than the cost paid (vv. 13–18). Since wisdom is woven into creation (vv. 19–20), the virtues of wisdom will give life (vv. 21–24). The young person is urged to refrain from folly (vv. 25–31) and to choose wisdom, since the Lord is actively at work in bringing about good consequences for those who do so (vv. 32–35).

E. A plea to embrace wisdom (4:1–27)

Context

There are three sections in this chapter, each introduced by the familiar form of address, *my son* (vv. 1, 10, 20, with a slight variation, *O sons*, in v. 1). Verses 1–9 act somewhat like a conclusion to the opening three chapters, especially with the lengthy quotation from the teacher's father (vv. 4–9) having a strong emotive tone and a real sense of urgency. The plural addressees (*sons*) may indicate a generalizing of the teaching developed earlier, and now applied to all. This section is a sustained exhortation to get wisdom, with no mention at all of the wicked. The second section (vv. 10–19) has a completely different shape. The advantages of the way of wisdom (vv. 10–13) are balanced by the warnings of going down the path of the wicked (vv. 14–17), and are capped off by a summary contrast of the two ways (vv. 18–19). The final section (vv. 20–27) is a sustained plea to let wisdom shape all areas of your life. This includes your inner self (v. 23), your speech (v. 24), what you look at (v. 25) and your actions (vv. 26–27).

1–9. The introductory call of verses 1–2 echoes many of the words of the previous lessons. There is the urging for sons to hear (which implies obey) the instructions or shaping of (their) fathers (as in 1:8). There is also the call to pay attention (2:2), to 'know understanding' (*gain insight*, ESV), and not to forsake the teaching that has been received (1:8), for the teaching (*precepts*, ESV, as in 3:1) is good. The repetition of terms, together with the plural *sons*, suggests that these words draw together the previous lessons into this sustained exhortation to get wisdom.[32] Verses 3–4a outline the setting of this section, locating it in the context of a father teaching his son, as part of a family where the mother is mentioned for her key role in the web of family relationships.[33] The mention of *tender*

---

32. Fox (2000: 172) observes that 'A father is ostensibly speaking to his son, but through him the author is actually addressing all boys.'

33. Indeed, Fox (2000: 173) suggests that the presence of the mother in v. 3 implies here that this is family teaching, rather than the words of a scribe or teacher.

(v. 3, *rak*) refers not to the mother's love, but to the impressionable young age of the son, who was still in his tender years. This setting is followed (vv. 4b–9) by a lengthy quote from the learner's father, who is mentioned as the one who teaches (v. 4a).

There are three groups of commands in verses 4b–9, followed by a reminder of the great benefit that comes from embracing wisdom. First, there is a need to hold on to the teacher's or father's words of instruction (vv. 4b, 5b). Second, there is the exhortation to get wisdom and insight (vv. 5a, 7). In particular here is the emphasis on the importance of gaining this wisdom, for it is both the beginning of the process (*the beginning of wisdom is this*, v. 7a) and of prime significance (*whatever you get, get insight*, v. 7b; NIV, 'though it cost all you have'). This is not different from the father's instructions, but is rather the content of his words. Finally, verses 6 and 8 describe the quest in terms of not forsaking wisdom, loving her, prizing her highly, embracing her. This is the language of the active seizing of what is attainable. Fox (2000: 174) notes that 'it is not enough to *do* wise things; one must *love* wisdom.' The benefits that flow from this mission in life are set out in verses 6, 8, where the teacher reminds his son that wisdom will keep you, guard you, exalt you and honour you. This is similar to the teaching of chapter 2 that the shaped character that results from embracing wisdom will have the power to preserve and promote you in daily living (see 2:8, 11). The image outlined in verse 9 is one of placing a garland or crown on your head, symbols of victory and exaltation (so Waltke: 2004: 282–283). The garland is literally 'a garland of grace', probably with the dual meaning of commending its wearer and characterizing the grace-empowered way a person deals with others. The crown speaks of public recognition and honour. The end result of embracing wisdom is thus not a life of restriction, but rather one of fullness.

10–19. Verses 10–13 set out the positive consequences of choosing the way of wisdom, beginning with a call to hear (v. 10) and concluding with a mini-summary in verse 13 – keep hold of instruction, do not let go, guard her, for she is your life. The observation is again made that wisdom leads to a long, rich life (v. 10; see 3:12; 9:11) not as a promise but rather as a common outcome of sensible living. The focus is not on the many exceptions (e.g. those caused by injustice, war or genetics) that we know about, but on the general

principle that, despite the many variables, living in accordance with
God's wise values will typically lead to good results. The teacher or
father describes this life choice as the way of wisdom and upright
paths (v. 11). It involves fundamental choices and an ongoing focus
on what is in conformity to wisdom.[34] The incentives are given in
verse 12 that such wise living will lead to a smoother, less trouble-
some experience of daily life (not being hampered or caused to
stumble). God's wisdom works in his world. Thus, the threefold call
of verse 13 is to value this wisdom so highly that you cling on to it
as a prized possession, that you refuse to give it up, and that you
wholeheartedly protect and guard it. So important is holding on to
wisdom that it is described as *your life* – the very core or essence of
what your life in this world is about.

Of course, choosing wisdom is only possible where there are
other options. The positive exhortations to embrace wisdom in
verses 10–13 are now balanced by the warnings against choosing
instead the way of the wicked (vv. 14–17). Verses 14–15 outline six
positive and negative exhortations in relation to the alternative path
of the wicked or the way of evil (or evildoers). Initially there are two
prohibitions: do not enter it in the first place, and do not continue
straight ahead on it (the more precise meaning of *walk*, v. 14). Then,
these are amplified by four rapid-fire commands (v. 15): actively
avoid it (i.e. choose to let it go); do not pass or cross over into it;
turn aside from it; and pass it by (the second and fourth commands
use the same verb cleverly in two different senses).

The daily life and practices of the wicked are then set out in verses
16–17. It is not a path of restfulness, for they cannot go to sleep
until they commit further wrongdoing. They are robbed of sleep (lit.
'sleep robs them') if they do not cause others to stumble (v. 16).
There is a drivenness, a discontent, almost an addiction to the
adrenalin rush they experience. As a result of their choice, they do
eat and drink of the spoils (bread/food and wine, v. 17), but its
source is from their wicked actions which have involved inflicting
harm on their victims (*the wine of* [which comes from] *violence*). There

---

34. Fox (2000: 179) notes that 'though *torah* in Proverbs is not law,
    it is authoritative.'

is the implicit admission that wrongdoers may gain from their evil (food and wine), but there is still no contentment or rest.

A simple contrast between these two options is drawn out in verses 18–19. The path of the righteous is one of great light (v. 18), while the way of the wicked is characterized by darkness (v. 19). The metaphor of light is used in the sense that light enables you to continue walking on your path, since it is darkness that causes the wicked to stumble or trip up, presumably because they do not see the obstacles or traps in their way of life.[35] The path of wisdom sheds light on daily life so that you can walk confidently and securely, while the way of the wicked makes everyday living more problematic.

20–27. The third and final section of this chapter (vv. 20–27) outlines a variety of areas of daily life in which wisdom is to be embraced and folly avoided. It begins with a familiar call to listen with full attention to the teacher's or father's wise words and sayings (see 1:8; 2:1–2; 3:1; 4:1, 10a). Verse 21 indicates that this teaching is to control *your sight* ('your eyes') and the very core of your thinking and willing (*your heart*).[36] These words are thus to shape you outwardly and inwardly: how you relate to the world and what you value within yourself. As earlier (1:8; 3:2), reasons are given for allowing wisdom to shape who you are. Verse 22 claims that the teacher's wise words bring life and healing. While wisdom sometimes speaks specifically of long life (*years of life*, 3:2; 4:10; 9:11), the focus here is rather on the quality of life – real life, true life. Elsewhere this is explained as embracing wisdom so that you may live (9:11), and that whoever finds wisdom, finds life (8:35), for she is a tree of life (3:18). Healing to all their flesh (as in the emended text of 3:8) implies a physical wholeness and health that will flow from being shaped by wisdom. Verse 21 specifically mentioned your eyes and your heart, and these are two of the four areas of everyday life now focused on. The heart – who you are on the inside, the centre of

---

35. Fox (2000: 183) suggests that 'light and darkness are metaphors for the happiness and good fortune that grace the righteous life and the misery and disaster that afflict the wicked one, respectively.'

36. Contra Fox (2000: 185), who thinks it refers to your speech, although he concedes that this is the expression of what is inside.

your being and thinking and will – must be protected or guarded carefully. It is not enough simply to modify your outward actions but not be changed on the inside. This is why the teacher's sayings need to be kept within your heart (v. 21b). There is the further explanation that wisdom in the heart is the source of life, or that life flows out from wisdom (v. 23).

Wisdom must also shape the various outward expressions of who you are. There is a need to discipline your speech, putting aside crooked/perverse words as well as deceitful or devious ways of speaking. Both terms found here of the kind of speech to avoid have been used to describe the actions of the wicked in 2:15. These are words that are twisted from the proper purpose of speech to build up others, convey truth and bring life. The eyes, or what you look at, is a common theme in Scripture, for what is 'eye-pleasing' is a source of temptation (6:25; Gen. 3:6; 1 John 2:16). The idea in verse 25 is not being distracted from living wisely by the various attractive possibilities in your peripheral vision. Just as there is to be straightness of speech (and of action in v. 27), so there is to be straightness of focus.[37] Finally, the metaphor of walking is used to describe your actions in verses 26–27. These too need to be shaped by wisdom, reflecting outwardly what you are like in your heart. Swerving to the right or the left is to leave the path of wisdom and to act like evildoers. While Jesus' language of the narrow gate/way (Matt. 7:13–14) is not used here, it does seem to refer to the same idea.

Meaning
In chapters 1 – 4 there is a continual call for the formation of a godly character that transforms every aspect of life. The sentence sayings later in the book (what they should do) cannot be dipped into by themselves, but are based on what kind of people they should be (their character). The real intention of Proverbs is to train a person, to actively form character, to show what life is really like, and how best to cope with and manage it. To miss this key insight is to miss the heart of the book. God, through wisdom, is active in this shaping process.

---

37. Fox (2000: 187) describes it as 'unswerving directedness towards a goal'.

This summons to embrace wisdom climaxes in chapter 4, where a more urgent tone is found. The father's extended speech in verses 4–9 is full of commands to love, gain and value wisdom. For a moment even the alternative of folly is ignored, as wisdom is the sole focus. In the remainder of the chapter the warnings against the evil way of folly reappear, but the emphasis remains on the positive value of embracing wisdom. In particular, the focus is on the life-giving nature of wisdom (vv. 13, 22–23).

F. Adultery as folly (5:1–23)

Additional note on the immoral woman in chapters 5 – 7

The theme of 2:16, the 'strange' woman, is taken up in surprising detail in chapters 5 – 7. In 5:1–23, 6:20–35 and 7:1–27 there are lengthy warnings against the adulteress. Certainly, sexual behaviour is a legitimate, even important, area for wisdom writers (e.g. 22:14; 23:27–28), but it is not extensively dealt with in the sentence proverbs from chapter 10 onwards. What are we to make of this puzzling emphasis in Proverbs 5 – 7?

The contrast in the opening nine chapters between wisdom and folly is crucial to understanding chapters 5 – 7. Wisdom – with its character-shaping demands – has been outlined from 1:20 – 4:27, and will be returned to in chapter 8. Chapters 5 – 7 explore the other option, giving an extended warning against folly, largely, but not exclusively, through depicting folly as an immoral woman. Chapters 5 and 7 are entirely about this woman, as is 6:20–35. Proverbs 6:1–19 is still concerned with folly, but in a different way. Verses 1–5 deal with the actual folly of being in debt; verses 6–11 concern laziness; verses 12–16 deal with the troublemaker; and verses 16–19 round off this section with a numerical saying describing many varieties of folly. In other words, folly is woven through both the major figure of the immoral woman as well as the other minor images. The various invitations of wisdom and folly that will come in chapter 9 are best evaluated in this broader setting.

This motif of folly first emerges in the warnings against keeping the wrong company of men (1:8–19). To choose to associate with those who ambush and steal (vv. 11, 13), who do evil and shed blood

(vv. 16–17), is to choose a path that leads to death (vv. 18–19). This is not the pathway to take; it is the way of folly. A similar description of it is given in outlining the ways of wicked men (2:12–15), and also as an aside in 4:14–17.

The theme of folly personified as a woman occurs as early as 2:16–19 – a warning against the 'loose' (NRSV; *forbidden*, ESV) or 'strange' woman, in parallel with the *adulteress* (2:16).[38] The strange woman of Proverbs 1 – 9 is, in the first instance, your neighbour's wife, but is also a metaphorical illustration of folly, which leads to death. The infidelity of adultery is seen as the opposite of wisdom or fidelity to the Lord. Perhaps such a woman is chosen simply because adultery is the clearest example of folly. Yet female figures play a significant role in the book, occurring at the beginning (1:8, 20–33) and the end (31:10–31).

One significant aspect of this motif is that quite commonly a connection is made between this woman and death. Her house sinks down to death (2:18–19); her feet go down to death and Sheol (5:5–6); the youth who follows her dies for lack of discipline (5:23); those who hate wisdom love death (8:36); the dead are there . . . her guests are in the depths of Sheol (9:18). Most extensively in 7:20–27, those led astray by her are pictured as various animals caught in deadly traps that will cost them their life (7:22–23), and she is pictured as slaying a mighty throng since her house is the way to Sheol and the chambers of death (7:25–27). By way of contrast, the call from wisdom personified is to embrace her and find life. Those who do so will dwell secure and at ease (1:33); the years of your life will be many (4:10); wisdom is your life (4:13); whoever finds wisdom finds life (8:35); and so the call to the unshaped is to turn from your simple ways and live (9:6).

---

38. On the debate about whether the woman is foreign, strange, an adulteress or a prostitute, see Tan (2008: 1–43). She concludes that it is not so much a geographical or nationalistic description, but rather connected with the idea of ethnicity. Longman (2006: 124, 159) says the 'strange woman' in chapters 5 – 7 as well as 2:16 is 'strange' in relation to legal and social customs, acting outside of community norms. This would include both an adulteress and a prostitute. Both seem in view in 6:26.

The prevalence of warnings against this immoral woman in chapters 1 – 9 suggests that the focus is not simply on sexual conduct, but on the broader contrast between wisdom and folly. This is reinforced by attention being drawn to the words of the seductress – she is smooth-talking (6:24; 7:5). Proverbs makes much of the seductive speech of the adulteress (e.g. 2:16; 5:3; 6:24; 7:5, 13–21; 9:15–17; 22:14). In relation to the strange woman of Proverbs 5 – 7, her weapons are not so much her beauty (mentioned only in 6:25) or sexually seductive wiles as her manner of using language. It is her 'coaxing words' (2:16; 6:24; 7:5, 21), her lips that drip honeyed words (5:3), her flattering speech (7:21), her mouth like a deep pit (22:14), that hold the power of entrapment.

Furthermore, much more attention is given to this figure than in the parallel Egyptian instructions, and the frequency of its occurrence in chapters 1 – 9 is out of all proportion to its mention in the rest of the book (22:14; 23:27). The figure of the strange woman is thus likely to be referring to more than sexual seduction, and so applies more generally to folly itself. It is interesting that in chapters 1 – 9 the emphasis is on wisdom personified and the immoral woman, with only a few references to woman as wife (5:15–19) and as mother (1:8; 4:3; 6:20). In chapters 10 – 29 the references to women are infrequent, but almost entirely refer to ordinary wives and mothers. Proverbs 31:1–9 concerns a woman who is the queen mother, while 31:10–31 reverts to the busy housewife, but also seems to mirror the image of wisdom in chapters 1 – 9. Personified wisdom is the antithesis of the 'strange woman' or 'immoral woman', and the opposite of folly personified in 9:13–18.

Another interesting aspect of the immoral woman of Proverbs 1 – 9 is the absence of God's intervening to punish the wayward youths who succumb to her ways. Even the passages that connect this woman and death do not say that if you commit adultery, God will strike you dead; it is simply an observation that those who go down this path are on the way to death (e.g. 2:18–19). Death is the consequence for those who embrace the adulteress, much like saying that if you take a fish out of water it will die, or if you jump off a tall building you will be dealt with according to the law of gravity! It speaks almost of natural consequences (e.g. 6:27–28). In other words, it is pictured largely as folly, self-destructive (6:32), being caught in a trap (7:22–23), a failure of discipline (5:12, 23). It is not generally even spoken of as a sin against God, and even where it does speak of sin (e.g. 5:21–22), the verses do not say that God will punish the sin, but rather that your sins will entangle or trap you. This reminds us that the function of these instructions is to urge us not to go down the path of folly, but rather to embrace wisdom, not with the threat of a big stick, but with the carrot of 'finding life' and 'avoiding death'.

Context

While the focus up to this point has been on the upside of wisdom, attention now turns to the downside of folly with a focus on her clear representative, the woman who entices a young man to commit adultery. The amount of vivid detail suggests that this operates at two levels. First, it warns against the specific act of adultery, commending instead a relationship of delighting in your spouse (vv. 15–19). Second, it also has in view the more general pathway of folly, with warnings of death (v. 5) due to lack of discipline (vv. 12, 23), and concluding with the observation that this has all happened *because of his great folly* (v. 23b).

In terms of the focus on female sexual predators (not the common pattern in our world), Longman (2006: 165) helpfully suggests 'that women readers transform the language to suit their context. In other words, instead of a honey-lipped female seducing a male reader, they should read in terms of a sweet-talking male trying to entice them into bed.' Proverbs was written with a particular audience in view (young men), but the principles apply to male and female alike. It is certainly not asserting that sexual sin is primarily the fault of females.

Comment

1–6. Verses 1–2 provide the introductory call to listen, followed by the reason to pay attention to this teaching. Again, the traditional form of address (*my son*) is used, showing that this is a continuation of the kind of teaching already found in chapters 1 – 4. The call is to actively pay attention to the familiar pairing of wisdom and understanding (e.g. 1:2; 2:2; 3:13, although here alone called *my wisdom . . . my understanding*), seeking to change who we are and how we think.

The purpose of listening (v. 2) is that it will help hearers to retain what they are already gaining – the virtue of discretion as part of their character, and relational knowledge that will determine their speaking.

The reference to *lips* (as an image for speech) in verse 2 leads well into the description of the immoral woman's lips/speech in verse 3.[39] The focus is not on her actions, but rather on how she uses words as weapons to entice those who are unformed.[40] The image of her lips dripping honey refers not to untidy eating habits, but is a sensual depiction of something that initially seems sweet and satisfying. The parallel description of her speech being *smoother than* [olive] *oil* also has rich and stimulating associations. The combined picture is of enjoying a rich banquet, a feast that promises no end to enjoyment. Of course, the reality is quite different from this projection. Her words are bitter and sharp, not just in their aftertaste, but in their very essence.[41] Wormwood (absinth) is a bitter, even potentially deadly, plant, while a two-edged sword is effective in cutting, but primarily has associations with death in battle. Immediately after the mention of the sword (v. 4b) is an assertion that such a woman leads you down the pathway of death (vv. 5–6; see 2:18; 7:27). While images of honey and oil suggest life in all its fullness, the reality is that the destination she takes you to is death or Sheol, the place of the dead in Hebrew thought (v. 5). Far from offering life, she gives no real consideration to what will lead to a life worth living (v. 6a). Her ways are those of instant gratification, of immediate pleasure, but not of a purposeful direction in life. Indeed, not only does she wander aimlessly in life, but she is not even aware that she is doing so (v. 6b). It is a thoughtless way of life that is not self-aware or worthwhile.

7–11. Advice and warning are given in verses 8–11, introduced by the generalized form of address, *sons* (as in 4:1, the plural form

---

39. Fox (2000: 191) notes that 'speech is both the danger and the antidote.'
40. Longman (2006: 159) suggests it has a double meaning, for lips are used for both speaking and kissing, with honey being a metaphor for tasting.
41. Fox (2000: 192) notes parallels between the language of v. 3 and Song 4:11, and between v. 4 and Ps. 55:21.

without 'my'), warning the young men to take notice of his teaching
(v. 7). They are to listen to his words, not the smooth speech of the
immoral woman (v. 3). His command (an imperative) is to distance
themselves (*your way*) from such a woman (v. 8a). The door to
her house (v. 8b) seems to be a common location for issuing her
seductive invitations. Her house is mentioned in other descriptions
(2:18; 7:8, 27), with an elaborate description of the young man
seduced as he passes by her house given in 7:6–20.

The negative consequences of not keeping your distance are set
out in verses 9–11. The NIV translates verse 9 to refer to the loss of
face ('lose your honour'), a concept well understood in an honour/
shame culture found in much of the Majority World. To succumb
to the immoral woman is to surrender your honour and your dignity.
However, the force of these words is likely to be different in this
context. Honour (*hôd*), more specifically splendour, refers to the
wealth and possessions that would be understood as the outward
signs of your character.[42] Dignity (NIV) is literally 'years'. The
reference here in verse 9 is to a loss of possessions and time that
would come from developing a relationship with someone who is
not your wife (who are not simply *others* but also 'cruel'/*merciless*).
This makes sense of the following verses as well. In verse 10 your
strength and your *labours* (this word normally means 'pain' or 'hurt',
but can be used to refer to toil or work which is painfully hard) do
not benefit you but rather strangers.[43] Verse 11 outlines that the final
consequence of developing such a relationship is that your life is
used up. The image of groaning at the end of your life pictures the
regret of a life that is wasted. Your physical life is 'spent' (NIV), but
your energies will have been wrongly directed.[44] Thus, all of verses
9–11 depict how a relationship with an immoral woman results in

---

42. Fox (2000: 194–197) suggests it refers to sexual vigour; Longman (2006:
    160) sees it as the life-sapping expending of sexual energy.
43. It could refer to either men connected to this woman, or members of
    her family. Longman (2006: 160) opts for 'pimps'; Whybray (1994: 88)
    proposes family members seeking revenge.
44. Fox (2000: 197) notes that it at least speaks of exhaustion, but may also
    include a reference to the effects of a sexually transmitted disease.

all your wealth, time, energy and hard work being used up in such a way that brings no benefit to you and your family (see vv. 15–20).

12–14. This small section continues the reflections of verses 7–11, but does so now in retrospect as it looks back over the situation and outlines the lesson learnt. Verses 12 and 13 say the same thing, but in different ways. This young man has resisted the rebukes and correcting words of his teachers and instructors. Proverbs 9:7–9 will later outline how someone's character (whether wicked or wise) is determined by how that person responds to correction and reproof. The identity or setting of these teachers is not the point, but rather there is a focus on how this young man has resisted their attempts to shape him. This section is rounded off by verse 14, which outlines the devastating conclusion reached by the young man who has gone down this path. The exact nature of his *utter ruin* (ESV; 'serious trouble', NIV) is not detailed, but the context of the assembled community implies at least an element of social disgrace and shame.

15–20. This is a crucial passage for contemporary believers because of its high view of human sexuality in a way reminiscent of Song of Songs. Some, however, interpret verses 15–18a as referring only to protecting your water rights. Thus, Kruger proposes that the passage has nothing to do with faithfulness in marriage, but is rather a reference to wells and cisterns being private not common property, continuing the loss of property theme of 5:9–11. On this reading, verse 18b is the first mention of a wife (Kruger 1987: 66). This is to miss the force of the water metaphor as an image of the husband's sexual energies and affections.[45] The use of the water metaphor is a discrete way of describing actions that are often described far more explicitly in much of the contemporary world. It depicts an evocative, sexual delight in making love to our spouse. Christians, who see the awful effects of sexual sin in the world, can

---

45. Toy (1899: 113) notes that water is a metaphor for sexual pleasure rather than reproductive power. Garrett (1993: 93) also argues that the springs and streams of water refer to the husband's sexual affections. Fox (2000: 199) notes that drinking water is a metaphor for sexual pleasure in 9:17, and the language of water and springs has this implication in Song 4:12, 15.

often give the impression that sex is too dangerous to be delightful. However, if we are going to take this passage seriously, we need to proclaim a positive view of sexuality and sexual expression within the context of an exclusive heterosexual marriage relationship. This needs to be done with the same clarity and conviction found in Proverbs, for anything less is to short-change God's people (male and female). If God has seen fit to include teaching about sexuality in Scripture, we must make room for such teaching in the church. In fact, 'the best defense (against committing adultery) is a strong offense (reveling in the joys of marital sex)' (Longman 2006: 158).

Different forms of water are referred to in verses 15–16. A cistern is simply a container for storing water, while a well is replenished by an underground source. Water can also come from visible springs, or streams filled by rainwater. The point is not the diversity of origins but rather the piling up of one image of life-giving water after another. The cumulative effect is that water (i.e. sexuality) is greatly valued, and the lesson is to delight in expressing your sexuality only in its God-given context of marriage (*your own cistern . . . your own well . . . your springs*). Thus, there is both restriction (only within marriage) and also encouragement to view sexual activity as one of God's best ideas! Verse 17 sets out the idea of exclusivity, but with a twist suggesting that you lose rather than gain by seeking to go outside the marital boundaries. In this context variety is not the spice of life, and more is not better. Verse 18a is simply the language of praise and delight in your spouse (*your fountain*). The church needs to rediscover and promote such a positive view of marital sexuality as an antidote to a sex-obsessed but not satisfied world.

The second half of verse 18 makes explicit the teaching of the whole section – that a young man should delight in his own wife.[46] The verb *fill you . . . with delight* (ESV, *rwh*) means to take pleasure in, or to enjoy, and the context of verse 19 suggests that it is not referring primarily to enjoying the general marriage bond, but

---

46. Tan (2008: 93) suggests that even the wife is metaphorical, a picture of personified wisdom to whom the man should remain faithful. However, the initial reference is to his literal wife, not just wisdom, just as the immoral woman refers to an adulteress, as well as to folly personified.

especially delighting in the physical and sexual relationship with your wife. As in the Song of Songs (e.g. Song 4:1–11), the language of praise (*a lovely deer, a graceful doe*) is found. Verse 19 speaks of *her breasts* filling you with delight, which is an example of synecdoche (using a part to mean the whole, like fifty head of cattle). The part chosen clearly implies that the teacher is talking of enjoying making love to your wife, in the whole variety of sexual expression from tender touch to intercourse itself. This sexual activity is within the context of marriage (*the wife of your youth*, v. 18b), and flows out from a relationship of love (*her love*, v. 19c). This is not simply a rational decision to be faithful to your spouse (although that is a good thing), but rather a physical and emotional 'intoxication', which so characterizes your relationship that it happens *at all times . . . always*. The verb *be intoxicated* (*šgh*, v. 19c) has a core meaning of 'be led astray', but here the image is of being so caught up in the delights of making love with your spouse that your thoughts are led away from other matters. There is a time, as Song 5:1 describes it, to 'be drunk with love'. In verse 20 the verb 'to be intoxicated/led astray' (*šgh*) is cleverly used in its negative sense of being led astray morally by this immoral woman first introduced in 2:16. Be intoxicated with the right woman, not the wrong one.[47]

21–23. The chapter ends with a motivational section focusing on the reality of God's judgment (vv. 21–23), although it does not specify when or how this will occur. While much of verses 3–20 has argued against adultery because its consequences make it a foolish option, the teacher's warning reaches its climax with a reminder of the deeper consideration of being accountable to God. This is a crucial part of wisdom and wisdom-affected ethics (e.g. Gen. 39:9; Job 31:2, 4, 6, 14, 23). Proverbs is not simply a pragmatic book without theological principles. In fact, verses 21–23 hold together the rich teachings of Proverbs on why to avoid wrongdoing. Verse 21 teaches that God both sees and evaluates all human actions. Even secret sin is not hidden from the Lord, who weighs up, assesses or

---

47. Lucas (2015: 71) comments, 'Women can transpose the teaching into their situation by replacing the honey-lipped woman by a sweet-talking man on the prowl for a one-night stand.'

ponders (ESV; 'examines', NIV) every deed. God is the one to whom all will give account, even in OT wisdom literature where it is not the dominant theme.

Verse 22 focuses on the more common teaching of Proverbs that an individual's actions often have natural consequences as well. The wrong actions (which include trying to trap others) end up trapping the wicked themselves. Sin, often with the tantalizing promise of freedom, leads rather to being held captive or tangled up by wrongdoing. We see this most closely with drug or alcohol addiction, but Proverbs insists that those who take the way of folly are addicts to their sin or wickedness. Wrongdoing is often enticingly captivating, but usually ends up being captivating in a different sense.

The final verse brings us back to the issue of character. The evildoer has made the wrong foundational choice – folly rather than wisdom. He is led astray (the same verb *šgh* translated *be intoxicated* in vv. 19–20) because he has chosen the path that leads to death not life. He will die because he has refused to have his character shaped by the *discipline* or character formation offered by wisdom.

Meaning

As seen in Proverbs 2, it is this wisdom-shaped character (2:11) that will protect a person from men and women who seek to lead someone astray (2:12–19). At the surface level, chapter 5 clearly alerts us to the dangers and consequences of adultery. The teaching here is both negative and positive. Negatively, reject the seductive enticements of a person you are not married to. Positively, delight in the God-given and enjoyable gift of sexual expression within marriage. Yet its setting in chapters 1 – 9 suggests that it is also a warning against embracing folly of every kind. This chapter sets out a theologically rich and multi-strand rationale for avoiding folly in the guise of the immoral woman. Folly is not only subject to God's scrutiny, but also deadly, self-destructive and enslaving (vv. 21–23).

G. Other examples of folly (6:1–19)

Context

The warnings against four snares or distractions in 6:1–19 are the only materials in chapters 5 – 7 that do not deal with the immoral woman. This raises the question of why these verses are located in this part of the book. A crucial hint is that the role of the immoral woman in chapters 5 – 7 is to personify folly. When you look again at 6:1–19, it seems to be moving beyond the personification of folly to some specific, concrete examples of folly, and warns against them. Perhaps this is in case some miss the significance of personification and say, 'Well, I haven't committed adultery, so I'm OK', even if the rest of their life is full of folly. So verses 1–5 speak of folly in financial matters with your neighbour; verses 6–11 target laziness; verses 12–15 refer to troublemakers, while the numerical sayings of verses 16–19 outline a miscellany of activities, climaxing in stirring up conflict in the community (v. 19). These examples of other forms of folly are a reminder that the real focus in chapters 5 – 7 is not adultery or the loose woman, but rather folly itself.

Comment
i. Financial folly (6:1–5)
1–5. The first snare concerns financial folly. Verse 1 outlines the action of being a guarantor for another, either a local neighbour or a stranger. The circumstances or reasons for doing so are not set out, but are more likely to be a result of seeking a large profit than to do an act of kindness. The consequences, however, are clearly described in verse 2 as being caught in a snare or trap. It is not even stated that the neighbour or stranger has defaulted, or whether this is just a possibility. The double mention of mouth in verse 2 draws attention again to the importance of right speech.

Verses 3–5 are then a sustained call to be urgent about getting released from this (actual or possible) financial bind. There is folly in putting up financial security for others, but there is further folly in not facing up to the resulting crisis. The goal is to *save yourself* (vv. 3, 5; 'free yourself', NIV) or deliver yourself from the financial obligation you have assumed for another. Since verse 3 urges you to go to your neighbour (the one who has taken out the loan), the goal is not to have the debt cancelled by the lender, but rather that the borrower should somehow pay or refinance the debt. This would only make sense if the neighbour had enough assets to do so, but chose to use yours instead.[48] The urgency is outlined in verse 4, with no time to sleep until the danger is removed. Verse 5 then compares the scenario to being like a trapped animal or snared bird, with death or captivity as the inevitable outcomes.

It is not stated that it is always wrong for believers today to act as financial guarantors for others. Many parents find themselves in this situation as children seek to buy or build their own homes. Yet even today there are many situations where people foolishly expose themselves to financial ruin as a result of being duped or naive. Folly comes in all areas of life, and money is a central idea in the book as a whole. In the sentence sayings the issue of acting as guarantor for another commonly arises (11:15; 17:18; 20:16; 22:26; 27:13) and is never viewed positively.

ii. Laziness and hard work (6:6–11)

6–11. This section is narrated in reverse order, with verses 6–8 outlining the solution of hard work, while the problem of the lazy person or sluggard is developed in verses 9–11. It may operate at two levels. Its surface intention is to encourage the lazy to work hard instead, but the setting in the contrast of wisdom and folly in chapters 1 – 9 may also suggest a further level of meaning. Those who do not bother much about pursuing wisdom may here be provoked to work hard in chasing wisdom (as in 2:1–4) and so embracing life.

Verse 6 gives three commands: the lazy person is instructed to act (*go to the ant*), think (*consider her ways*) and become (*be wise*). The action of going may be the hardest one in the light of the description in verse 9. It involves taking initiative and responsibility to bring about change. The assumption is that we can learn from observing the natural world, for there are many lessons there about how life

---

48. An alternative way of understanding these verses is to view the neighbour as the lender, with the stranger as the borrower in v. 1. Fox (2000: 211), for example, argues that this makes better sense of going to the neighbour (i.e. lender) in v. 3. However, the strong parallelism of vv. 1–2 implies that the stranger and neighbour are both borrowers. For further arguments in favour of the reading adopted, see Waltke (2004: 325, 331–332).

works. However, mere observation is not enough, for there is also
a need to consider or understand the way that ants live.[49] The logical
conclusion for the lazy and presumably unshaped person is to
embrace wisdom, to take a stand with wisdom not folly, and so be
wise. The cameo given in verses 7–8 draws attention to the diligence
or industriousness of ants. The significance of not having a chief or
ruler (v. 7) is that they do not simply work because they are told
or forced to. However, the reason why they do work so constantly
is not explained, and it does not seem to matter whether that is
simply their nature or if they just act communally (both of which
are probably true). What is important is their action of working
hard, and the positive consequences that follow. The ant both
prepares or builds up her food supply (better 'stores its provisions',
NIV than *prepares her bread*, ESV; the noun normally means 'bread' but
has a more general sense of food as well) and gathers in her food
at harvest time when there are abundant scraps.

The *sluggard* (ESV/NIV; 'lazybones', NRSV) is one of the stereotypical characters described often in the book (e.g. 10:26; 13:4; 15:19;
19:24; 20:4; 21:25; 22:13; and at length in 24:30–34 and 26:13–16).
He is rebuked for simply lying down and sleeping when there is work
to be done and wisdom to be pursued. Frequently he is pictured as
making excuses to avoid action (e.g. 22:13; 26:13) so that he does not
have to move from his bed (26:14a), and avoiding using his hands
to work (19:24; 21:25; 24:33; 26:14b). In this passage he lies down,
refuses to get up, and seems to imply that he is just having a little
sleep or rest (vv. 9–10a). The image of folding his hands (v. 10b, as
in 24:33–34; Eccl. 4:5) is adopting a posture that prevents any work
happening. Whether lying down or perhaps sitting up, no work will
get done. Verse 11 sets out the consequences of poverty and want
coming suddenly to the sluggard (but with ample warning), like when
being robbed by a thief or assaulted by an armed man.[50] Neither the

---

49. While it is lit. 'see her ways', the verb 'to see' (*r'h*) in Hebrew often means
    to 'come to see', 'think about' or 'understand'.

50. Waltke (2004: 339) notes that this word 'poverty' (*rēš*) is found only in
    Proverbs (10:15; 13:18; 24:34; 28:19; 30:8; 31:7) and 'denotes destitution,
    not merely the state of straitened means'.

fruits of hard work, nor the prize of wisdom, will be achieved by one who is too lazy to act, think and become wise.

iii. Troublemakers (6:12–15)

12–15. The third snare of troublemakers (what Waltke 2004: 341 calls 'the nefarious insurrectionist') has already been introduced in the book. The image of crooked speech (v. 12b) is the same as that used to describe the wicked in 4:24, and echoes the description of unruly men in 2:12–15. However, the images of verse 13 occur here for the first time and are not explained. He winks (NIV adds 'maliciously', presumably to avoid the impression that it may have been playful) with his eyes (see 10:10). He scrapes (ESV/NIV *signals with*) his feet on the ground, perhaps leaving signs there for other troublemakers who will pass by. He *points* (ESV; 'motions', NIV) with his fingers, as if to point something out or cause it to be seen. However, it is the descriptions surrounding this that make clear the general thrust of these otherwise-obscure actions. These are the deeds of one who is worthless and wicked (v. 12a);[51] they are the outworking of a *perverted heart* (v. 14a; 'deceit in his heart', NIV), and his actions continually sow discord (v. 14b), a theme picked up in verse 19b. In 'sending out' (*sowing*) discord, he spoils relationships with others. It may be that the acts of verse 13 are deliberately vague, for such a person often wreaks havoc by ambiguous and unclear signs that may not be self-evident at first. However, such a person – and the traits he embodies – should not be underestimated, for verse 15 outlines how a destructive and sudden end will come his way. His ways are not harmless but a serious threat to those seeking to honour God.

---

51. Fox (2000: 219) points out that the term 'worthless man', i.e. man of Belial or the related 'sons/daughters of Belial' is used of a wide variety of wrongdoers, including rabble-rousers and rapists (Judg. 19:22), apostates (Deut. 13:14), drunks (1 Sam. 1:16), political dissidents (1 Sam. 10:27) and unattractive, self-focused figures like Nabal (1 Sam. 25:17, 25) and the sons of Eli (1 Sam. 2:12). This collection seems to sum up those in view here. Garrett (1993: 97) describes him as 'someone who works to undermine social and personal relationships for his own benefit'.

iv. A numerical saying (6:16–19)

16–19. The final snare overlaps somewhat with the previous description, with both mentioning the sowing of discord (vv. 14, 19).[52] This is a numerical saying, a typical wisdom form found prominently in Proverbs 30 (30:15–16, 18–19, 21–23, 29–31). A clue to reading numerical sayings is that the focus of the message is often on the last item mentioned. The seventh example here, sowing discord in the community, draws together the remainder of the other descriptions. While they are initially a loose conglomerate of images, they can all be seen to contribute to a breaking down of the harmony and wholesome relationships which God intends to characterize people living together. Proud or haughty looks (*eyes*) imply that some are better than others. A lying tongue ruptures trust, friendships and families. The shedding of innocent blood undermines justice and causes needless grief. The mention of wicked schemes and feet rushing to do evil reveals some in the group who are concerned only for themselves, regardless of the cost to others. A false witness (as in 14:5, 25; 19:5, 9) can promote injustice and rip a good person's character to shreds. These are all socially destructive and anti-community activities. God longs for peace in community, and the thrust of the biblical idea of peace is not simply the absence of overt conflict, but more so the presence of wholesome relationships across human divisions. The language used in this numerical saying is very strong: God hates and detests such human failings. This gives some idea of the extent to which God is committed to building up community. Conflict, deceit and hatred must not be allowed to fester.

Meaning

Folly can be evident in many areas of life. Being foolish with finances can put us in a bind from which it is difficult to be disentangled. A failure to work hard, or perhaps strive for wisdom, leads to a lack of any achievement. Associating with troublemakers leads to irreversible disaster. The summary picture of verses 16–19 draws

---

52. Waltke (2004: 341) also notes the lying mouth/tongue (vv. 12b, 17), the eyes and hands/fingers (vv. 13, 17), feet (vv. 13, 18) and heart desiring evil (vv. 14, 18).

attention to folly leading to the breakdown of all kinds of relationships in the community. Folly has serious and deadly effects in these areas of everyday life.

H. The danger of adultery (6:20-35)

Context
This discrete unit continues from chapter 5 the focus on folly personified as an immoral woman, and will lead smoothly into a similar description in chapter 7. While the description in each chapter varies in how this woman is described, her role seems to be similarly negative in each case. In this section the man is specifically described as committing adultery with this woman (v. 32), making her husband furious (v. 34). She is a married woman (vv. 26, 29). The main lesson is that adultery is self-destructive and so makes no sense (v. 32). This description gives greater emphasis to the role of the woman's husband in seeking retribution than in the surrounding chapters.

Comment
20-24. Verses 20-21 are echoes of 1:8-9, with the mention of both parents teaching, as well as images of wearing the instruction like jewellery. As in 1:9, the image of wearing the teaching/ commands is one of accepting and adopting them so that they characterize your life. While binding them on your heart is not physically possible, it probably has the sense of wearing a necklace that will sit close to your heart. As a metaphor, it suggests incorporating these instructions into the very core of who you are. Tying them around the neck implies that they are to be lived out in your actions as well. There may be echoes of Deuteronomy 6:6-9 here.

Verses 22-23 outline the benefits of being shaped by the wisdom of this instruction (v. 22) because of what it is (v. 23, which is an aside or parenthesis in the argument), while verse 24 explains that the goal of being wise is that you will be preserved from the adulterous woman. The three settings of verse 22 (your walk/daily life, when you sleep, when you awake) are indications that the instructions given by the parents are useful at all times. They will usefully guide you in your daily activities; they will preserve you (one of the verbs used in 2:11) when you are vulnerable; they will give you input (lit. 'muse' or 'complain', but used in poetry to mean 'speak' or 'talk to') as the day begins. This assistance is based on the nature of this teaching (v. 23, the same words as in v. 20), for it sheds light or makes things clear like a lamp or a light. However, these instructions do not simply disclose the way life is, for they also work on shaping those who hear the teaching. They contain rebukes of (which come from, or consist of) discipline (NIV, 'correction and instruction'), which means that they are to correct and positively shape who you are and how you act. This dual process of shedding light on the way the world is, and shaping your character, is designed to preserve or guard (the same verb as *watch over* in v. 22, but here more active) from the immoral woman, who is here also described as either *the evil woman* (ESV) or 'your neighbour's wife' (NIV).[53] The other descriptions in this chapter make it clear that she is an adulteress (vv. 26, 29, 34). As elsewhere (e.g. 2:16; 5:3; 7:5), she is characterized by *smooth* or seductive talk.

25–29. This section begins with two prohibitions, warning the young man against both desiring (NIV, 'lust in your heart') and being captivated (lit. 'do not let her take you') by the immoral woman's beauty.[54] The *eyelashes* ('eyes', NIV: it probably means 'eyes' in 4:25 but 'eyelids' in 6:4, but is used elsewhere of the rays of light associated with the dawn – hence 'eyelids' or perhaps 'eyelashes' here) seem to refer to the fluttering of the eye(lashe)s as an attempt to entice the young man. Thus, like beauty in the first half of the verse, it refers to using her appearance as a way of seducing the youth. The reason for these admonitions is given in verse 26, introduced by *for*. The idea is that, although there is some small cost (*a loaf of bread*) in hiring a prostitute, adultery or sex with another man's wife may cost your very life. This is not an endorsement of prostitution, but rather setting out how much more deadly is adultery. Indeed, it is the

---

53. The exact translation depends on the translation of two similar small words ('evil', *rāʿ*, and 'neighbour', *rēāʿ*). The first is found in the Hebrew text, while the Greek version seems to assume the second.

54. Fox (2000: 231) notes that these two actions may not occur at the same time, but that the second may be the consequence of the first.

married woman, not her husband, who will chase after (*hunt*) your precious or valued life.

The point is made further by two rhetorical questions in verses 27–28, both of which expect the answer 'of course not'. Just as fire cannot be scooped into your lap (NIV, or *chest*, ESV) without burning your clothes, or walking on hot coals is impossible without scorching your feet, so too one who has sex with another person's wife is playing dangerously with fire and will not emerge unscathed (v. 29). The images are so vivid that they require no further explanation.[55] There are, however, two interesting features about verse 29. First, one who only goes as far as touching or perhaps striking her (presumably with a view to sexual contact) will still be punished.[56] Attempts at adultery are deadly as well. Second, the idea of punishment arises here for the first time in this description, which is otherwise focused on natural consequences. It is not clear if the punishment is meted out by God (as perhaps in 5:21), or by the aggrieved husband (as in v. 34), who could also be viewed as God's instrument. However, the language of punishment implies that this is more than simply the consequences of a foolish action. The conclusion of this section is that adultery is clearly dangerous and potentially lethal.

30–35. This section outlines the consequences of adultery. The starting point is the one who steals because he is hungry (v. 30), which at least makes some sense if the only alternative was to starve to death. Yet while such action could be understood, it is not endorsed, and the culprit, if caught, will need to pay the customary financial penalty (v. 31). This is the platform for a 'how much more' argument. How much more foolish is one who commits adultery, for his options were either abstinence or sexuality expressed in marriage. He would not die if he chose to reject adultery. Thus, the

---

55. Longman (2006: 179), however, suggests that the lap into which coals are scooped may refer to his genitals, as well as the 'feet' in the following verse.

56. Waltke (2004: 357), however, suggests that this might be a metonymy for having sex with her, as in Gen. 20:6. This seems to be reading too much into the word.

key verse (v. 32) concludes that the one who commits adultery both
lacks sense and destroys himself. The way in which he fails at these
two levels is not set out in the verse, but the unit as a whole makes
it very clear. One who plays with fire obviously lacks sense (lit.
'heart', *lēb*, but 'good sense' captures the image well). By his actions
he destroys himself, as outlined in verse 33. He will suffer physical
wounds or injuries, presumably inflicted by, or on behalf of, the
woman's spouse.[57] He will also be dishonoured or irrevocably
disgraced in a culture where loss of face matters even more than
physical injury. The final two verses of this chapter indicate that an
offended spouse will not be deterred from seeking revenge by
payment of a bribe.[58] This is a matter that money cannot fix.

Meaning
This part of chapter 6 depicts the practice of adultery – and the way
of folly behind it – as not only dangerous but also senseless. At the
level of both adultery and folly, it promises much, but it is deceptive
and deeply disappointing. Adulterous relationships may take place
in private, but the consequences that flow from them will be both
public and humiliating. The thrust of the passage is summed up well
in verse 32: *he who commits adultery lacks sense.*

I. The enticing words of the immoral woman (7:1–27)

Context
The woman of chapter 7 is presented in verse 5 in similar categories
to the descriptions of 5:20 and 6:24, although the specific details
differ in each case. While she is initially only identified as the 'strange'
(*zārâ*) or 'foreign' (*nokriyyâ*) woman (v. 5) – what we have called an

---

57. Fox (2000: 235) notes that the word translated *wounds* (ESV) can include a
    range of physical afflictions, injuries and diseases, but never refers to
    corporal or capital punishment imposed by a legal authority.
58. The phrase *when he takes revenge* (v. 34) is lit. 'on the day of vengeance'.
    Peels (1994), followed by Longman (2006: 181), has argued that this
    better refers to securing legal justice rather than taking personal revenge.
    This seems to make less sense of v. 35.

immoral woman – she too is a married woman (v. 19) who lives in the neighbourhood (vv. 6–8). So although she is never called the neighbour's wife or adulteress, she is identified in the chapter as such. She serves to round off the detailed emphasis given to folly personified in chapters 5 – 7. Accordingly, she alone has a long speech (vv. 14–20), which develops the flavour of her enticing words. This example, as part of chapters 5 – 7, provides a foil to the personification of wisdom in chapter 8 and leads into the two invitations of chapter 9. The purpose of folly pictured as a woman in chapter 7 is chiefly to remind us that to choose folly and her ways is not simply 'a lack of sense' (6:32), but is actually to choose the path of death rather than life. This theme will be picked up in chapter 8 with an extended description of wisdom personified, leading to the explicit choice between life and death (8:35–36) and reinforced further in the two invitations of chapter 9 (9:6, 18).

Comment
1–5. This section begins with the final use in the gateway chapters (chs. 1 – 9) of the address *My son* (*O sons*, ESV, is, however, later used in 7:24; 8:32). Verse 1 echoes the opening verse of chapter 2 (see comments there for more detail), with a focus on keeping (in 2:1 'receiving') the teacher's or father's words and treasuring up his commands. The young man is urged to start from the assumption that these words and commands are to be highly valued and become part of who he is (*with*[in] *you*). This emphasis on being shaped by this teaching seems to be so crucial that it is reinforced in verses 2–3. The result or purpose of keeping his commands is that you will live (v. 2a, the likely force of two imperatives). So the youth is called on to regard the instruction he has received as his most prized possession, the *apple of your eye*. This phrase (found also in Deut. 32:10; Ps. 17:8) is literally 'the pupil of your eye'. It speaks of the one thing that you choose as your favourite out of all the possibilities.[59] The

59. Longman (2006: 186) suggests that it may have developed from the fact that people can see themselves reflected in miniature form in the pupil of someone else's eye. It is not clear how this fits with the master's teaching being the apple of the young man's eye.

descriptions in verse 3 imply that the teaching is to be outwardly worn like jewellery, perhaps like a ring on the fingers and a necklace (*the tablet of your heart*), but designed to be visible reminders in order to be adopted within (*your heart*).[60] Verse 4 uses a relational metaphor to describe the same reality. The two parallel expressions of calling wisdom and understanding/insight your sister and your relative (ESV, *intimate friend*) is the language of full acceptance (a performative speech-act) and delight in the relationship.[61] The end result of embracing wisdom and being shaped by the teacher's words is, as in 2:16, that the young man will be preserved from being led astray by an immoral woman (v. 5). This example will fill the rest of the chapter.

6–13. A lengthy example is given in verses 6–13, 21–23, expanded in verses 14–20 by the enticing words the immoral woman uses to lead the young man astray. The scene is set in verse 6, with the teacher or father saying that he looked out through the latticed window (just like Sisera's mother in Judg. 5:28) as a vantage point for observing a scene of daily life.[62] Among the unformed (= *simple*) young men – those who could still choose the paths of either wisdom or folly – the focus centres on one young man (v. 7). He is described as lacking sense (lit. 'lacking heart', an idiom for understanding or sense), presumably from a moral or life experience point of view.

The story is told well. He is initially described as walking on the street *near her corner*, with *her* not yet explained but presumably referring to the immoral woman of verse 5. Anticipation builds up as he takes the road *to her house* (v. 8b, ESV; 'in the direction of her

---

60. Fox (2000: 240) notes that 'The triad of eyes-fingers-heart represents personality as a whole.'

61. Longman (2006: 187) notes that 'sister' is used as an image of romantic intimacy in Song 4:9, rather than as a reference to a sibling, and so is a term of endearment. Alternatively, both 'sister' and 'relative/kinsman' (as in Ruth 2:1) can be seen as relational terms describing people you are closely committed to.

62. Fox (2000: 252) comments, 'We are invited to join in the narrator's voyeurism as he peers out the window on the dark street.'

house', NIV).[63] While we expect an immediate meeting, verse 9 instead describes the setting. It is twilight, with the light fading and the night settled in. *At the time of night* is literally 'in the pupil [of the eye] of night', containing the word translated as *apple* in verse 2. This is an idiom for 'the middle/black of the night', the time when people's actions will not be as noticeable, hidden by the encroaching darkness, as in Job 24:15.

Suddenly the woman meets him, and she is at first described as 'made out like a prostitute' and 'guarded of heart' (v. 10, *wily of heart*, ESV; 'with crafty intent', NIV). Her intent is clearly to seduce someone like this youth. Verses 11–12 are an aside describing her characteristic behaviour. She is *loud* (used of folly personified in 9:13) and 'rebellious' (ESV, *wayward*; NIV, 'defiant', having the sense here of stubbornly resisting societal norms, in particular her obligations to her husband). As a married woman (not yet mentioned, but evident in v. 19) in that culture, her life should have revolved around her husband and her home, but she is a wanderer physically and relationally. She does not stay at home, but voyages into the streets outside and the market squares. This would be expected in much of our contemporary world, but her motive is not simply to be with other people. Verse 12b indicates that her sorties are hunting trips, for she is lying in wait for, or lurking to ambush, her prey on every street corner. She is on the lookout for men to seduce. Her actions make this clear. When this young man appears, she takes hold of him and kisses him (v. 13a) and speaks to him in a 'brazen' (NIV, or 'impudent', from the root 'זז, 'to be strong') way. She takes initiative to lead him astray.

14–20. This section is an extended recounting of her smooth and slippery words as she invites the young man to her house for sex. It is described as *seductive speech* and *smooth talk* in verse 21. It begins with an unusual pick-up line, the ancient equivalent of 'I have just been to church' (v. 14). It works on several levels. First, it accounts for why she is on the street, for the apparently noble purpose of fulfilling her religious obligations. She may even be trying to disarm

---

63. Fox (2000: 242) rightly points out, however, that 'the fact that she finds it necessary to come out toward him and implore him to enter shows that he had not set out to visit her.'

the young man by portraying herself as godly, although that is a little
difficult to square with her seizing and kissing him. Second, and
perhaps more importantly, it gives her a reason to invite him to her
home. While it literally reads, 'I have sacrificed my peace or fellowship offerings', an Israelite would know that some of the food
offered in this way would have been returned to the offeror to eat
that day or the next (Lev. 7:11–18; v. 16 links it with making a vow).
The NIV picks up this thrust well with its amplified translation:
'I have food from my fellowship offering at home.' However, even
this is simply a pretext, for the invitation of verse 18 is not to take
your fill of food, but rather of sex, misdescribed as *love*.

The offer is set out enticingly in verses 15–17. She has come
out to invite (lit. 'meet', *qr'*, but commonly with the sense of 'invite')
him to join her. She has been looking for him eagerly or with longing,
and has found him. The description of her 'bedroom' is opulent and
sensual. There are coverings and coloured linens imported from
Egypt (v. 16; see 31:22). The bed is perfumed and spiced with
expensive, delicious aromas (v. 17). She is painting a picture that
would arouse and stimulate desire, all as a prelude to her daring invitation to make love all night and delight in it (v. 18). She also seeks
to allay his possible fears that they will be surprised by her husband,
mentioned in verse 19. After stating he is not at home, she explains
that he is away on a long journey. The bag of money he took indicates that he had much time-consuming trading to do, and would not
be home until the next full moon (i.e. weeks away). She has cornered
the young man, embraced him, enticed him with images of luxurious
lovemaking and explained that it is all without risk of discovery or
danger. She is an effective presenter of her advertising pitch.

21–23. The example reverts to narrative in verse 21 with a
summary evaluation of the woman's words. As previously (2:16; 5:3;
6:24; 7:5), her smooth or flattering speech is the weapon of choice
to lead him astray. She also turns him aside from the right path by
her many words.[64] The words of verses 14–20 are effective in leading

---

64. Lit. 'she turns [him] aside [the causative form of the verb *nṭh*, to "stretch",
    having the sense of "turning aside from something"] by means of her
    abundant instruction.'

the young man to act on his aroused desires and to go with her. All at once he follows her (v. 22a).

However, the cameo ends with a description of the actual consequences he receives, rather than those that were offered to him. There are three images of death (vv. 22–23): an ox going to the slaughter ('lurching not to bliss but to butchery', Fox 2000: 252), a deer trapped until it is killed with an arrow (the Hebrew is difficult here, but this is probably the sense), and a bird caught in a snare. What began with the promise of making love all night has now degenerated into a scenario that is deadly. It will cost him his life, but he does not know it because he has been duped by her flattering words. The enticing offer promised much, but delivered only death.

24–27. The real consequence of death (in the sense of total loss not gain) is explained in the concluding lesson. The phrase *And now, O sons, listen to me* (v. 24) begins the final section, as it will in the next chapter (8:32), reminding us of the important truth learnt. Verse 25 warns against following the immoral woman, while verses 26–27 indicate that her pathway leads to death. The young man is urged not to let his thinking or inner longings (his *heart*, *lēb*) be turned aside to follow her (v. 25a), nor to stray into her paths by his actions (v. 25b). Four images of death and loss follow. Her victims have been brought down low, and are among many who are slain (v. 26). Her house, with its promise of delights (vv. 16–18), is actually the way of or to Sheol, the place of the dead in Hebrew thought, and is vividly pictured as going down to the chambers or domain of death (v. 27). The offer was inviting – as invitations often are in order to elicit a response. However, the reality was not only deeply disappointing, but deadly serious in its consequences.

Meaning
This warning example is meant to make clear to the implied reader that the path of adultery, or sexual intimacy outside of the God-given context of marriage, is extreme folly. What you think you see is not what you get. The outward form or enticements are not matched by the reality – *it will cost him his life* (v. 23). Furthermore, folly in other areas of daily living will also lead to a dead end, in contrast to the gift of life offered on the pathway to wisdom. The solution is to

embrace wisdom (v. 4) and prize her teaching (vv. 1–3), but not to
stray from her paths into the way of folly (v. 25).

J. A fuller picture of wisdom (8:1–36)

Context

The genre of this chapter is a wisdom speech (so Murphy 1998:
48–49), having departed from the instruction genre in order to offer
the student inspiration and encouragement to pursue wisdom.[65]
Waltke (2004: 386) calls the chapter an interlude and entitles it
'wisdom's self-praise to the gullible', while Longman (2006: 197)
entitles it 'wisdom's autobiography'. Within chapters 1 – 9, chapter
8 appears to serve as the companion piece to 1:20–33 (so Clifford
1999: 93). The wisdom speech contained here is best evaluated
against the deceitful speeches and promises of non-wisdom in
chapters 1 – 9 (e.g. 1:11–14; 2:16; 5:2–3; 6:24; 7:5, 14–21; 9:16–17).
In verses 22–31 it picks up the theme of wisdom's involvement in
the creation, which was first raised in 3:19–20. Appropriately, it ends
in verses 32–36 on the theme of the two pathways, with a strong
emphasis on wisdom as the way of life and thus the only sensible
choice to make.

Comment

1–3. Verses 1–3 set the scene by introducing wisdom personified,
in terms that echo 1:20–21. As earlier, wisdom is spoken about in
the third-person voice of a narrator. This voice is not actually identified, and may be the father or sage who is so dominant in chapters
1 – 9. Wisdom is calling for people to pay attention, and so she raises
her voice (v. 1). The twin terms of wisdom and understanding have
strongly overlapping meanings, and seem to be just slightly different
descriptions of the one reality. Verses 2–3 outline the public places
from and in which she calls out. In a way reminiscent of 1:21,

---

65. Even though it is not a lecture or instruction, Landes (1974: 280) still
    posits a *Sitz im Leben* of the teacher-pupil relationship, in which the
    pupil would be instructed in the nature, function, value and origin
    of wisdom.

wisdom raises her voice on the heights, beside the way/path, at the crossroads, beside the gates, at the entrance to the gates (vv. 2–3). The point of the heights is that she will be able to be heard on the path. Similarly, the crossroads and the gates (and their entrance) are the busiest parts of the town, with the gates also being the place where the important decisions of the town are taken. The overall image is one of wisdom making her call to people so public, that as many as possible will hear. No-one can respond, 'I didn't receive that email' or 'I was never told.'[66]

4–11. This is the most extended self-commendation that wisdom has yet made, a sustained invitation to listen, supported by reasons for paying attention. The groups addressed in this chapter are *men* and *children*/'sons of humanity' in verse 4. Longman (2006: 200) suggests that the audience, as previously, is actually (young) men at the beginning of their professional or married lives. This is possible, but not established simply by verse 4. Certainly there is a narrowing in verse 5 to a focus on two distinct groups: *simple ones* and *fools*. The *simple ones* are those not yet shaped by either wisdom or folly, and the fact of the appeal here suggests that they have not yet rejected wisdom either. However, if they do not embrace wisdom, they will become fools. What they are urged to gain is prudence (v. 5a), an issue of character and skill to find your way through the issues of life. The second group specifically addressed, the *fools*, are those who have rejected the path of wisdom, for they are those who *despise wisdom and instruction* (1:7). To the fools wisdom says, *learn sense* (v. 5b, ESV; Longman 2006: 199, 'take this to heart'). This reads more literally 'understand heart', where the heart would represent thinking. The phrase 'come to your senses' captures the intention of urging those who have rejected wisdom to change the core of their thinking. If the unformed *simple ones* are urged to have their character shaped by wisdom, the *fools* who have already rejected wisdom are challenged to do a U-turn and come to their senses by reconsidering wisdom and her claims.

---

66. Waltke (2004: 392–393) extends the setting to the end of v. 5, but it is better to see that the transition to a first-person speech by wisdom (as opposed to a third-person speech about wisdom in vv. 1–3) begins a new section.

Wisdom recommends herself because of the rightness and value of her teaching in verses 6–11. In verses 6–9 the moral quality of wisdom's words is highlighted. They are what is *right* (upright, v. 6b), *truth* (v. 7a), *righteous* (v. 8a; 'just', NIV), *straight* (v. 9a; 'right', NIV), *right* (v. 9b; 'upright', NIV) – and not wicked (v. 7b) or *twisted/crooked* (v. 8b). Wisdom is a trustworthy source, and so all her words and ideas can be relied upon. They are for the discerning/understanding, for those who have found knowledge, implying that they are intended to further shape those who have already chosen the way of wisdom.

This self-commendation ends with wisdom urging those who hear to receive or 'take on board' her instruction in preference to money, valuable metals or jewels (3:15). A number of scholars suggest that verse 11 is a gloss rather than an original part of the text (including evangelicals like Waltke 2004: 399). This is largely a text-critical debate, but if verse 11 is included, it is simply developing the value of wisdom in verse 10, and drawing out the obvious conclusion that nothing could be compared to her in value. The very objects that people treasure in this world are less valuable than what wisdom has to offer. Up to this point wisdom is exhorting her listeners to opt for the way of wisdom, without yet detailing what will flow from this foundational choice.

12–16. Wisdom introduces herself more formally in verse 12 and then proceeds to outline her character. She deals first with her positive characteristics (prudence, knowledge, discretion, v. 12) and then indicates what she distances herself from (evil, pride, arrogance, a perverse mouth, v. 13). There is parallelism between wisdom in verse 12 and the fear of the Lord in verse 13, as if they are different ways of describing the same reality, indicating how the fear of the Lord is foundational for the wisdom task.[67] As in 1:7, the fear of the Lord refers to the foundational choice of respecting God as God. Verse 13 makes it clear that this involves the decisive rejection

---

67. Fox (2000: 271) views vv. 12–16 as outlining wisdom's benefits to society and individuals, with a focus on wisdom's character in vv. 12–13, and on wisdom's contribution to statecraft (that it grants power) in vv. 14–16. Waltke (2004: 393) categorizes the entire section here as dealing with wisdom's role in civil order.

(*hate* is used twice) of *evil* and its component parts, pride and arrogance, evil behaviour (*the way of evil*, ESV) and twisted speech. All these have to be renounced if God is to be treated as God.

Verses 14–16 focus on the value of wisdom to those in positions of power. Verse 14 is a little more general than that, but in the context of verses 15–16, it is talking about advice, sound wisdom, insight and strength in order to rule well. There is a parallel between verses 15a and 16a (*by me kings reign* = 'by me rulers rule') and between verses 15b and 16b (*and rulers decree what is just* = 'and nobles, all who govern rightly'). The thrust of verses 14–16 is that wisdom will help those who wield power to exercise it in appropriate and beneficial ways in their community setting. This means that wisdom is intensely practical in leadership positions. The classic example of this is when Solomon asked for wisdom to govern God's people and discern between good and evil in doing so (1 Kgs 3:3–15, especially v. 9). Immediately after this is given, Solomon is tested in a legal dispute between two prostitutes over who is the true mother of a baby (1 Kgs 3:16–22). Solomon uses his wisdom by devising a shrewd test – ordering that the baby be dissected – to reveal the one woman who had true maternal instincts, with the result that all Israel understood that God's wisdom was with Solomon to do justice (1 Kgs 3:28).

17–21. Verses 17–19 operate similarly to verses 14–16, with a more generic introduction in the first verse before focusing on the real issue in the second and third verses. At one level, verse 17 is simply descriptive of the fact that wisdom loves those who love her, and is found by those who seek her. However, in light of the parallels in 2:1–6, it seems that the main task of this verse is to motivate people to seek and love wisdom. It is urging action, not simply describing the way things are. One key purpose of chapters 1 – 9 within the book is that its readers will strive to have their character shaped by wisdom as they reject the path of folly. This emphasis on pursuing wisdom makes sense of verses 18–19, which outline financial incentives for seeking wisdom: riches, honour, lasting wealth, prosperity (v. 18); better than gold or choice silver (v. 19). Honour (*kābôd*) can mean 'glory' and so refer to a glorious abundance of money and possessions, but may also imply here the notion of being held in respect by others. *Enduring wealth* suggests that what is gained from wisdom is not just short-term, 'flash-in-the-pan'

wealth that is conjured up today and disappears tomorrow. Of all
the descriptions in verse 18, the most interesting is *righteousness*
(*ṣĕdāqâ*). Although the NIV translates this as 'prosperity', this is a
common word for righteousness (it will be repeated in v. 20), and
makes sense within a wisdom mindset. The rich should be shaped
by wisdom, and a key component is a shaped character which will
include a commitment to the righteous use of their wealth and
power. Verse 19 states that the fruit or yield of wisdom is better than
precious metals like gold or silver. While this may be a way of
asserting that the by-product of wisdom is abundant riches, it may
also be that it is better in that riches as the outworking of a godly
character are better than riches alone. However, it is at least clear
that those who want to receive what wealth promises to give should
pursue wisdom instead. The message is 'embrace wisdom who
grants wealth and perhaps more'.

Verse 20 puts this wealth in the context of justice and righteousness. While wisdom will give wealth (Longman 2006: 195, 'substance')
to those who love her and fill their treasuries (v. 21), loving wisdom
involves being shaped by justice and righteousness, for that is part
of the way of wisdom (v. 20). Wisdom does not offer the promise of
dishonest gain, or wealth at the expense of those in need, but
of wealth rightly gained and to be used in conformity with wisdom's
nature and values. Justice and righteousness are a common pairing
in OT legal and prophetic texts, and the wisdom book of Proverbs
shows a similar valuing of these key values and priorities. Verse 21
projects a picture of wisdom being willing to give out rich treasures
that will be able to fill their coffers.[68] Anything less than wisdom is
worthless, or at least worth less than what wisdom can offer.

Additional note on interpreting 8:22–31

This key theological section has been debated at length by scholars.
Some suggest that the description of wisdom in 8:22–31 is so exalted

---

68. The idea of *inheritance* (ESV/NIV), derived from the verb *nḥl*, 'to grant/
    bestow an inheritance' in v. 21, is often used of the gift of the Promised
    Land as the most valued of all possessions.

that it is to be understood as a hypostasis, that is, a heavenly or divine being separate to God, even though it is described in human terms. However, wisdom is not depicted here as an actual heavenly being co-existing with God, but rather is an extended personification, an abstraction made personal for the sake of vividness.

The context favours the view that wisdom is here being personi-fied. Wisdom has previously been described in personal terms throughout this opening section of Proverbs. For example, she is portrayed as a woman crying out to the youth in the city in 1:20-33. In 3:16 she holds long life, riches and honour in her hands, making them available for those who seek her. In 4:6 the pupil is promised that if he loves her, she will protect him. In 4:8-9 she will honour and exalt those who embrace wisdom, putting a garland or crown on their head. Furthermore, she is one of two women in chapter 9 who personify the virtues of wisdom and folly respectively. Indeed, it is part of the teaching strategy in these chapters of Proverbs to personify folly as well. The immoral woman of chapters 5 – 7 (and 2:16-19) is at one level the embodiment of folly. Thus, there is ample evidence of the virtues of wisdom and folly being personified in the surrounding context. The juxtaposition of wisdom and the con-trasting figures in chapters 7 and 9 reinforce the view that wisdom is only personified, for the figure in 9:13-18 is certainly not a hypostasis (Kidner 1964: 78-79).

While later Jewish wisdom identifies the figure of Proverbs 8 with the Torah, a number of scholars have sought to identify the wisdom figure as a pre-incarnation appearance of the second person of the Trinity, later to come as Jesus. Along these lines, verses 22-31 are sometimes compared to John 1:1-18, or verse 30 is connected to Hebrews 1:2-3. Attempts to make a link with Christ are largely based on the relationship between this figure and the Lord in the much-debated verse 22 (see below). There is difficulty in knowing how the verb *qnh* is to be understood. The two viable options are 'created' and 'acquired/possessed'. Arianism (an early Christian heresy claiming that there was a time when Christ did not exist) used the former meaning to argue that Christ is a created being. However, if you adopt the more likely translation of 'acquired' or 'possessed', there are still problems connecting this figure to Christ. If this figure was 'acquired' or even 'possessed' by the Lord, then there still seems to be a time when he was not, or perhaps that he existed but was independent of the Lord. None of these options seems to fit orthodox Christology. If the NRSV is right in translating verse 22b as 'the first of his acts of long ago', this makes the objection even stronger.

The other obvious option is that it is not a reference to the pre-incarnate Christ (nor the Spirit, the view of Irenaeus), but simply to wisdom. Here it is an assertion that, since wisdom precedes the creation, it could be woven into every part of the created world. This makes sense of the examples of verses 24–26, highlighting the presence of wisdom before the creation. While there is a link between OT wisdom and Jesus, this does not require the figure of Proverbs 8 to be a depiction of Christ. Jesus fulfils and embodies OT wisdom, just as he fulfils OT law, prophecy and apocalyptic. This leads to Jesus being described as the 'wisdom of God' (1 Cor. 1:24, 30), without implying that every time wisdom is mentioned, it is really a hidden reference to Jesus. Similarly, the emphasis on wisdom in creation in Proverbs 8 is fulfilled in Colossians 1:15–20, where Christ is not only Lord in redemption (vv. 18–20), but also Lord over creation, bringing it into being and sustaining it (vv. 15–17). Wisdom is not separate from God's purposes, but the personified figure of Proverbs 8:22–31 is not a description of the pre-incarnate Christ.[69]

What, then, is the purpose of the personification in Proverbs 8? Goldsworthy (1987: 79) suggests that, 'Personification in Proverbs 8 is almost certainly a poetic way of highlighting the important

---

69. Steinmann (2009: 219–229), however, argues that a strong connection between this figure of wisdom and Jesus is made as early as the NT and the writings of Ignatius (AD 35–107). In particular, the early church picked up on v. 25 as a text supporting that Jesus was begotten before the creation. The orthodox response to Arius was that v. 22 needs to be read in the light of v. 25, which outlines that Jesus was 'begotten' before the creation. Others argued that v. 22 only refers to the creation of Jesus' human not divine nature. Steinmann gives a strong Christological reading for Prov. 8, seeing parallels between the wisdom attributes of the Spirit in Isa. 11:2 and Prov. 8, as well as between Prov. 8 and Eph. 3:8–10. He argues that vv. 24–25 teach Christ's eternal generation from the Father.

characteristics of wisdom as being both a gift of God and an activity of man.' Wisdom is best seen here as an attribute of God, one that he used as he wisely made the entire creation. To some extent, then, God's wisdom can be partially discerned by a close study of the created world. In addition, the precise identity of wisdom in its current context is to be found in the studied contrast in Proverbs 1 – 9 between wisdom personified ('Lady Wisdom') and folly depicted as a woman ('Dame Folly'). This common wisdom theme of the two ways is both how this chapter ends and is a theme further developed in chapter 9. The personification of wisdom in chapter 8 makes for a vivid contrast between these two fundamental choices in life. Thus, it is better to read the figure of wisdom as an extended personification, that is, an abstraction made personal in order to be remembered more easily. God possesses wisdom as one of his key attributes.[70]

22–26. This subsection outlines the beginnings of wisdom, first with a statement of God's action (v. 22), then a series of passive verbs in verses 23–25 (*I was set up . . . I was brought forth . . . I was brought forth*). God is the active participant here.

Of the two main possibilities of translating *qnh* ('created' and 'acquired/possessed'), the latter meaning is the core one and is adopted by KJV, ESV and NIV 1984 (contra NRSV = 'created'; NIV 2011 has 'brought me forth').[71] Some suggest that it may mean 'create' in

---

70. As in 3:19, where *the LORD by wisdom founded the earth*. Longman (2006: 212–213) helpfully notes the NT's use of this image of wisdom: 'Prov. 8 is not a prophecy of Jesus or any kind of literal description of him. We must remember that the text is poetry and is using metaphor to make important points about the nature of God's wisdom. Indeed, even in its OT setting where Wisdom stands for Yahweh's wisdom, we would be wrong to press the language of creation literally as if at some point God were not wise and only later became wise just in time to create the world . . . But – and this is crucial – the association between Jesus and Woman Wisdom in the NT is a powerful way of saying that Jesus is the embodiment of God's Wisdom.'

71. Longman (2006: 204) translates it as 'begot', but this is based on a Ugaritic parallel.

Genesis 4:1, when Eve speaks of the birth of Cain and says, 'I have created a man', but this could easily be translated as 'acquired' or 'gained'. Kidner (1964: 75) argues that of the verb's eighty-four OT occurrences, only six or seven allow the sense of 'create', and even they do not require it. Fox concedes that its basic meaning is 'acquire', but observes that the verb can mean 'acquire by creating' and so needs to be translated as 'created' here. Steinmann argues that the verb is nowhere used of *creatio ex nihilo*, which it would need to mean here, and so translates it as 'acquired' or 'possessed'.

Certainly, if it means 'acquired', this should not be understood as implying that there was a time when God was not wise. That would be to miss the thrust of this passage entirely. The rest of this section shows no interest in what existed prior to wisdom being created or acquired. Rather, it focuses on wisdom being infused into all parts of the creation from the very beginning. This bypasses the debate between those who wish to translate *qnh* as 'created' and those who prefer 'acquired' (and by extension, 'possessed'). The main point is not the process of acquisition of wisdom (by a new act of creation, or by acquiring an existing entity), but rather that God has wisdom and has used it extensively as he has made the world. In this light, *possessed* (ESV) is the most useful translation as it draws attention to the outcome rather than the process.

Wisdom then explains that she is the first of God's 'way' (v. 22). The word 'first' (*rē'šît*) has a variety of meanings, ranging from the first in importance (chief) to the first in a sequence (beginning). Since the context is one of the very commencement of creation, and since no rival virtues are mentioned or implied, 'first' most likely has a time sense here, and so means 'beginning'. 'Way' (*derek*), commonly used in Proverbs to mean your fundamental choice through life, here has the related sense of all that you do on this way, and so is usually translated as 'works' or 'deeds'.[72] The last part of verse 22 reads, 'his deeds of old, from then' (= 'from his deeds of old/ antiquity', a time phrase in parallel to 'the beginning of his way'.

---

72. Fox (2000: 280) describes it as 'a collectivity of actions – a pattern
    of behavior or a course of action . . . God's "way" and "works" include
    but do not end with the creation of the world'.

Both the NIV 'before his deeds of old', and ESV *the first of his acts of old* add a little to the text as a way of interpreting it.

In this time long ago, wisdom describes herself as being 'poured out' into the creation. The verb in the Hebrew text, 'poured out' (*nsk*), is often emended to read 'formed' (NIV) or *set up* (ESV).[73] However, the image of wisdom being poured out into the created world does parallel the verb used in verses 24–25 of wisdom being *brought forth* into the world. The idea in each case is that wisdom becomes an integral component used in shaping the creation. Verse 24 refers to this beginning period – in terms reminiscent of Genesis 1 – as the time when there were no *depths* or underground *springs* of water. Verse 25 describes this time as before the shaping of the mountains and hills (echoes of Ps. 90:2), while the following verse refers to the earth with its fields (lit. 'outsides') and soil (*dust*). The section from verses 24–26 thus gives a variety of descriptions of the same time period before the creation of the earth. In that setting wisdom was poured out (v. 23) and brought forth (vv. 24–25), so that there is nothing in creation that has not been wisely or skilfully made. It is therefore important to understand wisdom if you wish to make sense of the created world. This dovetails nicely into the affirmation of Genesis 1 about the original goodness of creation, and would have implications for the 'wise' use of our world.[74]

27–31. This subsection consists of two connected parts. In verses 27–30a we see wisdom's presence and 'involvement' with God the Creator and Sustainer. In verses 30b–31 wisdom is both the delight of God and the one who delights in God's creation.

Verses 27–30a contain various creational actions by God (vv. 27–29), which are bracketed by twin statements by wisdom

73. This is based on the view that the Hebrew root *nsk* makes little sense here, and could reflect a different root *skk*, 'to weave together' and so 'form'.

74. Collins (1980: 31–32) asserts that Prov. 8 'affirms without qualification that the created order is good' and that 'evil is not inherent in the order of creation, but results from human ignorance and the lack of wisdom'. Human sin, as set out in Gen. 3, is a further complication.

(vv. 27a, 30a) saying that she was there, that she was beside God as he was acting. If verses 22–26 describe the creation just before God made or shaped it, then verses 27–29 outline wisdom's presence *during (when)* the acts of creation.[75] These acts clearly echo the narrative of Genesis 1. Sometimes the descriptions use the words of Genesis 1 (e.g. 'on the face of the deep' in Gen. 1:2 and Prov. 8:27), but more commonly they simply allude to the Genesis account.[76] Thus, establishing the heavens echoes the creation of night and day, and filling them with the sun, moon and stars. Drawing a circle (ESV; 'marked out the horizon, NIV) on the deeps reflects the separation process of creation, while the firming of the skies (lit. 'clouds') and the fixing of the fountains of the deep refer back to the waters above the earth (sky) and those on the earth (Gen. 1:6–8). The assigning of limits to the sea (v. 29) echoes the gathering of the waters to make dry land (Gen. 1:9–10).[77] These are clear connections between the two texts. Against the backdrop of this account of the creation, wisdom makes two claims: *I was there* (v. 27a) and *I was beside him* (v. 30a). The phrase *I was there* (v. 27a) does not imply that wisdom was in the heavens/sky, but that she was part of that process. As Fox (2000: 284) points out, '"There" is a situation, not a location.' Wisdom was both present and actively involved in the work of creation. One key implication of this is that if wisdom is foundational to the creation of the world, it is also foundational to making a successful path through life.

---

75. Waltke 2004: 414 suggests that the sixfold use of 'when' (in all cases, the same Hebrew preposition) in vv. 27–29 draws attention to wisdom's presence during specific acts of creation.

76. On the echoes with Gen. 1, see Landes (1974: 279–293).

77. Longman (2006: 206) opts for there being five acts of creation in vv. 27–29, viewing v. 29b (marking out the foundations of the earth) as simply an expansion of the thought of v. 29a (assigning boundaries to the sea). His five acts are: the establishment of the heavens; the construction of the horizons on the depths; the firming up of the clouds; the intensification of the underground water sources; the setting of the boundaries of the sea.

Verse 30a needs to be discussed separately because of the variety of interpretations that have been offered, even if none of the possibilities undermines the basic point established above. The Hebrew word *'āmôn* has been variously translated as 'master worker/craftsman' (e.g. ESV), 'constantly' (e.g. NIV) or 'little child' (e.g. Waltke, Fox). The existence of this debate needs to make us cautious about drawing too much from whatever translation we think gives the best sense, but there is significant overlap of meaning in any event. Whether wisdom was by God's side constantly, like a master worker, or as a little child paying close attention, she is actively involved in the process as a co-worker or onlooker/admirer. Wisdom at least is present and learning from God's activity in creation, and perhaps also being used by God as he creates. While 'master worker' (or equivalent) seems to be the most commonly chosen in English Bible translations, the context in verses 22–31 favours an emphasis on wisdom's presence rather than her activity. She is active in the present (vv. 1–21), calling people to choose her, and claiming that she helps rulers rule (vv. 15–16). But the thrust of verses 22–31 is simply on wisdom's *presence* with God from the very beginning. If anything, wisdom is being used by God, woven into the fabric of the world, rather than herself being active.[78] In the end we cannot be sure, but it seems clear that it is primarily an echo of *I was there* in verse 27a.

The theme of delight is covered in verses 30b–31. Verse 30b could refer to God's delight in wisdom (so ESV: *I was daily his delight*) or wisdom's own delight, presumably at being beside God (so NIV:

---

78. On the linguistic arguments, see Scott (1965), who surveys the main possibilities for the word *'āmôn* (a hapax) and notes that all the following can be supported from either the text as it stands, or by just being revocalized: 1. master workman [RSV/NRSV/ESV; Longman = 'craftsman']; 2. cherished child [Waltke opts for this]; 3. guardian/foster-father [Scott opts for this]; 4. binding, uniting, fashioning [LXX, Syriac, Vulgate]; 5. true or faithful [Alden]. More recently, Fox (2000: 286–287) argues for a variation of 'little child', reading it as an infinitive absolute used as an adverbial complement translated 'growing up' = 'I was near him, growing up'.

'I was filled with delight day after day'). While it most likely refers
to wisdom being God's delight,[79] it is immediately followed by clear
statements that wisdom was rejoicing before God (v. 30c), rejoicing
in the whole inhabited world (v. 31a) and delighting in human beings
(v. 31b). There is a sense of playful exploration of the way the world
is ordered. While God delighted in wisdom's presence, wisdom itself
rejoiced in both God and those who fill his creation.

32–36. After this aside in verses 22–31, the key threads of the
chapter are drawn together in verses 32–36, and a suitable challenge
is given, introduced by the resumptive *O sons* (= NIV 'my children').
It consists of wisdom urging those who are still uncommitted to be
shaped by wisdom. The call to listen is, as often elsewhere, a demand
for obedience, evident in verse 32b by the parallel *keep my ways*. The
warning of verse 33 is not to neglect or ignore (lit. 'let loose') the
teacher's wise instruction or shaping. The one who listens/obeys is
called blessed in both verses 32 and 34, and the way to listen is to be
eagerly and expectantly watching out for lessons to learn (v. 34). There
is clearly nothing more important than being shaped by wisdom.

The final two verses (vv. 35–36) unpack the most severe consequences of accepting or rejecting wisdom, seeing it as a matter of
life and death. The contrast between verse 35a and verse 36b is
telling: *whoever finds me finds life . . . all who hate me love death*. There is a
careful balance between this simply being the consequence of their
choice (v. 36a, 'those who miss me injure themselves') and also the
active involvement of God (v. 35b, *obtains favour from the LORD*). From
one vantage point, the consequences naturally follow; from another,
God is actively involved in the process. The two ways to do life of
chapter 9 are thus anticipated in this final exhortation. Both will
speak of life as the outcome of embracing wisdom (8:35; 9:6), while
death is the consequence of choosing folly (8:36; 9:18). The promise
of life as it is meant to be is starkly contrasted with the shadowy
threat of death. Murphy (1966: 9) describes the kerygma of wisdom
as 'life' and sees it set out most clearly in this section.

---

79. Fox (2000: 287) notes that 'his' is supplied in the LXX, but is implicit
   in the Hebrew, for it is elsewhere used of being a *source* of delight
   to another (e.g. Ps. 119:24; Isa. 5:7; Jer. 31:20).

Meaning

Wisdom is portrayed here as an attractive, even irresistible, figure. Her call is unmistakable (vv. 1–3); her instruction is rich (v. 10); her foundation is the fear of the Lord (v. 13); her benefits are beyond measure (vv. 15–19); and her character is upright (v. 20). She is the ideal one to shape a young person's life. Furthermore, verses 22–31 describe her as so integrated into the creation that living in accordance with wisdom is the only way to live 'with the grain' (vv. 22–31). God's incredibly complex creation is riddled with the presence of wisdom. For this reason, the chapter concludes with a call to find true life through embracing wisdom, for the alternative is deadly (vv. 32–36).

K. Two invitations (9:1–18)

Context

The three sections of this chapter are clearly verses 1–6, 7–12 and 13–18, although verses 7–12 may be divided further. In the context of chapters 1 – 9, the call to embrace wisdom is actually part of a wider choice – which woman shall I embrace? Proverbs 9 contains two seemingly identical party invitations (vv. 4, 16), one from 'Lady Wisdom' and one from 'Dame Folly'. While the two invitations make a fitting conclusion to chapters 1 – 9, there is less clarity about verses 7–12. Byargeon (1997), however, points out that each individual mentioned in verses 7–12 corresponds to either wisdom or folly in the surrounding invitations.[80] Perhaps more significantly, the fear of the Lord sayings in 1:7 and 9:10 form an inclusio within chapters 1 – 9. The chapter does not end with a fear of the Lord saying simply because it is structured chiastically, in which the key point is made in the centre. The invitation of personified wisdom (vv. 1–6)

---

80. Several scholars regard vv. 7–12 as having been inserted into the text, with vv. 9–10 missing from one Hebrew manuscript and vv. 10–12 from another. The Greek version (LXX) even adds a few verses after v. 12, increasing the textual uncertainty. Garrett (1993: 114) rightly argues for the retention of these verses by noting the similarity between them and 1:20–33 and 8:1–36.

is balanced by the invitation of personified folly (vv. 13–18). The folly of the scoffer when corrected (vv. 7–8a and v. 12b) brackets the response of the wise person to correction (vv. 8b–9 and v. 12). This leaves the fear of the Lord and promise of long life at the centre and the structural key point of the chapter (vv. 10–11).

Comment

1–6. As in the parallel invitation in verses 13–18, there is an outline of the setting (vv. 1–3), the inviting words (vv. 4–6) and ending with the consequences of this choice (v. 6). Wisdom herself is introduced in the same, unusual plural form (with a singular verb) found in 1:20.[81] She has prepared well for the feast. The house that she has built is a substantial one, evident from the seven pillars she has quarried or carved (*hewn*, ESV).[82] The seven *pillars* or standing columns are described as belonging to wisdom (*her*, ESV, not 'it', NIV), so they may be decorative rather than structural. Solomon's palace had many cedar pillars (1 Kgs 7:2–6) and two decorative bronze pillars (1 Kgs 7:15–22), but simple homes may have had one or two wooden pillars in the centre.[83] The number seven may not have any particular significance (contra Garrett 1993: 115, who sees it as an echo of the seven days of creation), but if they are the pillars around the open courtyard in the house (so Waltke 2004: 433), then it is a grand house with plenty of room for more to come in. Her provision of a suitable place for a feast (v. 1) is matched by a description of the banquet itself (v. 2). The provision of meat (*beasts*, ESV) indicates a lavish meal since meat was a luxury item. The mixing of wine is not watering it down, but rather mixing in honey and spices

---

81. *DCH* suggests that it is a plural noun meaning wisdom personified.

82. Others make a slight emendation to the text here, based on the LXX, to read, 'she has erected/caused to stand', hence NIV: 'she has set up'. Prov. 14:1 explicitly describes the wise woman who builds her house.

83. McKinlay (1996: 50–51) notes that Israelite houses were pillared and that some large non-royal houses had seven pillars. Skehan (1967: 163 [469]) has argued that it is seven poems of twenty-two verses each which is her house of words, but this is unlikely.

for an even richer taste. She has also arranged or ordered the tables.[84] Wisdom is a generous and indeed perfect hostess. In the context of the book this is a celebration not to be missed. She has sent out young women as her messengers to ensure the invitation is heard. Dahood (1963: 17), citing a Ugaritic parallel, proposes that no-one would send out female servants to invite male guests, making it likely that she has sent them away or dismissed them. However, this is to press the details of a literary device too far, since wisdom is not an actual mistress with servant girls. The sending out of the girls is part of making the feast known. Wisdom calls out from prominent locations (as in 1:20–21, places chosen to ensure that all will hear), and issues her invitation through these girls.[85] Strictly, it is wisdom who calls out or invites (this verb means 'invite' in the context of a feast), but she does so through her messengers.

The words of the invitation are set out in verses 4–6. They are addressed to the *simple*, which refers as before to those who are not yet shaped by either wisdom or folly (see 1:4, 22), those who are still naive and easily taken in. In parallel with the simple is *him who lacks sense*, literally lacking heart (as in 7:7 and echoed in 8:5), which is an idiom for lacking sense or understanding. The invitation given in verse 4 will be repeated in identical words by folly in verse 16. It is a call to 'turn aside', to leave the current path and enter the house and way of wisdom. In other words, it is a plea to make wisdom the foundation of your life. The banquet image from verse 2 is repeated in verse 5, with a call to enjoy her food and carefully prepared wine. The reality behind this symbolism is set out in the transparent words of verse 6. The youth is invited to give up or leave behind his unformed or simple ways by making this foundational decision to base his life on wisdom. The double imperative (*leave . . . live*) is

---

84. The same phrase in Ps. 23:5 of preparing a table for David in the presence of his enemies.

85. Murphy (1998: 57) notes that *mĕrōmîm*, *highest places* (ESV), is found only here in the sense of heights, but must mean something like 'from the heights over the city'. *DCH* suggests that it perhaps means summit, but notes that elsewhere it means 'body'.

commonly a purpose construction in Hebrew, so the force is on
leaving behind your simple way (NRSV opts for 'lay aside immaturity')
in order to live (it could alternatively be a result clause: *so that/with the
result that* you will live). The second half of verse 6 adds another
imperative, 'go straight' (*walk*, ESV/NIV), which continues this
purpose (or result) construction: 'leave . . . in order to live and in
order to walk in the way of insight'. This explains the imagery of
verse 5 as a call to leave behind your past indecision in order to travel
wholeheartedly on the path of wisdom, to have your whole life
shaped by wisdom. This is an invitation to *live*, to find life as it is
meant to be, life in all its fullness – an idea picked up in the NT
where Jesus describes himself as the bread of life who gives life to
the world (John 6:32–35), a life that is abundant (John 10:10).

7–9. This middle section of the chapter (vv. 7–12) connects the
two invitations, compares the wise and the scoffer, and centres on
the fear of the Lord as the foundational principle for life.

A crucial clue to discerning the difference between those who
have embraced wisdom and those who have embraced folly is to
examine the way they respond to the correction of other people.
Those who choose folly (vv. 7–8a) do not know their own need – so
they react with insults and abuse. They have nothing to learn and
are unteachable. Those who choose wisdom (vv. 8b–9) know their
need to grow in wisdom, appreciate correction and are teachable,
since they seek to gain further knowledge.

In verse 7 the one who corrects or disciplines a scoffer or mocker
receives abuse or insults.[86] The second half of verse 7 claims that
the one who rebukes the wicked gets hurt. The word for 'hurt' or
injury is a term commonly used for animals unsuitable for sacrifice
because they have blemishes, but is here used as a parallel to 'insult'.
Thus, it could refer to either physical injury or being accused of
having (moral) defects (so Waltke 2004: 427, 'brings moral blemish
on himself'). Verse 8a warns against rebuking (a different verb from
that used in v. 7, but with a similar meaning) a scoffer, for the

---

86. Steinmann (2009: 238) notes that elsewhere in Proverbs *qālôn*, 'abuse',
     means insult (12:16; 22:10), and that receiving for himself dishonour
     is probably an idiom for 'invites insults'.

outcome is that he will hate you.[87] In each case, the wicked or mockers reveal their (lack of) character as they respond to correction, or being called to account.

The second half of verse 8 begins the contrasting description of the wise. Since the truly wise would aim to grow in wisdom and character, they appreciate any constructive criticism, instruction or correction, since it will help them to become the kind of people they wish to be. Thus a wise man who is rebuked will love the one who takes the risk of calling him to account. A rebuke therefore makes it clear whether a person wants to grow in character or simply to save face. The mention of a *righteous* person (v. 9b), in parallel to the wise one, emphasizes that this is not simply a matter of gaining knowledge, but rather an issue of character. Those who willingly embrace the instruction (implied) and teaching being given will increase or add to their learning (see 1:5a). In other words, the way in which people respond to correction and instruction is commonly a litmus test of their character and deepest commitments.

10–12. Against this backdrop comes an echo of the foundational principle of 1:7, acting as a kind of inclusio bracketing all of chapters 1 – 9. The fear of the Lord, or respecting God as God (see on 1:7), is the beginning of wisdom (v. 10). This is a different word for *beginning* from the one used in 1:7, and clearly has the sense of 'first in time', a word that occurs only here in Proverbs. This verse is the only place in the chapter where God is explicitly mentioned, but it is the crux of the teaching. Respecting God as God is the indispensable starting point, without which it is impossible to understand the various descriptions of daily life found in the rest of the book. To build a life or worldview without starting here is like building a house without foundations, or running a marathon without training. It makes no sense and will only lead to disaster. To interpret the sentence sayings that begin in chapter 10 without this hermeneutical key is to be like the fool in 26:7, 9, whose use of a proverb is ineffective and even dangerous.

---

87. Murphy (1998: 60) notes the parallel with the Egyptian *Instructions of Ankhsheshonq*: 'Do not instruct a fool, lest he hate you.'

In parallel with this *fear of the* LORD saying is a reminder about the importance of knowledge of God, or perhaps even 'knowing God' in a relational sense. The Hebrew words for knowing and knowledge are not simply about 'head knowledge', but often imply a relationship. Knowing God is crucial to understanding this world and how to live in it. God is described in verse 10b as *the Holy One* (actually the form is plural, but it is best to read it as a plural of majesty, since God is clearly in view). The term 'holy ones' is commonly used elsewhere to describe angels, but this sense does not fit the context or parallelism here. The language of holiness is not very common in Proverbs, used only here and in 30:3 (again *knowledge of the Holy One*). The book clearly does not deny God's holiness – indeed, here it assumes it – but it is not often focused on this aspect of God's character, which is dealt with more extensively elsewhere in the OT. The concern of this book is rather about how to act in daily life, built on the foundation of knowing and respecting God.

Verse 11 is closely connected with verse 10, giving a reason or motivation for grounding your life on respecting God as God (*for*/'because').[88] It makes sense to ground your life on the fear of the Lord because it is by wisdom that you will gain long life.[89] The expressions *your days will be multiplied* and *years will be added to your life* are parallel ways of describing a long life as the fruit of wisdom.

A further incentive is provided by verse 12, contrasting the wise person and the scoffer. The advantage of wisdom is set out a little cryptically, reading, *If you are wise, you are wise for yourself* (ESV), but the force of the final phrase is that you will be benefit from it. Clifford translates this phrase as 'to your own gain', in contrast to the outcome for the scoffer (similarly, NIV, 'your wisdom will reward you'). The

---

88. While the conjunction is usually translated 'for', Waltke (2004: 442) notes that it could be translated more emphatically as 'surely', and he thinks this fits better here. In fact, both senses suit the context well, and it is probably just introducing the motivation.

89. There is a textual issue here. The Hebrew text reads, *by* [means of] *me* (so ESV), as if wisdom is speaking, but it is sometimes emended to read 'by her' (underlying the NIV), as if wisdom is being described. However, on either reading wisdom is the means through which you gain long life.

outcome for the scoffer is that he alone will bear it, with 'it' sometimes understood as 'guilt' (e.g. Waltke 2004: 428), but most commonly as 'the consequences' (so Clifford 1999: 101; NIV, 'you alone will suffer'). Benefits flow from wisdom, and negative outcomes from scoffing.

13–18. This final section is the invitation by 'Dame Folly', the counterpart to, and opponent of, wisdom. Unlike Lady Wisdom, she has not prepared very much. She has built no house and sends out no servant girls. Instead, her character is outlined, whereas wisdom's was only implied by her words and actions. *The woman Folly* abstracts or personifies folly, which is the rejection of wisdom based on the fear of the Lord.[90] Verse 13 makes three crucial observations about her before her actions and words are described. She is pictured as making a loud, roaring noise (ESV, *is loud*; NIV, 'unruly', as in 7:11). This word can mean 'tumultuous' when applied to cities or lands, 'roaring' when applied to the sea, and 'growling' or 'barking' in relation to bears and dogs. When applied to this woman, it probably means 'bustling, boisterous' (Longman 2006) or 'stormy' (Murphy 1998). She is also described as 'simple' (NIV). The underlying Hebrew root means 'be wide, open, spacious', and while the noun, as here, usually means 'simplicity', the intensive (*piel*) form of the root means 'to persuade, seduce, entice'. A number of scholars therefore translate it as *seductive* (ESV).[91] If the word 'simple' is retained, it is no longer the simpleness of the unformed youth, but rather the rejection of wisdom's offer to shape her character. Another way in which she is opposite to wisdom is that she 'does not know what', which is probably elliptical for 'what there is to know' or 'what is going on' (hence ESV/NIV, *knows nothing*). The verb 'know' can also mean 'care about, be concerned about', and be translated 'she cares about nothing' (so Whybray 1994: 148, who cites Gen. 39:6; Job 9:21).

Verses 14 and 15 describe Dame Folly sitting in a prominent place in the city, calling out to those who pass by. In an Israelite walled

---

90. Steinmann (2009: 243) suggests that it is an epexegetical genitive, i.e. the woman who is foolishness, but it is more likely that folly is an attribute of the woman.

91. E.g. Whybray (1994: 148). Alternatively, Garrett (1993: 116) emends the text to read 'and seductive'.

city the doorway to the house would open into the street, so that she would be in public view. In parallel with this is the description of her sitting in the highest places in the town (see 9:3), which may be an additional location or simply the site of her house. Its significance is that the highest place makes it much more possible to be heard further away, so that her invitation can spread widely. The word *seat* could be translated 'throne',[92] but the emphasis here is not on her claiming undue honour, but on her making herself heard. Her purpose in sitting in this public location is to 'invite' ('call' takes this sense here) passers-by to her house.

The invitation of verse 16 is a repetition of wisdom's invitation in verse 4. Both invitations are addressed to those not yet shaped by wisdom or folly ('the simple'), and to those who lack sense or understanding ('lacking heart'). She is calling to those *going straight on their way* (v. 15) to turn aside into her house and what it offers. Her tempting offer is based on the insinuation that what is forbidden or hidden must be better than what is offered by wisdom. *Stolen water* is an enticing way of referring to adultery, the stealing of what belongs to another, as in 5:15–17 where water is used of sexuality. This is depicted as sweet or attractive. *Bread/food eaten in secret* (lit. 'of secrets') is in parallel with stolen water, and suggests that what is done in her house will not be made known to others. It happens in private, away from prying eyes, and is promoted as *pleasant* (ESV) or 'delicious' (NIV). This echoes the seductive speech of the immoral woman earlier in the book (e.g. 7:18–20). Her invitation started off in the same way as Lady Wisdom's in verse 16, but now in verse 17 it sounds more appealing, even seductive, as she offers forbidden fruit.

Verse 18 begins with *but*, indicating that the wrong impression given by Dame Folly's words will now be corrected. The one who is enticed into her house is not aware of the real and deadly serious consequences of embracing folly. While wisdom offers life, all other options are on the path to self-injury and death (8:35–36). The

---

92. So Murphy (1998: 56), 'enthroned on the heights of the city'; Steinmann (2009: 243–244), 'on a throne', noting it occurs in Proverbs only in connection with the king.

departed spirits (ESV/NIV, *the dead*) are there, as in 2:18. Another way of putting this is that those called/invited (*her guests*) are in the place of the dead, Sheol, with the *depths* making it clear that there is no way to return. While her invitation sounded very appealing, it is clear from verses 17–18 that it was dangerously deceptive.

Meaning
This chapter thus rounds off chapters 1 – 9, highlighting the funda-mental choice between wisdom and folly, and reminding us of the need to build on the right foundation of fearing God as God. Although the invitations from wisdom and folly begin in a similar way (vv. 4, 16), only that of wisdom leads to a life that makes sense. Folly offered what claimed to be sweet and pleasant (v. 17), but was actually the way of death, a place of rotting corpses (v. 18). To quote a proverb, all that glitters is not gold. Folly offers much but delivers little – then and now. Wisdom must be grounded in the fear of the Lord, and will be shown in the way we respond to correction and reproof (vv. 7–9). Only embracing the way of wisdom will lead to the 'good life' (vv. 5–6, 11). In the end there are not two ways to live, but rather one way to live, and another way that leads to death.

Looking back over chapters 1 – 9

What, then, do chapters 1 – 9 offer to the reader of the book of Proverbs? Fundamentally, they claim that the key to interpreting observations about daily life (found extensively in the rest of the book) is to make certain foundational commitments and choices. Life as God intended it must be grounded in respecting him as God (the fear of the Lord, 1:7; 9:10), and the path of wisdom must be followed and the way of folly decisively rejected. Once we respond to wisdom's gracious invitation, we must allow our character to be shaped by her and her values. Only then will we be ready to be God's person in God's world, living under God's rule in the many and complex situations of daily life. And only then will we be able to gain the benefit God intends us to have from reading the rest of the book of Proverbs.

2. THE SAYINGS OF SOLOMON (10:1 – 22:16)

The *Meaning* section in chapters 10 – 22 will usually not appear after the *Comment* section. This pattern has been chosen because the full meaning of a proverbial saying is generally not found in a cluster of verses, but rather when it is nuanced against other verses on any given topic. A study of some key topics is given in the Introduction.

A. The first half of Solomon's sayings (10:1 – 15:33)

10:1
Context
The title, *The proverbs of Solomon* (10:1), implies that this begins a distinct collection (ending in 22:16) of Solomonic proverbs within a broader range of other contributions. While 1:1 drapes a Solomonic covering over the book as a whole, there are non-Solomonic collections within the book, as is evident in the titles in 22:17; 24:23; 30:1 and 31:1. Yet this collection from 10:1 – 22:16 is Solomonic, perhaps in the sense that he authored many of them, adopted and adapted others, and gathered still more to give a comprehensive set of

snapshots and cameos that tell it like it is. A link is also implied between the wisdom of this book and the royal court.

Comment

1. The contrast between a wise and foolish person is fundamental to the book, and rightly begins the sentence sayings. Both parents are affected by whether their son chooses wisdom or folly (see also 1:8; 15:20; 23:24–25). In a patriarchal society a father is more focused on the public persona of his son, and the public wisdom of his son makes him glad (13:1; 17:21, 25; 28:7). We might have expected 'proud' (in a good sense), but *glad* (*śāmaḥ*, to be glad) captures the idea of delight and satisfaction. In that society the mother would have seen the son mainly at home, and the path of folly will spoil interpersonal and family relationships. *Sorrow* speaks of the grief that comes from ruptured relationships.

10:2–5
Context

These proverbs all concern financial prospering and want. While God's overt involvement in causing the righteous to flourish is usually not explicitly mentioned, it is a theological presupposition of the book that God is actively sustaining order in the creation. This makes it appropriate to introduce this idea early.

Comment

2. This introduces the key contrast in chapters 10 – 15 between righteousness (*ṣĕdāqâ*) and wickedness (*rešaʿ*), and the focus is often (as here) on the contrasting consequences of these two foundational stances in life. The point of the first half is not that ill-gotten gains do not last, but that they do not profit a person. What someone loses (e.g. integrity) in gaining wealth means that he or she has lost something more valuable than financial gain. This serves as a warning for those who think that it will be to their advantage to gain wealth by dubious means. The second half of the verse claims that righteousness delivers from death, but does not explain how. It refers to the general wisdom principle that trusting God is the pathway to life, outlined in 3:1–2 (also prosperity in 3:9–10) and mentioned in this chapter in 10:27 (see also 11:4). Finding wisdom is a matter of

life and death (8:35–36). Thus, the one who lives in conformity
with God's ordering of his world is less likely to suffer a premature
death. This is not a promise, but rather an observation that righteousness, a relational idea in Hebrew thought, is life-giving and
life-promoting.

3. This continues the same contrast as verse 2 between the
righteous and the wicked. God is active in this foundational need of
food, for people are either satisfied with, or lacking, food, because
God either *lets* or *thwarts*. However, this theological undergirding is
only one vantage point.

4. A person's own effort (the double mention of *hand*, which has
the sense of 'action') also has an impact on the resulting wealth, with
slackness leading to want or poverty, but diligence to plenty.[1]

5. The lesson is drawn out with a return to the *son* image of
verse 1. Here the contrast is between the prudent (= wise, skilful, prosperous) son and another son who brings shame to his family. The
difference is whether they work hard during the summer harvest (the
two terms are in parallel) or whether they sleep and do not work hard
during this make-or-break time. God's provision as set out in verse 3
does not remove the need for human effort (vv. 4–5), but rather
requires an ongoing response of diligent actions or even 'active
activity'.

10:6–7

Context

Both these proverbs contain a contrast between the righteous and
the wicked, linking the righteous with blessing (not just the
hard-working as in v. 4), and contrasting the enduring value of being
righteous with the self-destructive path of the wicked.

Comment

6. The blessings being on the *head* of the righteous is a way of
claiming that the plans, words and thoughts (i.e. what comes from

---

1. Whybray (1994: 158) suggests 'makes his fortune' and so to give
   economic security. Fox (2009: 512) adds the sensible observation
   that 'the present verse states a principle, not an absolute rule.'

the head) of the righteous lead to success (v. 6a). The focus appears to be on the thoughts that are expressed through words, since the second half of the verse points to the mouth of the wicked. The (dissembling) words of the wicked hide a real intent to tear down and destroy others (*ḥāmās*, *violence*, v. 6b). This is also repeated in verse 11b. The focus on the wicked in Proverbs and Psalms is often on their speech.

7. Contrasting outcomes are in view here. The lasting legacy of the righteous (continuing the blessings of v. 6) is to leave behind a pattern to follow (v. 7a), but the reputation or name of the wicked will decompose rather than endure (v. 7b). The NIV translates verse 7a as 'the name of the righteous is used in blessings', but the force of this section is rather that remembering a righteous person will lead to blessing, or that the memory of the righteous brings a blessing (ESV, *is a blessing*). The character or reputation of the wicked will not last or be remembered for long, for no-one will seek to emulate such a person.

10:8–10

Context

These verses are tied together by the mention of the babbling fool coming to ruin at the end of both verses 8 and 10. The contrast is between the wise (v. 8a; also one who *walks in integrity*, v. 9a) and the babbling fool (vv. 8b, 9b [*his ways crooked*], 10). The babbling (ESV) or chattering (NIV) fool is literally 'the fool of lips' (the dual form *śĕpātayim*), implying that fools use their speech to promote folly.

Comment

8a, 9a. The way to determine if people are wise on the inside is to look at their actions on the outside. What characterizes the wise is that they willingly receive instructions (v. 8a). While the word *miṣwōt* often means 'command(ment)', it also has a broader sense of 'instructions', and this is its general flavour in the wisdom book of Proverbs, which is more concerned with universal principles than with covenant regulations. Verse 9a reminds us that security or safety comes from a way of life (= walk, *hālak*) characterized by integrity (see also 28:18).

8b, 9b. The last half of each verse highlights the destructive consequences of living as a fool. It will lead to ruin (vv. 8b, 10b), and the crookedness of the fool's ways (contrasted with integrity) will be exposed (v. 9b), at least by others and perhaps also by God. There is a lack of explicit detail about what will happen to such a person – as if that is not the focus of the section – but simply bare statements of the outcome that the fool will come to ruin or be found out.

10. The image of winking the eye in verse 10a is less clear, but probably involves some secret deal or deceitful conduct (NIV, 'winks maliciously' seeks to capture this; it is linked with deceiving in 6:13; 16:30). Such dissembling will cause grief or trouble, probably to others. Some scholars, with support from the LXX, think that verse 8b has been wrongly repeated in verse 10b, and preserve a different ending to verse 10 (e.g. NRSV, 'but the one who rebukes boldly makes peace'). This is possible, and would make a contrast between a tiny destructive action (a wink) and the need for a much larger and bolder response to restore the situation. However, the repetition does serve to tie this small section together.

10:11–14
Context
These verses focus on the importance of speech for both good and ill. Verse 12 does not directly refer to speech, but the explicit mention of speech or organs of speech in the surrounding verses (vv. 11, 13, 14; also vv. 8b, 10b) implies that the hatred and love of this verse probably also refer to these attitudes being expressed in words.

Comment
11. The image of *a fountain of life* (*měqôr ḥayyîm*) is especially powerful in a society where the provision of water meant life and its absence death. The fountain of life is an image used in Proverbs to describe the teaching of the wise (13:14), the fear of the Lord (14:27) and good sense or prudence (16:22), often with the explicit mention of it preventing death (13:14; 14:27). It paints a picture of the righteous through their speaking creating life and building community. The speech of the wicked, by way of contrast, is destructive of community through violence, even though this may be hidden or concealed (echoing v. 6b).

12. Attitudes of hatred or love (which commonly become evident in words) will lead to either community breaking (strife/conflict) or community building (covers all wrongs). Loving words cover all offences or wrongs in that they seek to work for peace, not needless strife. This leads Whybray (1994: 164) to say that 'the proverb is thus an indirect exhortation to love one's enemies.' They do not dwell on the wrongs done to them, but rather on the need to restore broken relationships.

13. This picks up the connection between attitudes and words, explaining that wisdom on the inside will lead to speech that shows wisdom. Wise words come from one who has understanding – not just head knowledge, but one who has a character shaped by wisdom. However, only words that lack sense come from the foolish, so they need to be punished and corrected by the rod (*šēbeṭ*, v. 13b; 19:29b; 26:3b). In Proverbs the rod is associated with disciplining the foolish or untrained (13:24; 22:15; 23:13–14; 26:3; 29:15). While physical punishment is increasingly rejected in the contemporary Western world, the issue of discipline or correction is still crucial in forming values and character.

14. The words of the fool bring on disasters such as the strife or violence of verses 11–12. Fox (2009: 518–519) notes that the similar expressions in 13:3; 18:7 imply that the ruin in view here is what happens to the fool, rather than what he inflicts on others. The wise, however, seem to lay foundations for wholesome relationships through the pursuit of knowledge, and through speech based on that understanding. The verb *ṣpn* (*lay up*, ESV; 'store up', NIV) could also mean 'hide' or 'conceal', but is best rendered here in a positive sense. Words are powerful forces for either building up or tearing down.

10:15–16

Context

Both these verses concern the value of wealth. A rich person's wealth can provide a certain measure of safety and security.

Comment

15–16. A *strong city* in Israel was a walled city where those in the surrounding fields could go when under attack. This proverb is not arguing that people should trust in their wealth for security. It is simply observing that wealth provides insulation from setbacks in life, without any judgment about this being right or wrong.[2] For a person committed to righteousness, it will lead to life (so, rightly, ESV; NIV has 'is life' and 'are sin and death', but this is to miss the force of the preposition). For a wicked person, it will provide further funds for a way of sin (not 'and death', NIV). Wealth – just like words in verses 11–14 – can do harm or can be a great benefit, depending on a person's goals and values. Kidner (1964: 87–88) comments, 'A man uses his possessions according to his character: as tools for good or ill.'

Verse 15b might be easily glossed over, but it sets out an important idea in the book about poverty. Poverty here is not being morally evaluated, but its effects on the poor are being described. Poverty means that there is no buffer or protection when disaster strikes, and this leads to ruin. This description of the powerlessness of the poor (without moral evaluation) is picked up elsewhere: they are friendless (14:20; 19:7); their pleas are not listened to (18:23); they are dominated by the rich (22:7).

10:17–21
Context
These five proverbs all concern speech: words of instruction and correction (v. 17); lying lips/slander (v. 18); many words/restraining lips (v. 19); the tongue of the righteous (v. 20); and the lips of the righteous (v. 21).

Comment
17. This is a hinge verse, picking up the ideas of life and sin from verse 16 (where they were connected with character), but now linking them to how people respond to words that instruct and reprove. This picks up the thought of 9:7–9, where a litmus test of whether we have chosen the path of wisdom or that of folly is how we respond to correcting and rebuking (verbs from the same roots as

---

2. See Waltke (2004: 463). This is amplified in the thematic study on 'Wealth and poverty' in the Introduction.

the nouns *mûsār* and *tôkaḥat* in v. 17). The way of folly, of rejecting
correction, is not only damaging for ourselves, because our words
and example also lead others astray (v. 17b; better than 'goes astray',
NRSV; the *hifil* of *tʿh* means to 'cause to err' or 'mislead', as in 2 Chr.
33:9; Isa. 63:17; Jer. 23:32, but cf. Jer. 42:20), with *others* being implied
here.

18–19. False speech is here linked to folly, whether it is a person
who hates another but pretends otherwise (*lying lips*), or someone who speaks falsely about others to destroy their reputation or
place in the community (*slander*). In the first example, your speech
fails to match your heart; in the second, your words obscure the
truth. This leads naturally on to the need to monitor carefully all
that you say (v. 19). If you speak too much, it is easy to utter what
is false or unhelpful against others (*pāšaʿ*, better *transgression*, ESV,
rather than 'sin', NIV), so those who are astute exercise control over
how much they speak. The verb *ḥdl* (*is lacking*, ESV) normally means
'ceases/comes to an end' (= 'is ended', NIV), but ESV gives the better
sense. In the wisdom book of Job, Elihu is an example of a person
who cannot hold his words in, for they burst out to meet his own
needs (Job 32:18–20). As the outworking of this need to speak, he
rashly describes himself as 'perfect in knowledge' (Job 36:4, a term
he rightly uses of God in 37:16). His view that Job has not spoken
what is right is rejected by God (Job 42:7–8). The exercise of restraint
in speaking was also highly valued in Egyptian wisdom literature.

20. One consequence of controlling what we say is that when we
choose to speak, our well-chosen words are more likely to be of
value like choice silver (v. 20a). This is a strong contrast to the words
of the wicked, which reveal their thoughts or character (*lēb*, *heart*)
which are of little value to others (v. 20b). The contrast between the
tongue (of the righteous) and the heart (of the wicked) reminds us
that ultimately your character will sprout forth in your words, so that
both a wise character and wise words are of great value. By way of
contrast, the character (*heart*) of the wicked, and presumably the
words that result, are of little worth.

21. The benefits of this restrained or filtered speech are indicated
by a clever play on the word *lips*. The lips are the organ for speech,
but are also used for eating food, and verse 21a says that the lips
(speech) of the righteous feed or provide life and growth for many.

Reverting back to the path of life in verse 17, it is now pointed out that, on the other hand, fools are on the way to death (v. 21b). Their (presumably early) death is avoidable and therefore futile since it comes from not travelling on the right path. Here it is not God who actively brings fools to an early grave, but rather that their untimely demise occurs as a result of them 'lacking sense', without any description about how this might happen.

10:22–26

Context

These verses are a less cohesive section, but the contrast between the righteous and the wicked ties together verses 24–25. Moreover, it is preceded by a discrete unit on speech, and followed by another evaluating the wicked and righteous.[3]

Comment

22. This expresses the retribution principle (God rewards the righteous) by reminding us that God's blessing brings wealth. In the end it is not human effort that ensures wealth, for it is a gift from God. The blessing is pictured as not being mixed with adversity, for he adds no pain/sorrow/grief with it (ESV, better than NIV, 'without painful toil for it', although *'eṣeb* means toil in 5:10; 14:23). This is, of course, a general principle, not a promise (see Job or Jesus).

23. The characteristic practice of the fool is doing 'wickedness/wrong' (*zimmâ*, NIV, 'wicked schemes'), but this gives no lasting enjoyment, just the short-lived amusement of a joke. On the other hand, the person of understanding gains the benefit of pleasure or delight (implied from v. 23a) from his typical stance of acting wisely.

24–25. These are different ways of describing the same thing. *What the wicked dreads* is not a reference to 'whatever' they dread, but

---

3. Goldingay (1994: 81–82) sees a recurring literary pattern at the beginning of collections of sayings in chs. 10 – 15, suggesting that a better group is vv. 23–27. He argues that a new unit beginning in v. 23 makes more sense than one starting in 11:1. However, this seems to be undermined by the theme of speech binding together vv. 17–21, and the righteous/wicked motif suggesting that vv. 27–32 is also a unit.

rather what they dread most, which is that disaster will come upon them. This is called a *tempest* or 'storm' (*sûpâ*) in verse 25a, not in a meteorological sense, but rather referring to a life-and-death crisis. Both verses 24a and 25a suggest that the disaster that will come upon the wicked will lead to their death. By way of contrast, enduring life (*the desire* [or longing] *of the righteous*) will be given to the righteous who will receive ongoing days (vv. 24b, 25b). *For ever* (*'ôlām*) in verse 25b does not here have the sense of 'eternal', but rather 'ongoing' or 'enduring'.

26. This narrows in on one form of the wicked or fool – the lazy person or sluggard. Sluggards are considered at length in the rest of the book (e.g. 6:6–11; 26:13–16), where it is pointed out that their laziness does not benefit themselves. The point made here, however, is that when they are given a task, they will be an irritant (like the taste of vinegar, or smoke in the eyes), not a benefit to the those who chose and sent them. They will have many excuses, but the work they were asked to do will never be completed.

10:27–32

Context
Verses 27–32 return to the contrast between the righteous and the wicked found earlier.[4] Each proverb here explicitly mentions either or both of these two stereotypical figures, except for verse 29 which refers to the blameless and evildoers.

Comment
27. The point made here is similar to that of verses 24–25 – that the wicked will (characteristically) face premature death, but that the godly will have their life prolonged (echoing 3:1–2). The righteous are here described by their foundational life choice, the *fear of the* LORD (1:7; 9:10), which appropriately appears early in the sentence

---

4. Goldingay (1994: 75–76) points out the high frequency of 'righteous' (x19) and 'wicked' (x18) in 10:1 − 11:13; a lower but still significant number in 11:14 − 13:25; but thereafter quite thinly until ch. 21. He suggests that the concentration of these moral categories at the outset sets up an ethical context for reflecting on human behaviour.

proverbs. As in verses 24–25, there is no explanation of how the life of the righteous will be prolonged, nor how that of the wicked will be cut short. The emphasis is on the outcome, not the process or even the rationale.

28–30. This focus on the future then continues. What the righteous hope for is 'joy' (*śimḥâ*, NIV; ESV, *brings joy*) in their ongoing life, not just more days. However, the plans of the wicked will die with them rather than come to fruition. Another way of putting this is that God's purposes and plans (*the way* [*derek*] *of the LORD*, v. 29) will both preserve the blameless and destroy the evildoers. In the light of verse 28, these two types of people are the same as the righteous and the wicked. The stance of the righteous will lead to life and joy; that of the wicked will result in a life cut short and in hopes being dashed. This is further reinforced in verse 30, which also insists that the righteous will never be removed or uprooted (presumably from the earth; the verb *môṭ* has the core meaning of 'totter' or 'shake'), but that the wicked will die (i.e. not continue to dwell on the earth). The term *land* (*'ereṣ*) probably has the more generic sense of earth or world here in the light of wisdom's more universal concerns.

31–32. The final focus in the chapter is on the contrasting speech of the righteous and the wicked. The mouth and lips of the righteous utter what is wise (v. 31a) and appropriate (*rāṣôn*, v. 32a, *acceptable*, ESV; 'what finds favour', NIV), but the tongue and mouth of the wicked are distorting their intended purposes (*tahpukôt*, 'perversity', vv. 31b, 32b) and will be cut off (v. 31b), presumably as the wicked person dies and is therefore cut off from life. The righteous are using speech for its God-given purposes; the wicked twist speech for their own ends. Most importantly, there are set out here great incentives to belong to the righteous rather than be among the wicked.

11:1–4

Context

There is a general focus on character in this section, although in a variety of contexts.

Comment

1. When produce and goods were weighed, the use of wrongly marked weights would boost the profit margin of the seller at the expense of the purchaser. Honesty in daily work is an important aspect of character. This is put into a theological context (*an abomination to the* LORD, ESV; 'the LORD detests', NIV), which implies accountability to God in this area (16:11; 20:10, 23).

2. A different character contrast is picked up in this 'mini-narrative' (Clifford) – that between pride and humility (16:18). A person of pride will be disgraced (*qālôn*; Whybray 1994: 176 notes it is the opposite of honour, as in 3:35), which was very significant in an ANE honour/shame culture, and would bring shame to one's family or group. By way of contrast, the humble (*šĕnûʿîm*, i.e. those who view themselves and others rightly) will enjoy the successful life that wisdom gives.

3. A third aspect of character is uprightness or integrity, which involves living in accordance with what is right and true in one's whole life (*tummâ, integrity*, has a sense of wholeness). This is contrasted with *crookedness of the treacherous* (v. 3b; see also v. 6 where the upright and treacherous are compared). *Crookedness, selep*, is a different word from *perverse* in 10:31, 32, but has a similar meaning (15:4; 19:3). While integrity is a sure basis for guiding individuals in their life direction and decisions, the path of crookedness is one that leads to self-destruction.

4. The theme of wealth may be related to that of buying and selling in verse 1. In this light (also v. 3) it has in view riches dishonestly gained, and so contrasts with righteousness in the second half of the verse. Such wealth fails to provide any ultimate advantage (10:2). The *day of wrath* (*yôm ʿebrâ*, v. 4a) does not refer to an end-time judgment (not a focus in the wisdom books), but rather to a future time of disaster such as military invasion, famine or other crisis that can sweep away carefully gathered wealth. It is a parallel expression to being destroyed in verse 3b. In such situations, which raise the possibility of death (v. 4b), what is of value is a person's righteousness or character – what we cannot lose even if everything else is taken from us.

11:5–11

Context

Verses 5–11 involve a sustained contrast between the righteous and the wicked, picking up the motif of the value of righteousness in verse 4b and illustrating its worth in various settings of trouble. The different types of trouble are not detailed, but they are described as falling (v. 5b), needing deliverance (vv. 6a, 9b) and being taken captive/trapped (v. 6b). Their hope and the prospect of wealth or power are perishing (v. 7), destruction looms (v. 9a), and the city is endangered (vv. 10–11). Against such setbacks, righteousness is to be pursued and wickedness avoided. The righteous are said to be rescued/taken away (v. 6a), their ways made straight (v. 5a), delivered (v. 9b; also *delivered from trouble*, v. 8a), prospering (v. 10a) and blessed (v. 11a).

Comment

5–6. This highlights the importance of upright behaviour ('makes/keeps their way straight'). Verse 3 has already introduced this theme, as well as the self-destructive alternative of acting wickedly in the vain hope of gaining some advantage (Waltke 2004: 486: 'righteousness saves and apostasy damns'). It also recurs in verse 6, using the terms *upright* (*yěšārîm*) and *treacherous* (*bōgĕdîm*) from verse 3, and drawing attention to the contrasting outcomes, freedom ('delivered') and captivity ('trapped'). The same outcomes are described from a more theological perspective in 10:3, where God's active involvement in the process is asserted. The two ideas are both to be held in balance, for the consequences are both 'natural' and brought about by God. The precise scenario of verse 6b is not set out, but the unrestrained pursuit of lustful desires seems to be a weakness of the wicked which will be exploited by their enemies (5:22). Lust is both self-focused and insatiable.

7–8. The finality of death is an important reminder, as death puts an end to any future plans and money-making schemes.[5] *Wealth* (ESV, v. 7b, *'ônîm*) has a core meaning of vigour or strength, but can also mean 'wealth' as something achieved by someone's energy (possibly NIV, 'power'; cf. 'godless', NRSV). Certainly, any hopes or dreams will perish (mentioned twice) when a person dies. In whole Bible terms, we can see that the wicked will also have no hope

---

5. Van Leeuwen (1997: 117) comments that 'death is God's final "no" to evil'.

beyond the grave, but that is not the point being made here. There is instead a focus on deliverance from death in this life, which is picked up in verse 8a and contrasted with the lack of such deliverance for the wicked whose very direction in life is heading for destruction (v. 8b).[6]

9–11. A community perspective is now developed. Wickedness has earlier led to a person's own downfall (e.g. v. 5b), but now someone's wicked speech can also destroy a neighbour (v. 9a). Yet while the godless can destroy others, the righteous will themselves be delivered (2:12, 16; 14:3) by their knowledge, a key wisdom word (v. 9b). Verse 9b could also be translated 'the knowledge of the righteous will lead to deliverance', possibly of them and their neighbours mentioned in verse 9a, but the parallelism in the verse suggests that *the righteous* is the plural subject of the verb *ḥlṣ*, 'to be delivered'. The positive influence of the righteous in the community is then drawn out explicitly in verses 10–11. Both the prospering of the righteous and the downfall of the wicked lead to great delight in the city (v. 10), as people experience the moral and social benefits that come from true righteousness. These upright righteous people are described as blessing the city, which leads to it being lifted up in the esteem of others (*tārûm, is exalted,* v. 11a), but there is also the warning that this city could be overthrown if the wicked are listened to (v. 11b).[7]

11:12–15
Context
These proverbs all concern in some way how you are to act in community, although this is not a sharp demarcation as it is also in view in verses 10–11. Verses 12–13 deal with not exposing the faults of others, while verses 14–15 focus on safety and security. They are

---

6. Van Leeuwen (1997: 117–118) sees the poetic justice of this proverb illustrated in the lives of Haman and Mordecai (Esth. 5:14; 7:10; 9:1–10) and Daniel (Dan. 6:23–24). See Prov. 26:27; 28:10.

7. Whybray (1994: 180) notes that both vv. 10 and 11 refer to well-being in urban life, noting the other references in the sentence sayings to cities are 10:15; 16:32; 18:11, 19; 21:22; 29:8.

similar in form, with all having a strong internal contrast, and three of the four beginning with or containing a participle (often translated 'whoever').

Comment

12–13. Two practices to avoid are belittling/deriding (*bāz*) your neighbours (v. 12a) and slandering them (*rākîl*, v. 13a; see 20:19). In any community you become aware of the failings of others, but there is a real choice over whether to broadcast them publicly. A wise person (one of *understanding, tĕbûnâ*, v. 12b) remains silent about such matters. Living in community sometimes makes us aware of the secrets that others hide, which may have the potential to cause them great damage if the secret becomes more widely known. Those whose habit is to malign others (lit. 'walking slander', v. 13a, meaning that this is their way of life; NIV 'gossip' is a little weak) expose what was said to them in confidence or in secret. Verse 13b highlights that it is a matter of character (being *trustworthy in spirit*) to keep such a thing covered (provided keeping silent will not damage others), rather than delight in bringing another person down (10:12).

14–15. Safety was a big issue in a society where many larger disputes were solved by battle. In the face of an external threat (*a people falls*, v. 14a), the wisdom of many advisors is most likely to lead to the formulation of a wise way to respond to the crisis. This good outcome is called *safety* (ESV) or 'victory' (NIV), but is the common word for 'deliverance' or 'salvation' (*tĕšû'â*). Here it refers to being safely delivered from an enemy threat or attack.[8] At a more localized level, there is the financial danger created by acting as a guarantor for another, and verse 15 points out that such a practice exposes individuals to the insecurity of their future being determined by the actions and decisions of someone over whom they may have no control or influence (6:1–5). The one who refuses (*śōnē', hates*, ESV) to act as a guarantor is not in such danger.

---

8. Fox (2009: 536) observes that 'God or his representative is almost always the subject.'

11:16–22

Context

The proverbs in this section deal largely with the character of individuals, but the idea of retribution is in the background of some of the sayings. The final verse seems unconcerned with the idea of retribution, but may echo the description of the gracious woman in verse 16, and so round off or bracket this section.

Comment

16–17. An anomaly is recorded here. It is not problematic that a woman who is gracious[9] gains honour or respect, for that would be an appropriate outcome for her character. However, verse 16b challenges the blanket coverage of the doctrine of retribution, since here violent, not godly, men gain riches. This unexpected consequence reminds us that some proverbs are simply descriptions of the way things are, rather than endorsements of everything they observe. The contrast in verse 17 is between kindness which leads to benefit, and cruelty which leads to hurt. This receives an interesting twist in noting that people who are kind benefit themselves not others and, similarly, cruel people hurt themselves. The focus is not on God rewarding or punishing such people, but rather that a person's character leads to certain consequences.

18–19. The contrasting outcomes for the righteous and the wicked are then described in verses 18–21. Verse 18 is the subtlest, for it recognizes that the wicked can benefit from wages for their work. However, these wages are described as deceptive, which is explained by the contrast with the sure reward of the righteous (amplified in v. 19). The earnings of the wicked are probably uncertain because of the unreliable and dishonest people who employ them. The contrast in verse 19 is that righteousness (*ṣĕdāqâ*; Fox 2009: 538 suggests that it is a metonymy for a 'righteous person') is the way to the sure reward of life, but evil is on the path to (premature?) death, thus implying the value of being steadfast or persevering in righteousness.

---

9. Van Leeuwen (1997: 118–119) notes that *ḥēn*, 'grace', often means 'beauty' when referring to a woman, as in 5:19; 31:30.

20–21. God's attitude is now foregrounded. The wicked (i.e. those with a crooked heart or skewed set of values) are viewed as an abomination (i.e. destined for destruction), while God delights in the blameless ways of the righteous. As in 11:1, the expression of God's response implies that people are accountable to him. This leads smoothly on to the certainty of reward and punishment, which is emphasized in verse 21 (*be assured*/'be sure'; lit. 'hand to hand'). The parallelism is slightly different from what we may have expected. While it is not surprising that the evil person will be punished (16:5), it is unusual for him to be contrasted with the *offspring* or 'seed' of the righteous (so ESV).¹⁰ Perhaps this allows for the recognition that sometimes righteous people are victims of others, but that it would only be a temporary setback since the family will ultimately be delivered. While this sounds of little comfort, that may be due to the individualism of many Western readers. Even today, many first-generation migrants sacrifice their own hopes and comfort for the sake of the security and prosperity of future generations.

22. The contrast in this comic picture is between the limited value of physical beauty and the enduring value of discretion or, more broadly, character. Discretion has a core meaning of physical taste, but figuratively (as here) has the sense of 'discernment' (*ṭaʿam*; NRSV, 'good sense' seems slightly off the mark). Even a desirable attribute like beauty is worthless in the absence of the godly shaping of who we are. It may be a *gold ring*,¹¹ but it cannot make a defective character any more winsome than the snout of a pig emerging from a feeding

---

10. The NIV translates this as 'those who are righteous will go free'. This is less likely, and could only be justified if the implication was that the righteous were themselves descendants of other righteous people and so, in a sense, the seed of the righteous. This seems a little convoluted. An alternative is to follow the textual witness of the LXX and Targum to read 'those who sow righteousness' as in v. 18. The Hebrew text represents the harder reading, makes sense, and is to be preferred.

11. Whybray (1994: 185) mentions that 'nose rings were items of feminine jewellery', citing Gen. 24:47; Isa. 3:21; Ezek. 16:12. Murphy (1998: 83) comments that rings were worn in the ear as well (25:12).

trough. This is not a verse attacking women or beauty, but rather showing the crucial importance of a formed character.

11:23–31
Context
These verses interweave the topics of wealth and retribution. The section begins with verse 23 setting out both sides of the retribution principle. The final three verses explore the idea of retribution, with an interesting excursion in verse 30.

Comment
23. The desire of the righteous – which might include pleasing God, having your character shaped by wisdom, and treating others rightly – results in what is good. On the other hand, the self-focused hope or expected outcomes of the wicked lead only to *wrath*, which seems elliptical for (a day of) wrath or judgment (see also 11:5–8). The implication is clear: make your goals those of the righteous, not those of the wicked.

24–26. Generosity in giving to the needy is outlined in verses 24–26, and the danger of trusting in riches is addressed in verse 28, yet they are all evaluated through a retribution framework. In verses 24–26 the one who gives freely (v. 24a), who waters and brings blessing on others (v. 25), who sells rather than hoards grain (v. 26), will be enriched, grow richer, be watered and be blessed. In practical earthly terms, this is the way to prosper. By way of contrast, the one who *withholds what he should give* (ESV; 'withholds unduly', NIV; lit. 'refrains from uprightness', but the context is one of giving), rather than giving liberally, will suffer want/need (v. 24b; NIV, 'poverty').[12] Furthermore, the one who hoards grain (i.e. withholds it), and so is a curse to others, will also be cursed (v. 26). There is no explanation of how this righting of wrongs will take place, but it will happen.

27. The precise setting of this verse is difficult to identify, although the context suggests it concerns the use of wealth and is assessed on the basis of the idea of retribution. It contrasts those who

---

12. Longman (2006: 263) suggests that the seller might be withholding grain in order to get a higher price in a time of scarcity.

diligently pursue favour (that of God or others, *rāṣôn*) with those
who seek disaster/evil (presumably for others, *rāʻâ*), only to find that
it will come upon themselves not others. The implied exhortation
is to use what we have so as to promote what is good.

28. The implication is that being righteous is contrasted with
trusting in riches. Job too saw that trusting in wealth would be dishonouring to God (Job 31:24–25). This means, of course, that some
of the rich will not be righteous, and that wealth will be a source of
temptation. It is not a prosperity gospel here. Furthermore, one
attraction of wealth is that it holds out the promise of a flourishing
life, but this proverb sees that trusting in riches will lead to a fall,
while the person who instead pursues righteousness will thrive and
find life. God is the one who is to be trusted (16:20; 28:25; 29:25).

29. This makes good sense if finances are still in view, rather than
describing the kind of trouble people may bring to their household.
The foolish use of money would lead to them being shut out from
receiving any substantial inheritance – all they get is wind![13] Such a
person is the *fool* of the second half of the verse and will rightly be
only a servant to those who are *wise of heart*.

30. The plant imagery of verse 28b (*green leaf*) is developed with
the observation that the consequence (*fruit*) of a righteous character
is an abundant life (*a tree of life*). This may be an echo of the tree of
life in Genesis 3, but has already been used of wisdom personified
(3:18; see also 13:12; 15:4). The second part of verse 30 (*whoever
captures souls is wise*, ESV; NIV rearranges to read 'the one who is wise
saves lives') sounds at first like a commendation of evangelism, but
it is more literally translated as 'the one who takes/seizes [*lqḥ*] lives
is wise'. The idea is that the person who takes hold of others and
shapes them as righteous (who is, in a sense, an evangelist for
'wisdom') is acting wisely. In the light of the principle of retribution,
and against the backdrop of the empty temptations of pursuing
wealth for its own sake, comes this call to be shaped by wisdom, and
to be active in shaping others.

31. As a summary of the chapter, this verse affirms that the
righteous will be rewarded and the wicked punished in this life (*on*

---

13. Lucas (2015: 100) understands 'inherit the wind' as 'become insolvent'.

earth). This reveals that the focus of wisdom is on retribution in this life, which is developed in NT terms to focus also on the life to come.

12:1–4
Context
This is only a loose grouping of fairly discrete proverbs, although they do describe the varying consequences for contrasting characters.

Comment
1. This picks up the thought (seen earlier in 9:7–9 and 10:17) of different responses to discipline and correction. The idea of the first half is that discipline leads to greater knowledge (see also 9:9), while the implication of what follows is that those who reject or resist (hate) correction do not grow in understanding. It is not simply that they make a stupid decision in rejecting reproof, but that the result of their decision is that they end up being less wise.[14]

2–3. God has contrasting attitudes to those who are good and evil. One who is good attracts God's blessing or favour (*rāṣôn*), although the way in which this happens is left open. A person who practises evil actions (schemes or devices) is, however, condemned by God, but again the mechanism is not outlined. The focus is on God's evaluation of both types of people, rather than on explaining how God works it out. Verse 3 makes a similar point, but here with God backgrounded. Using the categories of the righteous and the wicked, the proverb claims that the righteous will be securely and firmly established (v. 12b), which wickedness cannot do for a person.

4. The description in verse 4a anticipates the more detailed picture of the *excellent wife* in 31:10–31. Here the focus is on her bringing honour (*crown, 'ăṭārâ*) to her husband,[15] and she is contrasted with a different woman, one who *brings shame* (*mēbîšâ*), and who is like a

---

14. Longman (2006: 269) points out that the sages' view was that 'mistakes provided opportunities for learning'.

15. Clifford (1999: 130) notes that the other objects described as a crown in Proverbs are riches (14:24), grey hair (= long life, 16:31), grandchildren (17:6), as well as the good wife here.

cancer (REB) at work draining away life and goodness. The contrast between honour and shame is not as well understood in a Western culture, but was a core contrast in the ANE. If the *excellent wife* of 31:10–31 is an exemplification of wisdom, then this verse might also allude to the contrasting effects of wisdom, which brings honour, and folly, which brings shame.

12:5–7
Context
This is a small group of proverbs about the righteous and the wicked.

Comment
5–7. A contrast is made between the 'plans' (NIV, *maḥšĕbôt*, better than *thoughts*, ESV) thought up by the righteous and the expressed thoughts (counsels/advice) of the wicked (v. 5). These thoughts are set out respectively as either *just* or *deceitful*. Verse 6 more vividly pictures how the speech of the wicked is intended to be life-destroying (like the youths' actions in 1:11), while the words of the upright lead to rescue or deliverance, and so are life-affirming (18:21; Fox 2009: 549 notes that 'words can kill and preserve'). Verse 7 gives a summary verdict of the outcome of these two competing options. The wicked who sought to ambush with their words (v. 6a) are themselves overthrown and destroyed (v. 7a), but the righteous will stand firm (v. 7b).

12:8–12
Context
These proverbs are largely independent sayings, but many of the actions and attitudes are weighed by the yardstick of common sense.

Comment
8. *Good sense* (*śēkel*; NIV, 'prudence'; it can mean intelligence, craftiness, success) is commended and contrasted with a mind twisted or made crooked – one that does not see things as they are. This provides a criterion for evaluating various thoughts and actions. Do they conform to *good sense* or are they the result of twisted thinking?

9. The issue of status emerges. A comical picture is drawn of the one who tries to project an image of being successful (v. 9b, *play the great man*, ESV; 'pretend to be somebody', NIV), but uses all his resources on keeping up appearances so that he has no food. In the first 'better than' proverb of the sentence sayings, such a person is contrasted with a lowly person of *good sense* who is content with his actual position, and so is still able to afford a servant. It is a contrast between image and real benefit.

10. This commends those who are concerned for (the Hebrew verb 'know', *yd'*, has the sense here of 'care for' or 'have regard for') the life and well-being of their animals. This is both the outworking of righteousness (dealing rightly with what you have stewardship over) and good sense (since treating an animal properly will prolong its life and usefulness). Caring for your animals is contrasted with the actions of those who lack sense (the *wicked*), whose 'kindest acts' (NIV, lit. 'their' *raḥam*; *mercy*, ESV) are still cruel.[16]

11. The issue of whether you spend your energy productively is now addressed. Working the land will lead to an ample supply of food (13:25; 20:13), but those who fritter away time on empty or unproductive activities (*worthless pursuits*, ESV; 'chase fantasies', NIV) will achieve little, and so are seen to lack sense.

12. The final proverb generalizes about the wicked and righteous, the categories used in verse 10 as well. Someone who has twisted thinking (the *wicked*, *rāšā'*) will envy the short-term dishonest gain of wrongdoers (v. 12a).[17] In the second half of the proverb the image is of the righteous person who shows good sense in sending down roots where he is (a tree seems in view) and so bearing fruit. The contrast appears to be between one who shows good sense by consistent, long-term thinking, and another who is enticed by the latest money-making scheme and flits from one mirage to the next.

---

16. Koptak (2003: 340) colourfully comments, 'Better to be the righteous person's horse than the wicked person's neighbor!'

17. There are two possible roots here: 1. *spoil*, ESV; 'proceeds', NRSV; and 2. 'stronghold', NIV, or 'siegeworks'. Even if the second root is chosen, it may refer to the wealth protected in the stronghold, but could focus on the protection itself.

12:13–23

Context

Many proverbs deal with speech here, explicitly in verses 13–14, 17–19, 22. This provides a hint for the setting of some of the other proverbs as well.

Comment

13–14. Verse 13a makes the initial observation that those who are evil are trapped by their wicked speech (*transgression of his lips*, ESV; 'their sinful talk', NIV), presumably because it provides an outward indicator of what they are like inside, or their lies eventually trip them up. The contrast in verse 13b is more general but, in light of the first half of the verse, should be read as claiming that the righteous reveal their character by their godly speech and so escape the disaster that comes to the evildoers.[18] This is confirmed by the descriptions of the righteous in verse 14 where both their speech (*the fruit of his mouth*) and their actions (*the work of a man's hand*) lead to them prospering ('filled with good things', NIV; 13:2a; 18:20a). Verse 14b is more literally 'the work of a person's hand will cause to return [or "return" if the variant reading is not adopted] to him', but the ellipsis needs to be filled, and in light of the first half of the verse it should be 'cause good to come to him' (= NIV 'brings them reward'). What is inside a person is shown in his or her words and deeds. The metaphor of speech as the *fruit of his mouth* is a telling expression, because fruit is the final product of the growth of a tree, and the tree's nature determines the kind of fruit it yields.

15–16. The main contrast here is between a foolish and a wise/ prudent person. However, the issue of speech is in the background and indicated by the mention of *advice* (v. 15b) and *insult* (v. 16b). Here someone's foolishness or wisdom is shown by how that person responds to the speech of others.[19] A wise person listens to, and

---

18. The NIV does not read it as a contrast, translating as 'and so the innocent escape trouble'. This implies that the consequence of the evildoers being trapped is that their innocent victims escape. This is less likely.

19. Clifford (1999: 131) notes that 'Fools are know-it-alls, certain that their path is straight and their decisions are correct.'

takes notice of, advice (v. 15b), but is not provoked to a foolish response by an insult (v. 16b). Verse 16b literally reads that a prudent person 'covers over' (*ignores*, ESV) an insult (10:12b; 17:9), which is to acknowledge that the offence is there, but not to meet it with a response in kind (19:11). The cycle of hate is broken. Proverbs 9:7–9 previously highlighted the different responses of the wise and the scoffer/wicked person to words of correction. The foolish think they do not need advice and so ignore it by trusting in their own views (v. 15a), but respond *at once* to an insult with obvious anger (*vexation, ka'as*, v. 16a). A crucial aspect of wisdom is acting rightly even when provoked.

17–19. Speech is clearly at the centre of this section, and the focus returns to the content of your words (with honesty, integrity), rather than on how you respond to the words of others. Verse 17 has a legal setting in mind, pointing out that a legal decision will only be fair if a witness declares the truth rather than lies (14:5, 25; Exod. 20:16). There is a broadening to a community setting in verse 18. Here reckless, hasty [words] (rightly implied) cause damage, depicted in a vivid image of piercing like a sword. However, appropriate speech is not just neutral, but actually brings healing and therefore growth. Words are a powerful tool to effect either great harm or great good. The precise nature of the contrast in verse 19 is not immediately apparent, but the point is that speaking truthfully builds up your enduring character (*for ever, 'ad*, can simply mean 'ongoing'), while a lie only gains a person an advantage for an instant.

20. In the light of verses 17–19 (especially the mention of *deceit* in v. 17), an observation is now made that the evil which is in a person's heart will be revealed in deceitful speech and plotting (v. 20a). On the other hand, those who are committed to promoting (by their words, lit. 'advices/counsels') wholeness and well-being (*peace, šālôm*) in the community will experience joy (v. 20b). Peace has a fuller sense than in English, implying not only the absence of harmful relationships, but also the active presence of wholesome attitudes and responses.

21–23. Verse 21 is at least making a general point about the prospering of the righteous and the floundering of the wicked, but the wider context of speech may suggest that one reason why the righteous prevail is because of their upright speech, while the words of the wicked can be their downfall. This is not a promise that nothing bad can happen to a good person (think of Joseph, Job or Jesus), but is an assertion that pursuing righteousness (in speech) is worthwhile and will commonly have good outcomes. This would lead nicely into God's verdict on different kinds of speech in verse 22. Lying lips (recalling v. 19) receive God's disapproval, but those who *act* (= speak) faithfully give him enjoyment. While God has not been explicitly mentioned in the previous verses, the ease with which accountability to him is introduced shows the theological under-girding of the book. The final point about speech, made in verse 23, is that our speech reveals our character of either wisdom or folly. Verse 23a implies that the prudent do not have a need to tell others how much they know, not that they refuse to let others benefit from their knowledge when it is needed. This is evident in the contrasting second half of the verse, where fools who open their mouth to speak folly lose any benefit of the doubt that may have been extended towards them. People then know without reservation of the fool-ishness of their character or heart.

12:24–28
Context
The emphasis in the final five proverbs of this chapter is more on deeds than words. Even where words are in view in verse 25b, the emphasis is still on the action of bringing a good word to another.

Comment
24, 27. Verse 24 outlines an ironic contrast in which those who work hard will rise to a position of ease where they can make others work for them, but those who want ease, and so refuse to work, will be put to work against their will. The *slothful* (*rĕmiyyâ*) are shown to be foolish and short-sighted (10:4–5), as they are forced to do what they sought unsuccessfully to avoid. Verse 27 picks up this same contrast between the diligent man and slothful person, and again high-lights how the (lack of) actions by the lazy person is self-defeating. While the hard-working person will achieve his goal (here wealth), the slothful person will not even cook his food to enjoy it fully.

25–26. The focus here is on the value of giving encouragement and guidance. A timely and supportive word can raise the spirits of

someone who is weighed down by troubles or anxious thoughts
(v. 25). At one level verse 25 is simply a description of the effects of
anxiety on a person, but the positive outcome from bringing a word
of encouragement gives an implied call to take such an initiative
(also the contrast between the verbs 'weigh down' and 'cheer up/
make glad'). A righteous person also cares for a neighbour by
modelling a godly lifestyle, thus giving guidance and direction (v. 26a,
more lit. 'a righteous person is searched out by his neighbour').[20]
This is in contrast to the wicked whose example will only lead them
down the wrong path (v. 26). Waltke (2004: 541) comments, 'A good
word comes from a good person.'

28. The conclusion is entirely on the righteous, with the wicked
and slothful figures being left behind. Righteousness (*ṣĕdāqâ*) leads
not to death but to life, a prominent wisdom goal (e.g. 8:35–36).

13:1–3
Context
A focus on words and speech is present in verses 1–3.

Comment
1. This chapter starts in the same way as the previous one, dealing
with how to respond to words of correction and rebuke (12:1; see
also 9:7–9; 10:17). The new element here is the concern with how a
son (perhaps student) listens to his father's (perhaps teacher's)
instruction. Such a call to regard your father's instruction was made
as early in the book as 1:8. A simple observation is made that a
scoffer does not take any notice of correction or rebuke (v. 1b). The
verb 'to hear' is not present in the first half of verse 1, but is rightly
implied from the second part of the verse. It often has the sense of
'obey', and probably does so here.

2–3. Good speech can bring life (v. 2a). The *fruit of his mouth*
(ESV; 12:14) is a vivid metaphor for the words that have come from
within. In this sense these words are like fruit that grows as a result

---

20. Many note the textual difficulties of v. 26a. Fox (2009: 559), with
    slight emendation, argues for 'the righteous man is released from
    misfortune.'

of who someone is, one's inner character. The image is at first confusing, since a person both speaks and eats with the mouth, but the lesson drawn is that if you use your mouth properly, you will prosper and so have plenty to eat. While the words of such a person are wholesome, a deceitful or treacherous person (NIV, 'unfaithful') seeks only destruction and violence (v. 2b). The implication is that the violent actions that will follow are the fruit of the treacherous. The contrast between the consequence of preserving life or leading to ruin is then drawn out in verse 3. Here those who control their speech (*guards his mouth*) show wisdom in choosing what to say and what not to say (21:23). The two verbs used in verse 3a, *guards* (*nṣr*) and *preserves* (*šmr*), are synonyms, which are often used as a pair (e.g. 2:11, where they describe how your shaped character protects you). This thoughtful, deliberate use of language is in their own interests, for the point being made is not that it will benefit others (although it will probably do this as well), but that it will preserve their own life. Opening wide his lips (v. 3b; 'speak rashly', NIV) is a picture of exercising no control over what you say, and this undiscriminating use of language will be self-destructive (10:14; 13:16; 17:27–28). Paul gives a similar warning and exhortation in Ephesians 4:29, which is developed by James (Jas 1:26; 3:1–12).

13:4–6
Context
The contrasting consequences of life and ruin are drawn out in these proverbs.

Comment
4. The lazy sluggard has cravings as a result of his (lack of) direction in life, but he produces nothing. However, the life choices (*nepeš*, *soul*, ESV, or 'life' here, and in the first part of the verse, means 'life direction' or 'way of life'; NRSV suggests 'appetite') of the diligent person result in ample provision of what is needed in life (v. 4, lit. 'is fat', a positive connotation in that culture). There is a real link between character/life direction and consequences.

5. One aspect of the righteous person's character (a hatred of falsehood/deceit) is highlighted. It is also observed that the wicked

will bring dishonour and shame, perhaps just to themselves but maybe also to those around them.[21]

6. It is an upright person's righteousness or wisdom-shaped character that will finally guard or preserve him or her (v. 6a; one of the verbs used in v. 3; 2:11). This is a way of insisting that there is real value in pursuing such priorities, and commending righteousness to readers. The alternative is to be among those not shaped by wisdom (the *wicked*), who will be overcome by their self-focus and rebellion (*sin*, v. 6b).

13:7–11
Context
Wealth is a theme of a number of the proverbs (vv. 7–8, 11) in this part of the chapter, but each makes a different observation about money. What emerges in this section is an acknowledgment of wealth's value, but also some mention of its downside and a reminder of the need to combine it with righteousness and wisdom.

Comment
7. People can project an image of being either rich or poor, but these appearances can mask a different reality. The idea of 'pretend' comes from the use of the *hitpael* of 'to be rich', *'šr*, and the *hitpolel* of 'to be poor', *rwš*. However, it could instead be a contrast between one who is rich and yet what he has amounts to nothing (of value) and the one who is poor but who has genuine riches or wealth in another way. Although Fox (2009: 563) opts for the customary translation, he notes that this alternative sense would parallel 11:24. The implication of this is that, given the doctrine of retribution, the show of wealth is not enough to establish a person's righteousness.

---

21. The object is not specified; NIV 'on themselves' is interpretive. The translation *brings shame*, ESV, requires emending the text to a similar-sounding verb, which makes a good parallel with the other verb, meaning 'bring disgrace/shame'. The NIV (1984) chooses not to emend, but uses a different root and translates as 'makes themselves a stench' (see Fox 2009: 562–563). On either reading the consequences are strongly negative.

8. Another qualification about wealth is given.[22] Here the presence of wealth is a threat to the rich, for they become a target for kidnapping and ransom. There is no point in kidnapping a poor person for ransom and so, in this case, wealth exposes the rich to a greater threat. This too is a qualification placed on the value of riches, even if rightly gained. The NIV translates verse 8 as 'A person's riches may ransom their life, but the poor cannot respond to threatening rebukes.' This implies that wealth provides an opportunity which poverty prevents. However, the verse is better read as pointing out a limitation of wealth.

9–10. These verses deal with righteousness rather than wealth. The image of light in verse 9 is a symbol of life, with the extinguishing of a lamp being an image of death. Since all die, the contrast is one of an early or untimely death for the wicked, while the righteous delight in their ongoing lives. Its placement here might suggest a warning to the rich to make sure they are also righteous. Verse 10 concerns interpersonal relations, with the valuing of advice by others being the hallmark of wisdom, and contrasted with a presumptuous self-confidence that rudely rejects the suggestions of others. Riches can also lead to self-sufficiency, but those who take advice acknowledge their need of others.

11. A particular way of gaining wealth is criticized. The ESV translates *mēhebel* as *hastily* but notes that 'by fraud' is also possible (so NIV, 'dishonest').[23] *Hebel* has a range of meanings, but its core meaning (outside Ecclesiastes) is 'vapour'. The image is thus one of wealth coming out of nothing (like a win in a lottery), and the warning given here is that it will disappear just as it came. Yet the steady, regular gathering of wealth (presumably through the diligent work of our hands) will endure.

---

22. Waltke (2004: 558) sees a shift from the previous focus on false riches and poverty to now examine 'the real advantages of wealth and the factual disadvantage of poverty'.

23. Whybray (1994: 204) notes that Proverbs warns about both hastily gained wealth (20:21; 28:20) and wealth obtained by fraud or other illegitimate means (10:2; 11:4, 18; 21:6).

13:12–19
Context

The central verses of this section (vv. 13–18) deal largely with instruction, bracketed by proverbs that focus on *a desire fulfilled* (vv. 12, 19; NIV, 'longing fulfilled'). Within this broad scope, a variety of issues are addressed.

Comment

12, 19. The common mention of a desire fulfilled suggests that this concept is crucial to both these proverbs. While the nature of the desire is not mentioned, the result is described as *a tree of life* (v. 12b, *'ēṣ ḥayyîm*) and *sweet/pleasant to the soul* (v. 19a). The image of the *tree of life* echoes the idyllic picture of Eden in Genesis 2:9 and is not uncommon in Proverbs (3:18; 11:30; 15:4). Together with the description in verse 19, it implies that a deep longing that has been met is something that sustains and encourages a person. A clear contrast is made in verse 12a with *hope deferred*, which drains energy from a person. More problematic is the expression used in verse 19b, *to turn away from evil is an abomination to fools*. This suggests that the desire that is fulfilled may be a desire for wisdom, which would make good sense of the images of the *tree of life* and *sweet to the soul*. Verse 19 would then describe the wise person who turned away from evil, embraced a desire for wisdom and found satisfaction, but such a course of action was an anathema to the fool who rejected wisdom. Such a view would also give a greater cohesiveness to this section, which would then clarify what is meant by embracing wisdom and the value of doing so.

13–18. Verse 13 explains that the *word* ('of instruction' implied) or 'command' (NIV, *miṣwâ*, better than *commandment*, ESV) is to be treated highly (revered) not lightly (despised), and the contrasting outcomes are an unspecified reward or self-destruction.[24] The word/ instruction or command of verse 13 is clarified in verse 14 as *the teaching of the wise* (= *the fear of the LORD* in 14:27). The image of the

---

24. The negative consequences are more woodenly 'is pledged to himself'.
   The phrase refers to being pledged to pay the penalty (or bear the consequences) himself.

tree of life in verse 12 is behind the description in verse 14 of the teaching of the sages being like a *fountain of life*, or a source of life as it is meant to be. The way of folly is depicted here as the *snares of death* (v. 14b, presumably an early or untimely death), and this is developed in the following proverbs as *ruin* (v. 15b), *trouble* (v. 17a), *poverty and disgrace* (v. 18a). The one who rejects wisdom is described as the *treacherous*/unfaithful (v. 15), the *fool* (v. 16) and *wicked* (v. 17). Yet the focus in this group of proverbs is on being shaped by wisdom, and how it is rewarding (v. 13b), is life-giving (v. 14a), wins favour (v. 15a), is based on knowledge (v. 16a), leads to healing (v. 17b) and brings honour (v. 18b). The differences between the two ways are shown in the areas of response to instruction/ teaching (vv. 13–14), right actions (vv. 15–16) and the use of words in bringing a message from another (v. 17). The lesson is thus to embrace wisdom and find our desires fulfilled through a positive outcome.

13:20–25

Context

Verses 20–22 and 25 focus on the theme of the contrasting outcomes for the wise and foolish, but verses 23–24 have only limited connections with the surrounding verses.

Comment

20–21, 25. Verse 21 states the general principle that the righteous are rewarded with good/prosperity ('good things', NIV; *tôb*), while sinners are so certain to come to disaster or trouble (a common meaning of *rāʿâ*, evil) that it is described as actively chasing after them. This is explained in verse 25 as the very basic level of having sufficient or insufficient food (10:3). Verse 20 pushes the contrast between the wise and the foolish in a different direction. Here the focus is on our companions, for we become like those we associate with. The reward of choosing to take your stand among the wise is that you become wise yourself, and so wisdom rather than prosperity is the good that follows. The flip side of this is that those who associate with fools commonly become foolish themselves, which leads to harm (v. 20b).

22–23. Verse 22a reflects on the ongoing prosperity of the righteous, saying that it is not only enjoyed in this life, but there is enough to make provision for future generations of your family. Grandchildren are not a big theme in Proverbs, but their value is also picked up in 17:6. There are, however, interesting twists to the doctrine of retribution in verses 22b–23. First, verse 22b allows for a sinner to gain temporarily (through wrongful means?) much wealth, holding this truth in tension with verses 21, 25. Verse 23b gives an additional qualification, by pointing out that sometimes people are poor not because of any lack of righteousness, but simply as a consequence of the unjust actions of others. Their fields could have produced crops or did so, but they are taken away. Such a scenario rings true to our experience of the powerful using their influence to oppress the needy and marginalized. While the righteous will be rewarded and the wicked punished, sometimes the unrighteous can be wealthy (at least for a time) and some will be poor because of the wicked actions of others (Fox 2009: 570 refers to 10:15; 14:20; 18:23; 22:7a and especially 30:14).

24. The focus here is on the importance of shaping as part of character. This verse (and others like it, e.g. 22:15; 23:13–14; 29:15, 17) receives bad press among many Western Christians who are hesitant about corporal punishment in the light of community concerns about child abuse. The focus is on the value of discipline much more than it is on the means used (in ancient Israel, corporal punishment, the rod). The lesson being taught is much wider. Children or youths who are left to follow their own desires will usually be self-indulgent rather self-disciplined. Echoing verse 1, we all need discipline to become the people God wants us to be, and this takes effort (e.g. 2 Pet. 1:5–8). The proper exercise of discipline is not an abuse of power, but rather the outworking of loving concern for those entrusted to our care.

14:1–9

Context

A contrast between wisdom and folly is found in most of the verses of this loosely connected group.

Comment

1. This stands over the section by making the general point that wisdom (personified as a woman building a house as in 9:1–6) builds up, while folly tears down.[25] The *house* built up by the wise woman and torn down by folly is not an actual house, but rather a household community. Folly too is personified as a woman (as in 9:13–18), but following her leads to destruction (as in 9:18). The implied warning of verse 1 is to pursue wisdom and reject folly, and this general theme is unpacked in the other verses.

2–3. The explicit contrast is between walking in moral uprightness or straightness, and being devious or crooked in one's ways. In verse 2a the term used for the wise person is one who *fears the LORD*, the foundation of wisdom and understanding (1:7; 9:10, which may also suggest it was wisdom personified in v. 1) in the sense of respecting God as God, treating him as he is in reality. Our characteristic way of life (*walks, ways*), not our isolated actions, makes us wise or foolish. Verse 3 highlights the importance of speech. When fools open their mouth, they enable others to discern their true nature, and the *rod for his back* is simply that their disclosed character will make it harder to deceive others. A more literal translation of the Hebrew for verse 3a is given in the ESV margin: *In the mouth of a fool is a rod of pride*. This is a more comic picture of the destructive words that will come from a foolish heart. On either rendering, a clear contrast is made with the wise, whose speech – reflecting their character – will protect or guard them (*šmr*, v. 3b).

4. A cameo of folly is contrasted with the consequences of wisdom. While keeping a clean manger (a stone feeding trough for animals) seems a desirable goal, if it comes as a result of having no working animals, then it is as futile as a hospital with no patients or

---

25. The translation *wisest of women* (ESV) is based on the assumption that the plural is used comparatively, which makes sense since the verb is singular. With a slight emendation, it would be identical with the form of wisdom personified in 9:1, and so would be an allusion to Lady Wisdom. This is made more likely by the use of an abstract noun for folly (i.e. folly personified) in 14:1b.

a school without pupils.²⁶ There is no productivity or output – it is neat but fruitless. However, having oxen, and using them to plough the fields, will result in the life-giving consequence of abundant crops.²⁷

5. The wise person does not lie, and so is a faithful or reliable legal testimony. The fool who lies is a false or deceptive witness. In the light of verse 3, there is an implication that the faithful witness will be preserved and the false witness come unstuck. The importance of being a true rather than false witness is a prominent theme in the book (6:19; 12:17; 14:25; 19:5, 9, 28; 21:28; 24:28; 25:18).

6. This verse considers the connection between character and further learning. If we adopt the stance of a scoffer (one type of fool, 1:22; 9:7–12), the quest for wisdom will be unproductive. A similar thought is given in 24:7a. On the other hand, a person of understanding is portrayed in chapters 1 – 9 as one who fears the Lord and has allowed wisdom to shape his or her character. Such a person will grow in knowledge, which is one of the purposes of the book (1:2, 7). Our foundational stance will make it either easier or harder to master living in the world.

7–9. The various images of verses 4–6 depict various versions of fools (the unproductive person, false witness, scoffer), but the language of wisdom and folly is not often used. However, this language is now made explicit in verses 7–9. First, there is a warning to avoid the presence or company of fools, echoing wisdom's call in 1:20–33. With fools, there will be no knowledge of what really counts in life, nor are their words trustworthy (lit. 'they do not know lips/words of knowledge', as in 20:15). This is why their folly is called 'deception/deceit' (*mirmâ*) in verse 8b. The contrast in verse 8a is

---

26. The translation *clean* (ESV) or 'empty' (NIV) are common renderings. *Bār* can also mean 'grain', adopted by NRSV, 'there is no grain' (also Garrett 1993: 141), omitting *manger*. The same point is being made, regardless of the translation.

27. Longman (2006: 297) concedes that 'a productive life is messy', while Kidner (1964: 106) makes the comment that many religious groups need to heed this proverb, and move to the farmer's perspective (the need for productivity) rather than that of the curator (pristine preservation).

important, for wisdom is described there as enabling people to discern their way or path in life. In other words, wisdom is not primarily academic but practical in helping us live sensibly in the world. In verse 9b the wise (now called *the upright*) enjoy acceptance or favour ('goodwill', NIV; *rāṣôn*), although it does not specify who accepts them. This at least includes acceptance by others, for it more literally reads, '[there is] favour among or between the upright', although this is also consistent with the favour of *both* the upright and God. The *guilt offering* could be rendered as 'a sacrifice for guilt' (as in Lev. 5:14–19) or simply as 'guilt' itself, for *'āšām* is used in both senses.[28] Yet in a wisdom context, *'āšām* most likely refers simply to guilt, which would give the sense of fools scoffing at the thought that they might be guilty. This guilt would include accountability to God, and consequent acceptance among other upright people to whom godliness matters.

14:10–14
Context
This is a loose cluster of proverbs around the twin poles of the heart and the idea of retribution. The heart is linked with joy in verses 10, 13, while retribution is clearly stated in verse 11. Verse 14 draws the two together with the description of the backslider in heart and the double mention of goodness and backsliding receiving appropriate consequences.

Comment
10–12. The idea of verse 10 is that no-one else can finally know what is going on inside the core of a person – the *heart* (*lēb*). The heart is not the centre of emotion, but what controls a person, particularly one's thinking. No-one (lit. *no stranger*, but with the sense of 'no other

---

28. The NIV adopts a midway position, translating it as 'making amends for sin'. It would be unusual if it were a reference to a guilt offering, since mention of specific sacrifices is uncommon in the book of Proverbs. However, the concept of sacrifice for sin or guilt before a god was common in the ANE, and so would have been readily understood by those both within and outside Israel.

person') can fathom the extent of a person's pain or bitterness, but nor can they comprehend the fullness of a person's joy.[29] Verse 11 is a classical expression of the biblical doctrine of retribution (12:7), with the character of a person (wicked or upright) leading to certain consequences (destruction or flourishing). The verb used for *flourish* (the *hifil* of *prḥ*) evokes a picture of a bush full of buds, about to burst in flower as the expression of its life. The focus is on character, not on isolated actions, and there is no mention of God's active involvement in the destruction or flourishing. It is simply a statement of the principle, but with an implied urging to choose to take a stand with the upright. The house/tent metaphor indicates where your base in life is. This is behind the warning of verse 12, for the *way* referred to there is that of the wicked person of verse 11. The proverb is not a general warning that you cannot always plan your future, but rather a reminder to the wicked person that the outcome of that destructive way of living is death (9:18; 16:25).

13–14. There is a return to the mention of heart and joy in verse 13, with the sobering observation that even when a person outwardly experiences laughter and joy, that is not the whole picture, nor will it continue for ever. Inside the heart may also exist a deep ache or grief, perhaps unknown to others in the light of verse 10, but which truly represents where that person is at. The second half of verse 13 uses the language of the *end* from verse 12, reminding us that grief can so commonly follow joy. The joy of loving others is followed by the grief of losing them; the delight in being reunited with family or friends leads to a greater sense of loss as you lose contact or proximity. Laughter and joy do not endure. This emphasis on what is going on inside a person (*the heart*) in verse 13 gives a subtle nuance to the reformulation of the idea of retribution in verse 14. The wicked is now described as the backslider in heart, one who used to be committed to doing good, but has now fallen away or 'turned his heart back' (*backslider in heart*, ESV, captures the sense better than 'faithless', NIV, or 'perverse', NRSV). This refers to what we are like on the inside, not simply how we act on the outside. The

---

29. Waltke (2004: 590) sees this as 'a merism representing the full gamut of emotions'.

parallel term of the good person is impliedly also a description of
someone's internal attitude, and so retribution in both its negative
and positive dimensions is based on a person's core character and
direction in life.

14:15–19
Context
Verses 15–18 deal with being careful about how you walk and act,
bracketed by a contrast between the simple and the prudent in verses
15 and 18. It is not entirely clear whether verse 19 belongs to what
precedes or follows, but it does serve as a fitting conclusion to verses
15–18 by indicating that the way of the good and righteous is to be
preferred to that of the evil and wicked. In this sense it unpacks
verse 18 and mirrors verse 17. Fox (2009: 580) suggests that it
continues the theme of the prestige that accompanies wisdom in
verse 18b.

Comment
15, 18. *Simple* refers not to someone of limited intelligence, but
rather to one whose character is not yet shaped or formed. In chapter
9 the *simple* person (*petî*) is one who has not made the decisive choice
between wisdom and folly, but is still considering both options (9:4,
16). The simple one is here portrayed as undiscriminating (v. 15a),
believing everything (or every word) rather than discerning what is
right or best. In verse 18a the simple are described as inheriting folly
– retaining what will lead to death instead of discarding it. By way
of contrast, the prudent (those who have embraced wisdom) give
thought to their steps (v. 15b; see v. 8a) and are crowned with knowledge (v. 18b). Proverbs 1:7 has noted that the fear of the Lord is
the beginning of knowledge, so the result of fearing the Lord (v. 16a)
is to be enriched or characterized by (= 'crowned with') knowledge.
These are descriptions of a thoughtful, wise and meaningful life,
which is built on the right foundation.

16–17. These verses then outline what will become of the simple
if they do not ground their life and character on wisdom. The wise
person fears (*yārē'*, the Lord, v. 16a; ESV, *is cautious*, but it is better to
retain the literal sense of the text) and turns away from evil. This
description of fearing (the Lord) and turning away from evil is

reminiscent of the wisdom figure Job (Job 1:1, 8). It describes those who have been shaped by Proverbs 1 – 9, who stand with God and allow their character to be shaped. If the simple do not accept this offer from Lady Wisdom, then they may become fools who are recklessly careless (v. 16b, probably a hendiadys), rather than astute and careful. Even worse, they could develop a short temper or have evil devices, which will lead them to act foolishly and attract only hatred (v. 17). *Of evil devices*, esv, or 'who devises evil schemes', niv, probably captures the sense of *mĕzimmôt.*[30]

19. This is a general statement that the evildoers will have to defer to or cower before those who are good, and that this will be shown publicly at the gates. Gates were at the centre of the community and legal life of a city, or less likely at the entrance to a grand home. If it refers to the city gates, it may have the setting of a legal dispute in which the righteous will prevail over the wicked.

14:20–24
Context
Poverty/wealth is a focus in four of the five proverbs in verses 20–24. Van Leeuwen (1997: 142) sees verses 19–24 as a cluster dealing with relations between 'people who differ morally or socio-economically'.

Comment
20–21. This begins with a wisdom observation that the rich have more friends than the poor (Murphy 1998: 105: 'riches create differences in social life'), without any implication that this ought to be the case. There is no command to follow, or goal to strive for. The proverb just describes the reality that those who are rich can lavish good things on their friends, but a poor person has little to give. While there is no exhortation in verse 20, this is supplied by verse 21, which is an encouragement to be generous to the poor rather

---

30. Whybray (1994: 217) notes that it commonly means 'cleverness' in Proverbs, but is used in 12:2 in the sense of 'wicked scheming'. The context suggests that this possible sense is present here. Clifford (1999: 146) comments that 'person of *mĕzimmôt*' has only a negative sense (12:2; 24:8).

than to despise them. Such a generous person is *blessed* (*'ašrê*), that is, honoured in God's sight. In both verse 20 and verse 21 the poor person is described as a neighbour, and verse 21a claims that we have a moral obligation before God to our neighbours (hence *ḥôṭ'*, *a sinner*), which is compromised by despising them.

22. Given the surrounding context of wealth and poverty, this is likely to be amplifying verse 21. Thus, despising your poor neighbour is now labelled as 'devising evil', and being generous to the poor is now reframed as 'devising good'. Likewise, the meaning of *blessed* (*'ašrê*, v. 21b) is now unpacked as meeting steadfast love and faithfulness. Blessing is not found in material terms but rather in committed relationships.[31]

23–24. The final two verses belong together, with a twin set of contrasts. Verse 23 contrasts the consequences of hard work as opposed to mere talk, while verse 24 reflects more generally on the result of each path. Talk alone (lit. 'a word/matter of lips') brings about nothing of lasting value, but effort will be rewarded (v. 23). The folly of fools (v. 24b) refers to talking but not working, and this will result in the person being shown to be a fool. Those who have worked hard will have their wealth to show, and this will be outward evidence of their wise choices. Given the idea of retribution in the book, their resulting wealth is a testimony to their wisdom. The image of crown implies a status visible to others, and recalls verse 18 (also 4:9).

14:25–27
Context
There is less overall structure in the rest of this chapter, with only occasional pairings such as the *fear of the LORD* sayings in verses 26 and 27.

Comment
25. This endorses giving truthful evidence at the city gates (where legal cases were decided) rather than uttering lies. Telling the truth

---

31. Van Leeuwen (1997: 142) suggests that this steadfast love and faithfulness may be from God, but it is not specified and so could refer to receiving these from God or others.

leads to saving lives, but there is no explanation as to how it does so. This may include the life of the person speaking the truth as well as the other person in the law case. The temptation in legal proceedings is to win at all costs, but a person of integrity will speak the truth regardless of the cost (see Ps. 15:2–4). At the very least, a clear connection is being made between truthfulness of character and life. The focus elsewhere is often that the lying witness will be punished (e.g. 19:5, 9), but here it simply indicates your character (see also v. 5).

26–27. The *fear of the LORD* is the foundational wisdom stance that shapes the book of Proverbs (1:7; 9:10), and sometimes comes to mean the godly life or piety built on this foundation (e.g. Job 4:6). It is life with a solid basis, and will lead to the protection of the next generation (v. 26). It is a great encouragement (and warning?) to parents to know that the godliness they teach and model will help protect their children as well as themselves. However, the fear of the Lord is not simply solid, but spectacular and life-giving as well, as it bursts forth like a fountain (v. 27a). This image is explained in the rest of the verse, where the fear of the Lord (treating or respecting God as God) works actively to turn you away from the clutches of death. There is positive protection in taking a stand with God in his world and shaping your character and life accordingly.[32]

14:28–35
Context
These proverbs have only a loose cohesion but are bracketed by two proverbs that deal with the king (vv. 28, 35), while the intervening proverbs concern matters of character that will affect the community, most explicitly in verse 34.

Comment
28. This makes the startling assertion that (at least in the context of a monarchy) the king and leader/prince need the people in order

---

32. Steinmann (2009: 337) notes that this verse is identical to 13:14 except for the first two words. What was asserted there about the teaching of the wise is repeated here about the fear of the Lord, which is central to the teaching of the wise.

to become great or prosper. While a hospital without any patients may be viewed by some as operating with perfect efficiency (as in an episode of the BBC television series, *Yes Minister*), the reality is that it cannot work for a community. The temptation of community leaders is to think that it is their brilliance that will make the group great. This is qualified by the reminder that without many people, the king or other leader will gain little glory and will effectively be ruined. There is a likely but unstated implication that rulers need to protect and promote the good of their people. While the explicit focus is on the king and a poetic equivalent, Waltke (2004: 604) is probably right in suggesting that 'The king serves as a type, an example, of any leader', so that the principle asserted here has a wider application to leadership in general.

29–31. What will make for a strong community? Being slow (lit. 'long', as in a long fuse; NIV, 'patient') to anger, rather than reacting with a hot (lit. 'short', as in a short fuse) temper, will lead to more considered decisions (*great understanding*), rather than knee-jerk ones (*folly*, v. 29). Similarly, an inner attitude of contentment (*tranquil heart*, v. 30), rather than the cancer of envy, will lead to life and growth rather than decay.[33] Caring for the poor is an important part of a working community (v. 31). It is often said that the goodness of a community can be discerned in how it treats its most marginalized members, but there is an added theological dimension in verse 31. Here, God as Creator (and therefore in biblical thinking, Sustainer) is *his Maker* (*'ōśēhû*), and whoever mistreats someone who is poor is actually committing an offence against God (*insults*, v. 31). We have an obligation not only to the poor themselves, but to the God who made them. In our globalized world this concern cannot be limited just to our own immediate community. The way in which we mistreat

---

33. Verse 30 is an interesting Hebrew sentence containing seven nouns and no verb. It reads lit. 'life flesh calmness of heart; rottenness of bones jealousy'. Such ellipsis (assuming, but omitting, words) is common in Hebrew poetry, and the relationship between the nouns needs to be supplied. In each half the verb 'brings' or 'results in': 'calmness of heart [brings] life [to the] flesh, [but] jealousy [results in] rottenness of [the] bones.'

the poor is by showing a lack of generosity, which is deemed to be oppressing them. In fact, generosity to the poor honours or shows grace to *him* (ESV; 'God', NIV, v. 31). *Him* could mean either the poor person or God, or perhaps both.

32. This is difficult to grasp fully, although it is unambiguous that the righteous person will find refuge and the wicked person will be overthrown or cast down. There is a clear structural parallel between the two halves of the verse, implying that the preposition (variously translated as 'in, with, by means of, through') has the same force in each part. It is best to see it used instrumentally in both cases, giving the translation: 'The wicked person is overthrown by means of (through) his wickedness, but the righteous person finds refuge by means of (through) his death.' Although believers often seek refuge from, not through, death, what is in view here is that the righteous persevere in their faithfulness to God right up to death. Thus, it is death (presumably not an early or untimely one) that gives the stamp of approval on those who have persisted in righteousness. The proverb as a whole then urges us not to take the path of the wicked, which is a sad end, but rather be committed to living in a godly way until the end of our lives.[34]

33–35. These final three verses all concern the community. Wisdom must be solidly rooted in a person's heart, the core of one's being and thinking (v. 33a), but it is not simply confined there. This foundation of wisdom – knowing how to live skilfully and success-fully – will make itself known (or 'is known') in the midst of others, even if they be fools (v. 33b). In other words, genuine wisdom will be preserved and lived out in the community, rather than become overwhelmed by others. The circle is drawn even wider in verse 34, which imagines the setting of a nation or an entire people. Right-eousness (presumably founded on wisdom) will benefit a nation, while sin will be a shameful reproach. Righteousness (*ṣĕdāqâ*) is largely a relational term in the OT and is seen in right relationships

---

34. For an alternative reading, based on reading the preposition as 'in', see the NIV: 'When [in] calamity comes, the wicked are brought down, but even in [perhaps "in the face of"] death the righteous seek refuge in God.'

with God, other people and the created world. Sin has ruptured relationships in all three of these areas.

Verse 35 picks up a number of themes from the preceding two verses: dealing wisely, acting shamefully and the setting of a nation under a king. The advice, directed to a servant of the king, is to act wisely. This would involve having wisdom in one's heart, and living it out in righteousness. By way of contrast, the one who acts shamefully, whose sin would bring reproach on the people, will experience the king's wrath. The way to live in community is to be a person grounded in wisdom and living in righteous relationships.

15:1–7
Context
These verses cluster around the theme of speech, with mention of *answer, word* (v. 1), *tongue, mouth* (v. 2), *tongue* (v. 4), *instruction, reproof* (v. 5) and *lips* (v. 7).

Comment
1. This concerns how to use words in response to others, for the words we use can change or create a situation of conflict. A *soft* (ESV, *rak*; 'gentle', NIV) answer can defuse a heated exchange, while a harsh or painful (*'eṣeb*, used of the pain of childbirth in Gen. 3:16; Whybray 1994: 205 suggests it is 'a word which *causes* pain') word can cause anger to flare up.[35] The implied lesson is for us to choose the tone of our words, for they can transform situations for good or ill.

2. Our speech is an indicator of our character, for what we are like on the inside (wise or foolish) determines what emerges in our speech. Folly pours out of the mouth of a fool, but the speech of a character shaped by wisdom adds something positive. It increases, contributes to or *commends* (ESV) knowledge.

3–5. Verse 3 is not explicitly about speech, but sets the important theological context that no action (and perhaps especially, no words) can be hidden from God, for he actively keeps watch over and assesses what is harmful (*rā'îm, evil*) and helpful (*ṭôbîm, good*). While

---

35. Clifford (1999: 150) points out the paradox here that a soft answer is hard (i.e. effective) and a hard answer is soft (i.e. ineffective).

how we live is therefore important, so is how we speak. Verse 4 contrasts a *gentle* (ESV) or 'soothing' (NIV) tongue with a perverse one. The former is a tree of life (3:18), an image of growth, flourishing and fruitfulness, while the latter has the effect of crushing the spirit. It is not specified whose spirit is crushed, but it at least refers to the one who is the object of this wrongful speech, and may also describe the distorting consequences on the one who utters it. Verse 5 picks up the theme from verse 1 about how to respond to the speech of others, although here there is a concern with our responses when others seek to instruct us. Again our character (foolish or prudent) is made evident by whether we take notice of a parent's instruction/disciplining words and correction/reproof. This echoes the content of 9:7–9 and will be picked up in verse 12.

6–7. Verse 6 does not explicitly refer to speech, but rather makes the general point (through metaphors of *house* and *income*) that the righteous possess something really valuable while the wicked person's path leads only to ruin. In a setting of proverbs about speech, one implication of this is that wise speech will be of value to others since it comes from their character, while the words of the wicked will be as destructive as their life choices. Verse 7a gives a summary commendation of wise speech in that it spreads knowledge, one of the purposes of the book (1:4). Verse 7b, with its mention of the heart, is a hinge verse that leads nicely into verses 8–15.

15:8–15

Context

The focus here shifts to the inner person. Verse 7b signals this change with the first mention of heart in the chapter. The heart (*lēb*) is explicitly mentioned again in verses 11, 13, 14, 15, but the attention drawn to the inner person is present in the other verses as well.

Comment

8–9. This couplet outlines what is an abomination to the Lord and what is acceptable to him. Both verses assume that God is the one who weighs up our lives and actions, with verse 8 focusing on worship and verse 9 on daily living. The contrast in verse 8 is not between sacrifice and prayer – both of which were appropriate responses to God in that culture – but between the varying character of the person

(21:27). The worship of the wicked one is rejected by God because of his wickedness, while uprightness in a person renders prayer acceptable to God. This contrast is also echoed in verse 29, while 12:22 mirrors an identical pattern in relation to lying lips and faithful actions. The contrast in verse 9 is between the life direction of the wicked and the one who pursues the relational concept of righteousness. The language of God 'loving' is remarkably personal.

10–12. The focus narrows to God's assessment of the wicked. Verse 11b ties all of verses 8–11 into the surrounding context by asserting that human hearts lie open before the Lord. This implies that the crucial difference between the upright and the wicked is not their outward actions but a matter of the heart, or what they are like on the inside. The word *discipline* (*mûsār*) can have a positive sense (e.g. *instruction* in 1:2–3), but the addition of the adjective 'bad, serious' (*rāʿ*) produces the sense of severe or stern discipline with a negative connotation. The consequences are set out as death (v. 10b), and in verse 11 as going to Sheol (the place of the dead) and Abaddon (death pictured as destruction). Their core fault is to *forsake the way* (understood as the path chosen through life, an outworking of the two ways to live in chapter 9) and to hate reproof (an echo of 9:7–9, and raised in this chapter in verses 5, 12). Verse 12 reinforces the idea seen in verses 5 and 10 that scoffers show their character by their negative response to being corrected.

13–15. The heart is explicitly central here. A *glad* (*śāmēah*, 'joyful') heart results in outward cheerfulness; sorrow within means that one's whole spirit is crushed (v. 13; 17:22). This is not a criticism of those who have sorrow in their heart, but is used as an illustration of the point that what people are like on the inside will be reflected on the outside. Verse 14 contrasts the one with understanding, who seeks to find out the way the world is (i.e. knowledge), with fools who fill their life with what is not true about the world (i.e. folly). Verse 15 speaks of the delights that come to the one who is cheerful or 'good of heart' (*tôb lēb*), an echo of the joyful or glad heart of verse 13, tying verses 13–15 together. The implication of this is that the daily life of the afflicted or oppressed is difficult because of their life choices, which suggests that it refers only to those whose heart has chosen the path of folly, rather than being a global diagnosis of all who are oppressed.

15:16–17
Context
These two proverbs are a pair in both their form and content. The 'better than' formula makes a connection with the previous verse (*cheerful*, v. 15, and *better*, vv. 16–17, both render *ṭôb*, having a core meaning of 'good'), and is a common Hebrew way of comparing the value of two items. There is a similar comparison in the next chapter (16:8). Both verses teach the virtue of being content with a little rather than striving after too much.

Comment
16. The contrast is between a small amount and a great treasure, but the reason why the smaller amount is better is that it is linked to the fear of the Lord (i.e. treating God as God). At this midpoint in the Solomonic collection, the fear of the Lord motif recurs (see 15:33; 16:6) and Yahweh sayings become prominent.[36] Unusually in this book, having few possessions rather than great wealth is linked to godliness (unlike 3:9–10), while excessive wealth is accompanied by trouble or worries (*mĕhûmâ* has the force of a deep disturbance). Fox (2009: 595) comments, 'Material wealth is good, but other things are more important. Piety compensates for its lack, and turmoil cancels its value.'

17. The simplicity of a vegetarian option (*herbs*, ESV; 'vegetables', NIV; *yārāq* can mean grass or plants) is contrasted with an elaborate and expensive fattened ox. Again the crucial difference is not in a little or a lot, but rather in a preference for love rather than hatred. In both verses, then, a little combined with a right relationship with God and others is not only enough, but much better than more 'things' with weaker relationships.

15:18–19
Context
These verses centre on two negative portraits of unrelated, but both foolish, stereotypical figures.

---

36. See Whybray (1990), who describes chs. 15 and 16 as a 'theological kernel'.

Comment

18. An easily angered person, one quick to flare up, will create strife and conflict (26:20; 29:22a). The contrasting figure, commended in the text, is of one who has patience and is not quick to react angrily, and such a person quietens disputes and divisions between people. In conflict, angry words are tempting to utter, but self-control leads to better relationships.

19. The lazy person (*'āṣēl*, *sluggard*, ESV) is compared to a hedge of thorns. This metaphor suggests that they act as a barrier or blockage impeding progress, which is confirmed by the contrast with a level highway in the second half of the verse. The comparison is that a lazy person achieves very little, but the purposeful pathway of the upright leads to significant advances.

15:20–24

Context

This cluster of proverbs focuses on the positive consequences of being wise, with the negative contrast (sometimes only implied) fading into the background.

Comment

20. The ESV/NRSV translations of verse 20a are ambiguous (they could mean that a wise son will grow up to be a glad father), but the Hebrew means that a wise son makes his father glad ('brings joy to his father', NIV). Children pay due respect to their parents by becoming wise in character and understanding. Those who choose the path of folly (again in character and thinking) despise or show little regard for their parents. The use of both father and mother reminds us that both parents are affected by the way their children live.

21–22. Success comes from being a person of understanding. The foil in verse 21 is one who lacks sense, a contrast seen previously in 10:13 and 11:12. The phrase *lacks sense* is paralleled with *destroys himself* in 6:32 (see also 7:7), but in 15:21 such a person delights in folly. A person of understanding – again a mixture of right thinking and discerning living – will have a life free of obstacles (as in 3:6). This is not an absolute promise, but a way of commending such a pathway in daily living. Verse 22 simply observes that plans do not come to fruition if you do not take advice, or perhaps even if you do not have a circle of friends working with you on a project (*maḥăšābôt*). However, many advisors will enable success to be achieved, as the accumulated wisdom of many is greater than that of any single individual (11:14).

23–24. Verse 23 does not contain an explicit contrast, but rather commends the ability to give a suitable response to others and a word in season ('timely word', NIV). The expression *apt answer*/'reply' (in Hebrew, an 'answer of his mouth') probably takes this sense from the parallel in the second half of the verse. Here there is delight over a word 'in its time' or a fitting/appropriate response. Verse 24 focuses on the positive direction in life of those with a character shaped by wisdom (the *prudent*). Their path will succeed or prosper (*leads upwards*, *lĕma'lâ*), which is clarified by avoiding an untimely or early death (symbolized by Sheol).

15:25–29
Context
This section begins and ends with a Yahweh saying, and the focus is predominantly on what people are like on the inside, especially the wicked. The wicked are mentioned explicitly in verses 26, 28, 29, but the plundering proud (v. 25; see the same word in 16:19) and those greedy for unjust gain (v. 27) are also variant ways of describing the same type of people.

Comment
25, 29. God's activity is in view in these verses, which bracket the section. God destroys what the proud and self-sufficient build up (v. 25a), and ensures justice for the marginalized (v. 25b). Boundary markers on land are not simply a concern in the Law and the Prophets, but also in wisdom material (Prov. 22:28; 23:10; Job 24:2; 31:38–40). While this is the only reference in Proverbs to widows, they are the object of special attention in Job (Job 24:3, 21; 29:13; 31:16, 18), and the marginalized in general (usually called the 'poor') are a focus in Proverbs. Verse 25 thus depicts God as standing up for the powerless against those who wield power in a self-centred way. Verse 29 describes how God distances himself from the wicked (so that they cannot call on him), but responds to the prayer of the righteous (15:8).

26–28. In between the brackets of God's activity in verses 25 and 29, there is a concentration on what the wicked are like on the inside. Their thoughts or schemes (NRSV 'plans', *maḥšĕbôt*) are strongly rejected by God, and contrasted with the purity (and therefore acceptability) of words that are gracious, pleasant or kind (v. 26). Verse 27 explores the inordinate desire for money (*greedy for unjust gain*). Such a person is contrasted with those who hate giving and receiving bribes (v. 27b). While greed promises life and ease, verse 27 observes that those who reject greed are the ones who gain life, while those who embrace it bring troubles or 'ruin' (NIV, *'ōkēr*) into their own households. Verse 28 describes the positive heart of the righteous that enables them to respond appropriately in varying situations. The implication is that the rightness of their heart will be disclosed in their words, which leads nicely to the contrasting situation of the wicked. Their inner person is also revealed in their words, which are full of evil things (the plural *rā'ôt* might highlight the many evil thoughts, or could be a plural of intensity showing how strong the evil is).

15:30–33
Context
Verses 31–33, with mention of reproof and instruction/discipline, all speak of being shaped by verbal input. Verse 30 does not fit as well, but appears to be a hinge verse, with the mention of the heart in verse 30a connecting back to the focus on the inner person in verses 25–29, while verse 30b, with its mention of good news (the word is related to the Hebrew root *šmʿ*, 'to hear'), connects with hearing words in verses 31–33.[37]

Comment
30. Together the two halves describe what gives encouragement and fresh life to a person. The light of the eyes refers to what someone delights in or what lights up the eyes, and this gives joy

---

37. Whybray (1994: 237) suggests that v. 30 is the only verse in vv. 25–33 that is thematically isolated. I prefer to see that vv. 25–29 and 31–33 are separate groups.

inside a person.[38] In verse 30b the receiving of good news builds up a person physically (lit. 'makes the bones fat or healthy').

31–33. Verse 31 endorses the value of listening to reproof as a way of becoming wise. The correction is described as life-giving (ESV, NIV; lit. 'the reproof of life' = 'which leads to life') or 'wholesome' (NRSV). The link between reproof and life is found in 6:23 (which also includes the word *light* found here in v. 30, and *instruction* found in vv. 32–33), where the idea is that heeding this correction will enable a person to resist the temptation of the adulteress. Such a reproof is life-giving in that it is character shaping. Verse 32 reinforces this negatively and positively. The one who ignores discipline or instruction is rejecting his inner self (*nepeš* or 'life'), while the one who hears (which may have the connotation of 'obeys') correction gains 'heart' (*lēb*, *intelligence*, ESV; 'understanding', NIV, NRSV). Clearly, a person's life benefits as a result of being shaped by this reproof. Verse 33 closes off this section by pointing out that the fear of the Lord (i.e. respecting God as God) is the basis and perhaps even the content of this discipline, and will lead to the practical skills of a wisdom-shaped character. In parallel with this is the virtue of humility (also paired in 22:4), which implies that a right view of oneself before God is essential for our prospering, here described as honour or glory.

Meaning in chapters 10 – 15
Looking back over chapters 10 – 15, many different topics have been covered, and it is difficult to tie the threads together. Yet it is clear that there is a fundamental divide in humanity between the wise and the foolish. In each subject area the resolution often returns to 'is this wisdom or is it folly?' Particular attention has been given to speech, but this has often been pictured as the outward expression of what people are like in the core of their being. The 'heart'

---

38. The NIV interprets *light of the eyes* as 'light in a messenger's eyes', which is also possible but more interpretive. It is likely based on a supposed parallel in the second half of the verse, but it overlooks the hinge function. Kidner (1964: 110) thinks that it might refer to the radiant face of a friend, which is equally speculative.

determines both a person's speech and action. It is not possible to
address only the things people say or do, but rather what they are like
in their heart. This is also a truth affirmed by Jesus (Mark 7:16–23).
The transformed heart reinforces two thrusts in chapters 1 – 9:
grounding our lives on the fear of the Lord, and embracing Lady
Wisdom. The heart is also strongly connected to character (another
key concern of the earlier chapters), as it provides the foundation
for the lifelong process of growing in maturity and integrity. All of
these factors are intertwined as a wide variety of topics are explored,
many of which are examined in the Introduction.

B. The theological heart of the sayings (16:1–9)

Context

Whybray (1990) has identified 15:33 – 16:9 as the 'theological kernel'
or heart of chapters 10 – 22, with an atypical concentration of verses
containing *the LORD* (all except 16:8). Proverbs 15:33 finishes off the
previous section as well as leading into this focus on what the Lord
is doing. Within chapter 16, verses 1 and 9 operate as a bracket, with
both outlining that people plan but God determines the outcome.
There have been Yahweh sayings in 15:25, 26, 29, 33 and also in
the two following sections (16:11, 20, 33), while the theme of the
bracketed verses (16:1, 9) is also echoed at the end of the chapter
(16:33). Signs of thematic unity in verses 1–9 include the mention
of the human heart in verses 1, 5 and 9, while the fear of the Lord
in verse 6 links the section to 15:33. The focus is not on occasional
actions but rather on the typical life patterns of people, seen in the
mention of ways (vv. 2, 7, 9) and similar words (*work*, v. 3; *turns away
from*, v. 6; *steps*, v. 9). Schwáb suggests that verse 9 has links with
verses 1–3 as a unit, noting that all but one Hebrew word in verse 9
is found in verses 1–3 (Schwáb 2013: 67). The negative mentions of
the wicked, the arrogant in heart and iniquity/evil in verses 4–6
suggest that this is the next section, leaving the more positive verses
7–9 as the final part.

Comment

1–3. Verses 1 and 2 are each made up of two contrasting halves
(divided by *but*), and in each case the second half, God's action,

determines the outcome. Verse 3, an example of step parallelism, announces the way forward. Human *plans* or arrangements (*ma'ărāk*, v. 1) seek to bring about a person's inner goals (*lēb*, *the heart*; 'mind', NRSV), but the one who says/decides what will happen (*the answer of the tongue*) is the Lord. This theme will be prominent in the second half of the Solomonic sayings (19:21; 20:24; 21:30–31). The ways of a person (v. 2) does not refer to one's moral ways, but rather one's intended plans as in verse 1. People can easily think that their intentions are not based on mixed or wrong motives (*pure in his own eyes*), but the Lord discerns the underlying aims and goals (*weighs the spirit*; see also 12:15a; 21:2). The obvious conclusion, set out in verse 3, is to hand over your actions for the Lord to examine, for this will lead to success. This is described here as *your plans will be established*, or made to stand or succeed. The word for *your plans* (*maḥšēbōtêkâ*) is different from the one used in verse 1, but the related verbal form (*ḥšb*) is found in verse 9. It often refers to skilful plans and thoughts. Schwáb (2013: 77) captures the essence of this reading in his paraphrase:

> Human beings plan their actions because they want to be successful. However, success is rooted in the LORD's decision and not in human preparation. The LORD knows what the true intentions of people are and he acts according to this knowledge. So, instead of striving for success, people should leave that to the LORD and refrain from using whatever (even unethical) means in order to achieve their aims. Paradoxically, when someone is willing to let success go, then God will provide success.

4–6. One obvious difficulty that could be raised about verses 1–3 is whether it sufficiently allows for the presence of evil and the actions of wicked people in the world. This issue is addressed in verses 4–6. Verse 4 claims that even wrongdoers are not outside God's control, with verse 5 adding to this, stating that such people will be punished. The way forward from our own wrong thoughts and plans is to put God in his proper place (the fear of the Lord) and through having our character shaped (v. 6). Verse 4 is a clear expression of the creation theology of the book – that God is a purposeful Maker of everything. The word *purpose* (NIV, 'proper end', *ma'ănēh*) is the same as *answer* in verse 1, but the underlying root has various streams (answer, afflict, be occupied with), so this is simply literary artistry using the same word but with a different sense here of 'purpose' (based on *'nh*, 'to be occupied with'). The wicked will face a day of trouble or reckoning (this could be the one they suffer or the one they inflict), but no mention is made of when or how. The wisdom framework of thinking would envisage an accounting in this life, not beyond death. No explicit mention is made of God's involvement in bringing this about, but the picture of the first half of the verse is of God actively running his world.[39] Similarly, verse 5 does not specifically state that God will punish the arrogant, but the fact of their punishment (rather than the when and how) is stressed. The mention of the *arrogant in heart* draws attention to people being accountable before God for their thoughts and not only their actions (developed in vv. 18–19). Godless plans and thoughts are described in strong language as an *abomination to the LORD*, and will be punished. Since verse 5 should lead to self-examination, verse 6 provides the way forward. In terms familiar from chapters 1 – 9 (also 15:33), there is a commendation of the fear of the Lord, or the foundational and ongoing respecting God as God. This core idea of Proverbs surfaces in the theological kernel of the individual proverbs because it undergirds the observations made throughout the book. The references to *steadfast love* and *faithfulness* are representative of the changed character insisted on in chapters 1 – 9. Thus *iniquity is atoned for* (in parallel with *turns away from evil*), in the sense of helping to purge wrong thinking and doing from our lives.

7–9. These verses resume the positive thrust of verses 1–3, as well as developing the image in verse 6 of a life of steadfast love and faithfulness built on the foundation of the fear of the Lord. Verse 7 describes the beneficial effect on relationships that flows from a life that seeks to please God, probably an alternative description of the reality set out in verse 6. Actions that are based on turning away from evil and pursuing committed love and faithfulness are

---

39. Lucas (2015: 121) rightly cautions that 'It is not saying that God predestines certain individuals to act wickedly so that they will be punished.'

ways that *please the LORD*. The picture of restored, wholesome relationships (the *hifil* of *šlm*, 'to be at peace') is described hyperbolically
as including even one's enemies. This is not a promise (it was not
true of Jesus, for example), but a way of saying that a godly life will
usually lead to healthier relationships with others. Verse 8 suggests
that contentment is more important than great wealth (picked up in
1 Tim. 6:6–10, 17–19; see also 15:16), especially if the money has
been obtained in unjust ways. The word for 'revenue/income/gain'
often refers to agricultural produce (Exod. 23:10; Deut. 14:22; but
note the different sense in Prov. 3:14), so it could have in mind wealth
gained by the unjust seizure of fields belonging to others. Verse 9,
recalling verses 1–3, concludes with an observation that a person's
direction and actions in life are finally determined by God. This is
not to deny human responsibility for our choices, but rather to
remind us that God is still in charge of his world. As such, it is a
fitting conclusion to this theological kernel.

Meaning
This small section is utterly crucial in understanding how to read
the individual proverbs of chapters 10 – 22. Its importance is evident
in its structural location at the seam between the two halves (chs.
10 – 15 and 16 – 22; see below), suggesting that its key ideas stretch
in both directions. Behind the various specific observations of
chapters 10 – 22 is the foundation that God is at work, ordering his
world and setting out how to act in daily life. This is not secular
wisdom, for this pivotal hinge section, together with the foundation
of chapters 1 – 9, provides the theological undergirding of the
proverbs. While God may not be explicitly mentioned in most of
the individual sayings, his behind-the-scenes activity and order are
to be assumed. This section helps to transform the many sayings
that do not specifically allude to God by providing them with a
theological context. God is at work in ordering daily life.

C. The second half of Solomon's sayings (16:10 – 22:16)

Context
This section lacks the (arguably) more observable structure and
groupings of chapters 10 – 15. However, there are a number of

features that mark them off from the earlier sentence sayings. First, the dominant type of parallelism in chapters 10 – 15 is antithetical (163 out of 183 verses, for those interested in statistics), with contrasting ideas in the two halves (often including 'but'). However, the parallelism in 16:10 – 22:16 is much more varied, with synonymous and step parallelism more prominent. Second, chapters 10 – 15 set out the basic principles about what flows from either a righteous or wicked character, but chapters 16 – 22 develop some of the exceptions to these rules as well.⁴⁰ Third, there is little focus on the king in chapters 10 – 15 (only in 14:28, 35), but the king is much more common in chapters 16 – 22 (16:10, 12, 13, 14, 15; 17:7; 19:12; 20:2, 8, 26, 28; 21:1). Fourth, there are few 'better than' sayings in chapters 10 – 15 (12:9; 15:16–17), but these are more frequent in chapters 16 – 22 (16:8, 16, 19, 32; 17:1; 19:1, 22; 21:9, 19; 22:1). This type of saying provides a form of prioritization or evaluation as one thing is judged to be superior to another. Thus, it highlights the foundational virtue of discernment, of being able to distinguish between things of a different type.

These observations do not provide evidence of structure in chapters 16 – 22, but they do suggest at least some attempt at grouping the collection and distinguishing it from the first half of the Solomonic collection.

16:10–15
Context
This section centres on the king, who is explicitly mentioned in verses 10, 12, 13, 14, 15. Verse 11 – the only verse that does not mention the king – links these verses with the preceding 'theological kernel' of verses 1–9 by the presence of *the* LORD. Verses 10–12 focus on justice (*mišpāṭ*) and righteousness (*ṣĕdāqâ*), with justice in trade (v. 11) fitting nicely between the mention of justice/judgment in verse 10 and righteousness in verse 12. Verses 13–15 all concern the king's reaction to those who appear before him. Verse 13

---

40. So Bartholomew (2001: 11–13); also Van Leeuwen (2005: 638): 'Prov. 10–15 teaches the elementary pattern of acts and consequences, while chs. 16–29 develop the exceptions to the rules.'

mentions speech that pleases the king (*righteous* lips, *ṣedeq*; 'honest', NIV; links with *righteousness* in v. 12). Verse 14 also deals with words, but only implicitly, for the wise man will appease the king by words. In verse 15 what will change a king's face and bring favour is often words. So verses 10–12 deal with justice and the king, while verses 13–15 concentrate on words before the king.

Comment

10–12. The king is a source of useful direction when he speaks with an authoritative word. *Oracle* (*qesem*, 'inspired decisions', NRSV) usually refers to a decision or prediction that is based on divination. However, pagan kings and mediums use divination (e.g. Ezek. 21:21; 1 Sam. 28:8). Even the prophets try to deceive by 'lying divinations' (e.g. Ezek. 13:6–9; Mic. 3:11). Divination is therefore unlikely to be commended here, and so the word *oracle* is best understood in a derived sense to describe a divinely given word of guidance. The parallelism with the second half of the verse makes it clear that this is a reliable word. The force is that when a leader is given a word from God, he will not err in a judgment (or justice) based on this word. A leader who walks closely with God can be trusted.

While verse 11 does not deal with the king, it uses the same word for justice (or judgment; 'honest', NIV) that is found in verse 10. Justice is present in the king (v. 10), but it must also be found among the people (v. 11) as they buy and sell their goods. Balances, scales and weights describe these commercial transactions. The need for commerce to be just is a frequent theme in the book (e.g. 11:1; 20:10, 23). Underlying this implied call for justice in business and daily life is the assumption that all things (including the objects we use to defraud others) belong to God, the Creator or Maker of everything. When we use what belongs to God, we are to do so justly.

Verse 12 returns to the king, and states that kings should or do regard wickedness as an abomination ('kings detest wrongdoing', NIV), because any lasting claim to power (*kissē'*, *throne*) can only be made to stand (*established*) through righteousness (see also 14:34; 25:5). Righteousness is a core biblical value that describes individuals fulfilling all the demands of their relationships. For rulers, it would imply building up the community, and a genuine concern for the well-being of those under them. This is godly leadership.

13–15. These proverbs seem to be interconnected, with the importance of right speech being established in verse 13, followed by two situations where suitable words produce more positive outcomes. Kings delight in, or approve of, righteous (NIV, 'honest') words. *Righteous* refers to the appropriate expression of your relationship or role. For a court advisor, it would involve keeping the king informed of relevant facts, providing astute analysis and avoiding foolish and self-serving ideas. In our different world and relationships, the same principle would remain, but might be applied in more contemporary ways. In the second half of verse 13 kings love (*'hb*, NIV, 'value') not just the words, but the person who speaks what is (up)right, or morally straight.

Verse 14 addresses a common complication of a powerful person being angry. The wrath of the king is described as terrifying (like the growling of a lion) in 19:12 and 20:2. Here it is a messenger of (something that brings) death.[41] In light of verse 13, it is the words of the wise that will avert or appease this wrath. It is not stated whether the anger will be directed against the advisor or others, but the focus is on the significant impact that wise words will have. A positive side of this is shown in verse 15, for such upright and insightful words can have a positive effect on the mood of a leader (*the light of a king's face*, ESV/NRSV; 'when a king's face brightens', NIV). The beneficial consequences of this are outlined as life and favour (*rāṣôn*, a noun from the same root as 'delight in/approve' in v. 13) and in the image of life-giving spring rain that will enable crops to survive. Wise, skilful words have real value in effecting change.

16:16–20
Context
Two 'better than' sayings (vv. 16, 19) highlight that this section is contrasting the path of the proud with those who choose the way of wisdom. The distinctive teaching of these proverbs is about the

---

41. Strictly *messenger* is plural. Fox (2009: 616) suggests that the underlying image is of a king in his wrath sending out many deadly messengers in all directions.

folly of pride (vv. 18–19), which seems connected to the pursuit of wealth (*šālāl*, spoil or plunder, v. 19b) but which is ultimately self-destructive (v. 18). Against this backdrop of pride, readers are urged to choose wisdom rather than wealth (v. 16), to avoid evil ways and preserve their life (v. 17), and to trust in the Lord (v. 20). The path of the proud is yet another example of folly when compared to all that wisdom has to offer.

Comment

16–17. This 'better than' saying points to the value of seeking the familiar pairing of wisdom and understanding. This is a key theme of chapters 1 – 9, seen in 2:2–4; 4:7–9, 20–22 and most specifically in the contrasts of 8:10–11, 19. The seduction of wealth is that it can give a sense of power and status, and so lead easily to pride. The focus is broadened out in verse 17 with references to a wise person's fundamental path through life (*highway*, *way*). The language used here of turning aside (13:14; 14:27; 15:24; 16:6) from evil, guarding one's way and preserving one's life has earlier been used of character (*šmr* and *nṣr* in 2:11). The foundational choice of those who choose the straight path (the upright) leads to a godly character which offers true life.

18–19. The contrast between this wise way of life and the path of pride is drawn out in the familiar proverb in verse 18. Pride and a haughty spirit are parallel terms, while the word for the proud in verse 19b is derived from the same root as pride. They are three descriptions of the one fault, not three separate groups. The attraction of self-seeking pride is hinted at in verse 19b, in that it can lead to much wealth at the expense of others. However, the core truth established by verse 18 is that it comes at great cost to oneself as well, for it is often a short-lived prelude to a destructive end. The lesson drawn out in verse 19 is that it is preferable to be of a lowly spirit, in contrast to the haughty spirit of verse 18b. Lowly of spirit refers to humility, and such people associate with those who are poor, afflicted or oppressed. The mention of the proud enjoying (temporary) plunder and the seemingly righteous poor indicates that Proverbs itself realizes that the wise do not prosper all the time, nor are the wicked punished without exception. Temporary suffering and prosperity can also be observed.

20. The positive thrust of this section is reinforced in this final verse. It commends the path of wisdom as trusting in the Lord. Such a person is *blessed* (v. 20b, *'ašrê*, ESV/NIV; 'happy', NRSV) or to be envied, and will prosper (NIV/NRSV; lit. 'find good', v. 20a). The first part of verse 20a is open to a number of translations. The general words used could refer to those who find success in a matter, those who pay attention to a word (ESV) or matter, or those who give heed to instruction (NIV). The parallel with trusting in the Lord suggests that it is not just pragmatic ('being attentive to a matter', NRSV), but rather being shaped by the way and character of wisdom and her words.

16:21–24
Context
This small section revolves around the positive value of speech, made explicit in verses 21, 23, 24 and perhaps implied in *instruction* in verse 22. There are a number of repeated words and phrases (not always evident in our translations): wise in heart (vv. 21, 23); sweet (vv. 21, 24); lips (vv. 21, 23); instruction (vv. 21, 23); adds (vv. 21, 23); prudent (vv. 22, 23). These verses commend wholesome speech as the outworking of a well-shaped character.

Comment
21, 23. These two verses parallel each other quite closely. The *wise of heart* (*ḥākām lēb*, v. 21) and the *heart of the wise* (*lēb ḥākām*, v. 23) both refer to the same reality of skilful living based on a godly character. Such people are *discerning* (able to make appropriate distinctions; Fox, 'astute') and their speech (lit. 'mouth', a common Hebrew habit of referring to parts of the body such as ears, eyes and mouth to describe hearing, sight and speech) is edifying ('make prudent', NIV; *make judicious*, ESV/NRSV). This speech is attractive or desirable and promotes instruction or persuasiveness (vv. 21b, 23b; most likely 'increases in learning' as in 1:5; 9:9). The loose woman also has persuasive speech (7:21), but it is directed to a less wholesome goal.

22. This verse is the least integrated into the cluster, and the second line is the only negative idea in the section. A person who masters 'prudence' (*śēkel*, NIV; 'wisdom', NRSV; *good sense*, ESV) –

literally the 'lord of prudence', one who is able to control his
character and actions – is described as a *fountain of life* (see also 10:11;
13:14; 14:27). In a desert culture where life depends on water, this is
an image of abundant, overflowing life as it was meant to be. The
second line of this verse is more ambiguous and variously rendered
(*the instruction of fools is folly*, ESV; 'folly brings punishment to fools',
NIV; 'folly is the punishment of fools', NRSV). However, the core
meaning of 'instruction' (*mûsār*) in Proverbs is 'discipline' or 'shaping'
(see 1:2), so it most likely refers here to using words (and perhaps
actions) to mould or correct the fool. This line concludes that it is
simply a waste of effort trying to change those who refuse to be
shaped by wisdom. Others suggest that it could mean that fools
need to learn a lesson by experiencing the consequences of their
foolish actions (so Waltke 2005: 30), or that fools themselves teach
what is foolish (so Fox 2009: 620).

24. This verse returns to the theme of pleasant words, with
a straightforward comparison of a honeycomb. Pleasant words (a
different word from that used in v. 21, but the force is similar) are
both attractive to the taste ('sweet') and beneficial (*health*) to the body
(lit. 'bones', but the whole body is implied). Perhaps it suggests that
wholesome words are not only pleasing to hear, but can also begin
to repair the damage caused by the hurtful words of others.

16:25–30

Context

In contrast to the previous and following sections, verses 25–30
(with the possible exception of v. 26) focus on negative images,
expressed in various forms of evil behaviour. They describe the
way of the wicked (v. 25), the worthless person or scoundrel (v. 27),
the perverse gossip (v. 28) and the violent person (v. 29) who acts
as a deceiver (v. 30). There is concentration on both their plans and
actions. Clifford (1999: 161) sees a progression in the second lines
of verses 27–29 from thought (v. 27) to speech (v. 28) to actions
harming others (v. 29). Indeed, each of verses 27–29 begin with
the same word (*'îš*, a person), binding them together. Even the
seemingly anomalous verse 26 may refer to someone being driven
by hunger to do something (unspecified) that he or she should
not do.

Comment

25. This proverb is identical to 14:12. The context of both proverbs is a group of negative characters. This is not a description of all people, for the focus is on the wicked, that is to say, those whose end point is the way of death. The wicked may think that they are in control of their life, but, like the guests of Dame Folly (9:18), it will end in an untimely death.

26. The thrust of this proverb is not transparent, in part because it is only an observation without an explicit evaluation (Williams 1981: 52 cites this verse to establish that proverbs can have multiple interpretations). On the one hand, it could simply mean that the hunger or appetite of workers (lit. life or soul, but sometimes it means hunger or appetite, as in 6:30; 10:3; 13:25) makes them keep on working in order to get food to satisfy their stomach. If so, it is just a description of a normal human process that we are geared to work in order to meet our physical needs. However, given the negative examples that surround it, it is more likely to imply that their hunger causes them to act in a way that is not right, but becomes desirable because of the extent of their hunger. If so, their needs are driving them to act wrongly.

27–30. Here are examples of a range of wrongdoers, echoing 6:12–19. In verse 27 a worthless person ('scoundrel', NIV, NRSV; see 6:12 for comments on a similar term) plans (normally 'digs'; Waltke 2005: 23–24 suggests 'prepares') evil for others and is characterized by destructive speech (compared to a fire burning out of control). Verse 28 describes a perverse person (ESV's *dishonest* is too weak) who spreads discord. The *whisperer* ('gossip', NIV; see 18:8; 26:20, 22) may be a separate person, but is more likely to be specifying the way such people twist or pervert the situation. As in verse 27, their speech is destructive, separating a close friendship by gossip. Violence has already been associated with the wicked (e.g. 10:6, 11; 13:2; also 1:8–19), and the role of the violent person is to entice (*pth* is usually translated 'deceive' or 'mislead', e.g. 24:28) another down a way of life that is *not good* – a parallel expression to the way of death in verse 25. Verse 30 also describes one who deceives. 'Winking the eye' has previously appeared in 6:13 and 10:10 (but using the verb translated as *purses* in this verse; also Ps. 35:19) to imply a negative action associated with deceiving. The expression of pursing ('compresses',

NRSV) the lips is not used elsewhere, but both the parallelism and the outcome suggest that it is deceptive conduct as well. Thus, in contrast to the wholesome speech of verses 21–24, the destructive speech and the twisted actions of the wicked lead to harmful consequences.

16:31 – 17:3
Context
After the negative images of 16:25–30, there is a more positive focus in this loosely arranged group. There are two sections (16:31–33 and 17:1–3), each of which contains a 'better than' saying, an antithetical proverb with a Yahweh saying, and a proverb containing step parallelism. While there is no common subject area, they are largely about character: righteousness, patience, self-control, submission to God, contentment, prudence and the heart.

Comment
31–33. Grey hair is a positive symbol of the aged (see 20:29), and there is in Hebrew culture a high view of the valuable contribution made by the elderly. Waltke (2005: 36) sees old age pictured here 'as a time of authority, status, and dignity symbolized by a crown'. The word 'splendour'/*glory* (*tip'eret*) is linked to the aged in 17:6 and 20:29, while the word *crown* (*ăteret*) is seen here and in 17:6. They are also both used in 4:9 to describe a gift from wisdom. Since the aged were so highly regarded, verse 31 describes those who have grown old 'gracefully' as having lived a life of right relationships (or righteousness).

Verse 32 endorses the virtue of self-control, by way of a 'better than' comparison. It is a good thing to be able to conquer and control a complex society like a city-state, but how much more of an achievement to *rule over his* [own] *spirit* ('one with self-control', NIV; see 25:28). As Clifford (1999: 162) puts it, 'Conquest of self is better than conquest of others.' In the first half of the verse this is expressed as *whoever is slow to anger* (as in 14:29; 15:18; Jas 1:19–20). They may feel angry on occasions, but they do not let their anger determine their actions.

Finally, in verse 33 there is an emphasis on another kind of control – God's planned, sovereign control over all that happens.

This theme has already been seen in verses 1 and 9 and perhaps in verse 25 as well. Contemporary readers often think of casting the lot as an expression of chance, but to the Hebrews it was a way of handing the decision-making back to God (see 18:18). It is clear that every *decision* (or 'judgment' about what will happen) is from the Lord (see Esth. 3:7; Acts 1:24–26).

This small subsection thus commends those who live righteously through a long life, those who exercise self-control and those who trust God to bring about the best outcomes.

1–3. Another 'better than' saying introduces this subsection by claiming that a life worth living is one of wholesome relationships, even if the food is ordinary (dry bread), rather than disrupted relationships, even where the food is ample and rich (feasting on meat offered in sacrifices). Right relationships are more important than prosperity, comfort or the other so-called good things in life (see 15:17). Alden (1983: 132) comments that 'the people you eat with are more important than what's on the menu.' The desirable state of *quiet* (*šalwâ*; NIV, 'peace and quiet') has the sense of peace and tranquillity, of relationships as they were designed to be. *Strife* (*rîb*), on the other hand, has the sense of striving, quarrelling or contending, and is commonly used to describe a breakdown of relationships that requires a legal case to settle.[42]

Verse 2 extols the virtue of being wise or prudent, and so successful in life. Even if you are only a servant, this skill or trait is so valuable that it outweighs the advantage that a son might have. The son is described as acting *shamefully*, which is not a natural opposite of wisdom for those in the West, but makes good sense in an honour/shame culture (so 10:5; 14:35). A wise servant's actions will add to the honour or reputation of a family, but a child who brings shame or dishonour on the family prevents life in all its fullness. The

---

42. Waltke (2005: 39) comments, 'The proverb instructs the disciple in several ways: (1) to prefer a frugal meal with family concord, not a sumptuous one with discord; (2) to accept a modest lifestyle of having not even sufficient produce and therefore a respect for the produce of others; and (3) to be ready to lower radically his economic expectations, and even his rights, to enjoy a feeling of well-being.'

wise servant is rewarded in outward terms by being included in the inheritance as if he were a son.

The final Yahweh saying (v. 3) speaks of God testing hearts. While this can refer to testing to punish the disobedient (as in 21:2), it is also used of testing metal to show that it is genuine or valuable (e.g. Ps. 12:6; Zech. 13:9). This is the very image of the first half of verse 3 (as also in 27:21), so it is likely referring to the positive testing of character in the whole section of 16:31 – 17:2 and perhaps beyond. God tests and approves of those whose godly character can be seen in their actions.

17:4–16

Context

Chapter 17 has little observable structure (Murphy 1998: 127 calls it 'a hodgepodge of sayings'). Even Heim concedes that 'there is a greater variety of themes in Proverbs 17 than in previous chapters, and obvious links are missing' (Heim 2001: 204). Yet verses 4–16 are predominantly about various kinds of fools and evildoers, with the exception of verse 6 and perhaps verse 10. The remainder of chapter 17 still has a focus on fools and wrongdoers, but there are more pictures of positive characters.

Comment

4–5. All the examples here concern wrong responses to other people. The two parallel lines in verse 4 both refer to listening or giving credence to destructive and false words (Waltke 2005: 41 thinks that it pictures the liar whose speech unleashes misery on the community). This could be gossip spread about another, or it could simply be words that will lead the impressionable astray. Those who promote such words by accepting them become evil and deceptive, that is to say, they become like the words themselves. Verse 5 outlines two situations of speaking words – mocking those least able to stand up for themselves (the poor), and rejoicing at the setbacks others suffer (i.e. *Schadenfreude*).[43] In both wrong listening and wrong

---

43. Fox (2009: 626) comments, 'God cares not only about visible offenses (v 5a) but about unspoken attitudes as well (v 5b).'

speaking, they reveal a lack of wisdom and character. Even more seriously, they dishonour God. This is seen most clearly in the mocking of the poor. Since God is described as their *Maker*, they show scant regard for the Creator God who has made all people in his image (14:31; Gen. 1:26–28).

6. This verse echoes 16:31 (*crown, glory*) and anticipates 20:29. The delights of being a grandparent are not the focus, just as having grey hair alone is not evidence of high status (16:31; 20:29). Yet they are both symbols of a long life, which Proverbs presents as coming from living a life of wisdom (e.g. 3:2). Thus, the *crown of the aged* is placed emphatically at the beginning of the verse. This makes sense of the second line. The parents of whom their children are proud, even boasting (NIV rightly picks up this sense of 'pride'), are – in light of 16:31 – parents who have lived righteously, their lives shaped by wisdom.

7–8. The focus here is on manipulating others by either speech (v. 7) or the use of money (v. 8). *Fine speech* (*śĕpat yeter*; lit. 'lips/speech of excess') probably refers to arrogant words (but Waltke 2005: 43 translates it as 'eloquent'; Fox 2009: 627 suggests 'excessive speech'). To speak like this is not appropriate for one who lacks wisdom. *False speech* covers deceitful words. A ruler should put the well-being of the people first. A modern equivalent would be to say that politicians should not lie to their constituency. Verse 8 deals with a related way of manipulating a situation through the offering of a bribe. The *magic stone* (NIV, 'charm'; lit. 'stone of grace/favour', ensuring a favour from others) is a vivid picture of the way a bribe can get you a favour. There is no explicit condemnation of bribery here, and indeed the only comment made is that it succeeds. A common practice in Proverbs is simply to describe the consequences of an action, rather than evaluate the action. The reader is meant to ask whether such manipulation is the outworking of wisdom or not. While other proverbs like 21:14 observe that a bribe can be effective, a bribe is also regarded in the book as undermining justice (17:23) and only working in the short term (15:27).

9–14. These proverbs deal generally with conflict, choices and broken relationships. In verses 9–10 both a positive and a negative response are outlined, but the focus is only on the fool or wrongdoer in verses 11–14. When a transgression occurs (v. 9), it exposes the heart of the one who responds. Those who try to cover over the offence, preventing news of it from spreading, are seeking to promote love (10:12), but if they pass it on like gossip, they betray a willingness for friendships to be broken (see 16:28). The person of understanding (v. 10a; see 1:5) allows a rebuke to sink deeply within (Waltke 2005: 43, 'penetrates'), presumably using the situation to help in maturity and growth. The contrast in verse 10b is that a fool learns nothing even from a major impact (a hundred blows or lashes). This echoes the observations of 9:7–9.

Verses 11–14 all seek to dissuade a person from the way of the fool or wrongdoer, but an imperative 'stop' is only explicitly found at the end of verse 14. In verse 11 evildoers only seek to rebel against those in authority (Whybray 1994: 257 notes that *měrî* almost always refers to rebellion against God), but their rebellion will be met by a cruel messenger (probably an 'enforcer' as in 16:14a, since that is where cruelty will show. This may be a divine passive, i.e. 'sent by God', and leads to death). Mixing with fools who indulge their folly (v. 12) is as self-destructive as approaching a female bear robbed of her cubs. This is not innocent behaviour, but rather a dangerous practice. Verse 13 draws attention to the consequence of a (wicked) person paying back evil for good. What evildoers try to inflict on others (evil) is the very thing that will always be present in their own house. The beginning of a conflict situation is described as *letting out water*, but the NIV captures the image well: 'breaching a dam' (v. 14). A bursting dam initially lets out only small amounts of water, but it is only a matter of time before a trickle becomes a flood. The advice of verse 14 is to nip conflict in the bud by stopping before the quarrel fully breaks out.

15–16. While many proverbs do not explicitly outline God's attitude to a variety of actions, verse 15 makes it clear that he detests both those (judges, so Whybray 1994: 258) who seek to justify (declare righteous) the wicked person and those who condemn (as wicked; there is the double use of *ṣdq*, 'to be righteous', and *rš'*, 'to act wickedly') the righteous. In strong language, God calls both practices an abomination (*abomination to the LORD* is also used in 3:32; 6:16; 11:1, 20; 12:22; 15:8–9, 26; 16:5; 20:10, 23). Verse 16 describes another anomaly of a fool who has shekels but no sense. In fact, the strange aspect of this (presumably observed) scenario is that the

fool is trying to acquire or buy wisdom, but (lit.) 'there is no heart'.
As seen in chapters 1 – 9, wisdom has to be sought earnestly in the
heart (e.g. 2:10), the very core of your being. It is folly to think that
it can be bought with money (e.g. 8:10–11; Job 28:15–19).

17:17–28
Context
In the rest of chapter 17 there is no coherent structure overall, but
there are some connections between verses. So *loves* appears in verses
17, 19; *friend/neighbour* in verses 17, 18; *heart* in verses 18, 20, 22; 'fool'
in verses 21, 24, 25 (and a different word for fool in v. 28); the idea
of injustice in verses 23, 26; restraining words in verses 27, 28.

Comment
17–19. These verses outline a number of issues that can be
helpful or destructive in relationships. Siblings and friends are
sometimes contrasted in Proverbs (e.g. 18:24; 27:10), but in verse 17
both show their value in difficult times. This positive note is
counterbalanced by verses 18–19. The scenario behind verse 18 is
a person who puts up financial collateral for someone he thought
was a friend (*neighbour, rēă'*, is translated *friend* in v. 17, and can refer
to either), and presumably suffers financial loss (see 6:1–5; 22:26–27).
Here the friend or neighbour creates the adversity rather than
helping in the midst of it. The verb *loves* from verse 17 appears twice
in verse 19. Now, instead of loving a friend, they love sin or transgression, strife or a quarrel (it is not clear from the Hebrew in v. 19a
which is the subject and which is the predicate; compare the NIV
and ESV/NRSV). Loving a friend brings support; loving a quarrel
leads to separation and sin. The image of making your door,
threshold or gate high is a way of saying that you are making it
difficult for people to enter your home. This is a rejection of friendship or relationship and, like loving strife, leads to destructive
consequences.

20–22. There is a contrast between one who is crooked of heart
(v. 20, see 11:20), who does not find *good* (i.e. fulfilment or success),
and one whose heart of joy (v. 22; see 15:13) is *good* medicine. Verses
20 and 22 highlight the negative side of this contrast, observing that
a perverted tongue (not being used for its proper purpose) leads to

disaster (v. 20b) and a crushed spirit dries up your life and vitality (v. 22b; lit. 'bones'). In between these two verses is verse 21, which outlines the same truth in both halves: those who have a foolish son experience sorrow but no joy (see also v. 25). This is actually the same contrast between one who is crooked of heart and the other who has a heart of joy.

23–26. This loose section deals at its borders with those who promote injustice (vv. 23, 26). While a bribe was described more neutrally in verse 8, here it is clearly set out as turning aside the ways of justice (as in Exod. 23:6). Two examples of injustice are given in verse 26: fining a righteous person who presumably did not deserve it, and physically striking a noble or honourable person (NIV, 'flog honest officials') because they have done what is right rather than any wrong. The one with understanding (v. 24, i.e. the discerning or wise person) focuses on wisdom (whose task it is to guard the *paths of justice*, 2:6–9; Steinmann 2009: 382–383, however, sees a connection rather to 4:25–27), but the fool looks at anywhere but wisdom – even to the ends of the earth (not so much a location but a contrast with where the discerning person is looking).[44] Verse 25 then expands the picture of this foolish son (echoing 10:1), suggesting that in avoiding wisdom and promoting injustice, he brings grief to his father and bitterness (or perhaps 'bitter grief'; this is the only time this word is used in the OT, but the common underlying root means 'to be bitter') to his mother.

27–28. The chapter ends with two verses concentrating on speech. Verse 27 does not initially identify the subject as a wise person, but those who exercise control or restraint over the words they speak are described as 'knowing knowledge', an emphatic expression highlighting their wisdom. In the second half of verse 27 a person of understanding is described as having a *cool* or 'fresh' spirit (this is based on retaining the *ketib* reading; the *qere* is a 'precious' or 'rare' spirit). Such individuals are not likely to 'lose their cool' and say words in a 'heated argument' that they later regret.

---

44. Whybray (1994: 262) suggests that 'his attention is always wandering';
     Waltke (2005:62) proposes that 'he orients himself to distant, godless,
     and unattainable goals instead of on attainable wisdom'.

Whoever has a *cool spirit* exercises self-control over what they say (see 16:32). Verse 28 is a kind of aside, giving some advice to the fool. Even if you are a fool, if you do not speak, people will not know how foolish you are (since your words would betray you), and so might give you the benefit of the doubt. If you say nothing, people may still assume that you are wise or intelligent.

18:1–8

Context

Words are connected to the first eight verses, linking with 17:27–28, which is also about speech. Verse 1 speaks of starting quarrels (NIV) by words, while verse 2 refers to airing one's own opinions. Verse 3 is not necessarily about words, but contempt, reproach and shame are often transmitted by words. The rest of the verses make fairly obvious connections: verse 4 – the words of the mouth; verse 5 – being partial through words; verse 6 – the lips of fools; verse 7 – a fool's mouth; verse 8 – the words of a gossip. So words or speech are used clearly in 17:27 – 18:2, 4, 6–8 and are implied in 18:5 and possibly in 18:3 (in partial qualification of Murphy 1998: 134, who writes, 'The structure, or better the lack of it, characterizes this chapter as well as the previous one').

Comment

1. Verse 1 can be variously translated because of the range of meanings for some of the key words. The subject is described as 'one being separated' (*niprād*), probably someone who goes off alone.[45] Such a person pursues or seeks *desire*, which can have a positive meaning as in 13:12 (*a desire fulfilled is a tree of life*), or something craved for or coveted. Most English versions translate it with a negative connotation here (e.g. 'self-indulgent', NRSV; 'selfish ends', NIV; 'goes his own way', Murphy 1998), and that makes good sense as the second half of the verse is clearly critical of the person.

---

45. As in Gen. 13:9; ESV here translates as *isolates himself*; NIV interprets this as 'an unfriendly person'. Longman (2006: 354) prefers to translate it as 'antisocial', someone who is internally divided, not separated from others.

Against all wisdom or sound judgment, such a person 'bursts out' – a verb found only in this section of Proverbs, being used of a quarrel breaking out, and parallel to strife or dispute in 17:14 and 20:3. So it has the sense here of 'starts quarrels' (NIV).

2–3. Fools need to learn much in order to be wise, but the nature of folly is that they do not listen to others, but simply proclaim their own (foolish) opinions (v. 2, lit. 'their heart'; see 12:23b). They have 'a closed mind and an open mouth' (Waltke 2005: 69). Most of us need to speak less and listen more. Verse 3 outlines a snowballing of folly from wickedness to a contemptuous dishonouring of others, to disgrace or shame. This is why our foundational choice of wisdom or folly (chs. 1 – 9) is so vital, as each leads to different consequences.

4–8. These verses describe some helpful (v. 4) or harmful (vv. 5–8) uses of words. The words of a person are described as *deep waters* (v. 4a), but the metaphor is not explained (but see 20:5a). There is debate about whether the two lines are synonymous or contrasting. While the former is more likely, if they are contrasted, then the image of *deep waters* is a negative one. It may refer to their hiddenness or strength, but the force of the second line is that a person's underlying wisdom gushes forth like a stream and brings life. At the very least, our words should reflect and express our wisdom within. Yet not all words are characterized by this wisdom. Verse 5 has a legal setting, and words used in that context can (wrongly) show partiality or favour to the undeserving wicked, stripping the righteous of the justice that should be shown to them. Words should rather be used to promote righteousness and bring fair consequences to the wicked, as in 17:15, 26. Verses 6 and 7 personify a fool's speech (lips and mouth) and list four negative characteristics. Such speech leads to disputes (ESV, *walk into a fight*), invites a response of a physical beating, is a cause for ruin (used in this sense in 10:14; 21:15), and is a trap for the fool's life (*soul* has the sense of 'life' here).[46] These

---

46. Waltke (2005: 73) comments, 'The wise person seeks to avoid conflict (cf. 17:1, 14; 20:3; 30:33) or to resolve it (cf. 15:18; 18:17–18; 25:9; 26:17, 21). In 20:3 avoiding controversy is equated with being held in honor (i.e., enjoying social esteem).'

are all consequences of speaking before thinking, and the fool's words reveal their real nature and life direction. Wisdom needs to be cultivated so that when we speak, godly wisdom will be the source of what we say. Verse 8 focuses on a specific misuse of words – to spread gossip. A *whisperer* (NIV, 'gossip') in Proverbs is one who spreads destructive gossip (16:28; 26:20, 22), destroying the reputation of others and provoking quarrels. It is something that Christians are not immune from in 'sharing prayer points' with others. In verse 8 the whisperer's words are described as being like choice pieces of food (in reality, Van Leeuwen 1997: 173 suggests, destructive 'junk food'), tempting us to do something we should avoid. Words can bring great benefit or great harm. Gossip thrives on the human desire to know something not known by others, and then to think of ourselves as better than others.

18:9–24
Context
There is no close cohesion in this section, nor any dominant emphasis. However, most of the proverbs concern life in society, and especially how to build up community rather than destroy it. A number of these observations are made without any explicit evaluation (e.g. vv. 11, 16, 17, 23). The community is not necessarily ideal in these verses, but a community is to be based on the Lord (v. 10), settling disputes (vv. 16–19), marriage (v. 22) and friendship (v. 24). Some of these emphases on community continue in chapter 19. As speech has an important role in community, words are again the focus in verses 13, 20–21, 23.

Comment
9. This proverb shows clear discontinuity with the preceding section. Those who reveal themselves to be slack in their work are described as belonging to the same group (lit. 'he is a brother to') as those who lord it over others (lit. a 'lord' or 'master', *ba'al*, but having a negative thrust here; hence *destroys*, ESV, NIV). Elsewhere in the book the lazy are seen to be hurting themselves by their lack of effort (e.g. 6:6–11; 19:15; 20:4; 21:25–26; 24:30–34), but this proverb suggests that their laziness affects others (as in 10:26), just like those who flaunt their power.

10–11. These proverbs address the issue of where people place their trust. Verse 11 describes the rich person who finds that wealth offers security and self-sufficiency, an ability to ride out the storms life presents (although *in his imagination* or 'conceit' may suggest some criticism. Waltke 2005: 77 contrasts the imaginary trust in visible wealth with the real security of trusting in the invisible God). The twin images of a strong city (see v. 19) and a high wall (see Isa. 30:13) are really two sides of the one scenario. In times of danger those in the countryside in Israel would flee to a walled (and thus strong) city which provided protection. It was generally an effective way to stay secure when danger threatened. This statement of material wealth giving self-sufficiency is not accompanied by any evaluation – such an attitude is seemingly just outlined and neither commended nor condemned. However, its juxtaposition with verse 10 suggests the need for a more foundational trust in God, rather than simply in wealth (see 10:15a). Verse 10 sets out the ideal of depending on God in times of trouble or danger. The name or character of God (Clifford 1999: 171 notes that this is the only time when the phrase 'name of Yahweh' appears in the book) is a strong tower (or fortress), and a righteous person runs there first and is truly safe (as in 29:25b). The phrase *is safe* (*śgb*) in verse 10 is the same verb (a participle used as an adjective) that describes a *high* wall in verse 11. While these proverbs do not undermine the role of wealth in providing security, they do remind us that this should be grounded on a prior trust in God for safety in a deeper sense. A community needs God at its core, and not simply money. Longman (2006: 357) comments, 'Wealth can help us navigate some problems in life, but it lets us down in the area of life's ultimate issues.'

12–15. Outlined here are a number of positive and negative attitudes that have an impact on living in community. Verse 12a is a variation on 'pride comes before a fall' (see also 16:18), observing the connection between a person's key attitude (haughtiness in the heart or core of our being, as in Ezek. 28:2) and the consequences that will often follow (breaking or wrecking). The idea of humility leading to honour or glory is also seen in 15:33 and 22:4, where humility (a right attitude to God, ourselves and others) is paralleled with the fear of the Lord, the foundation of wisdom (e.g. 1:7; 9:10). Since verses 10–11 focus on God as the proper foundation for trust, that suggests that *humility comes before honour* refers back to this crucial principle. The mention of honour in verse 12 also links with its opposite, shame, in verse 13. It is both foolish and dishonouring to the community (and to God) if we do not bother to listen to others, but instead focus only on what we will say (see vv. 2–3, although different words are used; see also 12:15). This would be a failure to treat others with the respect they deserve. The positive alternative is set out in verse 15, where an understanding mind (*heart*) and an ear given to wisdom seek to gain knowledge by learning from others. Whybray (1994: 270) comments, 'A desire for further education is the mark of the wise man.' The links with verse 14 are not as clear, but perhaps being regarded with contempt in verse 13 (by not being listened to) is the cause of the crushed spirit (note too the same sequence in verses 14–15 and 15:13–14). At the very least, a community that allows individuals to be crushed is lacking the wholeness that God intends for society (see also 15:13; 17:22).

16–19. These miscellaneous proverbs are all, at first glance, simply descriptions of the way of life in society, without any particular evaluation of whether it is helpful or harmful. A number of scholars (e.g. Whybray, Waltke, Lucas) see them as all having a courtroom setting. Gifts predispose others towards us (v. 16); it is easy to be persuaded by what we heard last (v. 17); having a decisive mechanism can resolve a dispute (v. 18); it is hard to overcome a quarrel when offence has been taken (v. 19). Yet there are some indications that not all these activities should be viewed neutrally. While there is room for gift-giving in society (e.g. to say thank you or express generosity), it can also become a bribe that seeks to pervert justice (e.g. 17:8; 29:4).[47] In the light of verse 11, offering a financial gift may also be an expression of trusting in wealth rather than in God. Verse 17 states no conclusion, but implies that listeners should not be convinced by the first person they hear. They should listen to other views as well. Verse 18 notes that the casting of lots can lead to a clear outcome in a dispute, but it does not necessarily say that

---

47. Kidner (1964: 129) notes that 'gift' (*mattān*) is a more neutral word than 'bribe' (*šōḥad*) in 17:8, 23. See Gen. 32:20; 43:11; 1 Sam. 17:18.

all disputes should be resolved in this way.[48] Verse 19 at one level simply describes the effect of quarrelling or taking offence, but this does not mean that matters should be left that way. It highlights the difficulty of overcoming disputes (especially with families), but the broader picture of the book is that it is worth working towards a positive end to any conflict.

20–21, 23. Since speech can have either a positive or negative effect in a community, the issue of words again reappears in both these aspects. The double mention of *is satisfied* in verse 20 makes it clear that speech can be fruitful (see also 12:14a; 13:2a). The idea of the first line is that those who speak well (e.g. carefully, truthfully, compellingly) can gain success and earn a living (e.g. by making a deal, motivating others, resolving problems). Their lips or speech produce a useful outcome which enables them to meet their needs (v. 20b). Similarly, in verse 21b those who *love it* (i.e. use the tongue in a right way, contra Whybray 1994: 273, who thinks it refers to being verbose) will prosper as a result. However, verse 21a tells us that the tongue can bring about either great damage (death) or very positive results (life). The implication is to make sure that our speech is used to build up rather than to tear down; to produce a good outcome rather than destructive consequences. Verse 23 also describes two different kinds of speech, one from the powerless (the poor) and one from the powerful (the rich). The poor ask and seek to persuade, for they are in need, but it is easy for the self-sufficient to be careless about their speech, since little rests on it as far as they can see. This is not an endorsement of these practices (especially the responses of the rich who answer *roughly*), but is an attempt to outline how society often works. The way forward for both the rich and poor is to use the tongue to bring life not death.

---

48. Van Leeuwen (1997: 174), followed by Lucas (2015: 133), suggests that the lot may have been used in legal proceedings when the argument was seen to be evenly balanced, although Lucas notes that there is no explicit example in the rest of the OT where a lot is used to resolve a legal dispute. Goldsworthy (1993: 133) suggests, 'The lot finds no place in the post-Pentecost church, as Christians today have recourse to the completed canon of Scripture.'

22, 24. Within a community there are also special relationships of great worth. Two are singled out at the end of this chapter: a wife and a close friend. The value of each is indicated by the accompanying descriptions. A wife is paralleled to 'what is good' (NIV), and this is qualified by *obtains favour from the LORD* (v. 22; see also 19:14). This latter phrase is used in 8:35 of finding wisdom, with *favour* (*rāṣôn*) having the sense of God's goodwill or pleasure. The gift of a spouse is a sign of God's goodness. So too is a friend. While the first half of verse 24 is elliptical, the ESV captures it well as *a man of many companions may come to ruin.*[49] The real point of verse 24 is to commend the friend ('one who loves') who clings to us closer than a brother (see also 17:17; 27:10). The love of a sibling ought to be a given, so an even stronger commitment than that is of great value.

19:1–3

Context

Proverbs 19:1–3 seems to deal with folly, explicitly in verses 1 and 3, but the image of feet missing the way in verse 2 also implies a fool. Waltke (2005: 93) sees 18:23 – 19:7 as a section concerning the moral ambiguities of wealth (although he concedes that vv. 1–3 is a subunit), with the rich attracting companions and the poor losing them, but the theme of wealth is not the core of verses 1–3. These

---

49. Lit. 'a man of friends', but the contrast with the exemplary friend in the second half of the verse implies a multitude of friends. Alternatively, the NRSV captures the sense as 'some friends play at friendship', as if it refers to those who pretend to be friends, but the translation of the verb is difficult to justify. Lucas (2015: 135) suggests that it requires a textual emendation. NIV has 'unreliable friends', but this is to make a different kind of contrast. The verb *rʿ* itself is difficult. It commonly means 'to do harm' (*rʿ* I); in the *hitpolel* (as here) it is likely to mean 'harm oneself/ one another', but it is not found elsewhere in that stem. Others see it as a *hitpolel* of *rʿ* II ('to break, shatter'), which could mean 'shatter one another', but the only other use in the *hitpolel* (Isa. 24:19) is not clearly reflexive. On either reading there is at least a possible disastrous outcome, in contrast with the second half of the verse.

verses explore the fundamental stance of the fool compared with that of a person of integrity.

Comment

1–3. The person of integrity is mentioned first in this 'better than' saying, but thereafter the focus is on the fool. Kidner (1964: 131) cleverly sees a distinction implied between one who is 'better' and one who is only 'better-off'. The image of walking in integrity is found elsewhere in Proverbs (e.g. 2:7; 10:9; 20:7; 28:6, 18), and in several of these other occurrences it is contrasted with the crooked or perverse person (10:9; 28:6 [poor/rich], 18; see also 11:3). The prevalence of this suggests a reference to a person's foundational attitude – as seen in chapters 1 – 9 – of choosing either wisdom or folly. Those who have determined their life direction have their character shaped by wisdom. While Proverbs often depicts a wise or righteous person prospering financially, both here and in 28:6 it is the poor person who walks in integrity.

The fool is introduced in verse 1, and his failings highlighted in verses 2–3. The distinguishing characteristic of fools in verse 1b is that their speech is crooked or perversely twisted from what it should be. Verse 2, linked to verse 1 by 'also/surely' (untranslated), criticizes the fool for acting without knowledge. The life or soul (*nepeš*, commonly translated 'desire', has in 6:30; 10:3; 13:25; 16:26; 23:2; 28:25 the sense of 'appetite'; see Waltke 2004: 90) needs to be shaped by content (knowledge). Otherwise, a person might not be heading in the right direction, or towards a helpful goal. So a fool can undertake much activity (*make haste*) but will be 'off-target' (e.g. 1:16). The word translated *misses his way* (ESV) is one of the common verbs in the OT for sin (*ḥṭʾ*), but can have the sense of 'miss the target' (8:36) or 'fail to attain a goal' (Isa. 65:20). The feet of fools have plenty of speed but they are heading in the wrong direction because they have chosen to follow folly, not the way of wisdom.[50] The destructive nature of folly is seen in verse 3, where the consequence

---

50. Clifford 1999: 176 notes that *nepeš*, which can mean 'throat', symbolizes the appetite, while 'feet' suggest physical movement, so that together they refer to the inner/thinking and outer/acting aspects of humans.

of people's folly is that their pathway is twisted or ruined (as in
21:12). The essence of their folly is that at the core of their being
(their *heart*), they are angry or enraged against God.[51] They have
missed the foundation of the fear of the Lord (1:7; 9:10).

19:4–9
Context
These verses are a likely section. The virtual duplication found in
verses 5 and 9, dealing with a false witness, draws the unit together
and gives a setting of a legal dispute. Verse 4, developed in verses 6
and 7, could also have in view a legal or court setting in which the
rich, or those offering a bribe, hold sway, while the poor are left
friendless. Verse 8 is less connected to the rest of the group, but it
may imply that the one who guards understanding (i.e. holds on to
the path of wisdom) will succeed in legal matters.

Comment
4, 6–7. These verses are comments on human behaviour that are
evident in the context of a legal tussle. In an ANE setting, where
community matters were decided at the city gate (see Ruth 4), the
wealthy have the means to win over friends to their side of an
argument. Money is often mentioned in Proverbs in the context of
a bribe or gift (e.g. 17:8, 23), and this accounts for verse 4. The
wealthy do not gain friends because they are nicer people (see 18:23),
but because they can offer some form of inducement – money now
or a favour in the future. Verse 4a is developed in verse 6, where
many seek the favour of a high-status or generous person (the
Hebrew word can mean a willing or generous person [ESV] or a noble
[NIV]; see 17:7, 26). The parallel in verse 6b makes the motivation
clear – such a person gives gifts (lit. 'a person of gifts'). This explains
verse 4b, since a poor person, by way of contrast, cannot afford to
give lavish gifts or promise favours. These are observations about
how society often works, with justice giving way to self-interest. The

---

51. Longman (2006: 365) and Lucas (2015:136) both quote Whybray (1994:
    276) with approval, noting that 'folly and blasphemy are closely linked
    here', but it appears to be anger against God rather than blasphemy.

proverbs are not endorsing these practices. Verses 6b–7 pick up the two categories from 18:24 (the friend and the brother), noting that even the closest of family members or friends *hate* (van Leeuwen 1997: 179 points out that it has the sense of 'shun'; Whybray 1994: 277 proposes 'dislike/avoid' here and in 11:15; 25:17) or 'distance themselves from' the poor person. The last part of verse 7 is more difficult to understand fully (many suggest textual corruption here), but the general sense is that the poor person unsuccessfully pleads for support from those supposedly 'close' to him. They are either not found, or unwilling to speak in his favour.

5, 9. These virtually identical proverbs have a clear judicial setting, with *witness* clearly being legal terminology. There is no concern with the process (how the false witness is punished, who orders it, etc.), but the verses simply focus on the fact that one who seeks to pervert justice will also justly receive punishment, and will not be cleared of guilt or exempt from punishment (see 6:29; 11:21; 17:5; 28:20). The passive sense might suggest that God will do this, but no special attention is drawn to his work. The second half of each verse describes this false witness as one who breathes out or testifies (the verb could mean either) lies (see similar language in 6:19; 14:5, 25). The sole variation in the two verses would be of little comfort for those who seek to twist justice. They will not escape/go free (v. 5b); they will perish or be destroyed (v. 9b).

8. The expression *gets sense* (lit. 'acquiring heart') is used elsewhere only in Proverbs in 15:32, but its opposite – to 'lack sense' – is very common (6:32; 7:7; 9:4, 16; 10:13, 21; 11:12; 12:11; 15:21; 17:18; 24:30). In 15:32 it is linked to accepting correction so as to be shaped into the kind of person who fears the Lord (15:33) and grows in character (Longman 2006: 367 is one of few commentators who thinks it means character here rather than mind). Lacking sense is often used to describe those who are not yet formed morally (e.g. 9:4, 16). In verse 8 it is the person who wants to be shaped by wisdom who is described as loving his [own] life. The parallel in verse 8b is that such a person guards understanding with the aim of finding what is good. Verse 8 thus describes the person of integrity mentioned in verse 1, and outlined in more detail in chapters 1 – 9.

19:10–19

Context

This loosely bound section deals with wisdom in community relationships such as the family (vv. 13–14, 18) and the king (v. 12). It deals with a number of positive virtues (e.g. being slow to anger, v. 11; godliness, v. 16; generosity, v. 17) as well as some problematic issues (e.g. laziness, v. 15; social confusion, v. 10; naivety, v. 19). A few of the verses deal with anger or wrath (vv. 11, 12, 19), which frequently destroys community.

Comment

10–12. Verse 10 outlines two scenarios that are *not fitting*: a fool living in luxury and a slave ruling princes.[52] The first is the obvious outworking of the wisdom principle that wisdom, not folly, will lead to success (e.g. 3:13–18), as 26:1 comments, it is not fitting for a fool to gain honour. However, the Hebrew intensifying expression beginning the second part of verse 10 (often in EVV, 'much less/worse') indicates that the real thrust of the proverb is in a court setting. This will also be picked up in verse 12, and may well be implied in verse 11. In light of verse 10a, the target of verse 10b is a foolish slave (30:22), not a former slave like the wise Joseph (Gen. 41:37–57). While verse 10b may involve a wider endorsement of an established social order, its primary focus is on the value of wisdom in ruling.[53] Verse 11 also has a wider application to all (wisdom leads us to be slow to anger [14:29; 16:32], seeking to overlook wrongs done to us [10:12; 17:9]), but the court setting of verses 10 and 12 gives a particular focus on those who have political power. Being in a position of power can lead to us acting too quickly to pay back our opponents and those who have offended us. Overlooking an offence and showing slowness to anger are signs that peace in the community is more important than our pride or status. It reflects

---

52. Fox (2009: 653) points out that this was 'enough of a possibility to warrant comment'.

53. Van Leeuwen (1997: 179) suggests it has 'an anti-revolutionary thrust', but this is to read too much of contemporary politics back into an ancient text.

the example of Joseph (Gen. 42 – 45) and Jesus (e.g. Phil. 2:3–8).
Strength of character (typical of one shaped by wisdom) is needed
to show others forgiveness and grace. Verse 12 describes rather than
endorses life in the royal court (16:14–15; 20:2). A lion growls to
warn off rivals or to intimidate its prey. In either case, this is a time
to avoid both a lion and a king. Yet a king who shows goodwill or
favour can be like the life-giving dew on grass (water symbolizes life
in the desert). There may be an implication to those in power to
bring life not death to those in their charge. At the very least, an
awareness of these two possible scenarios should make anyone
approaching people in power choose their timing well.

13–14, 18. In a family-based society members of a family can do
either great good or great harm to their relatives. A foolish child
(not just a son) can destroy a parent's reputation, circumstances or
even life. In Israelite society there was clear teaching about the
importance of disciplining as well as discipling their offspring (see
13:24). In verse 18 this practice is endorsed, with comment that there
is hope of change if they do so. The comment on not putting
children to death (v. 18b) seems strange to us, but perhaps reflects
the teaching of Deuteronomy 21:18–21. One of the principles
behind this passage in Deuteronomy is that rebellion within the
family can destroy the social fabric of the community, and so needs
to be addressed. Verse 18b could alternatively be translated as 'do
not make yourself responsible for his death' (so Steinmann: 2009:
403) by failing to restrain him from the way of folly.

The other relationship considered here is that of husband and
wife. A 'quarrelsome wife' (NIV; for justification of this, see Steinmann
2009: 404) is not simply a minor issue, but rather a constant
annoyance like the continual dripping of rain through a leaking roof.
Like the foolish child, she can ruin harmony in the family. However,
this criticism of a (foolish) wife in verse 13 is balanced by the prudent
or wise wife in the next verse. While some wives or women are
criticized in Proverbs (the loose woman of chs. 5 – 7; 11:22; 21:9,
19; 25:24; 27:15), they are not rebuked because of their gender, but
rather their character. The contrast in the book is not between men
and women, but between the foolish woman and the wise woman
(12:4; 9:1–6 and 13–18; 31:10–31). Thus, the focus in verse 14 is not
on the truth about inheritance in the first half, but on the wife who

serves as a contrast to the one in verse 13b. Such a wife is from the
Lord (emphasized in the Hebrew) and is (impliedly) a great gift to
receive (18:22), more important than wealth or property. Wisdom
again trumps folly.

15–17. Some vices destroy community, while virtues build it up.
Laziness (*'aṣlâ, slothfulness*, ESV) and idleness are singled out in verse
15 as destructive, leading to an unproductive *deep sleep* or simply to
hunger. If nothing gets done, nothing is achieved – even staying
alive. This is an example of folly. The theme of life versus death
continues in verse 16, where there is a contrast between the one who
keeps the 'command' and the one who *despises his* [or its] *ways*.[54] While
many view this as a reference to the commandments of the OT law
(and so *his* ways would be God's ways), the command or charge
(singular) more likely refers to God's fundamental instruction in this
book to seek wisdom as a matter of life and death (e.g. 8:32–36;
command is used in its plural form of wisdom's commands in 3:1;
see also Fox 2009: 655). *His ways* would then be God's ways as
expressed in Wisdom's teachings (13:13–14; it could secondarily refer
to the laws). Verse 17 mentions a particularly clear example of a
wisdom-shaped character – generosity to those in need. Although
in Proverbs the poor are often responsible for their own situation
(e.g. 10:4; but see 13:23; 19:1), giving to care for them is clearly
endorsed (e.g. 14:20–21, 31). Indeed, as here, explicit mentions of
God's attitude to the poor are often made (14:31; 17:5; 22:2, 22–23;
29:13). Here God expressly states that he will reward the poor with
generosity, although the means of this reward are not described.[55]

19. This verse describes those who are greatly hot-tempered
(reading the *qere* 'great' for the *ketib* 'lot'), in contrast with those who
are slow to anger (v. 11). They *pay the penalty* of being like this (NIV
translates, less persuasively, 'must pay the penalty') in the sense of

---

54. Some versions of the text have the passive 'will be killed', but it is best
    emended with textual support (*qere* and the Targum) to read *will die*,
    as in most EVV.
55. Whybray (1994: 181–182) notes that the five proverbs that deal with
    generosity, either explicitly or implicitly, promise a reward. In the NT
    see Luke 14:12–14.

bearing the community consequences that will come as a result of their attitude. The reason for this (*for* in the sense of because) is that such individuals will not (otherwise) learn from their folly, and will simply repeat the unacceptable behaviour. Tough love will confront them, not try to appease them. A wise person will know when to use a soft answer to turn away wrath (15:1) and when the community needs to halt the strife they cause (15:18; 29:22). In any event, it is good not to associate with such persons lest we learn their ways (22:24–25).

19:20–23
Context

These proverbs deal with a person's foundational inner life or virtues. Accordingly, they include two sayings explicitly mentioning the Lord, referring to his kingly plan for the world (v. 21) and the need to treat God as God, in other words, fear the Lord (v. 23).

Comment

20–23. Verse 20 is a call to listen to (lit. 'hear', which often has the sense of 'obey', or here 'respond to') to counsel or advice, and to accept discipline or shaping. Discipline (*mûsār*) can have the sense of intellectual discipline (hence *instruction*), but often in Proverbs (e.g. 1:3) conveys the idea of being shaped in character or core commitments. The second half of the verse makes it clear that this is not a general statement about the need to listen to advice from others (as in 12:15b; 23:12); rather, it is a call to accept the shaping that wisdom offers. *In the future* (better than 'at the end', NIV; contra Waltke 2005: 114, who sees a reference to a future hope even beyond death) reveals that this ongoing shaping is expected for the rest of the person's life. At one level verse 21 has a general application much like 16:9 (humans can make plans, but God's sovereign plan will prevail; also 16:1). However, the word 'counsel' from verse 20 (*'ēṣâ*) is repeated in verse 21, and is usually translated there as *purpose*, as in Job 38:2 where it refers to God's plan for how the creation is run. This suggests that verse 21 also insists that God's purpose in verse 20 – that people be shaped by wisdom – will prevail. This leads nicely to the focus on character in verse 22. *Desired* (v. 22a) can be understood negatively as a craving or coveting, but the sense here (as in 13:12) is something positive that is longed for. This is outlined as 'his loyalty' or *steadfast love*, which is essential for seeking the wisdom of the previous verses.[56] Since this is needed, a poor but impliedly wise or righteous person, that is, one of character, is better than someone of bad character such as a liar (e.g. 14:5). Verse 23 refers back to the foundational choice of the fear of the Lord, the basis of character in Proverbs 2 (as also in 10:27; 14:27). In chapter 2 understanding the fear of the Lord leads to a wisdom-shaped character (2:11), which will protect you from being harmed by evil friends (2:12–15) and the forbidden woman (2:16–19). Here in chapter 19 the focus is on what leads to life, and protection from harm. While the Hebrew of the second half of verse 23b is difficult, the sense is that those who fear the Lord can rest satisfied, and harm will not happen to them.

19:24–29
Context
The chapter ends with the description of a number of undesirable characters wrapped around a warning in verse 27. This verse sets out a key principle, which is the flip side of the positive truth expressed in verse 20. Steinmann (2009: 411) sees verses 25–29 'united by the contrast between discipline, which serves as a corrective, and punishment for those who refuse to be corrected'.

Comment
24–26. The picture of the lazy person or sluggard in verse 24 is a comical one. This negative portrayal is developed at length in the book (e.g. 6:6–11; 24:30–34; 26:13–16), but the distinctive picture here is that, after dipping his hand in the communal bowl, he is too lazy even to put the food in his own mouth. Clifford (1999: 179) notes that 'Lifting one's hand to one's mouth is an idiom for eating', as in Judges

---

56. Lucas (2015: 139) notes that *steadfast love* could alternatively come from a rare word meaning 'shame' (found only in 14:34 and Lev. 20:17), and *desired* is taken in a negative sense. This would ground the very different reading of the REB: 'Greed is a disgrace to a man.' While this makes a good counterpart to the second half of the verse, it has little to commend it otherwise and misses the focus on character.

7:6; 1 Samuel 14:26. The scoffer is introduced in verse 25 and contrasted with a person of understanding. The scoffer is a simple person (not simple-minded but unformed in character; see on 1:4; 9:4, 16) who has to be physically struck in order to develop any prudence. This is in contrast to a wise person who, when merely corrected, accepts the correction and gains in knowledge (see 9:7–9). In verse 26 the one who causes injury to his father and drives his mother away is a child who has so dishonoured his family that he brings shame on them (10:5; 17:2). While this sounds minor in an individualistic Western society, in a community-focused, honour/shame culture it is a grave offence that destroys the community (20:20; 28:24).

27. This self-defeating and community-harming behaviour happens when the warning of verse 27 is not heeded.[57] Once people stop being shaped by wisdom (lit. 'hearing/obeying discipline/ instruction'), they will go astray from words of knowledge. The lazy person, the foolish scoffer, the violent child and the wicked false witness are all examples of people who do not want to be moulded by wisdom and her life-giving words.

28–29. The catalogue of those who reject wisdom continues in verses 28–29. Witnesses are worthless or wicked when they subvert justice by giving false testimony. In so doing, they scoff at or mock the pursuit of justice. Verse 29 does not introduce any new figures, but pronounces judgment and punishment on these scoffers (the noun in v. 25; the verb in v. 28) and those described generically as *fools*. In contrast to verse 23 where wisdom leads to life, the way of folly in verse 29 is one of judgment and physical beatings. This gives further reasons to heed the warning of verse 27.

20:1–4

Context

Verses 1–4 give examples of the consequences of negative behaviour: becoming unwise, forfeiting one's life, losing honour and finding no

---

57. In its context this verse can be taken to be hypothetical (if you were to cease . . .), rather than an ironic command, the option chosen by many commentators. Longman (2006: 372) notes that this would be the only example of a father ironically instructing a son in chs. 10 – 31.

harvest. Verse 1 makes a link with the previous chapter by using the word *mocker* (*lēṣ*, placed first in the Hebrew text for emphasis), picking up on various forms of the word used in 19:25, 28, 29. Verse 2 repeats much of 19:12; verse 4 recalls 19:12, 24; while *strife* and *quarrelling* in verse 3 pick up on similar pictures in 19:13, 26.

Comment

1–4. In the previous chapter people were *mockers*, but now wine and strong drink are personified as mocking and brawling (v. 1a). This is clearly a rebuke for drunkenness, with the second line making it plain that those who are led astray by such self-indulgence have chosen the path of folly not wisdom. Verse 2a mirrors 19:12 (with a different word for wrath/terror), but the second line draws out a different inference: do not provoke a king, or else you will lose your life. So acting wisely in public life should lead to self-control when it comes to alcohol and provoking anger among those in power. In verse 3 a further warning is given, this time to avoid strife and quarrelling. It is the fool who will quarrel, but a wise person – one of honour (*kābōd*, 'glory/honour') – will rise above petty or pointless disputes. The *sluggard* or lazy person (v. 4) is given a multifaceted portrait in the book, but here a particular failing is being slack in ploughing the field in the autumn, with the inevitable result that there is no harvest to gather in. All these examples of folly lead to being disgraced or worse.

20:5–7

Context

In verses 5–7 there is a focus on more positive characteristics (understanding, steadfast love, faithful, righteous, blessed). This cluster of virtues (and the corresponding opposites) extends like an umbrella over the sayings that follow and offers a way forward. The question of verse 6b ('a faithful person who can find?') operates as a challenge to the reader to be that kind of person.

Comment

5–7. The image of deep water (v. 5a) is also present in 18:4, and its precise force is not explained in either setting. However, the key aspect of deep water (in the light of drawing it out in v. 5b) is that it makes an object harder to identify or find. The object in this case is the plan or purpose (*'ēṣâ*, as in 19:20, 21) in a person's heart – one's core commitment or goal in life – but even such an elusive reality is able to be revealed by one who is following the path of wisdom, the person of understanding (28:11). Lucas (2015: 140) puts it well: 'The wise person has the discernment to understand what is beneath the surface and express it in appropriate words.' Verse 6 announces that *being* a faithful person is rarer (and more valuable) than *describing oneself* as a person of committed loyalty or steadfast love (*ḥesed*). The implication is that faithfulness to others is a virtue to be sought diligently. The contrast is not between steadfast love and faithfulness, but between asserting a commitment and actually doing it. As Longman (2006: 378) says, 'Talk is cheap.' Verse 7 is a simple commendation of the righteous person, one whose life is characterized by integrity. Not only is such a one living in a way that builds up the community – his family especially gain from his positive role model and values. This integrity ('blameless lives', NIV) is not sinlessness (see v. 9), but a life genuinely good and shaped by wisdom. For his children in a communal culture, it is both taught and caught (22:6). How we live will have ripple effects in our family and community.

20:8–12

Context

The rest of this chapter is difficult to group, but there is repetition that suggests coherence, such as the wise king winnowing out the wicked in verses 8, 26, and the focus on deceitful measurements and weights in verses 10, 23. Although the king is mentioned only in verses 8, 26 and 28, he is also implied in verse 18 (since kings wage war). Many of the other sayings would be particularly apt and important for a king or those in a court setting (e.g. vv. 9, 13, 15, 19–22, 24–25, 29–30). The cluster of sayings around the subject of wealth in verses 13–17 suggests that this loose grouping – containing two Yahweh sayings – ends with verse 12 (similarly Whybray 1994: 291).

Comment

8–9. It was a core task of the king to secure justice (v. 26; 29:14). In his role of judge of right and wrong, he is able to sift out or winnow any evil actions performed by those who appear before him

(v. 8). While this is probably an ideal or aspirational statement, it stands as a deterrent to those who plan to do wrong and imagine they will get away with it. This leads on nicely to verse 9, which is not an abstract assertion of human sinfulness before God. Rather, it is an observation that all will do wrong, and that they will inevitably be exposed before human kings, judges or those in authority. None can say, 'I have made myself pure' (the factitive sense of the *piel* stem) or clean. Although this is ritual language, the reality referred to is moral wrongdoing, and the outcome is to stand before those who have the power to punish evil. The lesson implied is to avoid wrongdoing in the first place.

10–12. The idea of having our actions weighed and assessed continues in verses 11–12. In a culture where most goods were bought and sold by weight, a common way to short-change others was to use different (*unequal*, ESV; lit. 'a stone and a stone, an ephah and an ephah') measures for buying and selling (v. 10; see v. 23; 11:1; 16:11; Deut. 25:13–16). Such deceitful business practices, which serve only to cheat people, are described as not simply a disdain for justice but primarily an abomination to the Lord. Even in Proverbs, people are accountable to God for their financial and work practices. Van Leeuwen (1997: 186) comments, 'Often the use of money and material goods is the best indicator of the operative beliefs of a culture or a person.' Verse 11 makes it clear that our outward actions (if for a child or youth, how much more for an adult?) disclose whether our deeds are pure and upright.[58] This implies that our actions reveal whether our hearts or character traits are pure and upright. Another implication is that the way we act as a child will be a good indicator of how we will turn out as an adult. So Fox (2009: 667–668) comments, 'What his actions reveal is not so much whether

---

58. Whybray (1994: 291) notes that it is not stated explicitly whether this discernment is evident to God or to humans. The verb in v. 11a (*makes himself known*) could alternatively be understood to mean *dissemble* or 'disguise their nature' (see ESV footnote), as there are two Hebrew roots *nkr*. The second stream (*nkr* II) is found in 26:24. However, even if this was the sense, the point would be similar – even if children tried to disguise their nature, their deeds would show if they were pure and upright.

he is virtuous *now*, as what he will be like in the future.' Thus, shaping (encouraging and disciplining) children is time well spent. Verse 12 may be an unrelated comment (although both vv. 10 and 12 end with 'also the two of them') about God as Creator, but the recurring theme of judgment for wrongdoing suggests that it also refers here to those in authority being able to hear and see (and so discern) evil actions because God has given humanity the ability to do this. This suggests that God as Creator is ordering his world so that those who do wrong will be called to account.

20:13–17
Context
This is a group of sayings concerned with wealth. The mention of *eyes* in verse 13 echoes the mention of *eye* in verse 12, suggesting that the discernment of verse 12 needs to be used in relation to money as well. Each of the five proverbs is quite discrete, dealing with different aspects of wealth.

Comment
13–14. The theme of laziness is again raised in verse 13 (see 19:15; 20:4), with poverty (or dispossession of one's land, as suggested by the verb *yāraš*; but Fox 2009: 668 notes that in 23:21; 30:9 it simply refers to poverty) pictured as the likely consequence of sleeping when one should be working. Verse 13b provides a way forward for the lazy person – *open your eyes* (better than NIV, 'stay awake'). In light of verse 12, this will mean 'be discerning', use the abilities that God has given. The consequence of this change of attitude is an abundance of food (*leḥem*, *bread*, can mean 'food' in general). Verse 14 is reminiscent of bargaining in markets throughout the Majority World. While negotiating with a seller, the buyer points out all the defects of the goods and haggles about the price. Yet once the sale is complete, the buyer wants to brag about the great bargain. This is neither an endorsement nor a criticism of such bargaining; it is simply a description of how people buy and sell in commercial life. The proverb discerns that the bargaining is done as a way of ordering the world, and perhaps gives a warning not to be taken in by others.
    15–17. These proverbs concern our attitudes to possessions. Verse 15 puts a qualification on the value of wealth by comparing

it with something much more precious. Echoing 8:11, where the same word for *jewel* is used, wisdom is better than riches (also 3:13–15; 16:16). Whybray (1994: 295) suggests that 'stones/jewel' here and in 8:11 refers to a precious red coral, although it is sometimes translated 'rubies'. Longman (2006: 375) proposes 'pearls'. The focus in verse 15 is *lips of knowledge*, which refers to wisdom shaping our speech (it is used in 14:7 to mean the opposite of folly). Strive for this more than wealth. Verse 16 needs further explanation, and it is commonly read as a warning not to act as a guarantor for another. Yet it implies that people have a different obligation for how they might treat family, friends and fellow Israelites, compared with those who are strangers or foreigners. Together the *strangers/foreigners* describe those who do not belong to the community, or are un-familiar to them – perhaps travellers or merchants who warranted no special favours (see also 11:15; 27:13). Proverbs, like the rest of the OT, endorses care rather than exploitation for the poor and needy in their own community (14:31; 19:17; 22:22–23; 31:20; Deut. 24:10–13, 17). However, those who are outside these categories should not be entitled to the privileges reserved for those needing generous care. Verse 17 returns to the theme of *bread* or food (v. 13), and insists it must be rightly gained. Waltke (2005: 146) notes that bread 'may stand as well for satisfying any drive and appetite, including sex (see 9:17)'. While illegally or immorally acquired wealth (lit. 'bread of deceit') may give some pleasure (*'ārēb* can mean sweet or pleasant), it will later be as destructive and unpleasant as a mouth full of gravel (1:10–19; 9:17–18; 28:8).[59] In these proverbs wrong attitudes to wealth and possessions can lead people to lose their own integrity.

20:18–22

Context

Unlike the focus on wealth in the previous sayings, verses 18–22 all concern some aspect of speech, with the exception of verse 21, which returns to the theme of money.

---

59. Fox (2009: 671) comments, '"Bread of deceit" is bread gained by deceit, but at the same time it is bread that deceives.'

Comment
18. This concerns the positive value of wise speech. Plans are essential for the good life envisaged in Proverbs, and these are achieved by obtaining advice or counsel – wise words from others. *Counsel* (*ʿēṣâ*) itself sometimes means plan or purpose (e.g. 19:21), but can, as here, refer to advice (e.g. 2 Sam. 15:31). Waging war was one of the responsibilities of kings in the ancient world, and victory or defeat had major implications for their people. Thus, it must be entered into using wise guidance. This *wise guidance* (one word in Hebrew) is part of what the book of Proverbs is designed to achieve (1:5), and is commended elsewhere in the book (11:14; 24:6). Listening to the perspectives of those worth hearing improves the decision-making process, a truth not confined to the waging of war.

19–20, 22. Not all speech builds up a community, and these verses give examples of the wrong use of speech. Virtually repeating 11:13a, verse 19a comments that slander is harmful to the community as it (inappropriately) reveals secrets. This is not commending a cover-up when whistle-blowers need to speak out; it is discouraging the sharing of half-truths and innuendos that will destroy the reputation of others and divide communities. The person who engages in such actions is a *simple babbler* (ESV; 'anyone who talks too much', NIV; lit. 'the simple/unformed of lips/speech') – those who talk because they like the sound of their own voice, rather than because something is worth saying. The warning of verse 19b is 'do not mix with such people', but instead avoid them. Verse 20 observes that those who give cursing or shaming instead of the honour that is due (here to both parents) will die an untimely death. Their life will be snuffed out like a lamp (24:20), leading to the utter darkness of death. Verse 22 rebukes those who use boastful words of vengeance (24:29; 25:21–22; Deut. 32:35; Rom. 12:17–21). It is not clear if a person was wronged or only imagined it to be so (as if this did not affect the warning). What is evident is that such a one has taken the matter into his own hands, rather than trust God (hope in or wait for him). Words of bravado can leave our mouths before our theological principles, or even our brains, are engaged.

21. This is a puzzling and probably elliptical verse, which does not explain what is wrong with an early inheritance (assuming the *qere* reading 'be gained in haste' rather than the *ketib*, 'be acquired').

In the light of the general teaching of Proverbs, there could be two overlapping reasons for the warning. First, someone could receive an inheritance before his or her character was shaped, resulting in the person not using it wisely. Second, receiving an inheritance only once the parents have died would thus deprive the young person of the parental instruction assumed in the book (e.g. 1:8). Lucas (2015: 142) suggests it refers to 'a child somehow precipitating gaining their inheritance', perhaps while the parents are still alive, for example the prodigal son in Luke 15:12–16. See also 19:26; 30:11. In either case, the young person's lack of maturity may not enable wise use of the inheritance, and so he or she would not prosper or be *blessed* (see 13:11; 21:5).

20:23–26

Context

Since verses 18–22 focused on speech, and verse 27 begins a new section with more positive advice, these miscellaneous verses can be grouped together. A number of the proverbs reflect others found elsewhere in the book. There are 'Yahweh sayings' in verses 23 and 24.

Comment

23, 26. These proverbs echo verse 10 and verse 8 respectively and do not seem to add much to what has already been said. Perhaps verse 26 adds that God judges wicked *people* and not just evil *actions*, but evil people are probably also in view in verse 8 (*rāʿ*, *evil*, can mean 'evil person' there). The mention of *wheel* in verse 26 probably refers to the large cartwheels used in the threshing process (e.g. Isa. 28:27; see Fox 2009: 676).

24. The first half of this proverb recalls 16:9b, but it is given a different twist in the second line. Rather than continuing the focus of God's active sovereignty, attention is drawn instead to human limitations. Since God determines a person's way, how can human beings know where they are headed in life? No answer is given in the proverb, which suggests it is a rhetorical question pointing out humanity's lack of control of the future.

25. This verse envisages someone who has made a rash vow of dedication of some object to God. The verb *lʿʿ*, 'to speak rashly' is only elsewhere found in Job 6:3. It is the second line that indicates the nature of the rash behaviour. The person who has devoted the object to God has not properly reflected on it (perhaps on the consequences or the timing or the circumstances) prior to making the vow. This means that the proverb is only targeted at making vows or promises (to God, and perhaps by implication to others) without thinking the matter through and counting the cost.

20:27–30
Context
There has been a strong note of warning in most of the proverbs in verses 8–26, but this tone changes in verses 27–30 with some positive and upbeat advice.

Comment
27. This proverb is full of imagery, and it is hard to know what it means. Most English versions translate something along the lines of 'the human spirit is the lamp of the LORD, searching all his innermost parts'. The lamp of the Lord (placed first) and human breath (it doesn't mean 'spirit' anywhere else) are simply put side by side, so the verb needs to be implied. In 6:23 the father's command is a lamp, so the idea here could be that God's commands or lamp shed light on (for that is the appropriate verb for a lamp) human breath or life (*nišmâ*, 'breath', is used in Genesis 2:7 of the 'breath of life'; Waltke 2005: 157 suggests it is a metonymy for words or speech), searching out all the inner parts. Alternatively, *lamp* can mean 'life' (v. 20; 13:9; 21:4; 24:20), but is not so used about God.[60] However, it may mean that human breath is life from God, and he searches out its inner nature (15:11).
28–29. Mention of the king in verse 28 links it with verse 26, and this verse outlines how the king's throne or power are to be strengthened. This is done by committed, steadfast love or loyalty (*ḥesed*) and faithfulness, although the proverb does not specify whether it

---

60. Longman (2006: 382) suggests 'lamp' = 'life's energy'; Murphy (1998: 154) suggests it refers to conscience; Fox (2009: 672) sees it as 'a symbol of life, prosperity, spiritual illumination, and posterity'.

is the king's loyalty/faithfulness or that of his subjects or both
(Clifford 1999: 186 suggests it is God's loyalty and fidelity). It is most
likely to be the king's since in the parallel verse 29 it is the young
man's glory and the old men's splendour. As in 17:6, *glory* has the
sense of 'what you boast about'. The *young men* are not so much
'young' but 'choice' or 'in their prime' (and so young). Just as those
in their prime glory in their physical strength, so it is that the grey
hair of the old men is what shows their honour (16:31). It is interesting that honour and strength (*kōăḥ* and *hādār*, the words used
here) are worn as clothing by the wise woman of Proverbs 31 (31:25).
Grey or white hair is a symbol of long life, during which time a
person can grow in wisdom and character. It is not long life on its
own that brings someone honour (that is just good genes); rather,
it refers to those who have used their life to grow in wisdom. This
would be so for kings as well as others.

30. This final proverb speaks of how discipline improves our
life. The image of verse 30a is that blows (physical or otherwise)
received can cleanse or scour away evil within. The parallel in verse
30b suggests that defeats (*strokes*, ESV; 'beatings', NIV/NRSV, can
mean wounds, blows or defeats) make us clean within (13:24;
23:13–14). What is not explained is the process by which this
happens, but there is an expectation here that one who is wise
rather than foolish will learn from the setbacks and hard times in
life in order to become a better person (cleanse away evil, clean
us within).

21:1–5

Context

The weak coherence of the previous section continues into chapter
21 and as far as 22:16. Verses 1–5 deal with the plans of the human
heart (vv. 1, 2, 4) and the purposes of God. The Lord is explicitly
mentioned three times (vv. 1, 2, 3), and his presence in evaluating
human conduct is also seen in verses 4–5.

Comment

1–5. The heart is used to teach a number of different lessons in
these verses, but in each case it refers to the core or essence of a
person. God directs or turns the king's heart to wherever it pleases

him (God), since he can guide it as easily as one can channel a flowing stream of water (v. 1). The focus is not on the king bringing life-giving blessings (water in a desert culture, so Waltke 2005: 168; Isa. 32:1–2), but rather on God being able to determine how a king will act. Murphy (1998: 158) notes that 'the saying aims at glorifying the Lord, not the king.' If God can change the inner commitments of the most powerful human figure, how much more can he do this in others? Verse 2 raises the issue of God judging or weighing up the hearts of people (24:12). While humans try to justify their own actions (they are right in their own eyes), God assesses us in truth and discloses what we are really like (14:12; 16:2; 30:12). The way of a person (v. 2) is similar to the lamp (v. 4) and the plans (v. 5), all describing how we live our everyday lives. The criteria by which God evaluates people are set out in verses 3–4. God is not bought off with a lot of religious activity (*sacrifice*, v. 3), but accepts those who pursue righteousness and justice (*ṣĕdāqâ ûmišpāṭ*, v. 3). This does not mean that religious actions such as sacrifices were worthless, but they are of little or no value if not combined with a determination to live justly and rightly – to treat others as God sees them (15:8a). Righteousness and justice are contrasted with pride (lit. 'wide of heart'; Ps. 101:5) and haughtiness (v. 4), which come from an attitude of not valuing other people. This is the lamp (24:20) or essential life of the wicked (*rĕšāʿîm*), and it is labelled as sin or missing the mark (*ḥaṭṭāʾt*).[61] The use of these common words (*right-eousness, justice, wicked, sin*) highlights the choice of two paths through life that has been outlined in chapters 1 – 9. This contrast is also reflected in verse 5, where the thoughts and plans of those who apply themselves to the task will prosper, but those who are only looking for a quick shortcut will find that their haste results in poverty.[62] This echoes teaching found elsewhere in the book (e.g. 3:9–10; 10:4; 28:22).

---

61. The word commonly translated 'lamp' is a defectively written form. The NIV sees it as a defective form of the word for 'untilled ground', but this does not suit the context.

62. Waltke (2005: 172) notes that elsewhere the contrast is between the diligent and the lazy person, not the one who acts rashly or in haste.

21:6–19

Context

Verses 6–19 outline a series of negative characters and actions, in marked contrast to verses 20–23, making this a suitable grouping, even though there is a wide range of blameworthy descriptions. In the light of the contrast in verses 1–5, it develops the picture of those whom the Lord weighs and finds wanting (v. 2). The wicked are mentioned in verses 7, 10, 12, 18, suggesting that this is the dominant category.

Comment

6–8. These verses critique the liar, the wicked and the guilty before pointing to a way forward in verse 8b. The Hebrew root *p'l*, 'to do or make', binds this section together, being the first word of verse 6 (*getting*, ESV; 'made', NIV) and the last word of verse 8 (*conduct*). Verse 6 picks up the theme of gaining riches from verse 5, but reflects on the unjust acquisition of them. The lying tongue refers to using deceit, fraud or deception in order to obtain money from another person. While in many parts of the world this would be a criminal, defining what is deceptive might vary from culture to culture. However, the concern of verse 6 is that such treasures are both ephemeral (a mist, *hebel*, being driven away) and dangerous (lit. 'seeking or asking for death'). Wealth gained wrongly does not satisfy (28:22). The violent, oppressive actions performed by the wicked were presumably intended to sweep their victims away, but ironically, the wicked themselves will be dragged away by them. Verse 7 does not specify how this will take place, but it does explain why – because they refuse to do justice. The implication is that justice will ultimately prevail, and so their choice not to act justly will not succeed. Verse 8a contains two words found only here in the OT (*crooked, guilty*), so their meaning is not certain. However, the contrast in the second half of the verse (*pure, upright*/straight) highlights that a life marked by justice is to be preferred.

9, 19. These 'better than' sayings about a quarrelsome wife are often referred to flippantly, but do have a serious point to make. Discord is not only sown by the (largely) male characters mentioned in the surrounding verses, but also by members of either sex, and especially in the context of family life. Like the wider community, the home is intended as a place of peace. It is better to have a small place (corner of a flat rooftop, v. 9; not sharing the whole house), or no place of comfort at all (*live in a desert land*, v. 19), than it is to live with a wife who is quarrelsome (vv. 9, 19) and fretful (v. 19; 'nagging', NIV). The same word 'woman' or 'wife' is used in both verses 9 and 19, despite the ESV using *wife* in verse 9 and *woman* in verse 19. In the context of living together in an ancient culture, it should be understood as wife in both verses. The word *quarrelsome* has the sense of being judgmental (it is related to the Hebrew root *dyn*, to judge or pass judgment, 19:13, or in a man, 26:21). Relationships prosper when they are based on building up other people, not constantly pointing out their faults.

10–11. The wicked (lit. the 'soul', or better, 'life' of the wicked, but referring to the person as a whole) desire evil (v. 10), which is reinforced in the fact that they do not extend grace or mercy to their neighbours. This is wrong because such lack of generosity destroys community. Verse 11 contrasts the scoffer and others. Scoffers are fined or penalized for their attitudes or actions, seemingly having learnt nothing (9:7–8a; see also 10:17; 15:5). Yet the simple or unformed will learn from the scoffer's fate (19:25), and the wise will typically acquire further knowledge when they are corrected (9:8b–9). The scoffer is the real loser.

12–13. In this section there has been no explicit mention of God being involved in the righting of wrongs, but his activity has simply been backgrounded. Verse 12 describes God as *the Righteous One* and gives the assurance that he sees all and acts to bring an appropriate disaster to the wicked.[63] This describes in general terms the just activity of God in punishing wrongdoing, but does not mention the specific details. One example of his work is outlined in verse 13. Those who reject (close their ear to) the cry (commonly used of a cry for justice) of the poor receive the same treatment when they cry out (to God), but they are not answered (by God). This is poetic justice – God at work in his world.

14–15. Reading these two proverbs together is important. The effect of a bribe or gift is sometimes observed quite neutrally in

---

63. Clifford (1999: 191) points out that in Proverbs the righteous do not punish the wicked, but only God does (e.g. 13:6; 19:3).

Proverbs (e.g. 17:8; 18:16; 19:6b), but when it is given *in secret* or *concealed* (lit. 'in the bosom'), it is linked to perverting justice (17:23). Thus, while verse 14 indicates that a bribe or gift can effectively turn aside the anger of another, verse 15 introduces the wider concept of justice that acts as an implied critique of this form of bribery. The doing of justice (v. 15) is an alternative to securing unwarranted favour by bribery, and when justice prevails, the righteous delight but wrongdoers are terrified or dismayed.

16–18. All three verses show the futility of living apart from wisdom. *Good sense* (ESV; 'understanding', NRSV; 'prudence', NIV; *haśkēl*) was introduced in 1:3 to describe wise living, following wisdom not folly and so being the path to life not death (8:35–36). This earlier teaching is recapitulated here, making the point that one who departs from wisdom's way finds that death is the hidden destination of the way of folly (7:25–27; 9:18). Verse 17 makes the straightforward observation that those who spend their money on expensive pleasures will have little money left. Pleasure (*śimḥâ* can also mean 'joy', but here has the sense of 'pleasure/feasting'), wine and (olive) oil are good gifts from God, but the problem is with the verb *loves*. People need to love God and use his gifts, not the other way around. The scenario behind verse 18 is not as clear, but the general sense is that the wicked and the betrayer lose out rather than gain from their way of life. Instead, the righteous and upright are preserved at their expense. In each of these three proverbs, pursuing a path other than wisdom is shown to be the choice with the worst outcome.

21:20–23
Context
In contrast with the preceding and following verses (vv. 6–19, 24–29), the focus of verses 20–23 is on positive values and actions to pursue. They provide a glimmer of light to show the way forward.

Comment
20–21. Verse 20 echoes the issues raised in verse 17, but the emphasis is instead on the positive consequences for the wise person. Again the process is not outlined, but the wise retain their valuable wealth (NIV opts for 'choice food', but the idea is wider)

and goods. Oil, probably olive oil, is representative of produce in general. By contrast, fools use up (lit. 'swallow') all their resources. The wise person of verse 20 continues as the subject of verse 21 – the one who pursues righteous living (*ṣĕdāqâ*) and steadfast love (*ḥesed*). Those who have these virtues as their goal find ongoing life (life as it is meant to be), relationships made right (*ṣĕdāqâ* has a relational sense) and honour (a prized goal in an honour/shame culture). Individuals who chase after such virtues add value to their community.

22–23. The wise person is again the explicit subject of verse 22 and the implied subject of verse 23. The wise go up to (better than *scales*, ESV) a strong city (lit. 'a city of warriors/strong men') and bring down ('cause to go down', to balance, 'go up') 'the strength/stronghold of their trust'. The image – grounded in warfare language – speaks of the public usefulness of the wise. Figures such as Joseph, Daniel and the wise woman of Abel Beth-maacah (2 Sam. 20:14–22) are helpful examples. Wisdom is not simply for private or personal use, but for the good of the community. Verse 23 commends guarding what we say. Restraint in speech is not just using few words, but speaking words that have been weighed up and found to be helpful. This is not simply the silent man of Egyptian wisdom writings, but is a more positive picture of the one who uses fewer, well-chosen words wisely. 'Guarding' the mouth is a matter of exercising quality control on our speech – saying what is worth saying, and not saying the rest.

21:24–29

Context

The stereotypical negative characters of verses 6–19 (see also 19:24–29) reappear in verses 24–29. This will be followed by a focus on the Lord in verses 30–31, marking this off as a small group of sayings. In three of the proverbs their folly is shown more clearly by pointing forward to a better way (vv. 26, 28, 29).

Comment

24–26. The familiar figure of the scoffer or mocker reappears in verse 24. Proverbs elsewhere tells us that God mocks proud scoffers (3:34), that they will be punished (19:29), and that their activity is destructive (22:10). Here there is a focus on their central failing as they are twice described as arrogant or presumptuous, with two other words referring to their pride or haughtiness. In their pride they cross over appropriate boundaries; this is the force of the Hebrew word for *pride* used in verse 24b (*'ebrâ*; NIV translates less helpfully as 'fury'). The subject of verse 26a is not specified, but the double use of *craves/desires* links it with the related noun (*desire* or 'craving') in verse 25, suggesting that the sluggard or lazy person is in view from verses 25–26a. A common description elsewhere is that such individuals reap the consequences of their laziness (e.g. 19:24; 20:4), and that is the case here too. The refusal to work leads to death, presumably because the sluggard does not work to provide enough food to stay alive (v. 25). Yet the craving (for more food) lasts right through the day (v. 26a). The contrast of the righteous giving and not holding back does not refer to them giving to the lazy person. Rather, the idea is that the righteous one works hard and so has food to spare, and thus is in a position to give generously.

27–29. These verses give examples of wickedness in practice, explicitly in verses 27, 29. The wicked person's religious activity (here a sacrifice) is called an abomination (v. 27a), meaning something detested by God. It is such a person's character and foundational choice that render it unacceptable, not even any defect in the religious practice itself. However, verse 27b makes a further point that when offering a sacrifice that comes from a devious or evil intention, it is so much worse. It makes it an abominable abomination. Verse 28 has a courtroom setting, with both *witness* and 'hearer' describing a legal role (19:5a, 9a). A number of English translations render the word 'hearer' as 'listener' (NIV, 'careful listener'; NRSV, 'good listener'), but this is to miss the legal context. It is a term elsewhere used of a legal official who hears and judges a dispute (2 Sam. 15:3; Job 31:35). This gives a nice balance to the verse: a false witness will perish, but a person who brings justice (a hearer) will subdue them completely.[64] Verse 29 contrasts the wicked and the upright. While a wicked person might put on a bold or brazen face (the same term is used in 7:13), the morally upright

---

64. Longman (2006: 389, 399) argues for the sense 'subdue/destroy them completely' rather than 'speak forever'.

person is different. There are two textual issues in verse 29b, with most English versions opting for the *qere* reading ('understands/ gives thought to' instead of 'causes to stand') for the first, and the *ketib* reading for the second ('their ways' instead of 'their way').[65] Either rendering of the verb would be a useful contrast (the second issue is not a major difference), but the concept of giving deep thought to our way of living rather than putting up a show certainly gives the sharpest picture.

21:30–31
Context
Just as there were three occurrences of *the* LORD in verses 1–3, the chapter ends in verses 30–31 with two further Yahweh sayings. The theme here is that God's purposes will prevail.

Comment
30–31. The threefold repetition of 'there is no' in verse 30a is an effective way of saying that nothing at all (wisdom, understanding or plan) can overcome God's intentions. It reads literally: 'There is no wisdom, there is no understanding, there is no plan, opposite to/against the LORD', but many translations insert an implied verb like 'succeed' (NIV) or *avail* (ESV, NRSV). The force of the sentence is that nothing can stand, prevail, succeed or happen against God and his purposes.[66] Verse 31 expresses a limited version of the same truth, using the example of a military battle. While humans can make their preparations (getting their horses ready), victory or deliverance will be determined by God.

22:1–6
Context
These verses are diverse in their content, but largely positive in their descriptions, with the exception of verses 3b and 5a. However, even

---

65. The *ketib* refers to what is *written* in the Hebrew Masoretic Text, while the *qere* refers to the Masoretic suggestion of what is to be *read*.

66. Lucas (2015: 148) comments, 'True wisdom flows from Yahweh, and so any "wisdom" that seeks to oppose him is false and will fail.'

these exceptions are used to emphasize a contrast with the figure in
the other half of the verse.

Comment

1–2, 4. The subject of riches links these three verses. Two comparisons are made in verse 1. First, a (good, implied) name is worth
choosing (lit. 'is to be chosen') more than great riches. Second, grace
or favour ('to be esteemed', NIV; presumably by other people) is
better than money (silver and gold). One's name is a reference to
reputation or character, suggesting that who we are is more important
than what we have. Verse 2 is ostensibly about both the rich and the
poor, but the real focus is on the poor. No-one would think that
the rich are not made by God, but in practice many treat the poor
as if they do not have any significance derived from being made by
God. While there is a difference, there is no distinction in value (so
they lit. *meet together*, ESV = 'have this in common', NIV, NRSV). A
common theme in Proverbs is that God has created the poor (14:31;
17:5), while other sayings remind us of our obligation to the poor
because of God (19:17; 22:22–23; 29:13). In verse 4 the consequence
of, or reward for, humility/the fear of the Lord is described as
riches, honour and life. The relationship between humility and the
fear of the Lord is not set out, but most versions insert 'and', as if
they are separate items. Waltke (2005: 193) reads them in apposition,
namely, 'humility, that is the fear of the LORD' (= 'humility is the
fear of the LORD', NIV). Certainly, the foundational stance of fearing
God or respecting God as God is grounded in humility, and it is
right to see them closely linked (15:33). Riches (3:9–10), honour
(3:35; 8:18) and life (8:35–36) are desirable consequences of the path
of wisdom (joined also in 3:16). It is in our interests to have a godly
character (here, humility), based on the right foundation in life (the
fear of the Lord).

3, 5. The shaped character of the wise will shield them from
potential danger. Giving prudence to the simple was one of the
goals of the book (1:4). In verse 3 those who are shrewd or prudent
see a (looming) disaster and conceal or hide themselves from it,
while the morally unformed (i.e. simple) keep on going full steam
ahead and bear the consequences. There is an implied exhortation
to be shaped by wisdom rather than persist in folly. In verse 5 life's

difficulties (*thorns and snares*) are in the life path of those described as crooked or perverted – twisted away from how they are meant to be. Yet individuals who keep or guard their life (*nepeš, soul,* usually means 'life') will distance themselves from these traps and snares (the plural suffix suggests 'from these traps' rather than 'from a perverse person'). An important part of wisdom is being able to navigate a course through life, and here it means avoiding obstacles and difficulties in the way.

6. This is one of the best-known but most easily misused proverbs. Some find here a *promise* that if they bring their children up in the ways of God, then they can guarantee that their children will be believers. Yet this is confusing a *proverb* with a *promise.* A proverb describes what is typically true, not what is universally true. Not all children of godly parents do follow God, and it is simply not in our power to make someone else trust in God – that is God's work. This proverb gives us encouragement to value the influence we can have on our children and youth by noting that godly training has a real lasting effect on how they turn out. The church needs to devote resources to youth and children's ministries, and parents need to make the Christian training of their children a priority in their use of time and money. Yet this proverb should not be pushed so far that we are judgmental on those parents whose children do not follow God.

22:7–12

Context
This is only a loosely bound section, but the next group of sayings (negative attributes) begins at verse 13. In broad terms verses 7–9 concern wealth and power, while verses 10–12 focus more on internal attributes and character. There are strong notes of contrast, opposites and reversal, sometimes within a verse and sometimes between verses.

Comment
7–9. Verse 7 outlines a society stratified by power linked to money, but neither condemns nor commends it. It simply observes that economic power is real, whether that is the greater opportunities the rich have compared with the poor, or the dependency that results

when a person takes out a loan from another. In this culture loans were a matter of last resort, taken out only to survive, not to build an investment portfolio. However, while verse 7 describes the scenario without any evaluation, the following proverbs provide a warning and a way forward for the rich and powerful. The warning in verse 8 is not to use power unjustly. The imagery of sowing, and reaping what we sow, builds in accountability to the rich not to use their wealth in an unfair and self-serving way. Those who act unjustly will reap trouble or disaster. The second part of verse 8 repeats this warning by noting that their symbol of power (their staff or club or sceptre) will come to an end and be no more (*kālâ*, a verb that has the sense of being completed, used up, finished; *fail*, ESV, NRSV; 'broken' NIV). Power used in the wrong way will become powerless. Verse 9 provides instruction for the rich about a positive way to use wealth. The solution is generosity (lit. 'good of eye' = an eye to do good; ESV, *a bountiful eye*) to the poor, giving food to keep them alive. Generosity to the poor is repeatedly encouraged in Proverbs (e.g. 19:17).

10–12. While these verses mention people like the scoffer (v. 10a) and the faithless betrayer (v. 12b), their focus is more on a number of desirable character traits: rejection of scoffing, purity of heart, gracious speech and knowledge. The expulsion of those mocking or scoffing will remove strife, quarrelling and abusive behaviour (v. 10). It will be replaced by an inner commitment to what is morally clean and free from impurities (*purity of heart*), and a way of speaking that is full of graciousness ('grace of lips/speech'). These virtues are so winsome that those who value them are metaphorically described as having the king as their friend (v. 11). They also experience the favour of God, expressed as the eyes of the Lord watching over them (v. 12a). *Knowledge, da'at*, here refers not to academic content, but rather to knowing how to live well – the kind of living characterized by a clean heart and gracious speech. Verse 12b is not clear about whether God or the person pictured in verse 11 is the subject of the verb *overthrows*/'subverts'. This could be a deliberate ambiguity, for both are true. God is at work in frustrating the faithless words of the wicked, but he often uses the speech of those whose character has been shaped by wisdom.

22:13–16

Context

The collection of Solomonic proverbs closes with several short cameos about some negative stereotypes. This is a call to heed the warnings of the book and not to be like these figures.

Comment

13–16. The sluggard or lazy person has already been prominent (6:6–11; 13:4; 15:19; 19:24; 20:4), and will be picked up again in 24:30–34; 26:13–16. The comic theme of verse 13, echoed in 26:13, is that a lazy person wants to justify doing nothing with an unlikely and preposterous scenario (there is a lion outside). The unlikelihood of the event happening reveals the great lengths a sluggard can go to in order to avoid work. Verse 14 is striking because of the absence of a focus on the adulteress in the rest of the Solomonic sentence sayings. This does not reflect a lack of concern about adultery, for so much of the foundational chapters 1 – 9 use the adulteress as a clear example of the path of folly (2:16–19; 5:1–23; 6:20–35; 7:1–27; 9:13–18). As elsewhere, the emphasis is on her (smooth) speech (*mouth*, 2:16; 5:3; 6:24; 7:5, 21) and that following her is like falling into a deep pit of death and destruction (2:18–19; 5:5, 22–23; 6:27–28; 7:22–23, 25–27). Verse 15 is more general in character, observing that the natural state of an unformed youth is not wisdom but folly. The solution is not so much the rod (or staff or club) but discipline (*mûsār*). This word (one of the goals of the book, 1:3) refers to the training or shaping that comes from embracing wisdom, and which causes our natural folly to be left behind us. The final verse (v. 16) deals with an example of wickedness – using wealth and power not to benefit others, but as a way to act unjustly towards them. The injustice envisaged is the 'haves' helping themselves to what belongs to others in order to 'have some more' wealth for themselves. The irony reflected in verse 16b is that, in their pursuit of riches, they will only become poor, or lose their money in other ways to those richer than themselves. Exactly how this will happen is not explained.

Meaning in 16:10 – 22:16

Using a plethora of examples, this section is drawing a contrast between wise and foolish responses to life's challenges. There is

further exploration in this section of various exceptions to the
principle that God rewards the righteous and punishes the wicked,
but the retribution principle is still upheld. The difference is that
sometimes it may require a long-term view, for retribution does not
necessarily happen immediately. The picture that emerges of the
community is one where violence, injustice and anger can play a
part, but where the wise need to speak up and choose a wise
response. Issues of character lie behind all these outward actions
and words. There is an increasing focus on kings and courts, so a
pressing issue was clearly how to use power within the community.
Self-serving and destructive attitudes are held up to criticism, and
the ongoing embrace of the path of wisdom is again commended.

3. THE SAYINGS OF THE WISE (22:17 – 24:34)

A. The thirty sayings of the wise (22:17 – 24:22)

Context

Chapters 22:17 – 24:22 form a discrete section based (especially 22:17 – 23:11) to some extent on thirty 'chapters' from the epilogue of the Egyptian wisdom text, the *Instructions of Amenemope*, but filtered through a grid of Israelite faith (e.g. 22:19; 24:21). Most of the parallels are confined to 22:17 – 23:11, but the specific nature of the examples makes the borrowing clear. Israel's wisdom movement is part of a broader international interest in wisdom, and it is clear that some insights gathered from outside Israel have been incorporated into Scripture. Their truth – and adoption into the book – makes them authoritative rather than their source.

Thirty sayings are explicitly mentioned in 22:20. Of course, Egyptian deities and deified ideas (e.g. *ma'at*) are appropriately omitted, and the sayings are rearranged and developed in fresh ways. They can usefully be discussed in these thirty sections (see the headings in the NIV). There are some slight differences in the ways various scholars have divided up 22:17 – 24:22 into thirty sayings. Some treat 22:17–21 as an introduction and do not number it; some combine 23:12–14; some combine 23:15–18; some divide 24:8–9 into two; some separate 24:10 from 24:11–12. This commentary prefers the view of Waltke, which is reflected in the NIV numbering. Within these words of the wise, there are three subsections after the introduction in 22:17–21: 22:22 – 23:11; 23:12–35; and 24:1–22. Clifford (1999: 199) proposes that the first part is addressed 'to young people ambitioning a career', while the second deals with the concerns of youth, and the third covers the destinies of the righteous and the wicked.

Comment
i. Introduction (22:17–21)

17–21. Some versions (e.g. NRSV) see the *words of the wise* in verse 17 as a heading like the others at the beginning of each section of Proverbs. However, while this acts as a heading for a discrete group within the book, this phrase is actually the object of the verb 'to hear/obey' and already follows the call to listen (lit. 'extend/stretch out your ear'). Yet the focus of the verse is that what follows are words handed down by tradition among the wise. They are in parallel to *knowledge* in the second half of the verse. Those listening are urged to hear, obey and set their mind (lit. 'heart') to the content of these sayings. Keeping these teachings within you (lit. 'in your womb', used metaphorically of the inner self for young men as in 18:8; 20:27, 30) is pleasant (v. 18a), an adjective used in this section to describe words (23:8) and wealth (24:4). In the book as a whole wisdom's ways are pleasant (3:17), while wisdom and knowledge in our inner being are described by the related verb (2:10). The picture of verse 18b is that these wise words are so much a part of us, that they are also on our lips as we teach others. These proverbs are not for us alone. Even this is not the end of the process, for verse 19a outlines the purpose of all this – that we may trust in the Lord (Longman 2006: 416 calls this 'the theological motivation for the teaching of wisdom'). There is a close link between the fear of the Lord, embracing wisdom, and trust in the Lord. These instructions, which have their origin in an Egyptian wisdom text, have been selected and reworked so that they will help us to trust in Israel's

particular God, the God of the Bible. Clifford (1999: 206) notes that
'the Lord' is the centre word in verses 17–21.

The focus of verses 19b–21 is on describing the thirty sayings
and their role. The sage (now singular, '*I* have made them known';
cf. *the wise* [plural] in v. 17) has, in collecting and editing these written
sayings of advice and knowledge, made them known to his readers
(vv. 19b–20). While there is a textual issue about the word translated
thirty sayings, it is rightly adopted by most modern translations (e.g.
NRSV, ESV, NIV) and it discloses the link with the Egyptian text, the
Instructions of Amenemope, written in thirty (short) chapters.[1] This was
an earlier work than this section of Proverbs, and has also been
filtered and adapted for the people of Israel. Verse 21 sets out the
purpose of the rest of this section – to disclose right and true words
(Van Leeuwen 1997: 204 suggests 'a reliable answer'; Fox 2009: 712,
'the truest of words') so that the listeners might return with words
of truth (emphasized by repetition) to those who sent them. The
sayings that follow are commended for their truth and usefulness.

ii. Key life choices (22:22 – 23:11)

22–23. The theme here is caring for the poor and downtrodden,
because the God of justice will act on their behalf (14:31; 17:5).
No-one should rob from the poor, for it is not fair to take away the
little a person has. Nor should those who have been struck down
be attacked again (*crush* is the physical equivalent of 'oppress'). The
idea of retribution, an aspect of justice, is prominent, for God will
'plead their pleadings' and *rob . . . those who rob them* of life ('soul', in
the sense of life). In other words, God will act to stop wrongdoers
by treating them the way they have dealt with their victims.

24–25. This is a warning not to make friends with those predisposed to getting angry (15:17–18). A person easily angered or
given to anger (lit. 'a lord of anger') is one whose life is characterized
by this response, like the closely related 'lord of wrath' (29:22) who
is overcome with bursts of temper. These two characteristics, both
mentioned here and in 29:22, are not always unhelpful (God

---

1. On the textual issues, and the other options of 'formerly' or 'noble
things', see Waltke (2005: 219–220).

experiences anger and wrath), but are destructive when they so dominate a person that they drive out love, compassion and forgiveness, and make no room for self-control. That is why there is such a strong warning to neither befriend nor associate with such people. The reason is given in verse 25: you become like them, and get trapped in their dangerous way of life.

26–27. An appeal to self-interest lies behind this section, with the key rhetorical question being 'why would you act in a way that could be so harmful to yourself?' (6:1–5). The idea is that when you act as guarantor for someone (thinking that the person will pay the debt), you can expose yourself to a situation where you have an obligation to pay, but no means by which to do so. This is not an attempt to discourage people today from acting as a guarantor, which in many societies is commonly done for family and sometimes friends. Rather, it is an exhortation to count the cost before doing so, and especially to factor in the real possibility that a person might (even if unintentionally) default on a loan. If the amount of the guarantee is greater than your liquid assets, such an arrangement should not be entered into lightly. Prudent individuals would not risk their ability to provide for their own needs and that of their family. This is not to deny the role of generosity among the people of God, but it is a warning against recklessness. Fox (2009: 717) notes that there is nothing comparable in *Amenemope*, so this seems based on Israelite traditions.

28. This verse is unusual in Proverbs as it contains only a negative command or prohibition. No reason is given, no metaphor used and there is no mention of any consequences. There seems to be some respect for tradition or the previous generations. Moving landmarks was prohibited in the law (Deut. 19:14; 27:17), but the form here is different (a weak prohibition, rather than an absolute prohibition or curse). The concern is the same, but the expression is different. When moving landmarks is mentioned in other wisdom texts (Job 24:2; Prov. 23:10–11), the setting is one of injustice motivated by greed or other wickedness, especially against the powerless (15:25), and that is probably the case here too.

29. Here is a commendation of skilful labour (see 18:9), but the exact kind of work is not specified. The stated consequence of the skill is that such a person will prosper or succeed, and be stationed before the king rather than before those less prominent. These workers will find themselves in a position where they can be amply rewarded, and their level of workmanship actually noticed. The implication is that there is value in skilful work. Van Leeuwen (1997: 205) reminds us that 'Wisdom is concerned not with piety alone, but with responsible excellence in all of God's creation.'

1–3. The setting envisaged here is an invitation to a banquet with a ruler (v. 1a). This is not a situation most of us face (but present in *Amenemope* XXIII.13–20), but there is a clear lesson here about the value of self-control at a time when it is easy to indulge. A meal before a ruler (or employer or official, etc.) can be a test as well as a gift. The advice given is to 'understand well' (an intensifying expression in Hebrew, the infinitive + imperfect of the verb 'to understand' [*byn*]; *observe carefully*, ESV, NRSV; 'note well', NIV), which is a call to explore all aspects of the setting (or the person, as it could mean either 'what' or 'who' is before you) in order to act wisely (v. 1b). The action urged is cloaked in hyperbole. Putting a knife to your throat (the word *throat* occurs only here in the OT, but is related to the root 'to swallow') is a dramatic way of saying 'curb your eating'. The danger is if we are predisposed to over-indulgence with food (lit. 'lord of soul'; 'soul/self' [*nepeš*] can mean appetite, as in 6:30; 'lord of' here means 'inclined/given to', as in 22:24). While it is quite natural to desire the fine food served, it can come with strings attached. It is described as 'food of lies' or *deceptive food*. It pretends to be a gift, but as a modern proverb says, there is no such thing as a free lunch. A ruler may have a hidden agenda, perhaps buying our loyalty or silence for some future occasion.

4–5. These verses warn against trusting in riches. The listener is urged not to work hard in order to become rich, as if that were the appropriate goal or 'all-consuming purpose' (Murphy 1998) in life (v. 4a). The second half of verse 4 is elliptical, and reads literally, 'from your understanding, cease'. It could mean 'as a result of your understanding, stop (trying to become rich)' (so NRSV, ESV: *be wise/ discerning enough to desist*) or alternatively, 'stop trying (to become rich) by means of your understanding' (so NIV: 'do not trust your own cleverness'). Both are legitimate ways of reading the Hebrew text, and fit the context, so it may be a deliberate ambiguity implying both possibilities. Fox (2009: 723–724) argues it should be translated as 'staring' here; in other words, stop staring at or fixating on wealth. Verse 5 emphasizes the fleeting nature of riches, which gives a compelling reason for not trusting in or chasing wealth. As soon as our eyes focus (lit. 'fly, hover, light upon') on riches, they are gone (similarly, *Amenemope*, ch. 7). Wealth quickly ('surely', NIV; *suddenly*, NRSV/ESV; a Hebrew intensifying expression that does not specify the exact way in which the verb is intensified) sprouts wings and flies off like a wild eagle into the sky.

6–8. This section echoes verses 1–3, but broadens the concept out to one who offers food begrudgingly. The precise character of this person is not immediately clear. Some versions opt for *stingy* (ESV, NRSV, HCSB), others for 'begrudging' (NIV 1984), while some older versions pick up the more literal sense of 'him who hath an evil eye' (KJV). It refers to someone who is the opposite of one who has a good eye, which in 22:9 describes a generous person. The phrase *do not desire his delicacies* (v. 6b), a reference to desirable food, is also found in verse 3a. Verse 7 indicates that such a person has a façade of being generous, but is not like that on the inside. The only other place where the expression is used in the OT is in 28:22, where it refers to one who chases after wealth. So it describes someone who is greedy and not wanting to share, yet still wanting to have a name for being generous. Verse 7a does not clarify the matter, as it has been variously translated (see NRSV: 'for like a hair in the throat, so are they', and ESV: *for he is like one who is inwardly calculating*). The ESV probably best grasps the sense, but the verb 'think' or 'calculate' occurs only here in the OT. Although these stingy people urge you to eat and drink, they do not really mean it in their heart or inner self (v. 7b). The meaning of verse 8 is clear (you will vomit up what you have eaten and waste your kind words), but the reason for this is not set out. There may have been something bad about the food, but more likely it is a vivid expression for being revolted when you realize the hypocrisy of the host.[2]

---

2. Whybray (1994: 334) suggests that the vomiting is to be taken figuratively, meaning being revolted by a situation; Alden (1983: 168) similarly notes that 'the whole course of events is nauseating'.

9. The teaching here is reminiscent of another proverb: 'do not throw your pearls before pigs' (Matt. 7:6). The reason for refraining from speaking in the presence of fools (those who have rejected the way of wisdom) is that they will treat wise words as of little value (1:7b; 9:7–8a; 18:2). They will refuse to be shaped by them, and so speaking to them is actually a waste of time and effort. Fools will not be educated into God's kingdom.

10–11. Verse 10a is identical to 22:28, but the rest of this section expands and justifies this warning. Here readers are not only told not to move an ancient boundary marker (the equivalent of a surveyor's peg, but more longstanding), they are also prohibited from encroaching on (lit. 'entering', but the context suggests disentitling) the fields of orphans. Orphans are objects of God's special provision in Israel (e.g. Exod. 22:22; Deut. 10:18), echoed in wisdom (Job 29:12; 31:17–18). The reason given in verse 11 for respecting the land rights of others is that they have a strong friend. *Redeemer* often refers to a legal figure, as in Job 19:25, and here refers to God, who is depicted as intervening in a court case (*cause* or 'case' is a legal term, as is *plead*, ESV, or 'take up', NIV) on their behalf in order to secure justice.

iii. The temptations of youth (23:12–35)

12. This is a general call to be shaped by wisdom, beginning a new section not borrowed from *Amenemope*, but including some sayings echoing other Egyptian sources (Fox 2009: 733 notes those from Ahiqar and Anii). Readers are urged to 'bring their heart', that is, apply their mind to instruction (*mûsār*), a key word in Proverbs from the introduction (1:2, 3, 7) and constantly thereafter. It can mean 'discipline' (e.g. 15:10), but in parallel with *words of knowledge* (as also in 19:27) has the sense of being shaped and instructed by wisdom. Being shaped involves both discipline and instruction. The second half of the verse calls on them to listen carefully (*apply* or 'bring' covers both halves of the verse) to words of knowledge. While *instruction* is wider than verbal instruction, listening to the words of the teacher is clearly crucial.

13–14. The word *mûsār* found in verse 12 also occurs here, but with the sense of physical *discipline*, expressed as striking with a rod. Contrary to many contemporary notions of the innocence of

children, Proverbs works on the assumption that folly is bound up
in the heart of a child (see 13:24; 22:15), and so children will need
to be corrected and redirected. Physical punishment of children is
a contentious issue today, but the underlying principle of the need
to shape, restrain and limit them is an essential counterbalance with
other legitimate calls to encourage and nurture our children. It is
not simply one or the other, but both. The precise form in which
this discipline will take place may vary from culture to culture, or
from subculture to subculture. The goal is not for parents to let off
steam, vent their anger or show their power or control. None of
these is endorsed in the book. The purpose of discipline is to save
their soul (*nepeš*, life) from an early death (Sheol, the place of the
dead). This discipline is not meant to be cruel or vindictive, but
rather life-giving. Waltke (2005: 252) rightly observes, 'Parents who
brutalize their children cannot hide behind the rod doctrine of
Proverbs.'

15–16. Like verse 12, this is a general call to the student or son
to be wise. As in verse 12, there is a focus on an inner reality (the
heart/mind) and an outer expression (speech). In verse 12 the outer
manifestation was listening, but here attention is given to the other
important aspect of speaking the things that are right/righteously
(*mêšārîm*). The other way in which these verses develop verse 12 is
by the double reference to the teacher's/parent's response. They will
rejoice in their inner selves (their *heart*) if their student/son is wise
in their heart (v. 15b). Their inner being (lit. 'kidneys', the seat of the
emotions) will exult (a different but parallel word to 'rejoice') when
they speak what is right (8:6). The willingness of the young to be
shaped by wisdom leads to joy and delight in those who are training
them.

17–18. The focus on the heart continues in verse 17a, with a
discouragement from being jealous of sinners (3:31; 24:1, 19). Verse
17b uses an emphatic expression (*kî-'im*, 'indeed' = *but*) to point to
a positive alternative: live/continue/remain (the verb is only implied
here, and not actually present) in the fear of the Lord all (your) days.
This is a call not to move away from the foundational stance in life
of treating God as God (1:7; 9:10) in order to follow the enticements of folly (9:13–18). A motivation for standing firm is given in
verse 18, with an assurance (again *kî-'im*, here often translated

as *surely*) that there is a time after the present (a *future*), and that the certain hope that comes from building on the right foundation (the fear of the Lord) will prevail rather than be cut off.

19–21. These verses begin with an introductory exhortation (v. 19) to listen in order to be wise and in order to go straight ahead in the right way (a series of imperatives as purpose clauses). The specific focus is then on avoiding the company of those who drink and eat excessively, and not to be with/among those who drink wine in excess (20:1; 31:4–5) and eat meat gluttonously (v. 20). Many Christians heed the warning against too much alcohol, but ignore the danger of overeating. The reason for these warnings is given in verse 21 (introduced by *kî, for*): those who adopt such behaviour will be impoverished or dispossessed (land as their means of wealth taken from them). Their excessive consumption and drunkenness, and the resulting drowsiness or slumber, mean that nothing will be achieved, and they will only be able to afford rags for clothes (lit. 'they will be clothed with torn things/garments'). Self-control is the missing virtue here, as the drunkard's and glutton's self-indulgence will only lead to further misery.

22–25. A number of proverbs mention both father and mother (1:8; 4:3; 6:20; 10:1; 15:20; 17:25; 19:26; 20:20; 28:24; 30:11, 17), but this small section is bracketed by calls to have a positive attitude to them. Children are to have a right regard for them – listening, not despising, making them glad (vv. 22, 25). The father is described as the one who gave you life (v. 22), while the mother is the one who bore you (v. 25). There is a strong note of joy in verses 24–25: *greatly rejoice* (an emphatic expression in Hebrew, *gyl*), *be glad* (twice, *śmḥ*), *rejoice* (*gyl*). The key idea is to listen to and respect parents in order to make them glad. The exhortation in verse 23 to buy (or gain/acquire) truth, wisdom, instruction and understanding (see 4:5, 7; 16:16) needs to be interpreted in this context. A right attitude to parents is part of the shaping that wisdom wants to bring.

26–28. The heart has been a recurring image in this part of Proverbs (vv. 12, 15, 17, 19) and has been coupled with an outward expression in listening (v. 12), speaking (v. 16) and now looking (v. 26) – ears, lips and eyes. Keeping our eyes (focus, attention, what we look at) on wisdom and her ways is a key to the warnings that follow about the loose woman. Sexual unfaithfulness often has its origin in what we look at, and where our heart is. Two examples of loose women are given in verse 27: the prostitute and the adulteress. The adulteress is literally a 'foreign' or 'strange' woman, but it is a term that is characteristically used of an adulteress in the foundational chapters of the book (2:16; 5:20; 6:24; 7:5). The prostitute is also used in chapters 1 – 9 as a clear example of folly in practice (6:26; 7:10).[3] The language of her being like a deep pit and, its parallel, a narrow well, are images of danger and death from which it is difficult to escape (22:14). The loose or forbidden woman is elsewhere linked to death (2:18–19; 5:5, 22–23; 6:27–28; 7:22–23, 25–27). She is pictured as lying in wait (7:10–12) for her victim like a robber ('bandit', NIV), and increasing the number of 'betrayers' (*traitors*, ESV; 'unfaithful', NIV) among men. What she does, and how her targets react, has an effect on others who are entitled to faithfulness and loyalty.

29–35. The theme of this section is the self-destructive nature of drinking excessive amounts of alcohol. This is not a major idea in the book, but is certainly present (20:1; 21:17; 23:19–21), and there is a particular warning for those in positions of power and influence (31:4–5). The concept is cleverly introduced by 'a riddle in six questions' (Clifford 1999: 213), beginning with *who* (v. 29), in which a set of negative outcomes (woe, sorrow, strife, complaining, wounds) is described, but not their cause. There is a hint in the last of the six: *Who has redness of eyes?* Our focus is not meant to be on each of these separate consequences, but simply on the barrage of one after another. In verse 30 we are led to the identity of those with such troubles – those who drink excessively. They spend a lot of time drinking (the verb *'ḥr* has connotations of delaying, lingering; Whybray 1994: 340 notes it is used of late drinkers in Isa. 5:11) and sampling new mixtures of wine. Mixed wine is not diluted wine, for it was common to mix rich spices with the wine to bring out a richer flavour. They were the ancient 'wine snobs'. There is a clear instruction given in verse 31: do not spend so much time lingering over

---

3. Waltke (2005: 247), with a number of scholars, emends *zônâ*, prostitute, to *zārâ*, unchaste wife (strange/married woman). This does not change the thrust of the passage significantly.

wine. Looking at wine when it is red (there is no suggestion that we should all drink white wine instead) is really a matter of continually looking at the wine, presumably because they always have a cup in their hand. The expression *it sparkles in the cup* is literally 'it gives [puts forth] its spring in the cup', a way of describing the wine bubbling up like mineral springs.[4] It seems full of life and fun. It tastes rich and mellow in that it *goes down smoothly*, so it is tempting by both its appearance and its taste. Ironically, *smoothly* translates the Hebrew word *mêšārîm*, used in verse 16 in its normal sense of righteousness, but it is also used of wine going down smoothly in Song 7:9 (7:10 Heb.). Verse 31 indicates that drinking can often be an enjoyable – even enticing – experience at the time, but the rest of the passage then sets out the forgotten consequences of excessive drinking.

The sobering realities of verses 32–35 are meant to deter us from indulging in the pleasures of drinking. Verse 32 acts as a summary, observing that the effects are painful like a snakebite or sting. This is then itemized by a series of examples. In verse 33a there will be visions of *strange things* or perhaps even (lustful) images of 'forbidden women' (*zārôt* is used of the strange or forbidden women in 22:14 and other places). The inner thoughts (*heart*) of excessive drinkers will be expressed in perverse or twisted speech (v. 33b), presumably as they lose self-control. They will put themselves in situations of reckless danger (v. 34, lying down in the sea; sleeping on top of a mast or rigging – a hapax so its precise meaning is not certain, but it is clearly foolish). They may be physically injured or beaten up, but not aware of the damage done (v. 35a). The pain will certainly be felt after they have sobered up. The lack of direction in life is seen in that when they wake up from their drunken stupor, all they can think about is the next drink. There is no further purpose in life beyond this downward spiral.

iv. The destinies of the wise and the wicked (24:1–22)

1–2. This is a general warning not to envy evil people or aspire to joining with them, building on 23:17 and anticipating 24:19–20

---

4. Alternatively, Koptak (2003: 549) suggests that the wine is personified, and is here described as sparkling or winking its eye in a seductive way.

(perhaps also 3:31). The nature of their *evil* (*rāʿâ*) is not specified in verse 1, but it involves what they are like on the inside (*their hearts*) and their outward speech (*their lips*). They internally 'plot/plan' violent destruction (*šōd*), and use their speech to create mischief/ trouble (*ʿāmāl*, v. 2; 1:11–16). *Trouble* commonly has the sense of 'work' or 'toil', but here means mischief or harm (as in Job 4:8; Ps. 10:7). We need to choose our friends well, and seek out a helpful group of companions.

3–4. An analogy of a house is used to describe a person's life (see 9:1). It is created (echoing 3:19) by means of practical skill in living (= *wisdom*, *ḥokmâ*) and caused to stand (= *established*) by understanding (*tĕbûnâ*). The analogy of a house continues with the reference to its rooms (v. 3) being filled with wealthy objects that are valuable and give great pleasure (15:6). The exact nature of these objects is not identified (Garrett 1993: 198 is probably wrong to argue that these must be viewed primarily as metaphorical), but it is a picture of delighting in life's overflowing blessings (see 3:9–10). There is simply no other way to build a life that makes sense.

5–6. The positive value of wisdom is set out in these verses, which claim that the guidance wisdom gives is stronger than physical or military power. Real strength is found in a wise person, a man of knowledge (v. 5). Strength must be harnessed to some goal, and the wise have the power to live the good life to its fullest extent, which will include self-control, humility and concern for the community. Similarly, military battles are not always won by the army with the most resources, because it is the tactical decisions that hold greater sway. Thus, verse 6 affirms that proper guidance, part of the goal of the book (1:5), is crucial for military success, as is the advice of many counsellors (11:14; 20:18; 21:22). A key element of being wise is knowing the limits of our wisdom, and therefore looking to wise advisors. If this is so for times of war, it can also be applied to other occasions as well.

7. Fools can be smart, but they cannot be wise. In chapters 1 – 9 those who choose the path of wisdom reject the way of folly and build their lives instead on the fear of the Lord. One practical application of this occurs at the city gate, the place where public and legal decisions were made in a community. The second half of this verse could be read as saying that a fool *will* not speak in such a context (so ESV, NRSV, probably because it would show his folly), or that he *should* not speak (so NIV, because he will have nothing worthwhile to contribute). While either is possible, the latter seems more likely in the light of the first half of the verse.

8–9. Most scholars read these verses together (although Lucas 2015: 159 sees them as separate sayings), even though the scoffer of verse 9b is arguably a different figure. However, *plans to do evil* (v. 8a) seems to be very similar to the *devising of folly* (v. 9a), so it is best to consider the verses as parts of one saying. The one planning to cause evil or injury is rightly viewed as a schemer ('mischief-maker', NRSV). While *schemer* (*ba'al mĕzimmôt*, 'lord of plans') can be a neutral description, doing evil suggests otherwise, as does the labelling of such planning as *sin* (*ḥaṭṭā't*) in verse 9a. Sin here primarily has the sense of missing the mark or falling short of what we should be. The precise connection of verse 9b with what precedes is not clear, but it certainly continues the critique of the scoffer found in the rest of the book (e.g. 1:22; 9:7–8a; 14:6, 9; 15:12; 19:25; 21:24). Most likely the schemer of verses 8–9a is also the scoffer of verse 9b.

10–12. These verses concern how to act towards those suffering adversity.[5] Those who show themselves to be slack (as in 18:9, the *hitpael* of *rph*) in the time of trouble (*ṣārâ*) reveal that their strength is small (*ṣar*). This implies that they should have tried harder in those circumstances. While the day of trouble could refer to the person's own troubles, they lead nicely into the discussion of the sufferings of others in verse 11 and so more likely have this is view. This also accounts for the imperative (*Rescue . . .*) at the beginning of verse 11, where the specific trouble refers to those who are being taken in order to be put to death, or perhaps are on the path of folly that leads to death. This is in parallel with holding back those who are stumbling or tottering to being slain or slaughtered (v. 11b). Verse 11 acts as an exhortation to act on behalf of those who are in peril, rather than be slack and give up. Behind these ideas is the principle of taking initiative to help others, even if it is not our specific

---

5. Some scholars, e.g. McKane, Fox and Lucas, have v. 10 as a discrete saying separate from vv. 11–12. This commentary prefers the divisions suggested by Waltke.

responsibility (see the parable of the Good Samaritan in Luke 10:25–37). This leads nicely on to the reason for being proactive in our care of those who are suffering. We are going to face an evaluation of our lives by God (v. 12). God is described obliquely as the one *who weighs the heart* (21:2) and the one 'who guards your life' (similarly, 2:8, but often using wisdom, 2:11). We cannot plead a lack of knowledge of the need, because God knows and evaluates not simply our words but our inner beings (the *heart*). God guards our life (so NIV), rather than our *soul* (as in ESV/NRSV), since he is keeping watch over all of our life, not just one part of it. Verse 12 climaxes in the clearest expression of our accountability in the retribution principle that he will repay us according to our earthly work. This is also a NT principle (e.g. 2 Cor. 5:10), and one that does not undermine the doctrine of grace.

13–14. These verses exalt wisdom by describing it as sweeter than the dripping honey from the honeycomb (an image also used in 5:3; Ps. 19:10 [11 Heb.]). Honey is pictured proverbially as the sweetest food (Judg. 14:18), but it is described so positively in verse 13 simply as a backdrop to the value of wisdom in verse 14 (16:24). This is a 'how much more' kind of argument. If honey is so desirable, how much more is wisdom! The kind of energy and sweetness that wisdom adds to our life (*nepeš*) gives us a future and a sure hope. While Christian readers might see here a further meaning, the proverb more likely has in view a future that comes from a full, ongoing life in this world (3:16a; 8:35). It could even refer to their descendants or posterity, as in Psalm 37:37. Similarly, the hope (*tiqwâ*) that will not be cut off is not beyond death, but a long life shaped by purpose and value (19:18).

15–16. This section is important not only for its prohibition of attacking the righteous, but also for its reflection on the righteous and their rewards. The negative commands in verse 15 are very clear, reminiscent of 1:10–19 (see also 23:28). They warn not to act like the wicked and ambush the dwelling or resting place of the righteous, nor do any destructive violence to it (and impliedly to the righteous). More interesting is the reason given in verse 16. Some readers think that the doctrine of retribution in Proverbs – that God will reward the righteous and punish the wicked – means that the righteous will always prosper. This view, echoed by Job's three friends, takes no account of this verse, nor of other proverbs that describe property being unjustly taken by violence. The idea of retribution is not that righteousness is always rewarded on every occasion, but rather over the course of one's life. Verse 16 makes it clear that a righteous person can *fall* (suffer a setback, reversal or difficulty) seven times (symbolic of completeness), even though that is not the end (Ps. 34:19 [Heb. 20]). This makes it important for us not to judge a person's righteousness only by their current circumstances. Of course, life also tells us that there are many other reasons (famine, being born in a poor country, etc.) why people do not prosper materially. Yet there is a truth that those who live in a way intended by God will find 'the good life' (including in its fullest NT sense), while those who take the path of folly will experience obstacles in their pathway.

17–18. The advice in verse 17 is a typical expression of wisdom righteousness in treating your enemies (20:22; 25:21–22; Job 31:29; Matt 5:43–44). It is discouraging even an inner delight (*your heart*) when your enemy stumbles (*Schadenfreude*). Yet the reason given in verse 18 is quite unexpected for a proverb. We are to avoid gloating over our enemy's setbacks lest the Lord sees us gloating, is displeased by our attitude, and turns back his anger from our enemy. In other words, if we delight in our enemies tripping up, God will help them. God is even prepared to aid those who oppose him.

19–20. This section is a call not to worry about, or be jealous of, wicked wrongdoers. The reason for this confidence in the face of evil is set out in verse 18, introduced by *for* (*kî*). *Future*, as in verse 14, refers not to life after death, but rather a long and full life on earth. This is what the evil person will not have. Confirmation of this can be found in verse 20b. The *lamp of the wicked* (as in 13:9; 20:20; 21:4) is their life, and being *put out* refers to their early or untimely death. Evildoers are not to be envied or feared as they have no prospect of a life that can be enjoyed (23:17–18; 24:1–2).

21–22. The words of the wise conclude with both a positive direction and a pathway to avoid. In verse 21 there is a commendation of the underlying wisdom foundation of fearing the Lord, which means to respect him for who he is. Twinned with this is a call to fear (which probably also means 'respect') the king. Negatively, this means to turn away from those who act differently. Verse

22 provides the reason (again introduced by *for*, *kî*). Disaster will arise among those who do not fear their God and the king (v. 22a). Verse 22b is more difficult, in that the 'two of them' are not identified. While it could refer to two opponents, the only twosome mentioned here is the Lord and the king. If these are the source of the ruin, it will be a punishment imposed on those who have failed to respect them. The opponents are not those who will create a disaster, but those who will experience disastrous punishment that will be imposed on them. This is a good reason to avoid such people.

Meaning
These words of the wise are a recapitulation of themes found earlier in the book. The introduction in 22:17–21 has strong echoes of chapters 1 – 9, and calls on the young person to embrace wisdom as the path through life. This is followed in 22:22 – 23:11 by a series of examples of the kind of choices that young people need to make in order to stay wise, with a particular focus on finances. Attitudes to the needy, friends, money, property, work, food and speech are all considered. The second major section (23:12–35) covers a number of temptations that young people will encounter – refusal of parental discipline, gluttony, sexual immorality and drunkenness. This leads nicely on to a description of the differing destinies of the wise and the wicked (24:1–22), peppered with clear exhortations to choose wisdom.

B. More sayings of the wise (24:23–34)

i. The role of the judges in administering justice (24:23–25)
A new heading is found in 24:23, which introduces further sayings of the wise in 24:23–34. These sayings are distinct from what precedes in that there is no father's address to the son, nor any mention of the Lord or wisdom (Koptak 2003: 564). However, this may be because it is a very short section of only twelve verses. There are two useful ways of structuring the material. It can be grouped into verses 23–25 (the role of judges in administering justice); verses 26–29 (promoting community in speech and work); and verses 30–34 (the folly of laziness). Alternatively, there could be two parallel sections (vv. 23–27, 28–34), each starting with a focus on the law

courts (vv. 23–25, 28–29) then moving on to daily life (speech and work in vv. 26–27; laziness in vv. 30–34). Perhaps it is part of the cleverness of Proverbs that both structures seem grounded in the text, but the first has most to commend it.[6]

Context

Some scholars (e.g. Garrett) see verse 26 included in this section which involves behaviour in court. However, the focus in verses 23b–25 is on judging not witnessing (so Waltke). Even if verse 26 had in view lying in a court setting, it has more in common with verses 28–29 (including the word *lips* in vv. 26, 28) than with verses 23–25, and so belongs in the next section. This gives a single thrust to these verses, set out clearly in verse 23b as 'showing partiality is not good'.

Comment

23–25. Verse 23b is not a command to avoid partiality (lit. 'recognizing the face', i.e. preferential treatment), but rather a wisdom warning that showing favouritism in a court setting is not wise or right (*good*). Fundamental to a just legal system is that cases are decided according to the evidence, not for other, often self-serving, reasons such as the offer of a bribe. The idea of unfairly favouring the wicked is also condemned in 18:5; 28:21, while the broader principle of partiality is also found in 17:15, 23, 26. There is no concern here with the unfair favouring of the righteous, although this too would be unjust. Rather, verse 24 deals only with the wrong acquittal of a wicked person. Those who are guilty of committing a crime (the sense of 'wicked' in a legal setting, so Waltke) are to be confronted and condemned. This right attitude is commended in verse 25a. The varying attitudes to the wicked/guilty are then evaluated by their consequences in terms of cursing and blessing.

---

6. The second view is a slight modification of Garrett's structure (he places v. 26 with vv. 23–25). He sees a parallel structure for organizational purposes, with a focus on the law courts in vv. 23–26 and 28–29, with v. 27 concerned with economic priorities, and vv. 30–34 concentrating on laziness.

Those who wrongly acquit the guilty will be cursed and denounced (v. 24b), but those who rebuke or convict the wicked will gain a great blessing (v. 25b).

Meaning

When responsibility is given to a person to decide right and wrong, this must be based on the facts, not on our feelings for the person, or our personal benefit. Right action on such matters will lead to blessing.

ii. Promoting community in speech and work (24:26–29)
Context

These verses all deal with some aspects of being members of the community, either in what we say (vv. 26, 28–29) or how we work constructively (v. 27). While verses 28–29 address how to behave in a court setting, they deal with how to act as a witness not a judge. The principle behind the exhortations will also have a wider application in society.

Comment

26. An honest answer is commended. The absence of any legal language, and the surrounding community setting, suggest that verse 26 has honest speech in general in view (so Clifford 1999: 217). The phrase *kisses the lips* (v. 26b) is not found elsewhere in the OT. Kissing is sometimes an action of affection or homage, neither of which suits the context here. *DCH* suggests it means 'seal' and so 'be silent' (as in similar expressions in Gen. 41:40; Job 31:27). Certainly, the act of kissing involves putting the lips together, so the idea here is that once you have said all that needs to be said, you add nothing else. This seems better than the NIV suggestion that an honest answer is 'like' a kiss on the lips (i.e. something delightful). While this is also true, the preposition 'like' is not part of the Hebrew text, nor does it seem implied. Waltke (2005: 293) argues that the 'saying instructs the disciple to express his devotion to his superiors or peers by giving a straightforward, not devious and/or distorted, answer'.

27. The idea of building a house in verse 27 is used in 14:1 of building a community or household, not the physical building – a home rather than a house (McKane 1970: 575–576 notes that it can mean 'build a family' elsewhere). The saying clearly endorses hard work and diligent preparation, but it also requires an appropriate set of priorities. At the very least, as Garrett (1993: 201) suggests, it means that 'one should not provide for personal comfort until a means of income is established' (similarly McKane 1970: 576, 'Wealth must be produced before it is consumed'). Doing tasks in the right order is also an important aspect of wisdom.

28–29. These verses seem to be a proverbial pair. Themes of being a false witness (v. 28) and the danger of taking revenge (v. 29) are combined here. Other sayings about being a false witness are more descriptive (e.g. 12:17; 14:5, 25; 19:5, 9, 28; 21:28; 25:18), but this proverb explicitly prohibits being a deceptive witness, making groundless (*ḥinnām*, *without cause* or 'without success') allegations against a fellow member of the community. The prohibition against revenge in verse 29 echoes 20:22, which reminds us that God will exercise retribution. While verse 28 endorses truth in speech, the exhortation in verse 29 not to stoop to paying someone back also speaks of the need for us to be gracious in speech – treating people better than they deserve.

Meaning

Honest and gracious words are not only good work priorities, but also build up our community. Benefiting others strengthens our society, while being self-serving and vindictive does not.

iii. The folly of laziness (24:30–34)
Context

The sluggard or lazy person is a prominent figure in Proverbs, and is dealt with at length here, in 6:6–11 and 26:13–14. Verse 32 indicates that this is an example story, told in verses 30–31, in which the point is established by the proverbs quoted in verses 33–34 (so Garrett). The conclusion of verses 33–34 is a virtual quotation of 6:10–11, while the agricultural imagery in verses 30–31 echoes similar pictures elsewhere in the book (6:8; 10:5; 20:4).

Comment

30–31. The parallelism in verse 30 makes it clear that the sluggard (lazy person) is someone who is lacking sense ('stupid', NRSV). The phrase *lacking sense* (*ḥăsār lēb*, lacking heart) is a distinctively wisdom one, used in the OT eleven times in Proverbs, once in Ecclesiastes and nowhere else. It can refer to those led astray by folly (6:32; 7:7; 9:16), or who have not yet embraced wisdom (9:4). The setting in a field or vineyard is suitable for a society where the means of producing wealth were largely agricultural. The observations of verse 31, introduced by 'see' or *behold*, testify to neglect. Even basic maintenance of a vineyard would involve clearing away thorns and weeds/nettles (see the mention of the sluggard and thorns in 15:19). In the hill country of Israel stone walls were used to terrace slopes, enabling trees to take root and preventing water from running away. Failure to maintain such walls was self-destructive (see the positive pattern in Isa. 28:24–29, using wisdom language).

32–34. In verse 32 the speaker begins to draw out the lesson (*mûsār*), gaining instruction from what has been observed. This is a typical wisdom practice of learning lessons based on observing the created world (see 6:6–11). The conclusion in verses 33–34 is that lack of effort will lead to poverty and want (19:15; 20:4). Verse 33 appears to be a proverb that the lazy could use to justify their way of life. We all need rest, and the threefold repetition of *a little* (*mě'aṭ*) makes it sound balanced and responsible. However, the lazy person is only making excuses, for such people love sleep (20:13), and their laziness puts them into a deep sleep (19:15). As in 6:10–11, their idleness means that they have nothing to eat, and so the consequence of their laziness is poverty and want.

Meaning
As seen elsewhere in the book, laziness is not criminally wrong, but simply self-destructive. Failure to work or produce anything leads to the possession of no food, and no means to buy any. While sluggards are described in comic terms, their life is really a tragic mistake.

4. MORE PROVERBS OF SOLOMON COMPILED DURING THE TIME OF HEZEKIAH (25:1 – 29:27)

Chapters 25 – 29, the second grouping of sayings linked to Solomon (25:1), are best seen as two separate collections – chapters 25 – 27 and 28 – 29. The first section contains many striking comparisons and stark metaphors, as well as the 'contradictory' proverbs of 26:4, 5, but few references to God and relatively little antithetical parallelism (often pivoting on *but*). Toy (1899: x) notes antithetical proverbs only in 25:2; 27:6, 7, 12, but on thirty-three occasions in chapters 28 – 29, the familiar *but* reappears, and the old righteous/ wicked and rich/poor divisions are again prominent. The admonitions in this section presuppose that those being addressed already possess significant assets (27:23–27; 28:19) that need to be managed wisely. Chapters 28 – 29 may indeed be a manual for future monarchs (Malchow 1985). These chapters contain some proverbs already in a previous collection (e.g. 21:9 and 25:24).

Van Leeuwen's (1988) careful analysis of chapters 25 – 27 identifies the following components:

1. 25:2–27 – a 'proverb poem' addressed to courtiers, about social rank and social conflict;

2. 26:1–12 – a 'proverb poem' dealing with the fool, and life situations that call for a wisdom approach;
3. 26:13–16 – a 'proverb poem' about the sluggard;
4. 26:17–28 – a poem developing themes taken from chapter 25;
5. 27:1–22 – a collection of miscellaneous proverbs, set out in couplets (vv. 1–2, 3–4, etc.), although Waltke sees here two parallel sets of instructions on friends and friendship;
6. 27:23–27 – an admonitory poem, which can be read as advice to a farmer, but on a deeper level is addressed to the king as 'shepherd' of his people.

A. Living wisely in public (25:1 – 27:27)

i. Living in the community and in the court (25:1–28)
Context
After the title of verse 1, Bryce (1972) and Van Leeuwen (1998) have shown that there is an introduction in verses 2–5 (the king in vv. 2–3 and the wicked in vv. 4–5), followed by two sections. Verses 6–15 deal with the king and his subjects, while verses 16–26 concern the wicked. Verses 2 and 27 serve as an inclusio, focused on glory. Verse 28 falls outside the structure, but does not really belong to 26:1–12 either.

Comment
1. The heading in 25:1, echoing 1:1 and 10:1, describes these five chapters as *More proverbs of Solomon*, which the men of Hezekiah *copied* (ESV, NRSV) or 'compiled' (NIV). Solomon ruled from about 961 to 922 BC, while Hezekiah was king from around 715 to 687 BC. This means that the individual sayings that follow have their origin in the time of Solomon or before, but that the process of gathering and editing them was not completed until more than 200 years later. Proverbs is a predominantly Solomonic book, but it has grown over several centuries.[1]

---

1. Van Leeuwen (1997: 217) helpfully distinguishes between proverb creation and proverb collection. Many of the words in this book of Scripture have been shaped over long periods of time.

2–3. Kings are mentioned in both verses, and each reference is linked to searching. It is the God-given task for those in authority to explore and discern God's glory hidden in the created world (v. 2). The same Hebrew word is used for what God conceals and what kings are to search for. Such matters are hidden not to remain undiscovered, but rather to give rulers a quest in life. However, the inner thoughts (lit. *heart*) of kings are so complex to fathom that they are pictured as difficult to search. It is like finding an object in a location as high as the sky and as low as the earth's depths (v. 3; *'ereṣ, earth*, may here mean 'underworld'). Putting these two verses together suggests that while kings' intentions are seldom clear (and this may be a riddle), their key task is to explore God's glory.

4–5. While the king is also mentioned in verse 5, the focus is now on the wicked, and how their presence impedes the work of the king. They are depicted as dross that needs to be removed from the silver in order to make it pure (v. 4). The parallel is clear: take away the dross and the silver material can then be used; take away the wicked and the king can have a sustained rule that embodies righteousness (v. 5; 16:12b). A variety of wicked characters will be explored in verses 16–26, and these will all impede a king's righteous rule, which is an equivalent expression to searching out God's glory.

6–15. The focus here is on how to conduct yourself in the king's court. The king (*melek*) is explicitly named in verse 6, while the ruler (military or political leader, *qāṣîn*) rounds off the section in verse 15. However, all the intervening examples imply the same setting. Bryce (1972: 151) notes that there are six parallel sections in both verses 6–15 and 16–26, the first dealing with the ruler and the second consisting of six wicked characters.

6–7b. There is a warning here about the danger of self-promotion. The young men in the court are admonished neither to claim honour for themselves ('exalt yourself', NIV; *put yourself forward*, ESV/NRSV), nor to do this physically by standing among those (presumably in the court) who are important. As Jesus was later to say (Luke 14:7–11), it is better to be invited up higher than to be told to get to the end of the queue where you belong.

7c–9a. The last phrase of verse 7 (*what your eyes have seen*) belongs to the beginning of verse 8, as in most English versions. Here is another warning, this time not to be hasty in going to court rather than sorting a matter out with your neighbour. It is tempting to think that we must be right if we have seen something with our own eyes (v. 7c), but there may be more to the story that we are unaware of. The legal system is riddled with half-baked cases that fall apart in the end. The issue here seems to be hasty litigation (as in 20:3) rather than a deceitful process (as in 24:28). This haste is envisaged in verse 8, when a neighbour's response to a legal claim ends up reversing the outcome. The self-righteous litigant is shamed or dishonoured as the whole picture emerges. A better way forward would be to speak personally to the neighbour to see if the matter can be resolved or explained, before hastily dragging the information out into the public arena. This teaching is also echoed at the beginning of the process set out by Jesus (Matt. 18:15–20).

9b–10. The main goal here is the avoidance of shame (as also in v. 8) and a bad reputation. The loss of face implied here is often regarded as a minor irritant in the West, but is a major community issue in an honour/shame culture. The trigger for this undesirable loss of community respect and status is revealing another person's secret (v. 9b; in Ps. 25:14 it refers to being in the inner circle where you hear the most private of conversations). Few things are as destructive of community as gossip and betrayal of trust (11:13; 20:19).

11–12. The wise use of words is commended here. Various kinds of jewellery are referred to – a brooch or necklace of golden fruit[2] in a silver setting, a golden ring, a gold ornament – each an object of great beauty and value. Equally valuable, these verses say, is a word fitly spoken. The word *fitly* (*'ōpen*, NIV, 'rightly given') occurs only here in the OT, but the parallel with verse 12 implies some form of appropriateness (in timing, content, etc.). Wise reproof or correction addressed to one willing to listen (lit. 'a hearing ear') is also greatly commended and a fundamental attitude of the wise (9:8b–9).

13–14. Vivid weather imagery is used here of two contrasting types of speech. A messenger who faithfully (*ne'ĕmān*) passes on a

---

2. Van Leeuwen (1997: 218) suggests that *tappûaḥ* is more likely 'golden apricots' than apples. Whybray (1994: 364) notes that apples had not yet been introduced into Palestine. Kidner (1964: 158) suggests a quince.

(?long-awaited or important) message refreshes the 'life' (*nepeš, soul*, life; NIV/NRSV, 'spirit') of his master (13:17). This is compared to the cold of snow at harvest time – not a destructive cold, but one that is a refreshing change from summer heat. Snow at harvest time would be unlikely, but it may refer to runners bringing down compacted snow or ice to the valley to cool down their masters (Van Leeuwen 1997: 219). A negative image of speech is given in verse 14, when a gift spoken or boasted about ('I'll bring it on Sunday!') is never actually delivered. In many non-Western cultures gift-giving is fundamental to the community. These words give the impression of a generous giver – and are probably meant to do so – but no benefit comes to the person who was promised the gift. These words are as futile as cloud and wind, which promise rain for the farmer, but it never actually rains on the crops (see a similar idea in Jude 12). Longman (2006: 454) calls this 'all show and no results'. Faithful speech is life-giving; empty promises only increase frustration and result in shame for the 'giver'.

15. While the illustrations in this chapter all make sense in a court setting, this is made explicit again in verse 15, linking this section to verses 2–3. In the ANE rulers had near absolute power, so they needed to be persuaded, and their thinking shifted, by the astute use of words. Clifford (1999: 225) notes that 'persuade' has a negative sense in its four other uses in Proverbs, but it is positive here and in Hosea 2:16 and Judges 14:15. The two virtues of patience and persistence in speech are commended. Just as water can wear down rocks over many years, gentle and determined words of counsel can change rulers.[3]

16–27. In this section on wicked characters, there appear to be six sections with negative figures mentioned: a hateful friend, false witness, faithless man/tormentor, enemy, backbiter/bad wife and the wicked (so Bryce 1972). Verse 27b operates as an inclusio with verse 2, while verse 27a picks up the honey imagery of verse 16.

---

3. Van Leeuwen (1997: 219) comments that 'the softest organ, the tongue, breaks the hardest organ, the bone'. Fox (2009: 784) notes that 'Gentle, patient speech is so powerful that it can overcome even a hardened, stubborn official.'

16–17. Self-control of our appetites is commended in verse 16, with the figure of the glutton implied as the alternative. Honey is not only used for survival in a desert culture, but can also be added to rich food as an extra touch (honey is viewed positively in 16:24; 24:13). However, excessive consumption of any food is unhealthy. This may lead to vomiting, which involves the loss of any nutritional value, as well as the unpleasant experience of bringing up food. Verse 17 has a different scenario in view, but the repetition of 'have one's fill' in both verses 16 and 17 ties them together. It refers not to the friendly action of dropping in on a neighbour or friend (most of us probably do this too seldom), but rather of constantly being there (lit. 'make your foot precious', i.e. rare). As in verse 16, the neighbour may have 'had his fill of you' and, in the relational equivalent of vomiting (wanting you out of their lives), start to hate you.[4]

18. Relating to our neighbours is also in view here, but this time the problem is bearing false witness against them. The false witness is a common figure in Proverbs (e.g. 6:19; 14:5, 25; 19:5, 9; 21:18; 24:28), and such behaviour is often a cloak for greed or vindictiveness. In this verse it is said to be (*like* does not appear in the Hebrew text as it is a metaphor not a simile) a destructive weapon (club, sword, arrow) able to damage a person greatly.

19–20. Verse 19 is fairly straightforward, describing the folly of trusting in those who are treacherous or will betray us. Again this is a metaphor, but the force of calling someone a bad tooth or an unstable foot is to make a comparison. Do not rely on what is unreliable. An unstable foot might collapse as we put pressure on it, and a weak tooth might break if we eat something hard. In order to be useful as a foot or tooth, there needs to be good grounds for trusting them. A treacherous person – one given to betrayal – is even less trustworthy. Verse 20 is more difficult, as can be seen by comparing the ESV and NRSV. The ESV speaks of taking off a garment on a cold day and putting vinegar on soda; the NRSV puts vinegar

---

4. Clifford (1999: 225) comments, 'Too much of a good and delightful thing, honey or friendship, can be a bad thing.' Waltke (2005: 327) cites the English proverbs, 'familiarity breeds contempt' and 'guests, like fish, stink after three days'.

on a wound, and replaces taking off the garment with 'like a moth in clothing or a worm in wood, sorrow gnaws at the human heart'. The NRSV is based on the significantly different LXX text, but the Hebrew text can make sense as it stands. The incongruity of singing songs (usually songs of joy or praise) to someone with a heavy heart is the key idea of the verse, and this is seen to be as odd as taking off some clothes on a cold day, or pouring vinegar on a wound (which would irritate, but not bring relief). The word 'wound' (*neter*) could alternatively mean natron, a form of sodium carbonate used in making soap (hence ESV *soda*), but 'wound' fits better with the anomaly in the verse.

21–22. This section deals with how to treat our enemies, and the clear teaching of verse 21 is that we meet their needs (of food and water) rather than satisfy our wishes for revenge (20:22; 24:29; Fox 2009: 787 comments, 'Mercy is the best revenge'). We must treat them rightly, that is, as human beings. What is less clear is the motivation behind verse 22. The most likely explanation is that acting rightly towards others holds them fully accountable for how they then respond. We have done right, and so will be rewarded by God (v. 22b), but our right actions have turned up the heat on our enemies, asking how they will now respond. Shame now may prevent more serious loss in the future. Paul picks up these verses in Romans 12:17–21 in a context of peacemaking, and urges his readers not to take revenge, leaving that with God, but to act honourably even when others have wronged us, and to pursue peace. It takes on a similar thrust here.

23–24. These verses 'portray things that *precipitate* conflict' (Van Leeuwen, 1988: 85). As surely as the north wind brings rain (this may suggest an Egyptian origin, since in Israel the rain comes from the Mediterranean to the west), so backbiting speech creates anger in others (v. 23). Backbiting – hidden words spoken behind someone's back – provokes a strong reaction in return when the truth comes out. Suggestions, comments and other words, whose purpose is to undermine another and gain something for ourselves, destroy trust and community. Verse 24, similar to 21:19, alerts us to how destructive marital discord can be, initiated by either the husband or wife. We are urged to stay away from such conflict, probably for our own good as much as for the rest of the household.

25–26. A balance of two contrasting 'water images' (Lucas 2015) is presented in these verses. Good news from a distant land is refreshing and energizing, in the same way that a drink of cold water revives a person who is thirsty (alternatively, *nepeš* could mean 'throat' that is parched). News from a far land could be about a friend or family member, or even business interests established a long distance away. Without news there is anxiety; with good news there is fresh encouragement. The second image is one of a valuable thing spoiled. A fresh source of water like a spring or fountain is life-giving, but when muddied or polluted (corrupted, made useless), it can no longer fulfil its purpose. Righteous people can greatly benefit a community, but this is frustrated if they give way to (lit. 'totter, shake, slip') or crumble before the wicked. Whybray (1994: 370) sees here a recognition that 'the wicked do sometimes triumph over the righteous.' If the righteous cease to live righteously, they will allow wickedness to spread. Edmund Burke famously said, 'The only thing necessary for the triumph of evil is for good men to do nothing.'

27. The first half of this verse closes off the section beginning at verse 16 with another reminder about self-control. While it is specifically about honey, it is meant to deal with issues of gluttony in general. The second half of the verse forms an inclusio with verse 2 and its focus on God's glory.[5] Here, the corollary of searching out God's glory is that we should not try to seek our own glory (so ESV). This half consists of three nouns without a verb (lit. 'searching of their glory/honour is glory'), and it could refer to seeking too much glory (so NRSV: 'seek honour on top of honour'), but the pronominal suffix ('their') suggests that it refers to seeking their glory rather than God's.

28. This verse is strictly outside the proverbial poem identified by Van Leeuwen, but its content fits better with the preceding material than with 26:1–12. Since the theme of self-control brackets verses 16–27, this verse adds further endorsement of self-control. A lack of self-control leaves us defenceless in times of (unspecified)

---

5. Van Leeuwen (1988: 86) notes that '*every* word in v 27b is derived from vv 2–3'.

attack. Safety would have been found in a walled city, so a city without walls would be unable to keep intruders out.

Meaning

Bracketed by a concern for God's glory, this section draws attention to how to behave in the presence of those in authority. Carefulness rather than self-indulgence is the key to such potentially dangerous yet rewarding opportunities. The largely positive advice of verses 6–15 is about knowing our place, seeking to resolve broken relationships and speaking wisely, faithfully and patiently. Furthermore, verses 16–27 warn us about actions and characters to avoid if we wish to do well in such a setting. We need to have self-control, avoiding false witness and false trust. Our actions and words need to be appropriate to the context, and seek to be transformative. If we do this, we will bring life and promote the well-being of the community.

ii. How to deal with a fool (26:1–12)

Context

The fool (*kĕsîl*) is a particular focus in this section and appears in every verse except verse 2. There is no detailed attempt to outline the specific type of fool in view, for the focus is fairly broad. Instead, there are a variety of general observations about what all kinds of fools have in common, as well as some indication of how to treat them. This section contains the famous contradictory proverbs (vv. 4–5), as well as two crucial sayings about fools using proverbs (vv. 7, 9).

Comment

1–3. All three verses are sayings with striking nature comparisons. The first two verses are similes. Most people do not associate Israel with snow, but places like Mount Hermon today have ski-fields on their slopes, and it occasionally snows in Jerusalem. Yet it never snows in the dry, hot summers. Slightly differently, while it can rain at harvest time, it does not normally do so, and it is destructive when heavy rain falls at this time (e.g. 1 Sam. 12:17–18). Thus, the two images are of objects that do not belong together. Previously, fine speech has been described as not fitting for a fool (17:7), and also living in luxury (19:10). The point of verse 1 is that it is not appropriate to treat a fool with honour or glory. Verse 2 is the only verse in the section not specifically referring to the fool, but it acts as a complement to verse 1. Verse 1 spoke of *honour* (something good) being given to an undeserving fool; verse 2 mentions an undeserved *curse* (something bad) aimed at an implied innocent person. Verse 3 describes something bad happening to someone who deserves it.[6] What is clear here is that the classical doctrine of retribution (the righteous are rewarded; the wicked are punished) is not always seen to apply in Proverbs. The images in verse 2 are of small birds flitting about and flying but never landing for long. It is as if they never landed at all. Similarly, a curse (words designed to damage someone) that is undeserved (*ḥinnām* can mean either, as here, 'without cause' or 'without success') does not come to a(n impliedly innocent) person.[7] Verse 3 describes a number of actions that are fitting: a whip to spur a horse on, a bridle to control a donkey and a rod or cane to punish a fool (10:13b). Clifford (1999: 231) comments, 'By implication a fool is a stupid animal.'

4–5. Unlike the descriptive sayings in the rest of the section, these two verses are admonitions, and they seem to contradict one another at first glance. Are we to answer fools according to their folly (v. 5) or not answer them (v. 4)? This actually helps us to see the nature of proverbs. Few proverbs are designed to cover every situation. 'Too many cooks spoil the broth' and 'many hands make light work' both seem to be true, but they cannot both apply to the same situation at the same time. Similarly, Proverbs tells us that we need wisdom to know when not to answer fools according to their folly (v. 4) and when to answer (v. 5). Both are true and helpful as proverbs, but we need to discern which is the best proverb for any specific

---

6. See Van Leeuwen (1988: 92). Lucas (2015: 168), following Van Leeuwen, comments, 'The reason for the apparent anomaly of v. 2 not containing the word "fool" is because the pattern of good thing – bad person, bad thing – good person and bad thing – bad person did not allow this.'

7. The *ketib* reads *lōʼ*, 'not', which is better than the *qere* which reads *lô*, 'to him'. Murphy (1998: 197) suggests that the *qere* is obviously to be followed, but gives no reasons.

circumstance. So, if we try to reason with fools, we can get caught up with their pointless talk and so become foolish ourselves (v. 4). We are not to do that. However, sometimes we need to show that a fool's argument leads logically to undesirable conclusions, or to rebut it by reasoned argument. This will alert fools to the fact that their views are untenable. The difficulty is knowing when to rebuke and when to ignore.

6–11. These sayings are full of imagery and contain several similes and other implied comparisons. Verses 7 and 9 help us to see some restrictions on how proverbs can be used by explaining the effects of *a proverb in the mouth of fools*. The Hebrew preposition *like* is not present in either verses 7 or 9, but a comparison is intended. The point of the implied comparison in verse 7 is that the legs of a lame person cannot function as legs should (i.e. be useful for walking). Similarly, a proverb has its purpose set out in 1:2–6, but this cannot be achieved if the person using the proverbs is a fool. In verse 9 the picture is of a drunk person waving around the branch of a thornbush, which has the potential to cause real harm to others. The ESV translation (*a thorn that goes up into the hand of a drunkard*) suggests that fools harm themselves, but damage caused to others is probably in view (so NIV, NRSV). If verse 7 describes a proverb in the mouth of a fool as useless, verse 9 adds that it can be dangerous as well. In other words, you can receive or pass on wisdom simply by quoting proverbs. Within the book as a whole, this makes perfect sense. Chapters 1 – 9 have insisted that the way of wisdom involves starting with the right foundation, the fear of the Lord; choosing to follow Lady Wisdom rather than Dame Folly; and allowing wisdom to shape our character. We cannot bypass any of these steps without slipping back into folly. Only when we have put these elements in place will we be able to use the proverbial sayings to convey wisdom and bring life. Fools disqualify themselves from using proverbs rightly.

The remaining verses of this subsection highlight how we should treat, and in most cases avoid, fools. Verse 6 discourages from using fools to pass on a message. Since fools cannot discern the folly of violence, they may speak a message (or add their own comments) in such a way as to provoke a response of violence. Drinking violence (4:17) is an image of taking part in the violent conflict that might follow. Cutting off our feet – which would mean that we could never deliver a message ourselves – is a vivid way of describing what will happen when we entrust our words to a fool. Our message will never arrive, largely because it may be changed and distorted as it is presented. In verse 8 showing honour to a fool (discouraged in v. 1) is to make society ineffective. A stone is meant to leave a sling, much like a bullet must leave a gun, in order to perform its function. Giving honour to a fool will mean that nothing productive will be achieved. Instead of being honoured, a fool should be thrown out of society. Verse 10 cautions against hiring a passing fool (a drunk is one kind of such a fool). Their work (which may be to pass on a proverb or message in the light of vv. 6, 9) will only result in them wounding other people (lit. 'all'), physically or otherwise (*rab* means *archer* here and in Job 16:13, Jer. 50:29). Hiring a fool can cause great harm. Moreover, fools will not learn from their mistakes, so again we should avoid relying on them. Verse 11 compares them to a dog returning to its vomit (2 Pet. 2:22). The problem is not that fools need to be instructed; they need to have foundational and ongoing change as outlined in chapters 1 – 9. They need to embrace the way of wisdom and decisively turn away from folly.

   12. This final verse avoids the imagery of verses 6–11 and builds on the depiction of a fool in these verses. In the light of verses 6–11, a fool has no prospect of a worthwhile and productive life. Now verse 12 adds that people who are wise in their own eyes are worse off than a fool (see also 29:20). The phrase *wise in his own eyes*, used of a fool in verse 5, elsewhere describes a fool who will not listen to advice (12:15), a lazy person (26:16) and a rich person lacking understanding (28:11). It refers to those who are self-sufficient rather than grounding their lives in wisdom.

Meaning
There is further ammunition here to discourage young people from taking the way of folly, and relying on those who have chosen that path. Folly is not only a pointless option; it is a deadly one. Life is too valuable to be wasted on folly. Yet even the wisdom of proverbs needs to be used properly. In the hands of a fool it can be useless or dangerous. The fundamental step of rejecting folly and embracing wisdom, grounded in the fear of the Lord used to shape our character, is absolutely essential.

iii. The lazy person (26:13–16)

Context

The sluggard (*'āṣēl*) or lazy person is developed fairly extensively in the book as a whole, and is given full treatment not only here but also in 6:6–11 and 24:30–34. This passage builds on some of the other sayings as well. The idea of there being a lion outside is found in 22:13; the sluggard burying his hand in a dish and not even bringing food to his mouth occurs in 19:24; the link with excessive sleep is made in 6:9–10; 19:15; 20:13; 24:33. Even the phrase *wiser in his own eyes* is adopting language just used to describe a fool (vv. 5, 12; see also 3:7; 12:15). The lazy person, then, is a clear example of what Proverbs means by 'a fool'. Van Leeuwen (1988: 110) observes that a key idea is that sluggards are stuck motionless to one place – they will not go outside (v. 13), even get out of bed (v. 14), and so they are stuck to their table (v. 15) and will not budge when given advice (v. 16).

Comment

13–16. The lazy person's excuse for not going out to do work is that there is a lion in the street (v. 13). While we can see from 22:13 that the fear is of being killed, the comic nature of the portrayal suggests that this is not a legitimate concern. More likely, it is someone who is taking advantage of any excuse not to go where useful work will be required. This is reinforced in verse 14 by the implied comparison to a door on a hinge.[8] It is appropriate for a door to remain connected with the rest of the house, but the sluggard is as attached to his bed or couch as a door is to a house. This is unnecessary and inappropriate, and means that such individuals do nothing productive for themselves or their community. Alonso Schöckel comments, 'Moving in order not to move appears to be the height of laziness' (cited in Murphy 1998: 201). It is like trying to drive a car with the handbrake on and the chassis chained to a fence. The most comic picture is found in verse 15, echoing

---

8. Doors were hung differently in those days. Waltke (2005: 356) suggests a 'door pivot' fixed top and bottom in holes in wood or stone. However, this word occurs only here in this sense, so its meaning is uncertain.

19:24. Here laziness so clearly damages sluggards, as they are too lazy to feed themselves from food in a common dish put in front of them. It is too much effort to lift their hand from the dish to their mouth, even though they need to do so in order to live. Verse 16 makes the link with the fool of 26:5, 12 (*wiser in his own eyes*), demonstrating that such laziness is a parade example of folly. The comparison with seven people who can answer sensibly (i.e. with wisdom) shows the extent of their miscalculation: they think that they are wiser than seven others combined, even though each of them is more astute than the sluggard.

Meaning
The lazy person is perhaps the most comically drawn character in the book. With this section coming immediately after the one about fools, it draws attention to laziness as a clear instance of folly. Laziness hurts the lazy, not just those around them.

iv. The damage done by false words (26:17–28)
Context
This section is a pastiche of sayings about quarrels, gossip, lies and deceptive words. Whybray (1994: 370) suggests that it describes a range of people 'who damage social relations by injudicious or malicious speech'. Each idea is interwoven with the others, so that quarrelling is considered in verses 17–21, but gossip is introduced in verse 20 and explored further in verse 22. Lips, speech and tongue are mentioned in verses 23–25, 28, and deception in verses 19, 24 and 26. All contribute to the mosaic about actions that serve to destroy community.

Comment
17–22. Quarrels and gossip dominate this section. The first three verses are designed to show people the folly of joining in or, even worse, provoking a quarrel. One of the problematic aspects of quarrels is that they spread quickly. Joining in on a dispute simply escalates matters. Verse 17 outlines the danger to ourselves of intervening, using a vivid analogy. It is like grabbing a stray dog by the ears. While the outcome of this action is not specified, it implies that the dog will turn to attack the one who has hold of its ears. This

could lead to injury and (from a stray dog) disease. An even more graphic image is used in verses 18–19 to describe deceiving our neighbour then turning around and saying, 'I was only joking.' Having provoked a person to anger by our deceit, we sometimes imagine that it will all go away by saying, 'Just kidding', but that only makes people angrier. It is like adding a match to petrol. This makes sense of the simile in verse 18. A mad person or fool ('maniac', NIV/ NRSV; the meaning is not certain except from the context, as it is used only here in the OT) is pictured as shooting fiery and deadly arrows (lit. *firebrands, arrows and death*; Waltke 2005: 341 notes that 'arrows and death' are a hendiadys or cluster term meaning 'deadly arrows') at an object (25:18). Fire is a good image to use, since it is so difficult to control once it has started and it causes great damage.

The mention of fire continues in verse 20, with the new theme of gossip (as previously, *whispering*) introduced. Just as wood keeps a fire burning, and without it the flames would die out, so gossip acts as an accelerant to a quarrel. The point is repeated in verse 21, with both charcoal and wood acting as fuel for the fire. A quarrel-some individual is a person of strife or contention (both the *qere* and *ketib* readings have a similar meaning), not a person of peace who builds up society, and is described as causing a dispute or quarrel to keep burning. The idea of gossip, introduced in verse 20, is explored in verse 22 in another vivid image. Gossip is peculiarly attractive and enticing – making ourselves look better by putting others down. It is so seductive that it sometimes happens even as we 'share a prayer point' about a situation. Thus, gossip is compared to delicious bites of food that fill our body with delight (18:8). Of course, it is implied that this is self-deception, since gossip worsens and sometimes creates disputes.

23–28. A negative heart is explicit in verses 23–25, and implied in verses 26–28. As elsewhere in Proverbs, the problem is not confined to what we do, but who we are on the inside. In verse 23 two items are juxtaposed, making an implied comparison. An earthenware pot covered by a silver glaze looks so much more impressive than it actually is. Similarly, speech on fire (for a cause? lit. lips 'burning/set ablaze' or perhaps 'pursuing'), but underneath this apparent zeal is an *evil heart*, describes a person whose core goal in life is not to promote good in the community. The point is clarified in verse 24 by referring to one who *hates* ('enemy', NIV/NRSV, but the emphasis is on hating). Such people try deceitfully to disguise their real nature by their speech, but again the real issue is in their inner person (not the same word for heart that is found in v. 23) – and that is full of deceit. What you see is not what you get (Fox 2009: 800 calls it 'feigned friendship'). Even more sharply in verse 25, we are admonished not to believe or trust their apparently gracious words, for there are seven (the symbolic number of completeness) abominations in their heart. The apparent presence of grace does not mean its actual presence. Verses 26–28 then explain why such individuals should not be trusted. They may deceptively try to cover over or camouflage their hatred, but it will be ultimately disclosed in the assembly of God's people. This is not a reference to end-time judgment, but an earthly and possibly a legal gathering (5:14). The community of those who belong to God will see through the deception. The two images of verse 27 are based on the doctrine of retribution – that God will reward the righteous but, as here, also punish the wicked. There are many ways in which we can try to hurt others, but the two that are mentioned in this verse are digging a (hidden) pit or trap, and rolling a stone to cause damage. It both scenarios, those who seek to harm others are caught in their own wrongdoing, receiving what they intended to inflict on others. Verse 28 draws out the end result of this deceptive speech. A lying tongue, the focus of verses 23–25, causes great damage to (lit. *hates*) those crushed or oppressed by it (*its victims*). Also, speech that flatters on the surface, but has some other evil purpose behind it, still causes ruin. The obvious lesson of this final verse is to avoid mixing with those who speak like this, even when their words are 'garnished with grace'.

Meaning

There is great concern about the right use of words. At the very least, this means not using them to fuel gossip or quarrels that destroy relationships and communities. Even nice-sounding words can be used to wound and destroy, so we need to be on the watch for those who speak deceptively. Speech that builds up will come from a godly heart and a transformed character. We need to be careful to avoid speech that tears down and destroys.

v. Relationships, good and bad (27:1–22)

Context

While Van Leeuwen regards these verses as a loosely structured section, Waltke has shown that they divide into two parallel sections (vv. 1–10 and 11–21), with the hinge verse 22 (or Janus) at the end. He suggests that each section begins with 'to whom to listen', then defines 'impossible relationships', before outlining some 'positive teachings about friendship'. There are only two extended three-line verses (tricola), found in verses 10 and 22, again supporting a twofold division. Verse 11 begins with a resumptive address, *Be wise, my son*, which is also an indication of a new start. The theme of friendship is already prominent in the book (usually in individual sayings or pairs about friends or neighbours, e.g. 14:20–21; 17:17–18; 18:24), but is here developed at greater length.

Comment

1–10. Verses 1–10 consist of five proverbial pairs, largely with alternating positive and negative comments about friendship (so Waltke; vv. 7–8 may be exceptions), pivoting on the most crucial pair on the topic in verses 5–6. Waltke suggests that verses 1–2 set out the need for appropriate praise in friendship, while verses 3–4 explain that foolish, angry and jealous people cannot make good friends. Each of the three pairs in verses 5–10 offer positive insights into friendship: the need for rebuke (vv. 5–6); the causes of failed relationship (vv. 7–8; Waltke thinks it may refer to marriage – 'gratifying one's appetites in the right way, and . . . the loss of the most intimate of friendships, that of a husband and wife'); and the need for a friend's counsel and help (vv. 9–10).

1–2. The admonition of verse 1 is not to boast about tomorrow ('make a confident prediction of one's future achievements', Whybray 1994: 379). The force of this verb is not to gloat, indulge in self-praise or self-glory, effectively congratulating or praising ourselves for what we have done (the verb is the *hitpael* stem of *hālal*, 'to praise'). The word *for* (*kî*) introduces the first reason: we do not know what will happen on any given day (Jas 4:13–16). Part of the godly character promoted by Proverbs is humility (e.g. 22:4), and such boasting or self-praise is crossing over the line. Verse 2 offers a better way forward in waiting for others to praise you. Here is where friends come in, for a friend can affirm (*hālal*, *praise*) your achievements and plans. This means that we should be proactive in affirming our friends, but we are also encouraged to wait patiently and humbly for this approval from others rather than congratulating ourselves. The views of others are more likely to be an accurate reflection than our own inflated views of ourselves. Amazingly, verse 2 says listen to a stranger (*zār*, *another*, NRSV/ESV; 'someone else', NIV) and a 'foreigner' (*nokrî*), with the implication that how much more will a friend be willing to take this initiative.

3–4. There are certain characteristics which, amongst other things, damage or prevent the wholesome relationships on which friendship is based. The taunting or provoking from a fool is like a heavy dead weight; it is unnecessary baggage that prevents us from living life (v. 3). Such provocation is distracting and causes us to slow down, even though there is no need to do so. Anger and fury/wrath too channel our energy away from building relationships, as does the suspicion that is an integral part of jealousy (v. 4; 6:34). All of these characteristics urge us to respond defensively, and so close down rather than open up relationships. Two implications emerge. First, we should avoid these characteristics in our existing friendships. Second, we should not seek to develop friendships with those dominated by anger, jealousy or foolish provocation.

5–6. The warnings of verses 3–4 are followed by positive endorsement of other characteristics in verses 5–6. A 'better than' saying in verse 5 commends the place of overt (lit. 'revealed', *mĕgullâ*) rebuke within friendship. If friends are on our side, their words of correction will not be motivated by malice, but rather a concern for our well-being and improvement. As Lucas (2015: 173) points out, 'growth in wisdom requires openness to correction.' Friends will call us to account when we are self-indulgent, inconsiderate or rude. Of course, in doing so they risk the friendship (for not everyone likes to be rebuked), but they are genuinely seeking our best interests. Such bold and caring initiatives are better than *hidden love*, in other words, unexpressed care and friendship. Some people are afraid to voice their care for others, perhaps fearing that it will not be reciprocated. Yet this hidden love is of little value for others, and certainly of much less worth than a caring rebuke. In verse 6 the wounds afflicted by a friend are described as trustworthy or faithful (a *nifal* participle from the root *'mn*, 'to be [shown to be] trustworthy or reliable'). Hard words or rebukes from a friend still hurt, so they are appropriately called *wounds*. But some words of tough love wound in order to make us into the people that we want to become, and these words are in this sense trustworthy or faithful. The contrast in verse 6 is between these helpful rebukes and those who pretend love and affection even though they are 'haters' (the same word for enemies as in 26:24). Both an enemy's 'pretend love' and an un-expressed real love are less useful to a friend than the open, caring rebuke by one who wants the best for us. So too in our relationships we need to express correction – although in appropriate ways – even at the risk of being misunderstood.

7–8. While these verses need not be confined to a marriage rela-tionship,[9] this does seem to be their primary referent in view of the language of straying from our home in verse 8b. The idea is remi-niscent of 5:15 and its call to drink water from your own cistern, being delighted by your spouse's charms and intoxicated with her love (5:19–20). Here the image is of a honey pot, which is a genuine source of energy and refreshment. However, verse 7 makes two points. If we have too much honey (we are 'full' or 'sated'; 25:16, 27a), then we no longer discern the attraction of honey. On the other hand, if we are starved of food, anything will seem as sweet as honey. Our goal is not to be smothered in our marriage, nor is it to have a marriage that is distant and empty of intimacy. In such situations we may be tempted to 'stray from the nest' (v. 8a) and seek sexual and relational 'honey' from people other than our spouse. We need instead to value and nurture our marriage and its exclusive relationship.

9–10. In the ANE oil and perfume were evocative of a rich and enjoyable life. In verse 9a they are described as making the inner person glad. This is building a platform of something desirable, so that the benefits of friendship can bask in the afterglow. The real

---

9. Whybray (1994: 381); Murphy (1998: 207) sees them describing people who leave their homes and settle elsewhere; Steinmann (2009: 537) suggests it also covers those who fail to appreciate their family, or those who have an arrogant independent spirit.

point of verse 9 is to picture friendship as very sweet and desirable. The exact translation of the last part of verse 9 is disputed, but it is clearly a positive statement about friendship.[10] Verse 10 makes an amazing claim (from the viewpoint of an ANE culture) that friendship is stronger than a blood relationship. This is not to minimize fraternal responsibilities, but rather to lift up the value of a friend or neighbour. Verse 10a–b admonishes hearers not to turn away from ('abandon/leave'; Fox 2009: 808 suggests 'ignore' here) their personal or family friend in order to go to a blood relative (brother) when disaster strikes. We will receive better care from a neighbour who is physically close than a brother who is distant. In other words, we need to value strongly the support and help of friends and neighbours, for they will be of greater value in times of crisis.

11–21. In verses 11–21 Waltke's parallelism is perhaps not as strong as in verses 1–10. He suggests that verses 11–12 deal with 'to whom to listen', suggesting parents, but it could be interpreted as teachers instead. Verses 13–16 mention some figures with whom it is important to have a constructive relationship (the wicked, the hypocrite, the shrew), followed by positive teaching about friendship in verses 17–21 (clearest in v. 17).

11–12. The student or son is addressed by the parent or teacher at the beginning of this new section, and called on to be wise and make the teacher's heart glad (23:15, 25). Of course, this is not the end goal. An imperative followed by an imperfect is a purpose construction, and the aim here is that the teacher should respond in words to (i.e. answer) the one who reproaches him. The teacher wants to defend the wise character of the pupil, probably so that others will see him as wise and listen to him. There are two possible responses to life's dangers in verse 12 (22:3). The prudent or wise

---

10. The ESV and NIV translate similarly (the sweetness or pleasantness of a friend '[springs from] their heartfelt advice', NIV; [*comes from*] *his earnest counsel*, ESV), but the NRSV opts for 'but the soul is torn by trouble', which does not fit the flow of thought but is based on the LXX. *DCH* suggests that 'counsel/advice of soul', *'ăṣat nāpeš*, should be 'a tree of perfume', reading *'ēṣ*, tree, instead of *'ēṣâ*, counsel, and translating *nepeš*, 'soul, life', as 'perfume', a sense used in Isa. 3:20.

person sees the danger and hides from it, either by hiding himself (ESV), or taking safe refuge away from the danger (NIV; the Hebrew verb *str* could mean either). This choice is clarified by the different response of the simple or unshaped person. In the face of danger, the simple continue on (lit. 'cross over', 'go through'), but suffer the consequences of their refusal to avoid danger.

13–16. Verse 13 picks up the theme of not acting as guarantor for a stranger, virtually citing 20:16 and echoing 6:1–5; 11:15; 17:18. The parties are hard to identify (Waltke 2005: 382 sees a guarantor, a debtor and a creditor), but the feminine adjective used as a noun for foreigner (*nŏkriyyâ*) suggests that she is a foreign woman and so probably an adulteress (so ESV). However, what is clear is the warning to extricate ourselves from such an arrangement and the fools who have contrived it. Other people to avoid as friends are those who say the right words (a blessing) but at the wrong volume (a loud voice) and at the wrong time (early in the morning). Such people are so foolish that they do not understand that their attempts at blessing will be received as cursing. Finally, a quarrelsome or contentious wife (21:9, 19; 25:24) is compared negatively to a constant, repetitive dripping on a rainy day (19:13b). The image is of being worn down in a relationship. Verse 16 adds the further point that such a woman cannot be restrained or kept in place. This is clarified by the rest of the verse, comparing any attempt to restrain her as being as ambitious as controlling (lit. 'restraining' again) wind or grabbing hold of (lit. 'calling', *qārā'*) oil in our hands. Looking back over verses 13–16, it is clear that we should avoid friends like the fools of verse 13, the unaware neighbour of verse 14 and the quarrelsome wife of verse 15.

17–21. *Iron sharpens iron* (v. 17a) is not a statement about metallurgy but about friendship. This is made clear in the second half of the verse, which observes that one person sharpens another (lit. 'the face of their friend/neighbour'; Clifford 1999: 239 notes that the 'edge' of a sword or axe is called its face in Hebrew, as in Eccl. 10:10; Ezek. 21:21). One implication of this is that we do not need friends who just like us, or who never correct or challenge us. We need to have our rough edges knocked off, and we need to do the same to our friends. All of us are works in progress. Longman (2006: 481) comments, 'The wisdom enterprise is a community effort.' This

is the beginning of a list of positive characteristics that promote
friendship. Verse 18 describes those who are faithful and loyal to
their assigned task. The farmer who cares for the fig tree will be able
to eat its fruit, while the person who guards or looks after (*šōmēr*) a
master will be rewarded (lit. *honoured*). Faithfully performing a duty
of care to another is a valuable practice. Verse 19 is less focused on
the theme of friendship, but it makes the relevant point that it is
what we are like on the inside (our heart) that really counts. As
a reflection in water shows what we really look like (i.e. acts as a
mirror), our heart shows what we are really like. The NIV captures
it well: 'one's life reflects the heart.' The ESV turns it around to read
the heart of man reflects the man. Either of these is better than NRSV:
'one human heart reflects another', which misses the parallel with
water in the first half. Verse 20 also does not exclusively refer to
friendship, but it has implications for being a good friend. Sheol and
Abaddon, the bleak places of death and destruction, are made worse
by people not being satisfied or content (30:15b–16). Godly contentment is a precious gift to share with others, and will promote
healthy relationships, but it does not come naturally to us. Verse 21
introduces the theme of a tested character. We sometimes consider
that tests are designed to catch us out, finding out what we do not
know. But there is another sense of testing, seen most clearly (as
here) in the testing of metal. Precious metals like silver and gold can
be tested to show positively their level of purity (17:3a). A person
being tested by praise can have either sense. How people receive
praise can reveal whether they seek to be affirmed, or whether they
seek what is right. Yet who or what a person praises, or what people
praise about this person (depending on whether the suffix is subjective or objective), can also reveal what they are committed to.
Praise in friendship is a vital way of nourishing relationships with
others.

22. This final verse sits outside the section on friendship, but
as a three-line verse it rounds it off. It uses a vivid image of grinding
a fool with a pestle and mortar, but still not being able to remove
his folly from him. For folly is not simply something that can be
put on and taken off as we please (like a coat); rather, it is in-
grained in fools, part of their DNA so that it affects all that they
do and say.

Meaning

While not everything in these verses relates to the theme of friendship, they give both positive and negative information about being
a good friend, and what kind of friends we should seek or avoid.
Virtues like honesty, faithfulness and loyalty loom large, while
various forms of folly destroy friendships. In several verses we can
see that what we are like on the inside (our hearts) will show forth
in the way we treat others and develop friendships.

vi. Advice to leaders (27:23–27)

Context

Clifford (1999: 236, 241) describes the theme of this section as 'herds
and fields are the best wealth', but a wider significance is in view.
The image of a leader as a shepherd is used in both the OT and NT
(e.g. Jer. 23:1–4; 1 Pet. 5:1–4). The key admonition is given in verse
23 (look after your animals); a reason for the advice (beginning with
for, kî) follows in verse 24; while verses 25–27 elaborate on what will
happen when you do so, effectively operating as further motivation
to take notice. Verse 27, like verse 22, marks the end of the section
by a three-line verse.

Comment

23–24. A strong exhortation begins verse 23, using an emphatic
Hebrew expression (imperative + imperfect of the root 'to know',
yd'). It is a call to 'make sure you know' or *know well* the condition
(so most EVV, but it is lit. 'faces of', *pĕnê. HALOT* sees it as an idiom
for 'condition'; it could also be a metonymy, using a part to mean
the whole person) of your flock of sheep or goats. The parallel
expression is to put your mind (lit. 'heart') to your herds or flocks.
It is not necessary to determine whether sheep, goats or cattle are
in view (the Hebrew terms often do not distinguish) because the
exhortations here are meant to have a wider reference as well to
people under the charge of leaders. Of course, this saying endorses
care for our working animals, but it is not confined to such concerns.
The reason given for this proactive care is that our circumstances
can change, with examples given with regard to finances (*riches*) and
power (*crown*). Although there is no verb in verse 24 (just *not . . . for
ever*, 'to generation of/after generation'), the clear thrust of the verse

is that what we currently take for granted is not guaranteed to last. This is a good reason to look after those in our care in the present.

25–27. These verses describe the implied consequences of properly looking after our animals. The principles behind these observations (they will prosper when cared for, and provide benefits to us) have further implications for leaders in general. Time invested in those in our charge will benefit us as well as them. Verse 25 outlines the passing of time through the year, with the grass dying off in winter, the new growth of spring and eventually the produce harvested. As a result of providing food for the animals during this time, the lambs will produce wool and skin for clothing, and the goats will be able to be sold for a healthy sum (v. 26). Milk from some of the other goats will be enough to supply food for the household, including the servant girls who are attached. It is a picture of fullness, life as it should be. We care for the animals; the animals provide for us. Thinking more widely, as leaders provide for those for whom they are responsible, the community will prosper and all will be provided for.

Meaning
At the surface level, this section is a commendation of providing well for our animals, based largely on a self-interest argument that we will benefit from caring for them. However, its place in the book of Proverbs – where animals are not a major focus – suggests that the lesson we learn from the natural world is meant to be applied to human society. Whenever we are entrusted with responsibilities of leadership, we ought to act for the flourishing of those in our care. This will prosper both them and us. Malchow (1985: 243–244) points out that this small unit leads neatly into (and he thinks, introduces) chapters 28 – 29, which he argues are directed to future rulers.

B. The righteous and the wicked (28:1 – 29:27)

Context
A number of distinctive features set these chapters apart from the preceding material. Like chapters 10 – 15, but unlike chapters 25 – 27, they are dominated by antithetical parallelism (contrasts, usually indicated in the English by the word *but*). The strongest contrast in

these chapters is between the righteous (*ṣaddîqîm*) and the wicked (*rĕšāʿîm*). Bland (2002: 252) comments, 'The quality emphasized about the righteous is that they are socially responsible. The wicked are those who manifest antisocial behaviour, behaviour that destroys community life.' The importance of this contrast can be seen in the refrain of the wicked or righteous coming to prominence, found in four structurally significant proverbs (28:12, 28; 29:2, 16). These divide the two chapters into four clear sections (see Malchow 1985: 238–245; Finkbeiner 1995: 3–4). The refrains occur at the end of the sections in chapter 28 and at the beginning of the sections in chapter 29, giving the following units (28:1–12, 13–28; 29:1–15, 16–27).[11] If 27:23–27 has rulers and not simply shepherds in view, it may serve as a link or even an introduction (so Malchow) to chapters 28 – 29, which focus on a fundamental character divide (righteous versus wicked), and commend the faithful carrying out of their assigned tasks by those in authority.

Comment
i. The wicked (28:1–12)
These verses deal with both the righteous and the wicked, but there is a greater emphasis on the wicked. In most verses both are mentioned, but sometimes there is a focus only on the wicked (vv. 3, 9). The righteous are never the subject of an entire verse. The theme of this section is the importance and care of the poor. Although there are several mentions of *law* (*tôrâ*, vv. 4 [twice], 7, 9), the concern is not with any specific law, but rather with the attitude of being a 'law-regarding' person in general. As in wisdom literature generally, *tôrâ* can have the broader sense of 'instruction' (especially the teaching of the wise) and so is not confined to the Mosaic law. The emphasis is on being shaped by wisdom, and acknowledging your responsibilities to God and others in everyday life.

---

11. Finkbeiner (1995: 4), building on Malchow, views the sections as 28:2–11, 13–27; 29:3–15, 17–26, with the 'refrains' being transitions. Prov. 28:1 is then an introduction and 29:27 a conclusion, while 29:1, in the middle of the structure, is a key to the theme. These single verses have been added to the surrounding sections in our outline.

1. This preliminary verse introduces the two categories of the righteous (plural) and the wicked (singular adjective, *rāšāʿ*, used as a collective noun; the verb is plural). There is a comic picture of the wicked fleeing for their lives even though no-one is pursuing them (Lev. 26:17, 36), making it clear that they are among the foolish. Clifford (1999: 243) comments, 'Wicked behavior sets in motion a chain of ills that leads to a life of fear.' In contrast to the cowardice of the wicked, the righteous are bold and courageous, being compared with a lion.

2–11. The subject of verse 2 is a *land* (*ʾereṣ*) crossing boundaries/transgressing. While land most commonly refers to the physical land, here it is describing the people in the land (as in 1 Sam. 14:25; 'country', NIV). The idea is that when the people are rebellious, there are many vying for power, which unsettles the nation (as in times of revolution like the Arab Spring). Yet stability or order prevails when there is one person clearly in charge who is someone of character (*understanding and knowledge*; NRSV, 'intelligent ruler', puts the emphasis wrongly on brains not character). The Hebrew reads literally, 'so it will endure', but the thrust is that the society will be characterized by order and stability. In the remaining verses there is a twin focus on the rich/poor and those 'keeping the law'. The theme of oppressing the poor surfaces in verse 3, although ironically it is done by the poor (*rāš*; some amend this to *rōʾš*, chief or ruler, e.g. NIV, NRSV, but it makes sense as it is). While the poor may have expected help from their fellows who understood being needy, how much more burdensome it would be if they added to the oppression. Their actions are described as heavy rain that will destroy the crops (26:1), taking away even the last prospect of food from the grain that was planted. The rich and poor are contrasted in several verses. The 'better than' saying of verse 6 subverts the usual wisdom characteristics by commending a poor person who has a life of integrity rather than a rich person whose ways are crooked. This is a useful balance (also in 19:1) to the idea of retribution seen elsewhere, that is, that the righteous prosper and the wicked become poor (e.g. 15:6). This anomaly of the wicked rich is also present in verse 8, where the unrighteous rich have gained their wealth by 'exorbitant interest' (NRSV, a cluster expression of 'interest' and 'profit'). The irony this time is that such a person does not hold on to his wealth, but must pass it on to a different rich person who rightly shows generosity to the poor. The reverse evaluation of rich and poor apparent in verse 6 is also found in verse 11. More significant than the presence or absence of money is whether a person is only wise in his own eyes (3:7; 26:5, 12, 16), or whether he is genuinely a person of understanding. Such teaching about the rich and poor is an important qualification to a blinkered doctrine of retribution based only on passages like 3:9–10 and 8:18.

Being shaped by 'instruction' (NIV) or *law* (ESV, *tôrâ*) is addressed, explicitly in verses 4, 7, 9, but also in a broader focus on justice and uprightness in verses 5, 10. The contrast in verse 4 is between those who turn their back on or ignore (lit. 'abandon' or *forsake*) this instruction and those who keep/guard it, that is, put into practice as their basic stance in life. As in chapters 1 – 9, there are only two ways: one of wisdom, the other of folly. Verse 5 insists that this is a matter of rightly understanding justice (*mišpāṭ*; Clifford 1999: 244 notes that in Job 32:9 this means 'to be wise or act wisely'). Those who seek after the Lord know it entirely (lit. 'all', *kōl*), unlike those who are evil. Justice here is not a neutral category able to be comprehended by anyone, but must be based on the right foundation of trust in the Lord. Verse 7a combines these two ideas of keeping (a different verb from v. 4, but with the same force) the law and understanding, describing the person who keeps the instruction as characterized by (lit. 'a son of') understanding. This understanding, in the light of verse 5, concerns justice, or the fair treatment of others. Verse 9 picks up the negative portrait of the one who chooses not to be shaped ('hear', which can have the sense of 'obey') by *tôrâ*, which could mean here either God's law or the sage's instruction (or both). Again this shaping is pictured as an indispensable foundation, for without it the otherwise beneficial practice is fruitless. We cannot relate to God in prayer if we refuse to be obedient to his instructions (15:8, 29). Verse 10 commends those who are blameless, indicating that they will inherit what is good (3:35). Yet it also warns that those who lead the upright astray will fall into the trap they planned for others. The clear lesson is not to lead others into error, but rather enjoy living a righteous life.

12. The first refrain contrasts the different outcomes for the righteous and the wicked coming to prominence. When the righteous triumph (it can mean either 'exult/rejoice' or 'prevail/triumph'), the consequence is great glory or honour or reason for pride (perhaps even 'great elation', NIV). This is highly desirable. However, when the wicked rise (to power), this is a great shame or dishonour, and so the people are hidden, or hide themselves (alternatively, Waltke 2005: 396 proposes 'must be searched out'; Fox 2009: 825–826 suggests 'sought' in the sense of 'sought in vain'). The prevailing of the righteous brings great benefit to the community, while the rise of the wicked leads to a society scattered in shame.

ii. The character of the righteous and the wicked (28:13–28)

As in verses 1–12, there is never a focus on the righteous alone, but there are several verses entirely concerned with the wicked (vv. 15, 17, 21, 24). In verses 13–27 we see the character of both the righteous and the wicked. The latter are portrayed as those who hide their wrongdoings (v. 13); harden their hearts (v. 14); extort others (v. 16); murder (v. 17); have perverse ways (v. 18); follow worthless dreams (v. 19); greedily try to gain quick money (vv. 20, 22); show favouritism (v. 21); rob their parents (v. 24); stir up conflict (v. 25); trust in themselves (v. 26); refuse to care for the poor (v. 27). In contrast, the righteous confess their sins (v. 13); fear God (v. 14); hate wrongful gain (v. 16); live a blameless life (v. 18); work diligently (v. 19); are faithful (v. 20); rebuke wrongdoers (v. 23); trust in the Lord (v. 25); walk in wisdom (v. 26); give to the poor (v. 27; see a similar list in Bland 2002: 252).

13–14. Sin and confession are generally underemphasized (although never ignored) in wisdom writings, but they are present in verse 13 (Whybray 1994: 393 observes that 'this is the only verse in Proverbs which refers to God's forgiveness of the penitent sinner'). The wrong response to our transgressions (*pĕšārîm*, rebellion, sin) is to conceal or hide them, but this is only pretending they are gone. Such an approach will not succeed, for as Kidner (1964: 171) notes, 'sin buried is sin kept'. Confessing and abandoning our wrongdoings result in us being shown mercy. The full implications of this are only revealed in the new covenant inaugurated by Jesus, but this principle is right as far as it goes. This proper attitude to God in verse 13 forms the backdrop for verse 14, where the one who fears (God) continually is blessed. While the object of fearing is not explicit, the contrast with hardening the heart in verse 14b strongly suggests that the fear of verse 14a is the 'heart-based' foundational attitude of fearing God, that is, respecting God as God. While *pāḥad (fear,* be in dread of) is used instead of *yārē'* (fear), this is elsewhere used of the fear of God (Ps. 36:1 [Heb. 2]; 2 Chr. 19:7). In any event, the contrast in verse 14b makes it clear that those who have a wrong stance towards God (hardening their heart) will suffer calamitous consequences (lit. 'fall into disaster/evil'). Waltke (2005: 417) sees the impenitent sinner of verse 13a balanced by the hardened sinner of verse 14b.

15–16. These verses describe different kinds of people in authority. Wicked rulers – revealed as those who bring poverty to their people – are described in terms of the senseless damage they cause (v. 15), and are compared to a roaring, hungry lion, putting fear into everyone, or a charging bear on a destructive rampage. They boast about themselves, but do nothing to benefit the people over whom they rule. The ruler in verse 16a is just as bad. He has refused to choose the path of wisdom and so lacks understanding (3:13); he is described as an excessive extorter/oppressor (*cruel,* NRSV/ESV, is an over-translation of *rab,* 'much', 'greatly'). The contrast, however, shows that an ideal ruler is one who hates unjust gain (used of a bribe in Exod. 18:21) and will receive the reward that wisdom offers – lasting days (3:2).

17–18. The Hebrew of verse 17 is rather elliptical, and so needs clarification. It refers to a person weighed down or burdened (lit. 'oppressed', the passive form of the same verb used to describe the ruler in v. 16a) by the innocent blood he has taken (presumably the victim has died, as it is called 'blood of life'). The next part of the verse could be read as a statement (e.g. NIV, 'will seek refuge in the grave'; ESV, *be a fugitive until death*) or as a jussive (NRSV, 'let that killer be a fugitive until death'). The word for 'grave'/*death* is *bôr* (lit. 'pit'), which can be a symbol of death, or a physical pit or grave. The last phrase has the form of a prohibition plus a jussive ('let them not uphold/help him'), and this gives the best sense. Verse 18 commends those who walk in integrity, noting that they will be *delivered* ('saved', in the sense of 'kept safe'; 10:9). However, one whose ways are crooked or twisted will fall (lit. 'fall into one', rendered as *suddenly fall,* ESV, or 'fall into the pit', NIV/NRSV).

19–22. These verses revolve around hard work and wealth.[12]
Those who work their land will be satisfied with plenty of food, but
if their energies are diverted elsewhere ('fantasies', NIV; *worthless
pursuits*, ESV/NRSV; lit. 'empty things'), they will be 'full' of the
emptiness of poverty (12:11). Similarly, in verse 20 a faithful person
will have many blessings (which probably includes material ones,
10:22), but one who is in a hurry to be rich will be given a punishment of an unspecified kind (13:11; 20:21). Goldsworthy (1993: 174)
comments, 'Faith and wisdom come before riches, but riches without
faith lead a person astray.' Verses 21–22 zoom in on wrong attitudes
to money and possessions. Verse 21 declares partiality (probably
against the poor, as in 18:5; 24:23–24; lit. 'to recognize a face', but a
common idiom for partiality) as not good. Behind this is probably
greed, or a desire to benefit in some other improper way. The reality
is that people can be 'bought', although today it probably costs more
than a piece of bread. Related to greed is stinginess, with verse 22
claiming that a person 'bad of eye' (i.e. miserly, see 23:6) makes
wrongful haste to get wealthy, without knowing that poverty rather
than money will come to him.

23–27. A variety of interpersonal relationships are dealt with in
this final loose grouping. Verse 23 concerns speaking a hard truth
to another, pointing out that rebuking when a rebuke is due may be
hard at the time but will finally result in a better relationship ('find
favour/grace', *ḥēn*; 9:8b–9; 19:25b; 27:5–6). The tempting alternative
of telling people what they want to hear ('flatters with the tongue',
NRSV) will lead to fewer benefits. The argument, as often in Proverbs,
is not that it is wrong to flatter, but simply that it is not worth doing.
Verse 24 targets those who wrongly treat their parents by robbing
them but claiming to be innocent (see 19:26; 20:20; 30:11, 17; Mark
7:10–13; 1 Tim. 5:4, 8). What is in view here is taking some of the
family property and regarding it as their own, thus showing dis-
respect for their parents, with attitudes of greed and selfishness. All
of this is destructive for the community by undermining one of its

---

12. Finkbeiner (1995: 9–10) notes that they concern 'extra-personal
    relationships', a term he uses to mean 'one's relationship to things',
    unlike the interpersonal relationships of vv. 23–24.

key institutions. The theme of greed (lit. 'one who is wide of throat/appetite [*nepeš*]') is picked up also in verse 25, with the observation that a greedy person (by trying to gain what belongs to others) stirs up conflict (6:12–14). A better option, set out in verse 25b, is to trust in the Lord and so to use only godly means to provide for your needs (3:5–6). Such a person will not be aiming at riches at any cost, but will in fact be enriched (lit, 'be made fat', in that culture an image of prospering). A more general principle is given in verse 26, before a specific application in verse 27. Whoever trusts (only) in their own clever thinking (lit. 'heart') is described as a fool, and contrasted with the safety/deliverance that will come from walking in wisdom. This does not discourage thinking in itself, but rather urges against those kind of thoughts that do not lead to living wisely. The image in verse 27 of 'hiding their eyes' is initially a puzzling one. Elsewhere (Lev. 20:3–5; 1 Sam. 12:3) it means to pretend that a person or situation does not exist, so here it has the sense of ignoring those who are blind rather than providing for them. Those who give to the poor will not be in want themselves, but those who ignore the poor will find their life seems cursed rather than blessed (11:24–26).

28. This refrain rounds off the section. When the wicked rise to positions of power, ordinary people in the community steer clear of them, withdrawing from public involvement. However, when the wicked perish, the righteous will grow ('thrive', NIV). There will then be opportunity to prosper and to build up the community without having to fight with those in power.

iii. Wisdom in the midst of wickedness (29:1–15)

Again most of these verses contrast the righteous and the wicked, but there is a focus only on the actions or attitudes of the wicked in verses 1, 5, 9, 10, 12, and on the righteous alone in verse 14. Wisdom is prominent throughout, with wisdom or a wise man occurring five times (vv. 3, 8, 9, 11, 15; Finkbeiner 1995: 11 thinks it is the theme of these verses). Finkbeiner suggests that verses 3–15 can be divided as follows: verse 3 – wisdom in the family setting; verses 4–7 – kingly wisdom; verses 8–11 – wisdom under control; verses 12–14 – kingly wisdom; verse 15 – wisdom in the family setting.

29:1. Proverbs suggests that the way we respond to being rebuked or corrected reveals whether we are a person of wisdom or folly (e.g. 9:8, using the verb related to the noun here). Here 'a man of rebuke', a Hebrew way of describing one who has often been corrected, shows his folly in that he responds by hardening his neck, a phrase used in Exodus 32 – 34 for those who refuse to be shaped by God (Exod. 32:9; 33:3, 5; 34:9). The consequence of resisting this reproof is that we will be broken or fractured (to continue the imagery of bones) in such a way that there will be no healing or fixing. This verse fits outside the four subsections of chapters 28 – 29, and so functions as a key warning: do not refuse the shaping of wisdom, for the consequences of doing so are disastrous. Waltke (2005: 429) proposes that this verse is deliberately placed in the structural centre of Proverbs 28 – 29 in order to emphasize the danger of resisting the reproof of these chapters.

2. The third refrain is found in this verse. The contrast is between the righteous increasing (ESV; 'thrive', NIV, but it may also involve becoming more prominent; NRSV suggests, 'when the righteous are in authority'; the verb *rbh* means 'to be many, multiply, increase') and the wicked ruling. In the first case, the people rejoice; in the second, they groan or sigh, implying anguish or despair.

3. The motif of a son who loves wisdom making his father glad is common in Proverbs (e.g. 10:1; 15:20; 23:22–25; 27:11). However, there are a variety of ways in which this truth is built on in the second half of the proverb. It picks up the theme of 2:1–19; 6:20–24 that a character shaped by wisdom will help him reject sexual temptations. The particular twist in this verse is that hanging around prostitutes will have grave financial consequences – it will lead to squandering (lit. 'abandoning, forsaking') wealth, whether his own or that of his family. Longman (2006: 501) comments that 'prostitutes are expensive women'.

4–7. What does wisdom mean for a ruler? A king who uses the related practice of justice (*mišpāṭ*) will cause the land to stand ('gives stability', NIV/NRSV; *builds up*, ESV; 16:12; 25:5). Yet one who makes excessive financial demands on the people tears it down (v. 4). This second type of ruler is literally 'a person of contributions', but this is a Hebrew way of saying that his rule is characterized by demands for more money. This results in a variety of English translations (NIV, 'greedy for bribes'; NRSV, 'makes heavy exactions'; ESV, *exacts gifts*). The following three verses have clear application to a ruler (especially v. 7), but are not confined to rulers. Verse 5 deals with the issue of flattery ('smooth speech', 2:16), comparing flattering a neighbour to spreading a net or trap (nets were used to trap birds). Fox (2009: 835) sees flattery as 'a pretense of friendship intended to lower someone's guard'. The *his* (his feet) in verse 5 is ambiguous, since it could refer to the man's own feet or his neighbour's, but the context suggests that those going down the foolish pathway of flattery will themselves be trapped (1:17–19). This is made clearer in verse 6, where an evil person is snared in (his) transgression (12:13), while the righteous, who are presumably not trapped, shout or sing out for joy and rejoice. The path of the righteous – ruler or otherwise – is one of joy. Verse 7 is directed primarily at those in some position of authority, where a decision has impact on the rights of others. A righteous person knows (= acknowledges, acts in accordance with this knowledge; NIV, 'care about', as in 12:10) the pleas or rights of the poor, but the wicked do not have this commitment to them and their causes.

8–11. In these verses wisdom is more of a focus, with *wise* (*ḥākām*) found in verses 8, 9 and 11, and verse 10 having the related terms of *blameless* and *upright* (two descriptors of the wise man, e.g. Job in Job 1:1). Verse 8 contrasts the wise, who avert wrath or anger, and the 'person of scoffing', that is, one characterized by scoffing who destroys a town by blowing on it (NIV, 'stir up'), perhaps even setting it aflame by blowing destructive fire through it (hence NRSV/ESV, 'set a city aflame'). Verse 9 is a warning about the futility of having a sensible discussion with a fool (remember 26:4). While the wise would have something to offer, fools respond with outrage (*rāgaz* can mean 'agitating', 'being enraged', 'shaking') and mocking laughter that means that they are unable to hear this wisdom. In verse 10 the blameless and upright are the targets or victims. The *bloodthirsty* (lit. 'people of blood/bloodshed') hate them and seek their lives. Verse 11 rounds off this section by contrasting the fool and the wise person. Fools express ('bring out', in an implied bad sense of exercising no control over their worst thoughts and desires; NIV, 'rage') what they are like on the inside ('all their spirit'), but the wise calm down their anger and move on. Whether the divide is between the wise and the fool, or the righteous and the wicked, there is strong teaching about the two ways to live.

12–14. These verses are clearly addressed to those aspiring to rule. The ruler is mentioned in verse 12, the king in verse 14, and verse 13 refers to one who has the power to oppress others. There is great power in modelling. This is especially evident in verse 12, where the negative example of a king's behaviour (listening to false matters/words) results in all the lower officials becoming wicked. They put into practice what they see in the actions of those in authority. With power comes responsibility. Future generations will be right to condemn our failure in recent history to deal with issues like genocide or climate change. Verses 13 and 14 provide a rationale for how to deal with the poor over whom rulers have authority. Verse 13 describes what the rulers (potential 'oppressors') and the poor 'have in common' (NIV; lit. 'meet [together]', but NIV gives the sense well; see 22:2). Both are dependent on the Lord, since both were created by him. While there are differences, there are also commonalities. History tells us that those in power have often not treated those 'lower' in society with the equal human dignity that comes from all humans being made by God. A positive lesson is given in verse 14 (echoing v. 4a), where a king who acts rightly towards the poor (lit. 'judges with truth/faithfulness') will have his throne be established as long as he continues to act like this ('for ever' in most EVV is an over-translation).

15. This subsection ends where it began in verse 3 with a family setting. The value of parental discipline and correction is again affirmed (13:1; 15:5; 22:6; 23:13–14), with a reminder that leaving children to their own devices is not the path to freedom but to folly and shame. The apparent kindness of indulging children makes it more difficult for them to grow into the people God wants them to be. The language of shame reminds us that the OT culture was a community one where people were expected to promote honour and to avoid bringing shame on their family or community.

iv. Improper speech and attitudes (29:16–27)
After the familiar refrain in verse 16, there is less uniformity of content than in the previous sections. There are a couple of verses focusing only on positive scenarios (v. 17, a disciplined son; v. 26, the Lord as the source of justice), but a large group of negative portrayals in verses 19, 20, 21, 22, 24. Finkbeiner (1995: 13) divides

verses 17–26 into verbal speech (vv. 17–24, subdivided into necessary speech [vv. 17–18], improper speech [vv. 19–23], wrong speech and not speaking when one should [v. 24]) and the Lord's prominence over people (vv. 25–26). However, improper speech does not fully describe verses 19–24, which seem to include improper attitudes as well.

16. The contrast between the righteous and the wicked is again present, but this occurrence of the refrain only explicitly mentions the rise of the wicked, although the rise of the righteous seems implied in the second half of the verse. The first half reads 'in a rising of wicked people, transgressions rise', using the same verb (*rbh*) to describe both instances of 'rise' and implying a causal connection between the two events. When the wrong people come to power, the rest of society is not unchanged. The wicked values of those in authority are easily picked up by the wider community.

17–18. Verse 17 provides a picture of godly parental discipline of a child (building on v. 15), rewarded with a good outcome of rest or peace. Whybray (1994: 403) notes that this is the only admonition in the chapter. This discipline would include both words and actions, and both correction and encouragement. The second half of this verse adds that such a disciplined child will bring *delight* (this could also be translated as 'delicacies'; Clifford 1999: 253 suggests that it describes adult children caring for their elderly parents) to your whole being (*nepeš*, 'soul, life'; ESV/NRSV, *heart*). Another form of discipline (in relation to a servant) will be developed in verses 19, 21. Verse 18 extrapolates from family upbringing to the society as a whole. The community of God's people is meant to be shaped by (prophetic) vision, and by 'instruction'/*law*. Vision (*ḥāzôn*) is often associated with prophets (e.g. 1 Sam. 3:1), and can be used to describe an entire book of prophetic words (Isa. 1:1). Thus it can mean revelation (so NIV) or, perhaps in a wisdom context, authoritative words designed to shape us. Van Leeuwen (1997: 244) suggests it might refer to political guidance, as in 11:14. The parallel term in verse 18b is *tôrâ*, which commonly means 'law', but in Proverbs can mean the 'instruction' given by the sages or parents (1:8). So verse 18 at least refers to being transformed by authoritative words and instruction, but may also allude to the prophetic word and the law. In any event, those who accept this shaping are described as *blessed* (= 'happy in

God's sight', Ps. 1:1), while those who reject this teaching have cast off restraint (lit. 'let themselves loose, go out of control').

19–24. The positive function of discipline is set out in verse 19, with the explicit comment that words (alone) will not instruct a servant. The problem is that a servant could understand the message, but may not respond (the verb *'nh* can mean 'answer' but here has the wider meaning of 'respond with either words or actions'). The proverb does not make it clear (perhaps deliberately) whether the disciplining words need to be accompanied by actions, or whether the words on their own will not work without a change of heart in the servant. Both are true. The first is perhaps developed by verse 21 and so seems more likely in the context. It speaks of indulging or pampering (although the verb is found only here in the OT; Whybray 1994: 404 comments that it has this meaning in later Mishnaic Hebrew) servants rather than acting to discipline them. The second line of verse 21 is even more contentious (cf. NRSV, 'will come to a bad end' and ESV, *will in the end find him his heir*). Again this contains a hapax (a word used only once), but one commonly understood to mean 'insolent' or 'weak'. A negative outcome ('they will not turn out well') seems required by the sense. Verse 20 deals with a situation where words (although *dābār* can also mean 'matter' or 'thing' and so refer to actions) are used too hastily or impatiently. While Proverbs endorses the power of wise words to change people (e.g. 10:11; 12:18), it also reminds us of the need to guard our words (e.g. 13:3). Part of wisdom involves discerning what to say, but verse 20 deals with when to say something. Verse 22 might also in part refer to the wrong use of words (those spoken in anger), but most likely refers to both actions and words displayed by people who are controlled by their anger or hot temper (lit. 'a person of anger' and 'a lord/master of wrath'). When people have little self-control, their angry outbursts and responses promote conflict and many transgressions (15:18; 22:24–25; cf. 19:11). This focus on the whole person (not just one's words) is seen in the reference to underlying attitudes and issues of character in verse 23. Thinking too highly of oneself (pride) will lead to being brought low, but being *lowly of spirit* (humble) will cause a person to be honoured (11:2; 16:18–19; 18:12). What we are like on the inside (character) will have a great effect on how life turns out for us. Verse 24 deals with both actions and a failure to speak when one should. The cameo is given without much detail. A person who joins with a thief is described as hating his own life (8:36) or making a self-destructive choice. The second half envisages that during a robbery either the thief or the victim (NRSV, 'the victim's curse') utters a curse (the verb *'ālāh* can mean either to utter a curse, as in Judg. 17:2, or an oath, as in Hos. 10:4, but more commonly refers to a curse; so NRSV/ESV) but wrongly does not reveal the substance of what was said. The NIV translation less likely assumes that the person was put under oath but refused to reveal the truth. In either case, a person has refused to come clean by speaking out the truth.

25–26. These two verses differ from the previous ones in that they both explicitly refer to the Lord, commending trust in the Lord and seeing him as the source of justice. Both also view looking for human approval as an alternative to looking to the Lord. Verse 25 reminds us that fear of, or trembling before, humans (or perhaps even humans just being afraid, reading a subjective genitive here) lays a snare (a trap for birds), but safety (the verb implies being safely set on high) comes from trusting in the Lord. Trust in the Lord is often a synonym for the fear of the Lord, that is, treating God with the respect due to him because of who he is. His character and past actions invite a response of trust. The contrast in verse 26 is between those who try to gain a favourable judgment from a human authority (ESV, *seek the face of a ruler*) and those who recognize that ultimately justice for human beings comes from the Lord.

27. This closing verse links in with the focus on justice in verse 26 (although using different terms), but also reintroduces the divide between the righteous and the wicked that has been central to chapters 28 – 29. It describes the mutual strong dislike (lit. 'abomination') of the righteous and the wicked. The righteous person is paired with *one whose way is straight* or upright; the wicked one is equated to 'a person of injustice'.

Meaning
Crucial to chapters 28 – 29 is the divide of humanity between the righteous and the wicked. This is not the only way to describe the two ways to live of chapters 1 – 9, and in much of Proverbs the groups are seen to be the wise and the fools. Underneath the entire

section is an exhortation to be among the righteous rather than being found with the wicked. Those in authority or a position of power or wealth are especially encouraged to act righteously and so build up community. Righteousness needs to be displayed in our actions, our character and particularly in our words. This involves being shaped by wisdom, instruction and discipline, as well as working hard for the right personal and social goals.

5. THE SAYINGS OF AGUR AND LEMUEL
(30:1 – 31:9)

A. The sayings of Agur (30:1–33)

Context
The penultimate chapter (which has a heading in 30:1) is different from the preceding sentence proverbs. It includes a prayer (unusual in wisdom books, except in the lament prayers of Job), a selection of numerical sayings, and perhaps an instruction for a specific individual (see on v. 1). Chapter 30 is given the heading of *the words* [or sayings] *of Agur*. Scholars differ over whether the words of Agur extend only as far as verses 4, 9, 14 or whether they fill the whole chapter.

Comment
i. Testimony and prayer (30:1–9)
1–4. Verse 1 is difficult textually, but this does not significantly affect the meaning of the rest of the chapter. Whybray (1994: 408) comments, 'The only matter on which there is wide agreement is that this sentence contains the beginning of the speech which

continues in vv. 2–3.' That is not entirely true, for the opening part, *the words of Agur son of Jakeh*, are unproblematic. They are usually seen as non-Hebrew names (so Perdue 2000: 251), which reminds us that biblical wisdom is part of a broader international wisdom movement, and that an Israelite origin is not necessarily required for OT Scripture. One other suggested emendation is (with slight textual revision) to change an *oracle* ('inspired utterance, NIV) to 'from Massa', a reference to a tribe in Arabia (Gen. 25:14; 1 Chr. 1:30). While this would further emphasize the non-Hebrew origin of this section, *oracle* makes good sense in the light of *the man declares* which immediately follows. The rest of verse 1 has been variously rendered:

> ESV: *The man declares, I am weary, O God; I am weary, O God and worn out.*
> NRSV: Thus says the man: I am weary, O God, I am weary, O God. How can I prevail?
> NIV: This man's utterance to Ithiel: I am weary, God, but I can prevail.
> NKJV: This man declared to Ithiel – to Ithiel and Ucal.
> HCSB: The man's oration to Ithiel, to Ithiel and Ucal.

These five modern versions differ over whether to read proper names (NKJV, HCSB), Hebrew verbs (ESV, NRSV) or a combination of the two (NIV). The first three also disagree about how to translate the last clause – with a mood of defeat (ESV), questioning (NRSV) or triumph (NIV). It is best not to make one's view of the rest of the passage ride on any one chosen translation.

Verses 2–3 describe Agur's self-understanding, which is really self-humbling (Fox 2009: 854). He is not comparing himself to other humans, since it is clear from verse 4 that he is rather thinking of his standing before God. He considers himself foolish, more like a brute beast than a person, and limited in his understanding (v. 2). In particular, he has not learned wisdom, a key goal of the book (1:2), nor does he have knowledge of the 'holy ones' (NRSV, *qĕdōšîm*). While 'holy ones' could refer to angels, the plural is probably one of majesty or excellence ('the most holy one'), making this a reference to God (*Holy One*, NIV/ESV; see 9:10). Verse 4 indicates that this lack of knowledge is particularly about God's running of the world, in terms reminiscent of Job 38 (e.g. 'surely you know', Job 38:5). These are a series of impossible questions, with the implied answer: 'Only God. He alone knows and has done all this.' Only God can be at home in heaven and yet visit the earth. Only God can control the wind (Job 38:24b); he alone has authority over the sea (Job 38:8–11); only God can establish the ends of the earth (Job 38:4–6). The question *What is his* [and his son's] *name?* may make us think of God the Father and Jesus, but that is probably not in the mind of Agur.[1] Rather, it is simply a way of asking the identity of the one who has done all that verse 4 has outlined. In Job 38 similar challenge questions were designed to reorient Job and move him in a new direction. Here Agur is recounting these challenges to explain why he has moved on from his former lack of wisdom (vv. 2–3) to a firm foundation for wisdom and knowledge in God and his words (vv. 5–6).

5–6. These verses set out the firm basis for Agur's renewed understanding of life and knowledge. Every word from God is described as literally 'purified' or 'refined' (NIV tries to capture this with 'flawless'; NRSV/ESV opt for *proves true*). In the context of verse 6b, the image is that God distils what is true by removing the lies that sometimes obscure truth. Thus, the sense is that God's words (spoken and written) are both flawless and shown to be true. Wisdom about the world is not independent of God, but is based on the prior assumption that God is actively ruling over the world as King. Of course, mere knowledge of what God has said is not enough, and Agur understands that there is an implied invitation to trust in God or take refuge in the one who is like a protective shield (2 Sam. 22:31/Ps. 18:30). This is the fear of the Lord as outlined in 1:7; 9:10. For this reason, his words are not to be swamped and distorted by adding other words that lead away from truth and towards lies. Adding half-truths to what God has said undermines the solid foundation that God's words provide for those who take refuge in him.

---

1. Koptak (2003: 637) notes that some have interpreted the son as Israel or the king, but he suggests that the context implies 'any person who learns wisdom'. Garrett (1993: 237), however, suggests we 'cannot but think of the Son of God here'.

In the context of the book of Proverbs, one way of adding to God's words is to regard its proverbs as promises.

7–9. The sages' nuanced view of wealth is reflected in this section. While many 'prosperity gospel' teachers think that Proverbs promises that if you are wise or righteous then you will be rich, the book itself explains that there are dangers from both wealth and poverty. This instruction is in the context of a prayer, the only prayer in the entire book. Agur grounds his prayer on asking God (v. 7) to keep him from falsehood and deceit. Now that he has a solid foundation on God's words (vv. 5–6), he prays that God would cause lies and literally words of falsehood to be removed from him (v. 8a). Words matter, and he does not want false words to distract him from God's reliable words. His prayer, then, and the real focus of this section, is that he will not be seduced by having either too much money or too little (v. 9; 15:16–17). A key danger for those who have some wealth (which includes many of us in the West who are Christians) is that we value wealth too highly and become so self-sufficient that we no longer see the need to trust in God (v. 9a; note that the distinctively Israelite name of God, *the LORD*, is used here). Of course, that is not where we start, but it can easily be the final outcome of chasing riches (see Job 31:24–25). Sadly, Christianity in much of the Western world has declined as a rising standard of living has made many financially comfortable. The temptation of the poor is different but just as deadly (6:30–31). A solution to the brute fact of poverty is to take something that belongs to another person, dishonouring the name of the God we serve. The solution is set out in verse 8c – neither too much nor too little, but just enough. Being satisfied to have only our bread for the day will lead to contentment, making us responsible and generous with any excess, and patient and trusting when we experience a shortfall. Godliness with contentment is great gain (1 Tim. 6:6, 8–10; some also see echoes in Matt. 6:9–13).

ii. Proverbs and numerical sayings (30:10–33)

10. This individual saying is loosely connected to the following verses by the mention of cursing in verses 10 and 11. Behind this proverb is the idea found elsewhere that even the poor are valuable because God has made them (14:31; 17:5; 22:2), and the way we treat the poor matters to God (e.g. 19:17; 22:22–23). Servants would have no means of defending themselves from a false accusation, and would be easily dismissed by a master (see Gen. 39:6b–23). A servant who was forced into poverty in such a way would easily meet a tragic end (hence the slanderer is *held guilty*) and could curse the wrongdoer. The fundamental mistake was to treat others – even if 'only a servant' – as if they do not count. That is a failure of character.

11–14. Families were held in high honour in Israel, a reality made very clear in Proverbs, where both father and mother impart life-giving wisdom to their children (6:20–24; 10:1). Earlier examples of mistreatment of parents include assault (19:26), despising (23:22) and robbery (28:24). Verse 11, building on the teaching of 20:20, describes those (lit. 'a generation', *dôr* – it begins each of vv. 11–14) who seek to harm their parents by actively cursing, and passively rebelling by failing to bless them. Individuals have responsibility to their communities and especially to their families. This verse leads on to a section describing those who bring shame or dishonour to society as a result of their wrongdoing. Another group (*dôr*) – or perhaps even the same group described from a different vantage point – is deluded in that their self-perception of being pure or clean (*ṭāhôr*, 20:9) does not match with the reality of their actual filth (*ṣō'â*, a strong word elsewhere connected to vomit, Isa. 28:8, or faeces, 2 Kgs 18:27). Proverbs has earlier warned of the danger of self-deception (*in* his [singular] *own eyes* in 12:15; 16:2; 21:2; 26:5, 12, 16; 28:11), and so here the stench of their filth wipes away their denials. Verse 13 simply describes the proud or haughty, but in comical terms. They do not simply lift their eyes; they even flit their eyelids (or eyelashes, 6:25) high into the air (= arrogance, 21:4). Verse 14 rounds off the picture with images of those who violently attack the poor and needy (22:22). They are pictured as cannibals with sharp teeth, devouring (*'kl*, which has a literal sense of 'eating') those who are most marginalized in society. While these four verses form a group (each verse starting with *dôr*, 'a generation', or perhaps a person as representative of a generation), there is no outline of any consequences that they face. Their activities or shortcomings are simply described. Yet the strong negative or mocking tone of each verse, and the cumulative effect of all four juxtaposed, make this a strong description of the wicked. We are meant to evaluate them in the light of the previous critiques of the ungodly and fools.

15–16. This pair of verses includes a numerical saying (common in this chapter), whose function is to emphasize the theme of verse 15a. Those who are never satisfied with what they have are like the two daughters of a blood-sucking leech (Whybray 1994: 414 notes that a leech has a sucker at each end of its body; the word 'leech' occurs only here in the OT), who only cry out, 'Give! Give!' They are insatiable; they never have enough. Leeches are by nature like this, but human beings should not be. The numerical saying that follows in verses 15b–16 impliedly invites us to evaluate such people, by comparing them to four examples of things that are appropriately insatiable: Sheol, the place where the dead are found, always has room for one more (27:20); the woman who cannot have children always has an enduring longing (e.g. Gen. 30:1); the dry land of Palestine can soak up incredible amounts of water; and fire will continue to burn as long as there is more fuel. But for acquisitive humans, in the light of verses 8b–9, enough should be enough.

17. This verse is a unit on its own, although it builds on the assumption of honouring parents already seen in verse 11. Now mistreatment of parents is expanded to include mocking or scorning them. Since part of the role of parents is to instruct their children in wisdom (1:8), this includes rejection of the wisdom shaping ('obedience of a mother' = *to obey a mother*, ESV/NRSV) that they were seeking to impart. This failure to honour parents has real consequences, described (hyperbolically) as having their eye gouged out ('pecked out', NIV/NRSV; *picked out*, ESV) and eaten by predators such as ravens and vultures/eagles. The graphic nature of the image highlights that this is a serious matter, even a deadly one.

18–19. This numerical saying has the form x, x + 1 (three things ... four; a 'graded numerical saying'), and this structure often means that the emphasis is on the final element, in this case sexual love/attraction, the way of a man with a young woman (*'almâ*, a young woman of marriageable age; *virgin*, ESV). There does not appear to be any criticism of the way the man is behaving, but rather amazement at the complexities of life. Part of the wisdom movement is to study and observe the world, to notice features of everyday life, and to explore how things work in an orderly way. All four aspects mentioned in verse 19 are hard to fathom fully or describe. The way the majestic eagle flies; what drives the actions of a snake;

the many variables of sailing on the unpredictable seas; and then finally the nature of relationships between young men and women – all these are difficult to explain or outline. The sages cannot fully comprehend how such scenarios are ordered, and yet there appears to be patterns and familiar cycles. Life is both hard to understand, yet a wonder to explore.

20. Like verse 17, this verse is an isolated unit.[2] It concerns a shameless adulterous woman who does not see the harm her actions cause. For her the act of adultery is simply a matter of physical and sexual actions, with no relational implications. Yet for the man who sleeps with her, and for his wife and family, there are enormous relational issues (and also for her if she were married). This perhaps forms the background to Paul's teaching on sexuality in 1 Corinthians 6:12–20.

21–23. This numerical saying also has the x, x + 1 structure, but it is not clear that the focus is only on the last example. All four images seem to be anomalous and problematic, at least in some respects. Van Leeuwen (1988: 35–38) sees them portraying 'a world upside down'. These are four scenarios under which the earth quakes, or cannot bear up. The consequences seem potentially disastrous when their culture is more closely examined. While we might see a slave becoming a king as an example of the truth that anything is possible if we set our minds to it, that is not what it would have meant to its original hearers (19:10). The assumption of an ordered, stratified society, with everyone in their assigned place, made governing predictable and orderly. A cohesive community was more important than individual ambition. In such a community the righteous are rewarded and prosper, while the fools' sufferings include material want, and hence no food. Of course, one type of fool is the sluggard or lazy person who refused to sow grain and hence had nothing to harvest (20:4; see also 6:6–11; 10:4–5; 19:15). So a fool filled with food would not seem right (vv. 22b). Less clear is the example of an *unloved* (lit. 'hated', the passive participle of *śnʾ*,

2. However, Fox (2009: 873) sees it as 'the first interpretation of v. 19'; Waltke (2005: 490) connects them rhetorically, labelling them as 'four awesome ways and the awful way of the adulteress'.

'to hate'; in Gen. 29:33 Leah describes herself using this word)
woman getting a husband (v. 23a). The use of a participle implies
that the 'disliking' is continued, so the example in view is one of a
woman who is still hated (perhaps even by her spouse), yet he
marries her. It does not envisage a woman who was formerly hated
but now loved. A loveless relationship is in view, and such a marriage
is a recipe for disaster.[3] The final example is like the first in that it
involves a crossing of normal social boundaries, and is likely to
create upheaval. A servant girl replacing her mistress is suggestive
of broken-down and illicit relationships, and these often cause
division within a household or community.

24–28. The listing of four images without an x, x + 1 structure
suggests that all the examples illustrate the point being made. They
contain more details than the previous numerical sayings, with each
example having a separate verse. The common point is that each is
a small creature yet manages to master its environment well (Lucas
2015: 192 alternatively proposes that 'wisdom is more important
than size or strength'). The ant has already been used as a model for
hard work (6:6–8). Although each ant is small, it accomplishes the
enormous task of gathering food in summer so that it will survive
in the leaner months (v. 25). Rock badgers or hyraxes can still be
found in Israel in the barren cliffs around Ein Gedi (also the Golan
Heights). The cliffs are dry and inhospitable, but these creatures
have adapted well (v. 26). Locusts are able to be orderly even though
they cannot appoint someone as king or leader (v. 27). The prophet
Joel describes their army-like discipline as they feed on crops in their
path (Joel 2:4–5, 7). The last image is that of the lizard (v. 28).
Although a person can pick up a lizard (or perhaps 'spider'), no-one
can stop them going where they want to find food, drink or shelter.
While there is an illusion of human control, lizards can make their
way even into the most impregnable of human strongholds – kings'
palaces. These are four small and seemingly helpless creatures, but
they can achieve their goals by acting cleverly. They are described as

---

3. Longman (2006: 532) suggests a different scenario, which is also possible.
   He envisages a hated woman who gets married and now has a position
   of power from which she can get her revenge.

wise (*ḥākām*), which is not confined in the OT to intellectual sharpness, but includes living successfully. This is an observation about the animal and insect world, but there is a message here for people as well. Often humans find their environment overwhelming or too daunting, but we can learn from these creatures (as in 6:6–11) that our seeming insignificance need not preclude us from managing our environment if we act wisely. In the NT James talks about small objects having large effects (Jas 3:3–5).

29–31. The structure of this numerical saying (x, x + 1) suggests that the emphasis is on the fourth example, the king whose army is with him. The focus is on the appropriate stateliness of the king. The word usually translated *stately* is mentioned twice (v. 29) and is a *hifil* participle from the verb *yṭb*, which means 'to do good/be pleasing'. The sense here is that the people are pleased at the fittingly regal bearing evident in the way the king walks or goes about his tasks. The lion too acts as if he is king of the beasts (v. 30) and is not intimidated by any. The rooster (most EVV, based on the LXX; lit. 'strong of loins'; see Garrett 1993: 243) who struts in his domain acts similarly (v. 31a). No detail is given about how the he-goat fits in, but these creatures do have a leisurely and unhurried walk. A king with an army behind him is a picture of a ruler in his glory, going out to battle as kings were expected to do (2 Sam. 11:1). A king must be seen to be in charge, able to exercise his power and not be intimidated by others.

32–33. It is not clear whether these two observations are connected, but both urge their hearers to act more wisely by changing what they are doing. Verse 32 refers to the general category of being foolish, but also to two more specific attitudes: exalting yourself (the *hitpael* or reflexive stem of *nś*, 'to lift up') and devising evil (strictly speaking, it only means devising or planning, but the context suggests that a wrong action or goal is in view). It seems to refer to speech that is boastful and used to do wrong, and the solution is to put a hand over one's mouth, thus stopping any further destructive talk (Job 21:5; 29:9). Verse 33 operates in a different way, using the same uncommon word *pressing* (*mîṣ*) in three different images, a wordplay obscured in the NIV, which translates them as 'churning', 'twisting' and 'stirring up'. There is another wordplay on *nose* ('*ap*) and *anger* ('*appayim*, the same word with a dual ending; it can be

used of two nostrils). Pressing or churning milk to make curds is a
positive process, but the remaining two are not. Pressing the nose
probably means punching or twisting it in a fight, and results in a
bloody nose. Pressing anger is less clear, but most likely involves
stirring up someone's anger by forcing the person to act on it. The
end result is conflict or strife (*ríb*). The lesson seems to be that some
pressing produces good outcomes, while other forms of *pressing* are
harmful.

Meaning
The wise words of Agur cover a range of topics. He moves from
his former foolishness to his transformation by God and his words.
The rest of the chapter explores his new-found wisdom perspective.
This includes his attitude of contentment with having enough
money, rather than seeking either riches or poverty. He warns
against slanderous speech, lack of respect for parents, and the
dangers of both acquisitiveness and subverting the social order.
He also marvels at human relationships, the ability to manage the
environment, and the dignity of rulers. Wisdom reaches into many
areas of daily life.

B. The sayings of King Lemuel (31:1–9)

Context
The first section of this final chapter sets out an oracle to King
Lemuel from his mother.[4] They are words of warning, correction
and encouragement for him in his duties as a king. Lemuel was not
a king in Israel or Judea, so this 'foreign' material has been incorporated into this wisdom book because its truths need hearing. The
inclusion of this 'overheard oracle' implies that it is relevant to more
than King Lemuel alone. The attribution of the oracle to his mother

---

4. Another possible translation, e.g. Perdue (2000: 269), is that if *oracle*
refers to the tribe of Massa here and in 30:1, then it could be rendered
'Lemuel, king of Massa'. While this changes the translation and
reinforces the non-Israelite identity of Lemuel, it is not otherwise
significant.

also reminds us of the role of women in the wisdom tradition, and their significant contribution to training up the next generation.

Comment
i. The role of the king (31:1–3)

1–3. Verse 1 describes this section as the *words* or 'sayings' (NIV) of King Lemuel, but explains that he is not the originator of these words, for he is passing on what his mother had taught him. Mothers, like fathers, had important roles in teaching their children (1:8). Verse 2 reads literally, 'What, my son, and what, the son of my womb, and what, son of my vows', and has been variously translated (the Aramaic word for 'son', *bar*, is used). The NRSV views it as a call to stop ('no'), the NIV as a caution ('listen'), while the ESV elaborates the question (*What are you doing?*). It is probably a combination of all three – one small Hebrew word urging Lemuel to stop in his tracks, listen for a moment and reconsider what he should be doing. His task as king needs to be thought through and evaluated carefully. Verse 3 begins the specific teaching of the section, exhorting the king not to give his *strength* to women. 'Strength' (*ḥayil*) commonly means 'power' or 'strength', but can also mean 'wealth' or 'substance' (Gen. 34:29; Deut. 8:18). Later in this chapter (v. 10) it refers to a woman of 'ability' or an excellent woman (also 12:4). It can have a wide range of meanings covering all that a person has physically, financially and morally. The force here is 'do not expend all your energies and resources' on sexual self-indulgence, seeking to win the favours of the court women (Murphy 1998: 241 suggests 'the intrigues that are often associated with a harem'). The reason given is that they can destroy kings, probably by creating factions and divisions, or giving birth to rival heirs. Apart from these actions being self-focused, they are also a massive distraction to his real task as king. Power is to be used to serve others, not yourself.

ii. A potential distraction (31:4–7)

4–7. A particular temptation for kings seems to be the excessive consumption of alcohol, presumably paired with a self-indulgent party lifestyle. The rationalizations would be easy: I can afford it; I would enjoy it; perhaps even, I deserve it. Yet Lemuel's mother warns her son that wine and strong drink (NIV, 'beer') are not for kings or the wider category of rulers (v. 4).[5] Some reasons are given in verse 5. A king who drinks will forget the laws and decrees that build up the community, and he may use his power – when his inhibitions are removed – in a way that kings should not (20:1; 23:29–35). A king's power should be used to promote justice and the rights of the powerless, but a king who drinks and parties can change or pervert justice for the marginalized or afflicted. A self-focused party lifestyle impedes a ruler's commitment to the needs of his community.

Verses 6–7 at first glance seem to commend giving drinks to the poor and suffering. However, they need to be read as part of verses 4–7 as a whole. If there are people who should drink, it is not those who have authority over others and could abuse that privilege. Rather, it would be those who are only looking for a little (temporary) comfort in the difficulties of life. The focus is on the contrast between the two groups, not on the positive effects of drinking in the midst of life's hardships. Of course, it is clear that Proverbs should not be used to argue that Christians should never drink (as if they were laws), but it does warn of the dangers of excessive drinking. Verse 6 refers to those in difficult circumstances (*perishing, in bitter distress*/'anguish') and seems to envisage little harm and some good coming from their drinking. The good is identified in verse 7 – being able to focus on something other than their poor and miserable situation (or 'toil/hard work', *'āmāl*). If someone has to forget, this is a much better thing to be forgotten than the rights of the afflicted in verse 5.

iii. Do good for the poor (31:8–9)

8–9. These closing verses call for those in authority to speak out publicly for the poor and for justice. While it does not preclude any actions, the emphasis is on speech (*Open your mouth* begins both verses). The purpose of speaking up is not a self-serving one, for Lemuel is urged to advocate on behalf of the most marginalized.

---

5. The noun describes 'fermented drink' and it is related to the root 'to be drunk'. Waltke (2005: 505) notes that it 'denotes any inebriating drink with about 7–10 percent alcoholic content, not hard liquor, because there is no evidence of distilled liquor in ancient times'.

These include the dumb or mute (v. 8a), who may be unable either physically or socially to speak out for themselves. It is the king's role to judge righteously or with fairness (*sedeq*, v. 9a; 16:12; 20:28), and to act positively for (*defend*) those who are variously described as poor, needy (v. 9b) and 'those whom fortune has passed by' (*destitute*, most EVV, but the verb means to 'pass on, by, away', v. 8b). This is not simply a call to 'do no harm', but rather a rallying cry to 'do good'.

Meaning

While these words are addressed to a king by his mother, they are included in this book because they have a wider application. If kings can distort justice by drink-affected decisions, so can other officials and leaders, and they will need to take notice of the same warning. The underlying principle is that we need to use our influence or power for the benefit of others, not for our own self-indulgence, but to promote justice. The section ends with a reminder that it is not enough to refrain from unhelpful actions, since we also need to speak out for what is right and builds up the entire community. In the Holocaust History Museum in Jerusalem the words of the German essayist, Kurt Tucholsky, are a sobering reflection: 'A country is not just what it does – it is also what it tolerates.'

6. EPILOGUE: THE WIFE OF NOBLE CHARACTER (31:10–31)

Context

This poem is an alphabetical acrostic – with the twenty-two verses matching the twenty-two letters of the Hebrew alphabet. The first verse begins with the first letter of the alphabet, and each subsequent verse begins with the next letter in alphabetical order. It is an A to Z of wisdom.

In terms of subject matter, it concludes the book with the description of the wife of godly character. Some arrangements of the Hebrew canon have Proverbs followed by Ruth. Ruth is described by Boaz as a 'worthy woman' (*'ēšet ḥayil*, Ruth 3:11), the same description used at the beginning of this poem (31:10; also 12:4). The figure of the ideal wife or woman (the same word in Hebrew) is fascinating. Van Leeuwen (1997: 260) comments, 'Pious Jewish husbands still recite this poem every Sabbath eve in praise of their own wives.' She is described as bringing advantage to her husband (vv. 11–12). She is a person of high economic and social standing (vv. 21–22), whose husband is important within the community (v. 23). She makes practical business and commercial decisions (vv. 13, 16, 18,

24), and provides well for her household (vv. 14–15, 21, 27) and the needs of others (v. 20). She is virtuous as well as successful (vv. 25–26, 30), and is well regarded by others (v. 28).

In a number of ways she parallels Lady Wisdom in chapters 1 – 9:

- both are described as more precious than jewels (3:15; 31:10);
- whoever finds them will have material prosperity (3:13–14; 31:11);
- wisdom is found at the city gates (1:21), and she is praised there (31:31);
- wisdom laughs (1:26) at the results of folly, and the woman of chapter 31 also laughs (31:25) at the time to come, because she does not commit folly;
- the fear of the Lord characterizes her (31:30) and is vital in chapters 1 – 9 (1:7; 2:5; 8:13; 9:10).

While some view her as a depiction of wisdom personified (like Lady Wisdom in chs. 1 – 9), she is at least a woman who exemplifies wisdom, and puts it into practice.[1] At the end of the book, then, as a kind of *inclusio* with chapters 1 – 9, we return to the theme of embracing wisdom, and the reader is reminded of the benefits that wisdom will bring, and is urged to choose wisdom.

Verses 10–12 serve as an introduction setting of the value of this woman. The large central part (vv. 13–27) summarizes her many activities, while the final section (vv. 28–31) outlines those who praise her (see Waltke 2005: 515). The central part could be subdivided into her work in the home (vv. 13–19) and her involvement in the community (vv. 20–27).

---

1. Cox (1982: 253) describes her as 'a prototype – the ideal fulfilled'. However, Yoder (2009: 299) cautions that 'she embodies not *one* woman but the desired aspects of *many*'. Garrett (1993: 248–249) suggests that, unlike Ruth, Esther and perhaps Song of Songs, the original audience was not young women ('this is the kind of wife you should be') but rather young men ('this is what kind of wife you should get'). While this is true as far as it goes, there is a wider focus on wisdom itself.

Comment

A. Her great value (31:10–12)

10–12. The focus now turns to an amazing woman, variously described as an *excellent* (ESV) or 'capable' wife (NRSV, Clifford), a 'wife of noble character' (NIV) or a 'valiant woman' (Wolters). The Hebrew term, *'ēšet ḥayil*, can mean a woman/wife of worth or good character (Ruth 3:11), a woman of strength (used with reference to men in Judg. 3:29; 11:1; 1 Sam. 14:52) or a woman of wealth (the female counterpart of Boaz, Ruth 2:1). Since she is an example of wisdom, the focus is on her character or worth. Part of this woman's value is the realization that such women are uncommon (just to be clear, men like this would be even rarer – see 20:6b; Longman 2006: 541 draws attention to the male counterpart in the wisdom Ps. 112). Like wisdom, her worth far exceeds that of jewels (perhaps 'rubies', NIV; see 3:15; 8:11). Her husband trusts in her with every part of his being (lit. 'the heart of her husband trusts in her'; NIV, 'has full confidence in her'), and he will not lack in gain or profit (*šālāl* normally means 'spoil' or 'plunder' as in 1:13; 16:19, but has a more general sense of 'gain' here; also Ps. 119:162) from her actions and character. Her habitual practice (*all the days of her life*) is to pay back his trust with what is good, not harmful (v. 12). Details of this are given in the subsequent verses.

B. Her actions (31:13–27)

i. Her work at home (31:13–19)
13–19. This remarkable woman shows skill and dedication in her work at home. If she is wisdom exemplified, she reminds us that biblical wisdom is not just head knowledge, but rather practical skill in managing to live 'the good life' in the everyday world. Wisdom language is used about metalworkers and artisans building the tabernacle (Exod. 31:1–5; 35:10, 25–26, 30–35), a farmer knowing when to plant (Isa. 28:23–29), and a ship's pilot knowing how to guide a vessel into the harbour (Ezek. 27:8–9). In verse 13 she sources wool and flax/linen for her 'cottage industry' (Waltke),

and her hands delight in her work. In those days merchant ships were a risky and uncertain adventure, but if successful they brought great reward. She takes initiatives like that, and achieves a good outcome of providing food despite the possible perils of bringing it from afar (v. 14). Her diligence is seen in her rising early (lit. 'in the middle of the night', which does not mean the absolute midpoint, but simply that it is still truly dark, i.e. the middle part) and giving food (lit. 'prey/what is torn', probably referring to meat, which was a valuable food; Job 24:5; Ps. 111:5) to her household (v. 15). She also manages the servant women (v. 15c) either by providing them with food (*portions for her maidens*/'female servants', ESV/NIV) or by allocating them 'appointed tasks' ('tasks', NRSV).[2] Further examples of her enterprise are given in verse 16, both in planning to acquire property (*a field*) and using her previous profits (*the fruit of her hands*, ESV/NRSV; 'out of her earnings', NIV; the word for *hands* is that used in v. 13b) to start a new agricultural business (planting a vineyard). She is not simply domesticated and housebound, but also entrepreneurial and risk-taking. Verse 17 adds that she gets herself ready to work (lit. 'girds her loins with strength'; NIV, 'she sets about her work vigorously'; Steinmann 2009: 630, 'she rolls up her sleeves'), which is in parallel with 'she strengthens her arms/shoulders' (v. 17b). She works physically hard. She perceives that her trading is good (rightly *profitable*; the same expression is used in 3:14), and applies herself diligently to the task (*her lamp does not go out at night*, v. 18; Waltke 2005: 526–527 thinks that this rather signifies her enduring prosperity as she never runs out of lamp oil). She is 'hands on' in her weaving, reaching out for the distaff and holding the spindle in her palms (v. 19). This amounts to an impressive range of 'business' activities in a social setting where such initiatives would be difficult to attempt. In all she does, she shows wisdom, that is, practical skill in living, decision-making and risk-taking.

---

2. The word used is *ḥōq*, which normally means 'statute', but could mean either food or tasks appointed for them. Fox (2009: 894) notes that to 'give a *ḥōq*' 'is not used of individuals giving verbal orders', but *ḥōq* is used in 30:8 of a portion.

ii. Her involvement in the community (31:20–27)

20–27. This woman of worth actively cares for both her family and the broader community. Brown comments that 'the home serves as merely her base of operations for her activity in the community' (1996: 48). She is generous to the marginalized, variously described as the 'poor/afflicted' (*'ānî*) and the 'needy' (*'ebyôn*, v. 20). She opens her hand/palm to them, and extends her hands to give them what they need. She has no reason to be afraid of snow for her household. While Israel's climate is usually warm to hot, it does snow on the mountains to the north such as Mount Hermon, and every now and then in Jerusalem and the surrounding Judean hills. Snow is the extreme example of cold weather in this setting, and at such times the members of her household are warm because they are amply clothed (v. 21). 'Crimson' (NRSV) or *scarlet* (ESV/NIV)[3] in clothes represents more expensive garments, which would be warm enough if they needed to be. She is not confined only to cheap or readily available clothes. This detail is explained in the aside given in verse 22, with mention of her having coverings (7:16, perhaps for her bed, so NIV/ESV) to keep her warm, and clothes of fine linen and purple. Fox (2009: 896) notes that this is the only verse where she looks after herself, and that it is important to the portrait that she does not neglect herself. Purple and crimson are linked as colours of the finest material in Exodus 25:4; 35:6. There is mention of her husband (master/lord, *ba'al*) in verse 23, but his inclusion in her 'story' implies that this is in part because of her. The gates are the place of civic and legal affairs, and prominence there implies that he is an important and well-respected member of the community (Job 29:7–11). His wife's many activities would undoubtedly have contributed to his public standing. Her making of clothes has been mentioned or implied already (vv. 13, 17–19, 21–22), but now this is developed in the description of her activities in the marketplace. She not only makes linen garments and girdles/sashes (or belt, 1 Sam. 18:4), but

---

3. The LXX and Vulgate appear to read 'double' (*šĕnayim*) instead of *šānîm*, which might then imply the warmth of two layers (two-ply). However, there is no need to do this, and it would lose the parallel between the end of v. 21 and v. 22. See further Waltke (2005: 512); Fox (2009: 896).

is also actively involved in selling and delivering them to the merchants (v. 24; 'Canaanites', probably Phoenicians who were noted traders; Job 41:6). She is a person of enterprise. The poem also looks beyond her activities to her character and priorities in verses 25–27. Using the metaphor of clothing (Clifford 1999: 264 sees it as a metaphor for virtue), verse 25a draws attention to her persevering strength (*'ōz*) and her honour (*dignity*, many EVV). Her reputation or character is enhanced rather than undermined by the way she conducts her business and lives her life in the community. She is also not anxious about the future (*she laughs at the* 'days'/*time to come*, v. 25b; Job 5:22). This does not mean that she is frivolous and fails to plan ahead because disaster would not happen to her. Rather, it is because she works hard, has a profitable business (v. 18a) and has provided for any future downturn. She is secure for the future as a result of her careful and sustainable pattern of life. This is elaborated in verse 27, which notes that she keeps careful watch over the household affairs (the value of paying attention to detail!) and works diligently (described colourfully as not eating the bread of idleness, a word used only here in the OT, but related to the root *'ṣl*, meaning 'to be sluggish, lazy'). Verses 26–27 round off the portrayal of her character, commenting that the words she speaks are ones of wisdom, and when addressed to others are typified by the instruction or perhaps principle (*tôrâ*, law, instruction) of kindness. The Hebrew word for 'kindness' (*ḥesed*) is a rich one in the OT, variously translated at times as 'loving kindness', 'mercy' and 'steadfast love' (3:3: 21:21). She is wise not only in her actions, but also in her attitudes to those around her.

C. The praise she receives (31:28–31)

28–31. This final section rounds off the depiction of this worthy woman by outlining the ways in which others praise her, and specifically mentioning that she is one who fears the Lord. Her family are beneficiaries of her actions and character (vv. 11–12, 15, 21–23, 27), and so both her husband and her children ('sons') praise her and call her *blessed* (v. 28; the verb *'šr* in the *piel* means to pronounce or declare a person blessed, happy or successful). The content of her husband's praise is set out in verse 29. He notes that many women (lit. 'daughters') have acted worthily or excellently (*ḥayil*, the same word used to describe her in v. 10), but you have risen above (or surpassed) them all. Verse 30 then sets out what is her most salient characteristic, the aspect of who she is that is most praiseworthy. It is not her hard work, or her economic success, or her charm (*ḥēn* more commonly means grace, but has the sense of charm or elegance in 5:19; 11:16) or beauty (note her appearance is never the focus of attention in the poem, but nice clothes are mentioned in v. 22b, and a wife's physical features are commended in 5:19) that are the grounds for praise, but rather that she fears the Lord, that is to say, she respects God as God. This is, of course, the essential foundation of the good life in the book as a whole (1:7; 9:10), and helps to make this final poem a reminder of the core teaching of chapters 1 – 9. The final verse calls on all that she has made or done (the *fruit of her hands*; *her works*) to join in this public praise (*in the gates*). The praise spreads in these ever-widening circles to bear testimony to the way in which her character and life display such a clear example of how to live wisely in the world.

Meaning
This passage is a rich way to end the book on a high note. While it depicts wisdom exemplified in the life of a woman, it is not a lesson only for women, but for men as well. Both men and women need to be like the 'Proverbs 31 woman'! As with wisdom in the book as a whole, she establishes herself on the sure foundation of the fear of the Lord. She builds on this with productive activity that benefits her, her family and the community. Her character is shaped by wisdom as well, as she ignores a self-focused lifestyle and shows herself to be a person of great integrity, generosity and care. If we want to know how to live well in God's world, we need look no further than this passage. While it is developed in the other wisdom books, and indeed the rest of Scripture, her values, actions and character set out the essential elements of a worthy life shaped by wisdom. The 'good wife' points us to what Proverbs regards as 'the good life'.

Finding the Textbook You Need

The IVP Academic Textbook Selector
is an online tool for instantly finding the IVP books
suitable for over 250 courses across 24 disciplines.

ivpacademic.com